CONTRIBUTORS

FRANK DAWES was born in London and h[...] journalist on Fleet Street and for the BBC[...] *Not in Front of the Servants,* he is a membe[...] Guild of Travel Writers and the editorial [...] this guidebook.

ANTHONY BURTON has written several [...] industrial history of England—and one or [...] beer and pubs—and has written and pre[...] television series about England's industri[...] the BBC.

CATHERINE CONNELLY took up travel w[...] career in nursing. She has travelled exter[...] the world but makes her home near Londo[...]

BRYN FRANK is the author of *Everyman's [...] Short Walks in English Towns.* He contribut[...] Geographic's *Discovering Britain and Ire[...]* written for a number of other magazines [...] pers. He is the principal researcher for Sw[...] annual *Good Holiday Cottage Guide.*

SUSAN GROSSMAN was born in and lives in London. Formerly Travel Editor of *The Telegraph Sunday Magazine* and research officer on *Holiday Which?,* she has presented a program on food for the BBC, was the editor of *What Hotel?* magazine, and currently edits *Upbeat* magazine.

ALEX HAMILTON is the author of seven works of fiction and a travel book on the Trans-Siberian railway. He is a winner of the Fitzgerald Award for travel writing, and Travel Editor of the British national daily, *The Guardian.*

KATIE LUCAS, the author of a best-selling book on walking tours of London, runs a London-based specialized British tours company.

ANGELA MURPHY, a longtime London resident, is a freelance journalist who has contributed to a number of guidebooks, including the *Shell Weekend Guide Book* to England and *Hachette's Guide to Britain*.

DAVID WICKERS contributes regularly to several major British publications, is Travel Editor of *Marie Claire* magazine, and Travel Correspondent of the London *Sunday Times*.

THE PENGUIN TRAVEL GUIDES

AUSTRALIA

CANADA

THE CARIBBEAN

ENGLAND & WALES

FRANCE

GERMANY

GREECE

HAWAII

IRELAND

ITALY

LONDON

MEXICO

NEW YORK CITY

PORTUGAL

SAN FRANCISCO &
NORTHERN CALIFORNIA

SPAIN

TURKEY

THE PENGUIN GUIDE TO LONDON 1991

ALAN TUCKER

General Editor

PENGUIN BOOKS

PENGUIN BOOKS

Published by the Penguin Group
Viking Penguin, a division of Penguin Books USA Inc.,
375 Hudson Street,
New York, New York 10014, U.S.A.
Penguin Books Ltd, 27 Wrights Lane,
London W8 5TZ, England
Penguin Books Australia Ltd,
Ringwood, Victoria, Australia
Penguin Books Canada Ltd, 2801 John Street,
Markham, Ontario, Canada L3R 1B4
Penguin Books (N.Z.) Ltd, 182-190 Wairau Road,
Auckland 10, New Zealand

Penguin Books Ltd, Registered Offices:
Harmondsworth, Middlesex, England

First published in Penguin Books 1991

1 3 5 7 9 10 8 6 4 2

Copyright © Viking Penguin,
a division of Penguin Books USA Inc., 1991
All rights reserved

ISBN 0 14 019.936 5
ISSN 1049-1457

Printed in the United States of America

Set in ITC Garamond Light
Designed by Beth Tondreau Design
Maps by Mark Stein Studios
Illustrations by Bill Russell
Copyedited and fact-checked by
Cindy Rosenthal and Ann ffolliott

THIS GUIDEBOOK

The Penguin Travel Guides are designed for people who are experienced travellers in search of exceptional information that will help them sharpen and deepen their enjoyment of the trips they take.

The Penguin Guide to London 1991 highlights the more rewarding parts of the city so that you can quickly and efficiently home in on the right hotel and the best way for you to get the most out of the city.

The guides do far more than just help you choose a hotel and plan your trip. *The Penguin Guide to London 1991* is designed for use *in* London and on the most rewarding day trips from the city. Our Penguin writers (each of whom is an experienced travel writer who lives in or near London) tell you what you really need to know, what you can't find out so easily on your own. They identify and describe the truly out-of-the-ordinary restaurants, shops, activities, and sights, and tell you the best way to "do" the city and plan the day-trip destinations.

Our writers are highly selective. They bring out the significance of the places they cover, capturing the personality and the underlying cultural and historical resonances of a city or region—making clear its special appeal. For exhaustive, detailed coverage of cultural attractions, we suggest that you also use a supplementary reference-type guidebook, such as the Blue Guide or the Michelin Green Guide, along with the Penguin Guide.

Some sections of this book are based on parts of *The Penguin Guide to England & Wales 1991*—but are greatly revised and expanded. Most, including the array of day-trip options, are completely new to this book.

The Penguin Guide to London 1991 is full of reliable and timely information, revised each year. We would like to know if you think we've left out some very special place.

ALAN TUCKER
General Editor
Penguin Travel Guides

375 Hudson Street
New York, NY 10014
or
27 Wrights Lane
London W8 5TZ

CONTENTS

MAPS

THE PENGUIN GUIDE TO LONDON 1991

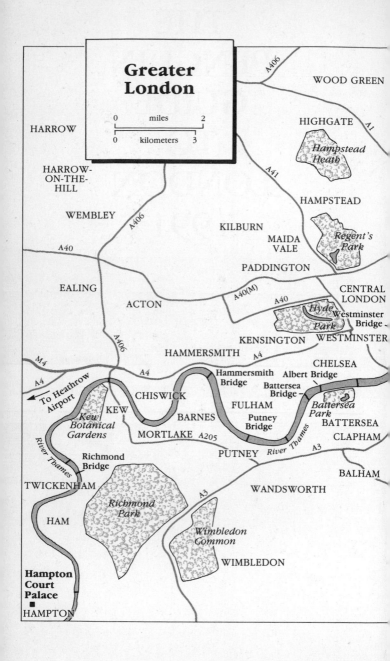

Greater London

miles 0 — 2

kilometers 0 — 3

HARROW

HARROW-ON-THE-HILL

WEMBLEY

A40

EALING

ACTON

A40(M)

A40

WOOD GREEN

A406

HIGHGATE

A1

Hampstead Heath

HAMPSTEAD

A41

KILBURN

MAIDA VALE

Regent's Park

PADDINGTON

CENTRAL LONDON

Hyde Park

Westminster Bridge

KENSINGTON

WESTMINSTER

HAMMERSMITH

A4

CHELSEA

Albert Bridge

M4

A4

A4

Hammersmith Bridge

Battersea Bridge

To Heathrow Airport

CHISWICK

Battersea Park

BATTERSEA

KEW

BARNES

FULHAM

Putney Bridge

CLAPHAM

Kew Botanical Gardens

MORTLAKE

A205

PUTNEY

River Thames

A3

River Thames

BALHAM

Richmond Bridge

TWICKENHAM

Richmond Park

A3

WANDSWORTH

HAM

Wimbledon Common

Hampton Court Palace

WIMBLEDON

■ HAMPTON

A406

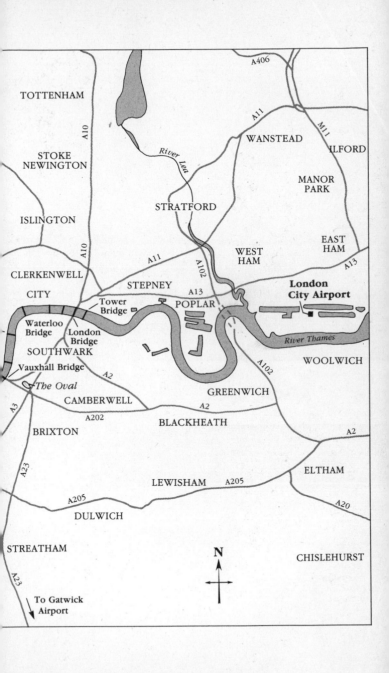

OVERVIEW

By Frank Dawes

Frank Dawes was born in London and has worked as a journalist for the BBC. The author of Not in Front of the Servants, *he is a member of the British Guild of Travel Writers and the editorial consultant for this guidebook.*

From an orbiting satellite 450 miles up, the **River Thames** is the most outstanding feature of London, a sinuous dark ribbon winding across the purple blotch of mostly built-up land within the circle of the M 25 motorway. And indeed London's river is *the* connecting thread through the kaleidoscopic pattern of widely varying localities stretching 35 miles from Heathrow Airport in the west to Dartford Tunnel in the east.

Since the once mighty Port of London moved downriver toward the estuary to accommodate container ships, the river has assumed greater significance for tourism. Pleasure-boat traffic is on the increase and ocean-going cruise ships have returned, the smaller ones mooring in the shadow of Tower Bridge. London City Airport, operating STOL flights to other cities in the U.K. and to Europe, occupies the site of the old Royal Docks, and eight square miles of East London waterfront is undergoing the greatest rebuilding operation since the Great Fire of 1666. This is nothing less than a new city grafted onto the old.

London's history may go back to Roman times, when as the walled city of Londinium it was the trading center from which all roads radiated, but it is now a capital gearing itself for the 21st century. The Beefeaters at the Tower of London, the Guards at Buckingham Palace, and the Household Cavalry still provide a flash of scarlet and

1

gleaming steel, the popular image of London along with double-decker buses and black cabs, but other familiar images have gone the way of pea-souper November fogs. Since deregulation the buses no longer have to be red and may well be green, gray, or even yellow. The sight of a City businessman wearing a bowler hat is rare enough to turn heads in busy streets where nothing is usually weird enough to merit a second glance. No longer does Fleet Street reverberate through the night to the roar of the presses spewing out millions of news-papers; their offices are now dispersed around the capi-tal, survived on the street by the journalists' church of St. Brides, the well-known pub Ye Olde Cheshire Cheese (where the sawdust on the floor is still changed daily), and the preserved façades of the Daily Express and Daily Telegraph buildings.

The importance of what jazz musician George Melly calls "the transpontine divide" cannot be over-empha-sized. The Thames is a cultural as well as a geographical frontier, whereas the traditional divide between East End and West End is becoming less and less relevant. It is no exaggeration to say that in modern London true Cockneys "born within the sound of Bow Bells" are hard to find. To a surprising extent, citizens who hail from other parts of the country or the world regard themselves instead as North of the River or South of the River people. While it may be true that the north has long enjoyed a monopoly on affluence (and visitors), the myth that South London is inferior and alien territory occupied largely by gangsters and used-car dealers is put about by folk who live north of the river.

They perversely ignore the existence of the South Bank Arts Centre, the reconstruction of Shakespeare's Globe theater on its original site on Bankside, the Oval for cricket and Wimbledon for tennis, the charming Georgian and Victorian suburbs of Dulwich Village and Blackheath, Greenwich (the maritime heart of England), and Rich-mond Park and Kew Gardens, to say nothing of numerous outstanding art galleries and museums. And while a few years ago it might have been difficult to find good places to dine in a South London dominated by fish-and-chips takeouts and ethnic Indian and Chinese restaurants, all that has now changed, most noticeably in places such as Clapham, Balham, and Wandsworth. Here, too, are some of the least-spoiled pubs, many serving Youngs bitter, a full-bodied South London beer. Captain Cook took a glass or

two of something even stronger at the Angel in Rother-
hithe between global explorations, and earlier the Pilgrim
Fathers had gathered at the nearby Mayflower (then The
Shippe) before embarking on their voyage to the New
World.

For the inquiring visitor, not all the jewels of London
are to be found in the Tower. Many of the historic buildings and country villages in the surrounding shires that
have been swallowed up by the expanding metropolis
survive and are worth seeking out. Eltham Palace and
Downe House (where Charles Darwin lived and wrote
On the Origin of Species by Means of Natural Selection)
are on the southeastern outskirts. The Baroque Moor
Park north toward Watford, the village clustered round
the famous school that Churchill attended at Harrow-on-
the-Hill, and the 500-year-old tithe barn in the village of
Harmondsworth half a mile from Heathrow's runways—
these are just a few of the many such examples.

Like all great capital cities, London can be overwhelming at first sight. Where to begin? Much depends of course
on the time available, but if possible let the river make the
introductions before you explore *both* banks in depth. To
the west, royal Windsor Castle and Cardinal Wolsey's
Hampton Court are reminders that the water by which
they stand was once the main metropolitan highway, at its
apogee in Tudor times. Embraced by the Thames as it rolls
along toward London is Richmond Park, 2,500 green acres
first enclosed as a hunting ground by Charles I in 1637 and
still roamed by red and fallow deer. Not far away, and also
overlooking the river, the Royal Botanic Gardens at Kew
were established in 1759 and now cover 300 acres, with a
magnificently restored Victorian Palm House and the new
multi-environment Princess of Wales Conservatory.

Most of the previously mentioned popular "sights" and
a good many others can be seen from a boat on the river
as it winds its way through the heart of the capital from
Chelsea Embankment under no fewer than ten bridges,
including the London Bridge that replaced the one now
to be found at Lake Havasu in Arizona. The Thames flows
past the palaces of Lambeth (spiritual) and Westminster
(temporal), where Parliament sits, and past the ancient
City of London, within whose square mile lies the Bank of
England and the Stock Exchange, and which has been
governed since the 12th century by a corporation of
aldermen and liverymen. Its boundaries are guarded by
iron griffons bearing shields embossed with heraldic de-

vices, and the policemen's helmets are distinctively different from those worn by the rest of London's "bobbies."

The best view of Tower Bridge and the Norman Tower of London is from the water, especially if the vessel you are on is large enough to require the opening of the bridge's twin bascules (which occurs only a few times a week these days). One of the most enjoyable excursions—and a rewarding introduction to London—is down the river from Charing Cross Pier to Greenwich on the south bank, where you can see something of Britain's seafaring tradition in the Maritime Museum, tread the deck of the *Cutty Sark* (the last remaining tea clipper), learn about the history of Greenwich Mean Time at the Old Royal Observatory and, in the courtyard, bestride a brass strip denoting the Prime Meridian (Longitude 000), with a foot in each hemisphere. The Queen's House in the Royal Hunting Park at Greenwich is one of the masterpieces of 17th-century architect Inigo Jones, and the first Palladian-style house in England to be restored to its original pristine elegance and opened to visitors.

An alternative and intriguing way of getting to Greenwich is to board one of the computer-driven trains of the Docklands Light Railway at Tower Gateway, where remnants of Roman Londinium are on display in the gardens. The train proceeds swiftly through the vast building site of the new London, symbolized by the towering green glass Daily Telegraph building on South Quay, to Island Gardens on the Isle of Dogs. On the opposite side of the river is an array of classical buildings, an inspiring prospect unchanged since Canaletto painted it two centuries ago, except that the sailing ships have gone. A foot tunnel, with access by a vast creaking elevator, runs under the river here.

The constant juxtaposition of ancient and modern is one of the fascinations of London. The Docklands Light Railway is an innovation, just as the tube was the world's first deep-level electric railway when it was first opened a century ago. In its heyday in the 1930s, it set the pace for graphic design as well as efficient operations, but today it is increasingly compared, not always favorably, to the underground systems of other major cities. For graffiti it occasionally outdoes even the New York City subway system.

Still, more than 90 percent of the nine million overseas visitors who come to London each year use the Underground to get about, and two-thirds use the buses. If you seek the old-fashioned civilities, with a little sightseeing along the way, go by bus. A Visitor Travelcard, available from your local travel agent before you leave home, offers virtually unlimited travel for up to seven days on the tube, buses, Docklands Light Railway, and British Rail within the London and suburban zone. The card comes with a set of discount vouchers for Madame Tussaud's, the London Zoo, and other tourist attractions.

Neighborhoods

For the visitor who wants more than the usual whistle-stop tour of the Tower of London, St. Paul's Cathedral, Westminster Abbey, and Big Ben, this guide covers a variety of up-and-coming neighborhoods in addition to those that are familiar to readers who know a bit about London already.

We range from the capital-letter City (that is to say, the area within the original Roman walls) to the West End and beyond, then to the new city of Docklands and on to Clerkenwell, Islington, Hampstead, Camden Town, and some of the other less well-known "villages" that make up the urban patchwork. Markets such as Smithfield for meat and Covent Garden for fruit and vegetables may have lost their original purpose but are as vibrantly alive as ever with new ideas and styles. Literary Bloomsbury, in contrast, has changed hardly at all, although the circular Reading Room at the British Museum will be no more when the library is relocated to a new site near St. Pancras Station sometime in the 1990s.

Ethnic quarters such as Soho, with its "little China," its strip shows, sleazy clubs, and good restaurants of many nationalities; Brixton; and Notting Hill, whose Caribbean carnival in August has become the largest outdoor festival in Europe, are where the pulse of London life is at its strongest. Even though violence and crime are on the increase, and the visitor should be aware of this, these are far from being "no go" areas.

The East End holds interest for anyone who wants to know about succeeding waves of immigrants, from the 16th-century Huguenots to the Jews and Irish Catholics of the 19th century and the Bengalis and Bangladeshis who make up a sizable minority of the population today. The Cockney dialect, or one version of it, can still be heard amid a variety of other accents and tongues.

The West End, Mayfair, and Knightsbridge are, as ever,

the magnet for those who come to London for dining and dancing, theater and entertainment, and, above all, shopping (see the relevant sections below). Chelsea, whose associations with royalty and the literati go back centuries, experienced its heyday as the birthplace of "Swinging London" in the 1960s and is now somewhat faded. However, Chelsea still has a "villagey" air, enhanced by the river flowing past its southern doorsteps, as do those parts of Hammersmith and Chiswick that are fortunate enough to have a frontage on the north bank of the Thames.

Seasonal London

The list of seasonal attractions never stops growing, and ranges from a tour of Lord's Cricket Ground to Rock Circus, a permanent waxworks exhibition of such stars as the Beatles and the Rolling Stones backed by music. London's calendar is always full, from the New Year's Eve celebrations in Trafalgar Square, where thousands gather to hear Big Ben, to the setting up of the annual Christmas tree from Norway and the switching on of the illuminations in Oxford Street, Bond Street, and Regent Street.

Spring comes to the river with the annual boat race between Oxford and Cambridge universities, run over a course from Putney to Mortlake. In high summer straw boaters, Champagne, and hospitality marquees line the banks at Henley—and the rowing seems almost incidental. In July the Worshipful Companies of Vintners and Dyers, accompanied by representatives of the Queen, conduct an annual Swan Upping, from Sunbury to Pangbourne, during which the birds are counted and marked.

The Easter Parade in Battersea Park, and the London Marathon from Greenwich to Westminster Bridge and the Chelsea Flower Show, both in May, are signs that what used to be called "the Season" can't be far behind. The latter arives with a fanfare and all the imperial pomp of two grand military parades: Beating the Retreat and Trooping the Colour (the latter celebrating the Queen's *official* birthday). Her Majesty lends that invaluable "royal touch" to the English summer when she rides in an open coach over the turf at Royal Ascot, greets the guests at a garden party in the grounds of Buckingham Palace, or appears unexpectedly in the Royal Box at Wimbledon.

Visitors with an artistic bent might be more attracted to the Royal Academy of Arts' Summer Exhibition, the

"Proms" at the Albert Hall, or open-air concerts in the grounds of Kenwood House on Hampstead Heath or Marble Hill at Richmond (best to take your picnic hamper and blanket). On August Bank Holiday, Caribbean carnival comes to Notting Hill and the streets are filled with spectacular floats and costumes and the beat of steel bands—a festive indication of London's multicultural mix.

The approach of winter is signaled by Fireworks Nights, held all over on November 5 to commemorate the foiling of Guy Fawkes's plot to blow up Parliament in 1605. Less than a week later the City of London lets its hair down for the annual Lord Mayor's Show, when the worthy elected to that office rides in a gilded coach to the Law Courts followed by a variety of floats and bands.

London Oases

London is full of quiet corners such as the Chelsea Physic Garden, which dates from 1673 and is the second oldest botanic garden in Britain (after Oxford's), and, five minutes from Marble Arch, Tyburn Convent, which offers peaceful sanctuary beside a replica of the Tyburn Tree, the gallows that stood nearby in Hyde Park Place. The nuns still pray for the highwaymen and martyrs hanged there. As well as these quaint oases, the capital has wide acres of parkland, commons, gardens, green spaces, and stretches of open water offering escape from the rush and the traffic's roar.

Hampstead Heath, with its panoramic views of St. Paul's Cathedral and the city from the northern heights, attracted such notable intellectuals and artists as Robert Louis Stevenson, Karl Marx, and John Constable. The commons of Wimbledon, Wandsworth, Clapham, and Blackheath are strung across south London like a necklace of emeralds, ever open to walkers, riders, and kite-flyers. But London's crowning glories are the royal parks that lie at its heart and were once the grounds of palaces. Hyde Park, originally a hunting ground for Henry VIII, has boating and swimming on a lake called the Serpentine, and horseback riding in Rotten Row. Its open tree-dotted grassland merges imperceptibly at the west with the more formal Kensington Gardens and the Round Pond adjoining Kensington Palace, where the Prince and Princess of Wales, Princess Margaret, and other members of the royal family have their apartments. Security is tight, but it's not unusual to catch a glimpse of them driving past, apparently unnoticed by the crowds at large.

Regent's Park, laid out by John Nash, who also designed many of the elegant Regency terraces encircling it, is the home of the London Zoo and an open-air theater. The canal that skirts it is used for pleasure cruises from Little Venice to the west and Camden Town. Green Park and St. James's Park, flanking Buckingham Palace—whose private grounds are discreetly hidden away behind a high, spiked brick wall—provide something like countryside between the traffic fumes of Piccadilly, Whitehall, and Grosvenor Place. Just off the Mall, the broad avenue that sweeps arrow-straight from Trafalgar Square to the palace, is Clarence House, where Queen Elizabeth, the Queen Mother (affectionately known as the "Queen Mum"), has her London home. The palace and its outdoor military rituals, spiced by the occasional wave of a white-gloved hand as the Queen rides by, are the focus of most visitors' attention.

The royal parks provide the green backdrop to the spontaneous and continuous entertainment that draws visitors to London from all over the world. Next to Old Father Thames himself, they are the city's most enduring inheritance, changeless and open to all.

Day Trips

The choice of fascinating places to visit within a day of London covers all points of the compass. Nor is the Channel that separates England from the Continent a serious barrier (see The Coast of France and Belgium section below).

If, however, you prefer to keep your day trips within the shores of England, there are plenty of famous and historic places to see within an hour or two by car, bus, or train. Motorways such as the M 25, which girds London, have made it easier to get around this relatively small and crowded island, but traffic can be heavy at times.

It is worth considering sitting back and enjoying the marvelous scenery from a train or the bus, which is even cheaper and just as convenient. In fact, our Day Trips from London chapter is designed primarily for rail and bus travellers.

We have spread the net as wide as possible to include lesser-visited places such as Warwick and Royal Tunbridge Wells along with the more popular places such as

Windsor, Stratford-upon-Avon, Bath, and Canterbury, which are crammed with tourists at peak times. Likewise, Oxford and Cambridge, those two ancient seats of learning that are always paired although miles apart geographically, are nonetheless each well within day-trip radius of London.

In what Paul Theroux called "The Kingdom by the Sea," you are never far from the lap of the waves on sand or shingle, and we have selected three places along the south coast within easy reach of London—Brighton, baronial Arundel, and Portsmouth.

Whichever trips you choose, you will find a vast array of museums, castles, historic houses, and exhibitions to fill a day, and guided tours galore to ease the way if that is more comfortable or convenient for you.

USEFUL FACTS

When to Go
There is never an off-season for London and southern England. Although many people prefer to come in May, when the azaleas and rhododendrons in some of the lovely gardens are in full bloom, other people prefer year-end holiday time, when they can enjoy a typically English Christmas, with all its connotations of log fires and pantomimes.

London's major tourist season is July and August, and as a result hotels, restaurants, and theaters are often booked full. The stately homes and gardens in the region also experience their full share of the tourist torrent then. All things considered, spring and autumn are much better times to visit.

The weather in the south is entirely unpredictable, but these two seasons are also often the nicest. Spring can be wonderful, with mild, sunny weather and the trees coming into leaf. Autumn, with its glorious, hazy-sunny days, often goes on until Christmas. But England is, after all, an island, with an oceanic climate subject to the winds and weather of the Atlantic.

What to Wear
London is a huge city, but don't let that put you off; most of the best-known sights are close together, enabling you to see a great deal in two or three days. (You could just as well spend the rest of your life trying to learn about it—and not exhaust its wonders.) It is really a collection of

small villages, each with its own heart and ambience. But London is definitely a walking city, so make sure you bring some sensible shoes.

The things you are least likely to need are very dressy evening clothes. The English tend to underdress rather than overdress, unless it is a very grand ball, at which time the family tiara gets an outing. If evening clothes are needed by visitors during their trip, it will probably be easier to rent rather than take up a lot of space in your luggage. There are several evening-dress rental shops listed in the Yellow Pages. However, even for the opera and the theater people here really don't dress up much, unless it is a gala or premiere. So many people go out in the evening straight from their place of work that day dress is the norm in the evening as well.

The climate in southern England is temperate, which means the temperature rarely rises above 80°F or below 30°F. For the latest weather report, telephone (0898) 50-04-01. Contrary to what most visitors have been led to believe, London does not have a great deal of rain. It does, however, have a lot of weather of every sort—and it is entirely unpredictable, so it is just not possible to tell anyone what they should bring to wear. Perhaps the most sensible thing to do is to dress in layers—the classic British compromise. Another solution is to travel light and buy when you get here, as the clothes, especially the knitwear, are of very good quality.

Getting In

From North America, there are now direct flights to London's Heathrow or Gatwick airports from Atlanta, Boston, Chicago, Dallas/Fort Worth, Los Angeles, Montreal, New York, San Francisco, Toronto, and other cities. Among the many major airlines flying the North America–Britain route are Air Canada, Air India, American, British Airways, British Caledonia, Pan Am, TWA, Virgin Atlantic, and World. Qantas and British Airways fly the long route between Britain and Australia.

The London airports are well connected to the central city by public transportation. Heathrow is on the Underground (Piccadilly line; 45 minutes from the airport to Piccadilly Circus, with stops in the hotel area around Harrods as well), which is very convenient. If you are planning on taking the Underground from the city center to Heathrow, however, it is essential that you know from which terminal you are departing. One Underground stop

serves terminals 1, 2, and 3; another serves terminal 4—
and if you get off at the wrong stop, you will end up
walking miles with your baggage. You can also take a
Green Line bus from Heathrow to Victoria Coach Station,
or Carline buses and vans to Victoria Coach Station and
Waterloo, King's Cross, Euston, Paddington, and Victoria
railway stations. London Transport's Express Airbus makes
stops throughout central London, ending at Euston, Paddington, and Victoria stations. The bus trip from Heathrow
to central London takes about 45 minutes. Taxis make the
trip from Heathrow to central London in about the same
time and charge about £30.

The best way to get from Gatwick to London is by train.
This extremely efficient service runs directly from the
Gatwick main terminal every 15 minutes, with trains
reaching Victoria Station in just 30 minutes. Carts are
available so you can push your luggage from customs to
the entrance to the train platform. Hourly Green Line
buses also connect Gatwick with Victoria Coach Station.

Ferries link southern England with dozens of ports on
the Continent and in Ireland. The two major Continental
lines are P and O, which serves Dover–Boulogne, Dover–
Calais, Dover–Zeebrugge, Felixstowe–Zeebrugge, Portsmouth–Cherbourg, and Portsmouth–Le Havre (Tel: 0304-
20-33-88); and Sealink British Ferries, which serves
Dover–Calais, Folkestone–Boulogne, Harwich–Hook of
Holland, Portsmouth–Cherbourg, and Weymouth–Cherbourg (Tel: 071-834-8122). The trip across the Channel
can take anywhere from a few hours to a full day or night,
depending on your destination. The fastest crossing is to
be had on one of the crafts of Hoverspeed, which make
the trip from Dover to Calais or Boulogne in just 35
minutes. The company has recently added the Blue-
Ribband Hoverspeed *Great Britain* to its fleet for the
Portsmouth–Cherbourg run (Tel: 0304-24-02-41).

Entry Documents

A passport is required of all travellers entering Britain,
with the exception of citizens of other EC countries, who
need only present an identity card. Citizens of the U.S.,
Commonwealth nations (Canada, Australia, and New Zealand), South Africa, and many other countries do not
need a visa. Britain imposes strict anti-rabies measures,
and all pets entering the country must be quarantined for
a minimum of six months; unless you are moving to
Britain, leave the pets at home.

Getting Around on Day Trips

If you are travelling from London on a day trip, be fore-warned that there are eight different train stations, each serving a different part of the country. Here are the ones you're most likely to use: Charing Cross serves southern England; Liverpool Street, East Anglia and Cambridge; Paddington, western England and southern Wales; Victoria, southern England; and Waterloo, southwestern England.

Several discount passes for train travel are available. The most popular is the BritRail Pass, available for both first-class and second-class travel, which allows holders unlimited travel through England, Scotland, and Wales for periods of 8, 15, 22, or 30 days.

National Express is Britain's nationwide bus network. Of special interest to overseas visitors is the Tourist Trail, which runs from mid-May through October and links London with major tourist spots—Stratford-upon-Avon, Bath, and so on—around the country. Travellers can follow the entire 14-day itinerary or make daily forays from London. The BritExpress Card is available only at British Rail offices overseas and offers a 33 percent discount on all bus travel in Britain for up to a month.

Most major car-rental agencies have offices at London's airports and train stations. You must be 21 years of age (25 with some firms) and present a valid driver's license; an international driver's license is not required. Driving is on the left, and drivers from the United States, Canada, and other countries where driving is on the right may have difficulty adjusting to this orientation. Be extremely careful. The same holds for pedestrians—remember to look both ways before stepping into a street.

(For getting around in London itself, see the section following London Museums, in the London section.)

Local Time

Britain observes Greenwich Mean Time (GMT), five hours ahead of the East Coast of North America (four ahead of the Canadian Atlantic Provinces) and nine hours behind Sydney, Australia.

Telephoning

The country code for Britain is 44. The London area has been split into two area codes: (071) for inner London and (081) for outer London. When dialing from outside Britain, do not include the initial 0 in city codes.

To make a public-telephone call, put 10p (pence) into

the coin slot in the telephone box if it has a *yellow* band on the exterior. Dial the number you require and speak; when you hear an insistent beeping tone you will need to feed more money into the box to continue the call. For a box with a *green* band on the exterior you will need a green telephone card, which can be purchased at most newsagents. You insert the card into the slot and make your call. From either type, if you wish to speak to the operator, dial 100. For London directory enquiries dial 142 (when you are in London), and for directory enquiries in other regions, dial 192 when you are within the area code.

Currency

The unit of currency in Britain is the pound sterling (denoted as £), which is divided into units of 100 pence. There are coins for 1p, 2p, 5p, 10p, 20p, 50p, and £1, and notes in denominations of £5, £10, £20, and £50. The rate of exchange fluctuates; check postings in banks and in daily newspapers for the current rate of exchange.

In the main hall at most airports there is a bank where you can change foreign currency into pounds and pence. Outside airports, banks are open Mondays through Fridays between 9:30 A.M. and 3:30 P.M. There are many Bureaux de Change around London, and most hotels will change money as well. However, both charge a higher rate than the banks do, so, if at all possible, change your money during banking hours.

Tipping

Always check on the menu in a restaurant to see whether it includes a service charge; if it doesn't, leave 10 to 15 percent. For porters and bellhops, 50p per bag is the norm, with the minimum £1. Tip hairdressers and taxi drivers 10 to 15 percent. Tip the hotel hall porter a suitable extra amount when you depart (beyond the service charge included in your bill) for extraordinary services rendered, if any.

Business Hours

Sunday is a day for strolling in the parks and going to church. As a result, very few shops are open, many restaurants are closed, and even museums don't open until 2:00 P.M. During the week most pubs now stay open continuously from 11:00 A.M. to 11:00 P.M. On Sundays they open

at noon and close from 3:00 to 7:00 P.M., then open until
the 10:30 P.M. closing.

Shops open at 9:00 A.M. and close at 5:30 P.M., except for
the one evening a week when shops in most districts of
London stay open until 8:00 P.M.—Wednesdays in Knightsbridge and Kensington and Thursdays on Oxford Street.
Shops and most banks are closed for bank holidays.

Holidays
Bank holidays are Christmas Day and Boxing Day (December 26), New Year's Day, Good Friday and Easter Monday,
May Day (the first Monday in May), Whit Bank Holiday
(the last Monday in May), and August Bank Holiday (the
last Monday in August).

Medical Problems
If you should need medical help or a doctor, ask the
concierge of your hotel, as most hotels have one they can
call on. If they don't, Medical Express, a 24-hour medical
partnership, can be reached at (071) 499-1991. For phar-
maceuticals, Bliss the Chemist, at Marble Arch, Tel: (071)
723-6116, is open from 9:00 A.M. until midnight. If the
worst happens and you need an ambulance, dial 999,
which is also the number for the police and the fire
brigade.

Electric Current
Voltage in Britain is 220/240, 50 HZ, which means that an
adapter or converter is necessary for North American
appliances, including adapter plugs.

Information
Offices of the British Tourist Authority, located in cities
and towns across Britain, provide maps, booklets on
sights and travel itineraries, accommodations listings, tips
on travel passes and tourist discount passes, and a wealth
of other information. BTA offices abroad are extremely
helpful when you are planning a trip. Major offices are
located at: 40 West 57th Street, New York, NY 10019 (Tel:
212-581-4700); John Hancock Center, Suite 3320, 875
Michigan Avenue, Chicago, IL 60611 (Tel: 312-787-0490);
Cedar Maple Plaza, Suite 210, 2305 Cedar Springs Road,
Dallas, TX 75201-1814 (Tel: 214-720-4040); World Trade
Center, 350 South Figueroa Street, Suite 450, Los Angeles,
CA 90071 (Tel: 213-628-3525); Suite 600, 94 Cumberland
Street, Toronto, Ontario M5R 3N3 (Tel: 416-925-6326);

123 Lower Baggot Street, Dublin 2, Ireland (Tel: 01-614-188); Suite 305, 3rd Floor, Dilworth Building, corner Customs & Queen streets, Auckland 1 (Tel: 649-314-46); and Associated Midland House, 171 Clarence Street, Sydney, N.S.W. 2000 (Tel: 02-29-8627).

—*Katie Lucas*

BIBLIOGRAPHY

PETER ACKROYD, *Dickens' London*. Ackroyd sets the scene and then leaves it to Dickens's writings and to excellent photographs to bring Victorian London alive.

————————, *Hawksmoor*. This powerful and atmospheric novel can best be described as a supernatural thriller, combining a vivid account of London life, centered on the work of the great architect Nicholas Hawksmoor, with an investigation into 20th-century murders.

NICHOLAS BARTON, *The Lost Rivers of London*. The story of London's rivers, other than the Thames, many now running underground—including the famous River Fleet, now covered over by Fleet Street.

ROBERT BAYLIS, *Pilgrim's London*. A guide to London's Christian heritage, this is not just a description of the capital's many churches but also covers monuments, portraits, and buildings associated with famous Christians.

GILLIAN BEBBINGTON, *Street Names of London*. This comprehensive guide explains the origins of the names of four thousand London streets.

JOHN BETJEMAN, *City of London Churches*. The former poet laureate was famous for his love of ecclesiastical architecture. Here he describes his favorite churches with his usual enthusiasm, at the same time demonstrating his special gift for identifying the odd and unusual detail.

MARY CATHCART BORER, *The Story of Covent Garden*. The whole story of this area in the heart of London, from convent garden to fruit and flower market on to more recent years and the battle for conservation.

ARTHUR BYRON, *London Statues*. A comprehensive guide to the city's outdoor statues and sculpture.

ROBERT CAMERON AND ALISTAIR COOKE, *Above London*. A collection of aerial views in color, with a lively and informative commentary.

JENNIFER CLARKE AND JOANNA PARKIN, *In Our Grandmothers' Footsteps*. An illustrated guide to the role of women and their accomplishments throughout history. This gazetteer lists sites associated with famous women, from houses to public monuments.

G. COUCH AND W. FORRESTER, *Access In London*. This is a guidebook intended specifically for the physically impaired and others who have trouble getting around.

EDWIN COURSE, *London's Railways*. A full and detailed description of London's rail system and its history.

ALIZINA STONE DAK AND BARBARA SLOAN HENDERSHOLT, *Mystery Readers' Walking Guide to London*. A series of fascinating walks around Central London, each one following the path of a well-known mystery writer.

W. R. DALZELL, *The Shell Guide to the History of London*. This very extensive illustrated guide tells the story of London from Roman times to the present day. The emphasis is on buildings and structures that can be seen today, and is particularly strong on architectural history.

ANDREW DAVIES, *Literary London*. A street-by-street guide to the authors who have lived in London and written about London, and so also a guide to the London they described.

ANDREW DAVIES AND FRAN HAZELTON, *Walk London*. The main section is devoted to 40 London walks, each one fully described and accompanied by a detailed map.

DANIEL DEFOE, *Journal of the Plague Years* (1724-1726). Defoe, best known as a novelist, was also a great essayist. He combined his talents to good effect in producing this convincing account of London during the Great Plague of 1664–1665.

CHARLES DICKENS, *Barnaby Rudge, Bleak House, David Copperfield, Dombey and Sons, Little Dorrit, Nicholas Nickleby, The Old Curiosity Shop, Oliver Twist, Our Mutual Friend, The Pickwick Papers*. No one did more to create the image we now have of 19th-century London than Dickens. His novels mostly portray a city of narrow alleys, dirt, and discomfort; but also a growing city, a place of excitement and exhilaration.

SIR ARTHUR CONAN DOYLE, *The Complete Sherlock Holmes*. 221B Baker Street, the home of Sherlock Holmes, is probably the most famous fictitious address in London. Doyle's novels and short stories are packed with descriptions of all aspects of London life in the last century.

NELL DUNN, *Poor Cow* and *Up The Junction*. These two novels, evocations of working-class London in the 1960s, present a vivid picture of life in the inner suburbs.

SUSANNE EBEL AND DOREEN IMPNEY, *Guide to London's Riverside*. The Thames has a central place in the story of London's development, and this guidebook tells the story in terms of the riverside of today.

S. FAIRFIELD, *The Streets of London*. A dictionary of London street names and their origins.

GEOFFREY FLETCHER, *The London Nobody Knows*. Fletcher is both artist and writer, and he illustrates this account of some of the byways and odd corners of London with his own sketches. A book for those who want to get off the beaten tourist track.

ALEC FORSHAW AND THEA BERGSTRÖM, *Markets of London*. London owed its early development to its role as a market center, and there are still markets for almost every kind of commodity in the capital. This guide tells you how to reach them and what they offer.

SHIRLEY GREEN, *Who Owns London*. Everything is owned by somebody—from Cleopatra's Needle to Berkeley Square. This book tells you just who owns what, and describes the property revolution of the second half of the 20th century.

GEORGE AND WEEDON GROSSMITH, *Diary of a Nobody*. A hilarious account of life in suburban London at the turn of the century.

JOHN HILLABY, *John Hillaby's London*. A very personal account of walks very much off the beaten track: as much the story of the people of London as of places.

HENRY JAMES, *London Life* (1889). The great American novelist is more usually associated with the country house than the city, but here he turns his refined attention to life among the upper classes at the turn of the century.

PAUL JOHNSON, *Aerofilms Book of London from the Air*. The title says it all.

MICHAEL LEAPMAN (editor), *The Book of London*. The story of London's development up to the present day, with sections on a variety of topics covering all aspects of life and work in the city.

KATIE LUCAS, *London Walkabout*. The author, who runs a British tours company, gives details of a number of walks through London, each one fully described and enlivened with historical notes and anecdotes.

IAN NAIRN, *Nairn's London*. The classic guidebook, revised by Peter Gasson in a new edition. The late Ian Nairn was one of the most idiosyncratic of architectural writers, always controversial and always stimulating.

IAN NORRIE AND DOROTHY BOHM, *Walks Around London: A Celebration of the Capital*. Another title that says it all.

SIMON OLDING, *Exploring Museums, London*. The Museum Association's guide to the museums of the capital.

L. M. PALIS, *The Blue Plaques of London*. Small blue plaques recording the fact that someone of note once lived there can be seen on many of London's buildings. This is a comprehensive guide to who lived where.

MARY PEPLOW AND DEBRA SHIPLEY, *London For Free*. A guide to all those places that can be visited without spending any money. It proves a vacation in London can be fun—and cheap.

SAMUEL PEPYS, *Diary*. These famous diaries cover the years 1660 to 1669, a momentous period that included the restoration of the monarchy and the disasters of the Great Plague and Great Fire.

NIKOLAUS PEVSNER, *Cities of London and Westminster; London (2): South*. These volumes in the Penguin "Buildings of England" series are indispensable guides for all serious students of architecture, with full details of all the buildings of note in the area.

CHRISTOPHER PICK, *Children's Guide to London*. It would perhaps be more accurate to describe this as a parent's guide to London; it describes 12 walks and one boat trip, all guaranteed to keep children entertained. Many of the walks are well off the popular tourist routes.

FREDERICK A. POTTLE (editor), *Boswell's London Journal, 1762–1763.* Boswell is best known for his biography of Dr. Samuel Johnson, which also depicts London life, but it is the journal that gives the more intimate picture of city life in the 18th century, life enjoyed to the full by the young Scotsman.

V. S. PRITCHETT, *London Perceived.* A classic description of London by a distinguished author.

ROGER PROTZ, *The Best Pubs in London.* A guide to both the best pubs and the best beer by the former editor of *The Good Beer Guide.*

PETER QUENNELL (editor), *Mayhew's London.* A selection from Henry Mayhew's great four-volume work, *London Labour and the London Poor,* which first appeared in 1851, the year of the Great Exhibition.

ANN SAUNDERS, *Art and Architecture of London.* A scholarly, fully illustrated treatment of the subject.

RICHARD TRENCH AND ELLIS HILLMAN, *Under London: A Subterranean Guide.* A fascinating guide to the world beneath London's pavements. A book full of surprises.

JOHN TALBOT WHITE, *Country London.* A guide to parks and commons, riverside walks and woodland. A series of walks is described, each one appropriate to a particular time of year.

GEORGE WILLIAMS, *Guide to Literary London.* A series of tours illustrated with maps, this guide describes the places where major and minor writers lived and worked; the sites occupied by historic theaters, book shops, and coffee shops; and the places that have figured in English literature.

—Anthony Burton

LONDON

By David Wickers
with Bryn Frank

David Wickers, a longtime resident of London, is Travel Correspondent for the Sunday Times *of London, Travel Editor of* Marie Claire *magazine, and a regular contributor to several other magazines and newspapers in the United Kingdom. Bryn Frank is the author of several books about Britain. He has also contributed to* National Geographic, *among many other publications and guidebooks. He is the former editor of the monthly travel and feature magazine* In Britain. *Both he and David Wickers are members of the British Guild of Travel Writers.*

Most people seeing Stonehenge for the first time say "Isn't it small!" Many a traveller who has somehow missed out on London before will exclaim "Isn't it green!" That simple statement will stop many a commuter in his or her tracks, but it's true. The City office worker—we use the capital letter advisedly, for "the City" denotes the square mile, the original London now devoted mainly to commerce—may *think* he has been shoehorned into his deskspace, but the fact remains that this great metropolis contains enough unspoiled parkland to make it seem like a garden city.

It's one thing to soak up the sun in one of the royal parks, and it doesn't take a sophisticated tourist to tumble across St. James's Park, Green Park, Kensington Gardens, or Hyde Park and lay out his or her picnic. But there are precious copses and greenery besides: in the Inns of Court (where young lawyers are schooled and household names among law firms have their chambers); in the

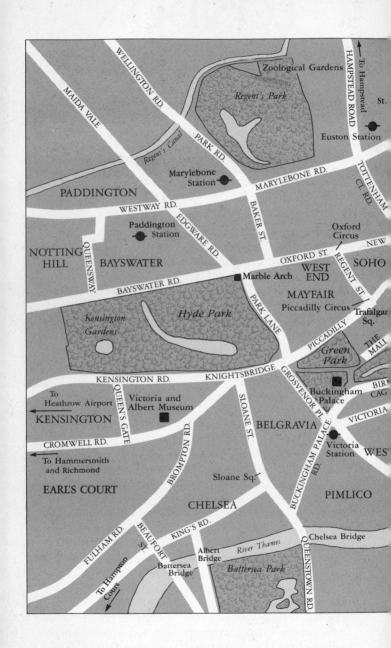

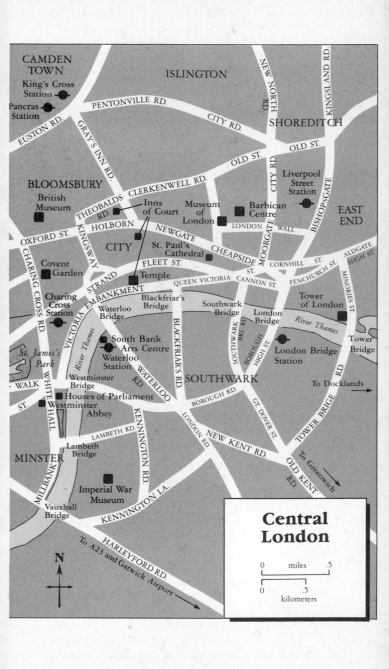

CAMDEN TOWN

ISLINGTON

King's Cross Station

Pancras Station

PENTONVILLE RD.

CITY RD.

NEW NORTH RD.

KINGSLAND RD.

SHOREDITCH

EUSTON RD.

GRAY'S INN RD.

OLD ST.

OLD ST.

CITY RD.

BLOOMSBURY

CLERKENWELL RD.

Liverpool Street Station

British Museum

THEOBALDS RD.

Inns of Court

Museum of London

Barbican Centre

BISHOPSGATE

EAST END

HOLBORN

KINGSWAY

NEWGATE

LONDON WALL

MOORGATE

OXFORD ST.

CITY

CHEAPSIDE

CORNHILL

ALDGATE HIGH ST.

CHARING CROSS RD.

Covent Garden

St. Paul's Cathedral

FLEET ST.

ST.

FENCHURCH ST.

MINORIES ST.

Temple

STRAND

QUEEN VICTORIA

CANNON ST.

Tower of London

VICTORIA EMBANKMENT

Charing Cross Station

Waterloo Bridge

Blackfriar's Bridge

Southwark Bridge

London Bridge

River Thames

Tower Bridge

River Thames

South Bank Arts Centre

BLACKFRIAR'S RD.

SOUTHWARK BRI. RD.

BOROUGH HIGH ST.

London Bridge Station

St. James's Park

Waterloo Station

WATERLOO RD.

SOUTHWARK

To Docklands

WHITE WALK

Westminster Bridge

BOROUGH RD.

GT. DOVER ST.

TOWER BRIDGE RD.

Houses of Parliament

Westminster Abbey

ST.

KENNINGTON RD.

LONDON RD.

NEW KENT RD.

To Greenwich

LAMBETH RD.

MINSTER

Lambeth Bridge

MILLBANK

Imperial War Museum

KENNINGTON LA.

OLD KENT RD.

Vauxhall Bridge

KENNINGTON RD.

N

To A23 and Gatwick Airport

HARLEYFORD RD.

Central London

0 — miles — .5

0 — kilometers — .5

Temple Gardens by the Thames, close to the Savoy Hotel; and in Berkeley Square.

Thus it is possible to find quiet in the heart of the city. For some it is the inner courtyard of the Wallace Collection (of fine art) in Manchester Square; for others it is a stroll around the expensive quarter that is Mayfair, or the somber granite banks and financial institutions of the City, or the London University enclave of Bloomsbury, easy on the eye and almost untouched by recent development.

They say London is a collection of villages. Understanding the difference between the City and the West End is a great help in London. Not knowing the difference is like going to Oxford or Cambridge and asking "where is the university"—it is actually all around you, in separate colleges.

Strictly speaking, "the City" means the area within the original Roman walls, and it is interesting to note that the original transmural expansion was made by those who were actually banned from the old city, such as actors and brothel-keepers, as well as certain privileged classes, including monks, aristocrats, lawyers, and foreigners, who could afford to ignore the protection afforded by the city walls. If you should visit the Smithfield market area (the streets around it, especially nearby Clerkenwell, have seen a massive financial investment, and the area is becoming stylish and interesting), remember that it first grew to prominence in the 12th century as a place where produce was sold just outside the city walls. Houndsditch, a street near Liverpool Street station (gateway to East Anglia), is another name that evokes memories of the City walls, and is so called because of the dead dogs that were often found in a stream that circled the walls.

By the 16th century London was bursting at the seams, as the capital grew on both sides of the Thames. Then came the Great Plague and Great Fire of 1665 and 1666, which, rather than bringing about the demise of London, paved the way for its rebirth.

But the term "City" remains, and for many people, as we hope to show, it is as full of interest as the West End, where the shops and conventional entertainment are located. Certainly, unless you venture into the famous "square mile" and beyond it toward the East End, you will never really feel the pulse of London.

There are several contenders for our opening pages, but we begin with London's river, "Old Father" Thames, and let the current carry us east to the City, the hub of finance, and its fringing areas. Then we leap back west into the center of town to feel the pulse of Covent Garden, with its historic roots but distinctly contemporary flavors. Nearby is Bloomsbury with its museums and literary associations, cosmopolitan Soho, and the West End's major stores. Mayfair, its neighbor to the west, could be dubbed American London, being home to the American embassy, but Westminster, the seat of the British Parliament and various government offices south of the West End, is undiluted U.K.

Moving still farther west, we take a turn upmarket to Belgravia and Knightsbridge, among the city's most affluent neighborhoods. Nearby Chelsea also has its share of wealthy residents, although the style is a shade more avant-garde. But this is just as well; otherwise the culture shock between Knightsbridge and Notting Hill, northwest across Hyde Park, famous for its annual carnival when its largely black population takes to the streets in a pageant of calypso and reggae, would be hard to take. Farther west still, both Richmond and Hampton Court, the palace of King Henry VIII, are green gems.

Not that the west enjoys a monopoly of urban greenery. In the north, Regent's Park, with its zoo, is one exception; it's also close to both Madame Tussaud's Waxworks Museum and Camden Lock's weekend market, both major tourist draws. Islington and Hampstead, farther north, are great places for exploring interesting small shops (Islington for antiques, Hampstead for clothes, though neither exclusively so). Hampstead also has the bonus of the best of London's open spaces: the rural landscapes of the Heath.

Back toward the east of the City is the epicenter of Cockney London, the East End, with its Jewish and, more recently, Indian and Pakistani populations. And nearby on the river is the newest "village" of London, the Docklands area, a vast landscape of formerly abandoned docklands that has been, and is still being, transformed into residential and commercial properties. From this newest neighborhood in London you can walk through a tunnel under the River Thames that will bring you face to face with Greenwich, one of its most historic.

MAJOR INTEREST

The Thames
A boat tour

Tower of London
South Bank Arts Centre

CENTRAL LONDON

The City
St. Paul's Cathedral
Museum of London
Fleet Street
The Strand
Inns of Court

Covent Garden
Royal Opera House
Courtauld Institute Galleries
Shopping

Bloomsbury
British Museum
Georgian London squares

Soho
Chinatown
Jazz
Ethnic restaurants

West End
Oxford Street and Regent Street for shopping
Piccadilly Circus
Royal Academy of Arts
Wallace Collection

Mayfair
Grosvenor and Berkeley squares

Westminster
Buckingham Palace (Changing of the Guard)
Churchill's bunker
Houses of Parliament
Westminster Abbey
St. James's Park
National Gallery
Tate Gallery

Dulwich Village
Dulwich College Picture Gallery

LONDON WEST

Knightsbridge—Belgravia
Harrods and other shops
Hyde Park

Notting Hill
Annual Caribbean carnival

Chelsea
Shopping on King's Road
Old houses of literary greats

South Kensington
Victoria and Albert Museum and other national
  museums

Richmond
Walks along the Thames
Kew Gardens

Hampton Court

LONDON NORTH

Camden Town
Camden Lock weekend market
Regent's Park and London Zoo
Nash terraces
Regent's Canal boat tours

Marylebone Road
Madame Tussaud's Waxworks Museum
Baker Street

Islington
Antiques shops and markets
Sadler's Wells Theatre

Hampstead
Hampstead Heath
Highgate hilltop village

LONDON EAST

East End
Cockney ambience
Petticoat Lane market
Kosher and Indian food

Docklands
Historic ships and buildings
New commercial and residential development

Greenwich
Old Royal Observatory
Maritime history

The Thames

Although there is no single London, there is a significant single divide between the north and south: the River Thames. Moving upstream (west) from Tower Bridge, there are more than a dozen bridges linking its northern and southern banks. Despite the ease with which one can cross from one side to the other, however, the emotional divide between north and south London is deeply rooted. While the south has always had its pockets of prosperity in such places as Dulwich Village and Blackheath, joined now by Battersea, Greenwich, Clapham, and a number of other recently gentrified boroughs, the north has long enjoyed a monopoly on affluence. But more to the point, as far as the traveller is concerned, south London has relatively little to offer the visitor compared with the wealth of attractions—from stylish shops to seasoned sights—north of the river.

London happened because of its river. Its commercial significance was the city's raison d'être. Today, although the forest of masts and rigging, vibrant warehouses, cranes, and general state of economic frenzy that dominated the area in the past have all but disappeared from the scene, the Thames is still the most essential element in London's chemistry.

Among the world's great rivers the Thames ranks very low. Its entire length runs only a little more than 200 miles, making it a mere stream in contrast to, say, the 4,000 miles of the Amazon or even Europe's 1,000-mile-long Rhine. And it is not always a pretty sight, especially at low tide when its muddy banks are exposed. But while a boat ride along the Seine may be hard to beat when it comes to romance, Paris's river cannot hold a candle to the Thames for the sheer interest sustained by the passing panorama.

The Thames was once the main highway of London, and in Victorian times people used to "take the water" much as we now "catch a bus"; the penny steamers were packed with day-trippers. With the development of the Docklands area, boating on the Thames has once again become popular, and both pleasure craft and river buses are plentiful. The fares on the riverbuses are reasonable, and the departures punctual. The best seats are at the front, where you can see the landmarks on both river-banks. (For more information, see the Thames Line, be-low, in the Chelsea section.) Likewise, in the 1950s the

Thames was so filthy that anyone who had the misfortune to fall in was rushed off to have his stomach pumped. Today perch, trout, and even the occasional salmon have been fished from its waters. The Thames has been granted a new lease on life, one in which leisure has taken the place of commerce, and its importance as a focal point of any visit to London is of greater significance now than it has ever been.

A sightseeing boat ride is one of the best ways to enjoy the Thames. Starting from **Westminster Pier**, right beside Westminster Bridge across the road from the Houses of Parliament, regularly scheduled boats depart in either direction. You'll drift past several of the most important sights in the city, and while most cry out for far closer scrutiny than from the rails of a passing launch, at least the ride—backed by a commentary—is an apt introduction to the London cityscape.

Less easy to arrange, but a big bonus if it does come your way, is the sight of Thames-side London from the air. Many a weary transatlantic passenger is enlivened by the sight of Tower Bridge dwarfing the White Tower, which was built by William the Conqueror as the earliest part of the Tower of London and renders the nearby City church of All Hallows by the Tower pathetically small. Naval history buffs will spot the HMS *Belfast,* the doughty World War II cruiser, and the child in all of us will probably think the Palace of Westminster looks like a toy fortress painstakingly assembled by a twelve-year-old. The tower of Big Ben is more noticeable for its clockface than its Victorian fripperies, and, as on the ground, a lot of people are surprised at the way the Victoria Tower, at the westerly, House of Lords end of the palace, dominates.

When the light is right, you will also notice from the air how flat the eastern approaches to the city are, and how serpentine the course of the Thames actually is (most maps simplify its progress). That flatness is one reason the spectacular Thames Flood Barrier, which is open to visitors, was built. Another thing the observant or regular air traveller will notice is how much greenery there is in the city. On one swathe of undeveloped land, Hackney Marshes, there is enough space to fit *one hundred* football fields side by side.

The most historically important riverside sight is the **Tower of London**. First built of wood by William the Conqueror in 1067, then converted to stone a decade later, it protected the king's capital from both invaders sailing

upstream from the Channel and from conquered Londoners who might challenge his authority. The tower's most
famous historical role, however, was as a prison to a score
of leading figures, including the Little Princes (both alleg-
edly murdered in the so-called Bloody Tower), Thomas
More, Anne Boleyn, Sir Walter Raleigh, Guy Fawkes, and,
the last in the line, Rudolf Hess. Many were to pass through
Traitor's Gate, the main entrance, never to see daylight
again.

Although the tower is one of those "obvious" sights that
the majority of Londoners probably haven't visited since
their childhood, its popularity with visitors is enormous.
Apart from the impressive antiquity of the place, there are
two other aspects of a tower visit that will linger in the
memory long after your knowledge of its history has
faded. First is the **Crown Jewels**, which include the five-
pound crown said to have been worn by all British monarchs, including Queen Elizabeth II, since Charles II (and
maybe even earlier), as well as the crown of the Queen
Mother, which incorporates the enormous Koh-i-Noor
diamond (a name now associated with dozens of mostly
insignificant Indian restaurants scattered throughout the
city).

The second memory will be of the **Beefeaters**—more
officially, the Yeoman Warders—whose history dates
from their role as bodyguards to Henry VII in the 15th
century. They parade every morning at 11:00 in the Inner
Ward, but you can see them at their most spectacular—
though you need to make a written application to the
Resident Governor of the Tower to do so—at the Ceremony of the Keys, the closing of the main gates of the
tower every evening at 10:00. Before you leave the tower,
be sure to count the ravens. There are six, and legend
dictates that when they no longer flap about the place, the
tower will fall. Try to arrive early to avoid the crowds—
re-entry tickets are available to enable you to go out to
eat. The earlier or the later in the day you go, the better.

Immediately in front of the tower is **Tower Bridge**,
probably the single most widely recognized landmark in
the entire city. Though your visit may not coincide with
the impressive opening yawn of its road section—or
bascules—as it only occurs roughly three times a week,
the bridge nevertheless makes a stunning picture. It took
eight years to build and was opened in 1894 with great
pomp and ceremony by the Prince of Wales, later King
Edward VII. At the time it was hailed as one of the great

engineering wonders of the world. In its heyday the bridge opened for river traffic some 50 times a day and required a permanent staff of more than 100, including a few whose only job was to collect the horse droppings (presumably so they wouldn't cascade down the opening bascules onto waiting traffic).

The bridge cost £1 million to build, and in the early 1980s £2.5 million was the price of converting it into a tourist attraction. Today you can get acquainted with the bridge from the walkway, the topmost, latticed structure linking the two great Gothic-Revival towers. The walkway and several tower rooms constitute a **museum**, with exhibits illustrating the history of the bridge (including, for those who miss it, pictures of the bridge with its jaws wide open for passing ships; one photograph shows a bus that failed to stop and was caught straddling the gap). Best of all, the museum affords one of the best views of the Thames to be had.

When describing London from the air we mentioned the **church of All Hallows by the Tower**. This is just one of the many exquisite city churches, overlooked by all too many travellers, that can be havens of tranquillity in an inevitably noisy and crowded metropolis—and they are repositories of London history. Among other favorites are nearby **St. Andrew Undershaft**, close to Leadenhall Street, which dates from about 1530 and is rich in monuments, and **St. Giles Without Cripplegate**, which is about 600 years old and is where Shakespeare is said to have attended the baptism of his nephew in 1604. ("Without" in the name denotes that it was built outside the city walls; St. Giles is in the Barbican Arts Centre northwest of the Tower.)

If you can only spare the time to see one such church, though, make it All Hallows, on Byward Street. For one thing, it combines well with a visit to the Tower itself. The foundation is A.D. 675, but the present building is 13th century. The registers give details of the marriage here of John Quincy Adams, who was to become the sixth president of the United States, and of the baptism of William Penn on October 23, 1644. In the undercroft is a Roman pavement *in situ* and a model of Roman London.

Having mentioned some favorite London churches, we should note that many people consider the handsomest London church of all to be **St. Martin-in-the-Fields**, on Trafalgar Square (see below under Westminster). Apart from its physical charms and its very popular lunchtime concerts, it offers visitors a rare chance every year—during the Harvest Festival service held in October—to see some or all of London's "Pearlies," an East End hierarchy whose "royal family" wear mother-of-pearl suits and collect vast sums for charity.

The place in Central London that offers the most intimate relationship with the Thames, however, is the **South Bank Arts Centre**, by Waterloo Bridge. In front of the Royal Festival Hall, built for the Festival of Britain in 1951, there is a broad promenade along which to stroll, lean, and watch the passing barge traffic or gaze at the Houses of Parliament. The **Royal Festival Hall** was an architectural triumph in its time, but you may not feel the same accolades can be applied to its neighbors. You will no doubt form a strong opinion about the newer buildings in the complex—the stark concrete presences that house the **Queen Elizabeth Hall**, the **Purcell Room**, the **Hayward Gallery**, the **National Theatre**, and the **National Film Theatre**. The Hayward Gallery generates much more pleasure inside than out, and is known for its imaginative but not outlandish contemporary exhibitions, as well as for its "borrowings" from major museums—for example, in 1990 an exhibition of Chinese paintings from the British Museum.

The newest attraction, opened in September 1988, is the **Museum of the Moving Image** (affectionately known as "MOMI"), the largest museum in the world devoted to cinema and television. It traces the history of film from the Chinese shadow plays of 2000 B.C. to the latest in optical disc technology. The style of presentation here is interactive; the museum is full of evocative images and cinema memorabilia, plus opportunities to get involved in activities such as editing a film and script reading from an autocue. There are also high-quality temporary exhibitions. Another new development here is Gabriel's Wharf, next to the National Theatre, which features a colorful food market on Fridays, with some stalls open on Sundays.

CENTRAL LONDON
The City

Unmistakably, **St. Paul's Cathedral** *is* London. Designed by Sir Christopher Wren, the great 17th-century church now sits rather uncomfortably in its surroundings, not unlike an aging, legally protected tenant who occupies a prime parcel of fast-appreciating real estate. Look at a selection of old paintings of London, and St. Paul's, with its curvaceous dome and squat twin towers, reigns magnificently over the skyline. Even in pictures taken during the Blitz, the wartime bombing inflicted by the Luftwaffe, the cathedral's environs lie around its ankles.

Today the cathedral is both hidden and dwarfed by clusters of uninspired office buildings, all fed by revenues from the City's commerce. Prince Charles has even gone on record as decrying such works as "carbuncles." Poor old St. Paul's looks pitiably ill at ease in this setting, and, architectural gem though it is, it no longer works the way Wren intended it to.

When you do occasionally catch a glimpse of the cathedral riding above the skyline of modern London—from the southern bank of the Thames near Blackfriars Bridge, for example, or looking east down Fleet Street or from a riverboat—it is superb. The dome, a giant pewter tureen from the outside, ornately painted within, is one of the cathedral's most impressive features. Depending on whether you are gazing at it from within or without, the size varies; the interior of the dome is actually a false ceiling, and is best appreciated from the less neck-craning perspective afforded by the famous Whispering Gallery, named after its unusual acoustics, which allow a *sotto voce* murmur on the far side of the dome to be carried around the circumference and be heard by an ear held beside the opposite wall.

If you have time after seeing St. Paul's, walk eastward along Queen Victoria Street and look out for the narrow Edwardian frontage of **Sweetings**, a classic London restaurant (lunchtimes only) little known to outsiders that serves top quality fish dishes to discriminating merchant bankers, some of whom eat at the counter. Best of all, because it's quick and informal it's not expensive.

St. Paul's is arguably more a symbol of the City of London than of London the city, a confusing matter for first-time visitors but a distinction that is easy to explain. The City of London is both the oldest section of town and, as London's financial heart, the place that bore the brunt of 1987's Black October, when share prices plummeted. It is an official city-within-a-city. Its foundation was laid by the Romans in A.D. 43, when they built the first bridge over the Thames and declared the existence of Londinium, defending their new outpost with a wall. Fragments of their protective perimeter can still be seen today (next

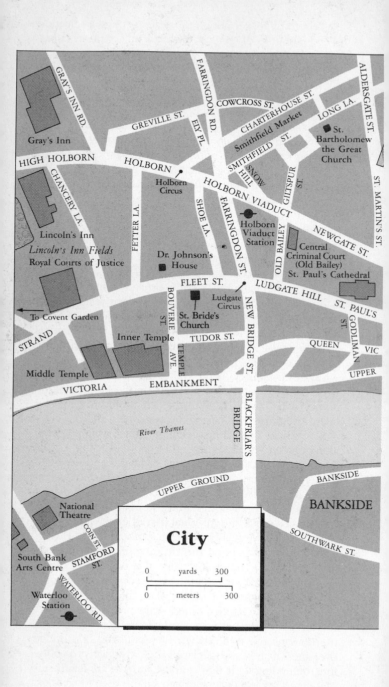

City

| 0 | yards | 300 |
| 0 | meters | 300 |

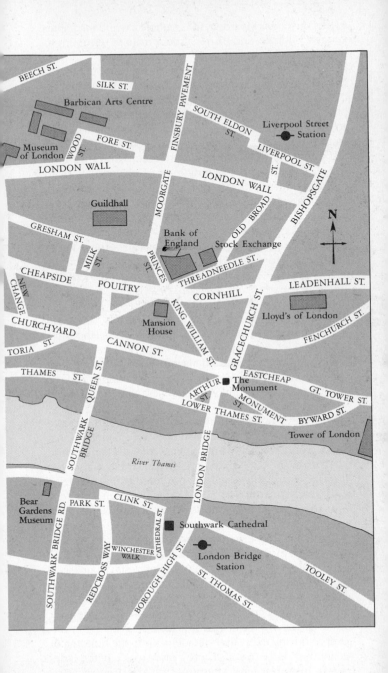

to the Museum of London, for example), while the names Ludgate, Aldgate, and Bishopsgate remain as testimony to the wall's existence.

Visitors with more than a slight curiosity about historic London should first stop by the **Museum of London**, on the street called (evocatively) London Wall, which explains the story of the capital from prehistoric times. It is an unprepossessing modern building at first sight, its entrance opening directly onto the pedestrian walkway that connects the Barbican Centre (see below) with the rest of the City. But the building's youth lends itself to exciting, contemporary displays and light, airy galleries.

Pity the unfortunate person whose task it was to whittle down a potentially mammoth collection into a few choice exhibits that would best portray London's history. The galleries are open-plan and chronologically ordered, so it makes sense to start on the upper floor with The Thames in Prehistory, followed by Roman, Saxon and Medieval, Tudor, and Early Stuart London. Downstairs, mock shop fronts, transport exhibits, and video screens are part of the Late Stuart, Georgian, early 19th-century, Imperial, 20th-century, and Ceremonial London displays (the latter includes the Lord Mayor's State Coach, built in 1757 and still used in the annual Lord Mayor's Show). Other galleries specialize in prints, drawings, and paintings of London, as well as costumes and textiles. Now move on to roam the streets.

In Medieval times the City expanded to roughly a square mile (677 acres). Today British and major international banks, insurance companies, commodity exchanges, and other financial firms have their headquarters within the historic Square Mile originally bordered by the Medieval wall. Nearly five million people pour in during the day from suburbia, but walk these streets on weekends or at night and you will hardly meet a soul.

The Great Fire of 1666 (described so vividly in Samuel Pepys's *Diary*), the wartime Blitz, and postwar redevelopment have proved to be in the worst interests of conservation. Evidences of old London are thin on the ground, although 3,000-year-old Celtic crematory urns have been found beneath Fenchurch Street, and the foundations of the Rose Theatre, built in 1587, have recently been uncovered during excavations made prior to the building of yet another office tower . There's more to see in the little-known **Bear Gardens Museum and Arts Centre**, Bear Gardens, Bankside, on the south side of the river more or less opposite St. Paul's. a reconstructed Elizabethan theater, a plan of the proposed new Globe Theatre, and a Rose Theatre reconstruction. And one of the finest collections of Elizabethan and Tudor London artifacts is the "Cheapside Hoard," the contents of an Elizabethan jeweler's shop that was buried, only to be rediscovered in 1912. It is now displayed, in a setting as it once was, in the Museum of London.

If you're blessed with a sense of imagination you can get a feel of the City's past from present-day names. Cheapside—the name comes from the Saxon "ceap," to barter—was the site of a market in the Middle Ages, while nearby Poultry and Milk streets had more specific retail functions. In the Middle Ages, the **Guildhall**, on Wood Street a short walk southeast from the Museum of London, was the nerve center of the City, with a cluster of Livery Halls (for example, the Apothecaries' Hall, the Goldsmiths' Hall, and the Haberdashers' Hall) around it. These were the headquarters of the Guilds of London, which looked after the interests of various merchant and artisan members, and maintained professional standards. Visitor access is sometimes possible by prior arrangement; Tel: (071) 260-1456 for further information (City of London Information Bureau). Dating from 1411–1435, the Hall of the Corporation of the City of London, to give the Guildhall its official name, is still recognizably Medieval in parts, although the lower section of the Great Hall, the porch, and the crypt were damaged by the Great Fire of 1666 and bombed in 1940; they were restored in 1952–1954. The Court of the Common Council of the City of London meets here every third Thursday, and the public is admitted. And within the contemporary fabric of City life you will still find numerous references to sheriffs, aldermen, and the early trade guilds.

Pepys is one of very few 17th-century writers who is read today. His description of the Great Fire is still riveting: "Poor people staying in their houses as long as till the very fire touched them. . . . The poor pigeons I perceive were loath to leave their houses, but hovered about the windows and balconies till some of them were burned and fell down. . . . The churches, houses and all on fire and flaming at once, and a horrid noise the flames made, and the cracking of houses and their ruine. . . ."

Signs that the City is a separate entity include the uniforms of local policemen, similar but not quite the same as those worn in the rest of London (they have red and white armbands, for a start), and various unique ceremonies, culminating in the Lord Mayor's Show to mark the annual election of the new top man. Even the Queen is traditionally escorted into the City by the Lord Mayor. And each December the Worshipful Company of Butchers presents a boar's head to the Lord Mayor in thanks for the City's giving the butchers access to the Fleet, once a tributary of the Thames, where they could clean the "entrails of beasts."

The **Barbican Arts Centre**, the City's newest grand-scale development, on Silk Street, grew out of an enormous hole in the ground, a 60-acre bomb site just to the east of the Museum of London. In addition to its trade exhibitions, concerts (it's home to the London Symphony Orchestra), stage plays (many by the resident Royal Shakespeare Company), conferences, and art exhibitions, the Barbican is a place where some 5,000 mostly wealthy people live. It is also a place that visitors love to hate, not only for its out-of-the-way location and overpoweringly harsh design but also for the confusion that any simple movement within its labyrinthine confines seems to involve. The name "Barbican" comes from the French/Persian "House on the Wall," which enabled watch to be kept on the northern routes of the city. There is little of the old Roman Wall left in the City, and the only structure extant, from the beginning of the second century, is the remains of a Roman fort at Cripplegate. The latter can be viewed from the Barbican Centre as well as from a window in the Museum of London.

Of course there are other City sights to see, including the Stock Exchange, the Bank of England, the Mansion House (the official residence of the Lord Mayor), and the futuristic Lloyd's insurance building (built like the Centre Georges Pompidou in Paris with its insides on the outside). Many of the buildings here will be of little interest to anyone whose working life is not plugged into the wheels and deals of commerce, however. The **Monument**, which commemorates the Great Fire (it started in a bakery that, at 202 feet, was situated as far from the base of the monument as the monument is tall), is a notable exception. It was designed by Wren, who, were he to climb to the top today, might well be tempted to leap to the bottom after seeing the clutter around his more famous edifice. It used to be one of the City's best known viewpoints, but it has been dwarfed by recent development. A Latin inscription at the base (with a translation) tells that Charles II—prompted by Wren—petitioned Parliament to rebuild while the ruins of the fire were still smoking. A nearby notice says "No lift. Just 311 steps." And there are encouraging notices on the way up!

Never does the City come so entertainingly alive for the ordinary visitor as on the day of the Lord Mayor's Procession, held on the second Saturday in November. You'll have every chance, if you stand along the well-publicized route, to see the newly sworn-in Lord Mayor, who in 1991 will be the 802nd person to hold the office. During his (or her) term the Lord Mayor will make about 1,000 official appearances, eat 600 formal meals, and make about 800 speeches. You can see the Lord Mayor's 244-year-old coach at other times of the year in the Museum of London.

Fleet Street Area

Before the development of the Docklands area, you would have found the office of nearly every national newspaper somewhere along **Fleet Street**, which runs west from St. Paul's and Ludgate Circus. Although the high-tech machinations of Wapping have milked Fleet Street of some of her most successful sons (*The Times, The Sunday Times, The Daily Telegraph, The Daily Express* and the *Sunday Express,* and the *News of the World* among them), a large number of the buildings here are still devoted to churning out newsprint. Don't ignore the offshoots, either; Shoe Lane, for example, is home to the International Press Centre. One of Fleet Street's most beautiful landmarks is the Art Deco former Daily Express building at number 121, a world of glass and polished chrome. If Fleet Street ever loses its media associations, it will be a momentous day; the printing trade has been linked with it since the beginning of the 16th century.

St. Paul's, towering above Ludgate Circus, forms an impressive eastern anchor to Fleet Street. Start walking the length of the street from there and, between the various media giants, you'll come across traditional tobacconists, topsy-turvy Tudor-gabled buildings, **Dr. Johnson's House** in Gough Square (open to the public daily except Sundays and holidays), where the famous dictionary was written between 1749 and 1759, and several large outdoor-clothing and sports stores. At its western end the road takes a sharp upturn in class as it becomes the Strand.

Halfway along Fleet Street, on the north side, look for a

tiny lane called Wine Office Court. Dr. Johnson would have turned this corner many a time, for it leads to an ancient inn called **Ye Olde Cheshire Cheese**, a remarkable throwback to the 17th century. You'll probably need to queue, unless you arrive at an odd time. Inside, there's sawdust on the floor, wood paneling, and traditional food and ale.

At the western, Strand end of Fleet Street look for London's last-surviving example in situ of a timber-framed Jacobean townhouse (number 17), known as **Prince Henry's Room**. It survived only because the Great Fire of 1666 stopped next door. While it would be nice to report that Prince Henry, son of James I, had lodgings here, the colloquial name seems to come from the fact that Henry became Prince of Wales in 1610 while the building, a pub, was being restored.

The Strand (or simply Strand) deserves a brief detour. It parallels the river (although its pedestrians cannot see the river), thus adding immense value to the buildings along its southern flank, most of which back onto the water. The world-famous Savoy Hotel is without doubt the grandest of these (try to have a breakfast in its delightful **River Room**), though its neighbor, **Somerset House**, is a close competitor. Built in white Portland stone, the latter used to be the headquarters of the Registrar General of Births, Deaths, and Marriages but now houses the less popular Board of Inland Revenue, the Probate Registry, and the very popular **Courtauld Institute Galleries**, which recently moved into new quarters here (see the Covent Garden section, below). The **Savoy Hotel** has as its forecourt the only road in Great Britain where you are obliged to drive on the right side. This dates back to a special privilege granted by Parliament to allow Savoy Theatre-goers (the theater stands adjacent to the hotel) to dismount from their carriages directly into the theater. If you are lucky enough to be invited to join a party dining at the Savoy, don't be surprised if you are seated next to Kaspar the cat; he is the Savoy's own model puss brought in to avoid unlucky parties of 13.

Other worthy sights in the area include the Wren-designed **St. Clement Danes** church (the bells ring out the "Oranges and Lemons" nursery rhyme at 9:00 A.M., noon, 3:00 P.M., and 6:00 P.M., Mondays through Fridays), the Royal Courts of Justice (see below), and the traffic-ridden semicircular street known as the Aldwych, with the BBC's Bush House, the **London School of Economics** nearby on Houghton Street, and the **Roman Bath**—an important source of cleanliness in its heyday, now owned by the National Trust. Restored in the 17th century, it is open to the public by appointment only; Tel: (071) 798-2063, 24 hours in advance.

Benjamin Franklin had lodgings at 36 Craven Street, off the Strand, during the time he lived in England as a man of substance and agent for Pennsylvania (from 1757 to 1762 and again, after a brief return to America, from 1764 to 1775). He had first come to London in 1724 after a family quarrel, and at that time stayed about 18 months.

The Inns of Court

In addition to its journalistic associations, Fleet Street (along with its offshoot, Chancery Lane) cuts through the heart of legal London. Any tour of the area should begin with the **Temple**, reached via Middle Temple Lane, one of the tiny side streets off Fleet Street. Apart from containing the 12th-century **Temple church**, one of four round churches still extant in England, the Temple is divided into Inner, Middle, and Outer temples. The last has long since disappeared, but the other two were developed into Inns of Court when the church reverted to the crown in the late 13th century.

Although the outside world rarely penetrates the privacy of London's Inns of Court (except as victims of some heinous deed), a stroll through the cloistered courtyards of the core of the country's legal community will reveal a tranquil world of fine stone buildings, manicured gardens, and elegant quadrangles. In a few steps you can leave the traffic hubbub of Chancery Lane and find yourself in an atmosphere more reminiscent of Oxford or Cambridge than the City.

The "Big Four," all a short stroll from one another, refers to the four Inns of Court: Gray's Inn, Lincoln's Inn, Middle Temple, and Inner Temple (the last two are part of the Temple complex, the other two, separate from each other, are off to the north). Together, they have been the linchpins of Britain's closely knit legal community since the 14th century.

In 1292 King Edward I declared that the country's legal system was a mass of shortcomings. Until then all matters of justice had been dealt with by members of the clergy. They were undoubtedly the most literate members of society, but they were still laymen so far as non-canon law was concerned. Edward's desire to professionalize the legal system led to the recruitment of top candidates from the aristocracy. At first the students were scattered around the country, but by the end of the 14th century all barrister pupils were brought to London and accommodated in hostels, or "inns."

A note of explanation is called for before delving into the inns' hallowed grounds. In Britain, unlike in the United States and most other countries, there are two distinct types of lawyer. Barristers represent the prosecution or defense in the high-ranking courts, whereas solicitors—who are forbidden to stand and be heard in these places—handle the nuts-and-bolts paperwork on a case and deal directly with clients. The barrister may never so much as meet those he subsequently represents in court. But the laws governing the law are beginning to change; in the near future solicitors are likely to be permitted to represent clients.

Today each inn is an autonomous entity with its own chapel, library, and dining hall. The latter, a richly decorated room, has always been the focal point; Queen Elizabeth I and her courtiers, for example, were wined and dined in the most northerly of the inns, above High Holborn Street, the Tudor-style **Gray's Inn**, on so many occasions that today's inmates still toast "Good Queen Bess" in a room adorned with relics of a vessel captured during the rout of the Spanish Armada. A number of Shakespeare's plays also debuted in the inns: Gray's Inn saw the first performance of *The Comedy of Errors* in 1594, while the magnificent Middle Temple Hall can claim the same honor for *Twelfth Night* in 1602. Nowadays you can still catch the occasional performance in the forecourt on clement summer evenings. (Gray's Inn is still commemorated by Gray's Inn Road, which runs from King's Cross to Holborn.)

The oldest of the four Inns of Court, **Lincoln's Inn**, just east of Kingsway, near the Holborn Underground station and off Lincoln's Inn Fields, can name eleven Prime Ministers among its members. Records date from the 15th century in this Inn, which was built partly on land owned by Henry Lacy, Earl of Lincoln, whose lion figures in the Inn's badge. The poet John Donne, Chaplain of the Inn and later Dean of St. Paul's Cathedral, laid the foundation stone of the chapel in 1619.

The college-like buildings of the Temple, just off Fleet Street, are home to the two other inns: the **Middle Tem-**

ple and the **Inner Temple**. Originally home of the Knights
Templar, a military order founded in Jerusalem in 1118,
the Temple was built after the knights, weary of the
Crusades, arrived in London in need of a home. At the
same time that Edward I was reshuffling the legal system,
the order was disbanded, and so the Temple was let out
to the law students.

While television's pompous, blustering Rumpole of
the Bailey is a caricature of British barristers, there is a
great deal of snobbishness attached to the inns, and the
members of each one adhere to a strict hierarchy. Their
interiors are sacrosanct, as they contain the offices (or
"chambers") of practicing barristers, whose names are
listed beside each doorway.

Over the years these lists have read like the pages of
Who's Who. Sir Thomas More and several other Lord Chan-
cellors were members of Lincoln's Inn, the place where
rival Prime Ministers Disraeli and Gladstone also qualified
as barristers. Sir Francis Bacon, Sir Winston Churchill, and
Franklin Roosevelt belonged to Gray's Inn, and Charles
Dickens was apprenticed to one of its lawyers at age 15. Sir
Walter Raleigh and Sir Francis Drake were both members
of the Middle Temple (it's even rumored that one of its
serving tables is made of timber from Drake's ship, *The
Golden Hind*). John Dickinson, a Middle Templar, was the
man who coined the phrase "no taxation without represen-
tation"; when the Declaration of Independence was drawn
up, five Middle Templars signed the final document. In
addition, many prominent North Americans are still honor-
ary members of the inns.

You will undoubtedly catch sight of barristers rushing
to and from court in twos and threes, each clutching a
bundle of "briefs." By tradition, they cannot use brief-
cases; all documents must be carried openly and bound
by a red ribbon (hence the expression "red tape").

Having prepared their cases, barristers have only a
short walk to work. The neo-Gothic **Royal Courts of
Justice** on the Strand, home of the High Court and the
Court of Appeal of England and Wales, pass judgment on
the most important civil cases. The vaulted, cathedral-like
Great Hall, supported by granite pillars and hung with oil
paintings of former judges and coats of arms, echoes the
hushed activity. Barristers, ticking on White Rabbit schedules, their black gowns bloated like sails in a gale-force
wind and frizzes (wigs) askew, emerge from one corridor, zip across the hall, and disappear into another. Don't

even attempt to follow them; five and a half miles of corridors lead off the hall, and that's a lot of shoe leather if you get lost.

Members of the public whose cases are scheduled for judgment in one of the 64 courts later in the day stand huddled in earnest conversation with solicitors. All the day's cases are listed in showcases, but that's as far as you can go. Though not legally restricted from entering, visitors are customarily not allowed to watch cases in progress. To witness a trial you have to make your way to the public gallery of the Old Bailey, the most famous criminal court in the world.

"Justice is not blind at the Old Bailey," declared the City of London Corporation 75 years ago when the **Old Bailey** (or the Central Criminal Court, to give it its proper name; located back east near St. Paul's, at Old Bailey and Newgate streets) was built on the site of Newgate Prison, which was demolished in 1902. To emphasize the point, they made sure that their version of the Goddess of Justice, the statue that sits on the building's green dome high above the traffic jams holding the scales of justice and the sword of retribution, was one of the only ones in the world without a blindfold.

The open area in front of the court building dates from 1783, when public hangings first took place here in an attempt to reduce the riots that often accompanied the journey of prisoners west from Newgate Prison along Oxford Street to the gallows at Tyburn. A plaque at the junction of Bayswater and Edgware roads, close to Marble Arch, marks the site of Tyburn Gallows, fashioned "in a triangular manner" in order to face each of the three roads leading to the junction, and where up to 24 people at a time could be hanged. (The last public execution in England took place at Newgate in 1868, when Michael Barrett was convicted and hanged for the bombing of Clerkenwell Prison, in which 12 died.) Many prisoners did not survive to stand on the gallows, dying as a result of the unsanitary conditions in Newgate, where gaol fever (a form of typhoid) bred. To hide the stench that pervaded the courts, and supposedly to protect against infection, judges held posies of sweet-smelling flowers. Today judges still carry posies on ceremonial occasions as a reminder of the appalling conditions of years gone by.

Criminal justice in England and Wales focuses on the Old Bailey, and within the walls of its 23 courts you can hear the verdicts of major trials, many of which are referred to the High Court judges as a last resort. The most famous and most important cases are heard in the surprisingly small Court Number One, a wood-paneled courtroom whose dock floorboards have creaked under some of the most notorious criminals in the history of 20th-century Britain. These include the American-born Dr. Crippen, accused of murdering his wife, Belle Elmore, and cutting her up into pieces before eloping with his mistress. More recent trials have included that of former M.P. Jeremy Thorpe, acquitted of conspiring to murder his ex-lover, and the "Yorkshire Ripper," the rapist and murderer who terrorized that part of the country in the late 1970s.

Not many townhouses begin life as a museum, but the house near Lincoln's Inn into which architect and antiquarian Sir John Soane moved in 1753 was actually designed to house his collection of architectural fragments, prints, antiquities, and paintings. **Sir John Soane's Museum**, 13 Lincoln's Inn Fields, is a museum with a difference. Instead of hurrying through marble halls you press the door bell, are admitted with some ceremony, and sign the visitor's book. You're then free to wander slowly through the many-roomed mansion and be impressed by the profusion of mirrors and play of light at almost every angle. There are some domestic touches on the first floor, but mostly you'll be astonished by the sheer flamboyance and originality of the decor.

Covent Garden

Within the space of a few years, Covent Garden, the city's old fruit-and-vegetable market (west of the Inns of Court area), has been transformed into one of the liveliest and loveliest urban centers in Europe.

In underground cellars once used to store bananas, young sophisticates now pick cherries off the ends of tiny paper parasols resting on the edges of cocktail glasses. From stalls in the central Apple Market, where Granny Smiths and Cox's Orange Pippins were once stacked, shoppers now buy elaborately patterned sweaters and scores of other products handmade by the craftspeople who sell them. And in high-ceilinged warehouses that once stored crates of carrots, parsnips, potatoes, and other roots, Filofax clutchers now dine on nouvelle cuisine served by bow-tied waiters whose own social back-

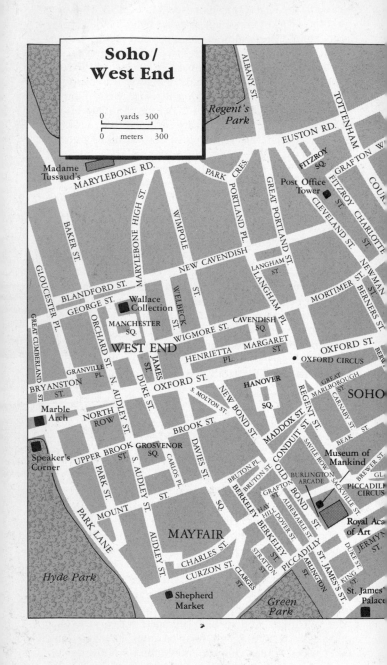

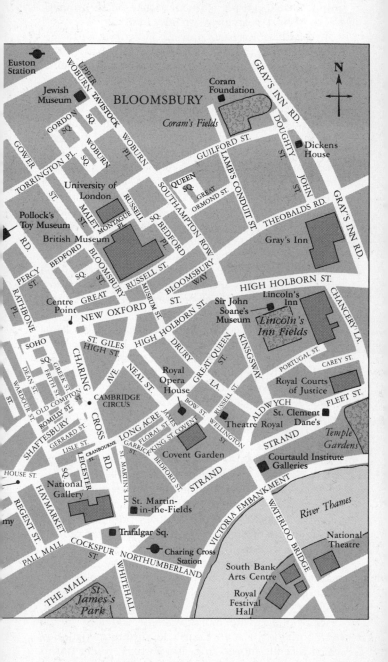

ground would not permit them to take on such menial and deferential roles anywhere else in Britain.

In an earlier incarnation Covent Garden was also a very fashionable part of town. Inigo Jones designed **St. Paul's Church**, popularly known as the actors' church, as well as the piazza on which it stands. The story has it that the earl of Bedford (the original landowner) told Jones that his budget would only stretch to cover a barn, so the architect promised the "most beautiful barn in the country." The church was completed in 1633 as part of London's first square, and was modeled after the Italian piazzas Jones had studied in his travels. It was later destroyed by fire but rebuilt to its original specifications.

The original Theatre Royal, where Nell Gwynn sold oranges, opened in 1662, and soon afterward the **Royal Opera House** opened its doors on Bow Street, off Long Acre. But the area's early elegance did not last long. The presence of the wealthy drew rogues—the poet Dryden was beaten up in an alleyway outside the Bucket of Blood pub, now the Lamb and Flag. It is no coincidence that London's first police force, the Bow Street Runners, was established just around the corner.

Fostered by the security of the strong arm of the law, a new wave of prosperity followed. This renaissance was marked by the construction of the Central Market buildings in 1830, when the duke of Bedford decided that something smarter was needed to replace the rows of shanty vegetable stalls that had stood their ground since the 17th century. Coffeehouses also flourished; Dr. Johnson first met Boswell in a small establishment, now fittingly called Boswell's, on Russell Street.

In 1974, after three centuries of commercial activity, the market vendors moved out to modern premises across the River Thames at Nine Elms. They left behind a mass of grimy buildings—and an enormous debate on just what to do with such a potentially prime site on the fringes of the West End. Restoration work on the old buildings was started, but the transition was not accomplished without opposition—mainly from neighborhood residents, who would have preferred to see the development of a simple residential community, not an upscale designer village.

Today one of the more welcome additions to the neighborhood is the **Courtauld Institute Galleries**, which recently moved from Bloomsbury, where only a third of the collection could be seen at any time, to

Somerset House on the Strand. Painters represented in this impressive collection include numerous 19th-century masters—Bonnard, Degas, van Gogh, Seurat, Manet, Monet, Cézanne—as well as Rubens, Michelangelo, Brueghel, Dürer, Tintoretto, Rembrandt, Gainsborough, Bellini, and Kokoschka.

The Covent Garden area offers some of the best of London's shopping—not for basics (there is only one butcher shop, and even that is mostly a purveyor of game) but for fashionable, boutique-type wares. Lots of old traders remain, including Anello and Davide, the theatrical shoemakers; the Drury Tea and Coffee Co.; and Stanfords, the map shop. Covent Garden itself and neighboring streets such as Long Acre contain scores of galleries and bookshops, clothing boutiques, epicurean and organic food stores, gift shops, and other establishments whose wares all bear a stamp of design that far exceeds the functional.

Many shop fronts are based on original designs, and in the north hall, site of the old Apple Market, a flavor of the old market days remains. Forty original wrought-iron stands, salvaged from the Flower Market, are now rented to traders and craftspeople, who sell their goods beneath the magnificent glass roof. As for the Old Flower Market itself—on the eastern side of the piazza, completed in 1872 and staffed entirely by women—it now houses the **London Transport Museum**'s collection of early buses, trams, trains, trolleybuses, and motor and horse buses; a collection of 1920s and 1930s advertising posters; videos, including one with recollections from people who worked on the London buses; a simulated driver's journey on the Underground during the First World War; and many interactive displays. The entrance to Britain's first **Theatre Museum** is next door on Tavistock Street, within walking distance of the Royal Opera House and many other theaters. The best place to start a tour here is in the strangely decorated tearoom, and then on to a dramatic show of the British stage and its development from Shakespeare to the present day.

Every lunchtime you will find performances by buskers, all carefully screened by the Covent Garden management, in front of the portico of St. Paul's Church, the very spot where George Bernard Shaw's Eliza Doolittle first met Professor Higgins, as well as under the 1830s roof of the Apple Market.

At night the activity moves to a different rhythm. When the stores close—most not until 8:00 P.M.—people drift to the pubs and wine-and-cocktail bars, then on to restaurants. You can eat inexpensive but sometimes bland African at the **Calabash**, Italian at **Orso**, American at **Joe Allen's**, Chinese at **Poon's**, classic English at the **Opera Terrace**, French at **Mon Plaisir**, Japanese at **Ajimura**, Mexican at **Café Pacifico**, and expensively at **Inigo Jones**.

Bloomsbury

Sinatra's rendition of Ira Gershwin's lyric, "A foggy day in London town," captures Bloomsbury, north of Covent Garden, in a surprisingly dramatic mood. The British Museum, he croons, has lost its charm—a curious attribute to apply to such a hefty, solid chunk of masonry, even on the sunniest of days. And, just to correct those misconceptions, London's traditional pea-soup fog, in which Ira Gershwin was no doubt once engulfed, is now only to be experienced in ancient horror movies (the air cleared as Londoners shifted from coal to other energy sources).

The **British Museum** (its façade on Great Russell Street but its entrance on Montague Place) is at the heart of Bloomsbury, a fitting edifice for this, the most cerebral area of town. This great repository of treasures, many blatantly stolen from Egypt and other lands at a time when Britain's imperialist arrogance, not to mention its archaeological light-fingeredness, exercised no ethical restraints, is invariably among the top half-dozen priorities of overseas visitors to London (although the last time most Londoners will have paid their respects is on a compulsory tour organized by a teacher who felt it would do his or her restless charges good).

Construction of the present building, with its ancient Greek influences (rather ironic, considering the recent tussle over the fate of the Elgin Marbles lifted from the Parthenon site), was completed in the middle of the last century. (It displayed the grime of all those years, too, until its recent cleaning.) The building houses a vast collection, spread among some 75 rooms, galleries, and landings. Museum freaks will obviously need to tackle the lot, devoting their entire vacation to poking around. Others will prefer to edit their visits to the essential exhibits. These must, of course, include the **Elgin Marbles**, if only to see the cause of the dispute between the authorities in Britain and Greece concerning their permanent home. You'll find them displayed in the Duveen Gallery. The

Grenville Library contains the **Magna Carta**, one of the most important documents in the annals of democracy, while the prize in the Egyptian Sculpture Gallery is the **Rosetta Stone**. All these are housed on the ground floor. In the Egyptian Gallery upstairs are the famous mummies, arguably the museum's most interesting exhibits. Save time, also, for a tour of the Reading Room (on the hour, 11:00 A.M. to 4:00 P.M.), a stunning library in which rows of desks radiate out from a central area beneath a 40-foot dome. The library is shortly to be rehoused, so see it here while you can.

Other Bloomsbury museums include the **Percival David Foundation of Chinese Art**, on Gordon Square, which includes superb porcelains; and the tiny one-room **Jewish Museum** in Upper Woburn Place, Tavistock Square, which in cramped surroundings displays artifacts from Jewish life and religion, including Torah scrolls, Ark curtains, marriage contracts and mugs, Hanukkah lamps, and a rich and elaborately carved synagogue Ark once used as a servants' wardrobe in Chillingham Castle, Northumberland.

Also worth seeing is **Dickens's house**, 48 Doughty Street, which contains memorabilia from every period of Dickens's life, not just the three years he lived here, much of it set out as it was in his time—with the kitchen a reproduction of the one in Dingley Dell, the study where he worked on *The Pickwick Papers, Oliver Twist, Nicholas Nickleby,* and the beginning of *Barnaby Rudge,* and the dining room where he held regular dinner parties. It also houses one of the most comprehensive Dickens libraries in the world. **Pollock's Toy Museum**, 1 Scala Street across Tottenham Court Road, displays the original "Penny Plain Tuppence Coloured" Toy Theatres, as well as a variety of 19th- and 20th-century toys, some of which can still be bought, though not cheaply. Here is a cornucopia of toys: early jigsaws, puppets, dolls, games, and those toy theaters, with examples from the 16th century to the present day, plus a collection of old teddy bears, including Eric, "the oldest known bear." There is also the **Wellcome Museum of Medical Science**, at 183 Euston Road, where entry is restricted to students in the field, although the entrance hall, with its mock-historical pharmacies, is well worth a peek.

If the British Museum represents Bloomsbury's seat of knowledge, the **University of London** is its seat of learning. American visitors, in particular, will be surprised at the relatively small acreage that such an important educational institution occupies. This is partly because there are no halls of residence as such, but also because several of the surrounding "ordinary"-looking buildings have been bought by the university for the use of individual faculties.

Located to the rear of the British Museum, on the southwestern side of Russell Square, the main part of the university is a relative newcomer to Bloomsbury—the tall Senate House was begun only in 1932—but because so many of its parts are found in older buildings, its geographical roots seem much older. Among the most important of the larger buildings are University College and, on the opposite side of Gower Street, University College Hospital.

Sadly, the tallest building in Bloomsbury also happens to be one of the ugliest. The Post Office Tower, west of Tottenham Court Road, dominates London's skyline (it's the second-tallest structure in London, after the NatWest Bank building in the City) and is widely despised, though it has a good reason for being here, as its ungainly stature affords the necessary ground clearance for its communication functions. At least, that's the excuse. Close by, on and around **Berners Street**, you'll find London's nearest equivalent to New York's garment district. Early in the morning you'll be jostled by people wheeling trolleys of new clothes destined for wholesale and retail outlets. Streetwise shoppers make individual purchases here, though not all businesses will allow retail sales.

On nearby **Charlotte Street** you'll be at the heart of a district of small ethnic restaurants that tend to be less expensive and less chic than those in Knightsbridge or Mayfair. The area is often associated with Greek restaurants, such as the long-established **White Tower** on Percy Street, but there is also a well-known French restaurant, **L'Etoile**, on Charlotte Street.

There are, as in any section of any city, certain monstrosities. But Bloomsbury is one of the most intact corners of Georgian London, its leafy squares little changed since their drawing rooms witnessed the frantic exchanges of artistic, literary, and philosophical banter between members of the early 20th-century Bloomsbury Group. Most members of this circle (Virginia Woolf and her sister Vanessa Bell, Rupert Brooke, D. H. Lawrence, art critic Roger Fry, Lytton Strachey, Clive Bell, Maynard Keynes, and E. M. Forster) didn't have far to travel when visiting—they lived on one or another of Bedford, Woburn, Russell, Gordon (Virginia Woolf lived at number 46 before she married), Tavistock, or Fitzroy squares. Sadly, Bloomsbury Square has lost all its original architecture; only **Bedford Square** and **Fitzroy Square** are still lined with their original tall, dark, and extremely handsome mid-18th-century terraced houses. However, the core of most squares is still a quiet patch of green, though when in the shape of lush gardens they are usually closed to the public (the residents have keys).

Brunswick Square is the black sheep of Bloomsbury— its dimensions have narrowed and its beauty has disappeared since the construction of an ugly housing block and a small, modern cinema, the Renoir, which was plunked in its center alongside a Safeway supermarket and other commercial outlets.

With all of its literary associations, it's little wonder that Bloomsbury sprouted a plethora of publishing houses, many now departed in the face of skyrocketing rents. To see what they produced, try some of the area's many bookshops—**Dillons** is the largest, built to serve the university, its distinctive navy blue and gold window display hogging the northern end of Malet Street. For browsing for secondhand or more specialized tomes, head south of Russell Square to the network of narrow streets around **Museum Street**.

Soho

Since the beginning of the century Soho has enjoyed a dubious reputation. Mere mention of the word still conjures up images of sleazy clubs, brothels, gambling parlors, and gang plots (both the Italian and Chinese variety). It is a world where, by night at least, tourists either fear to tread or do so with adrenaline pumping through their veins.

Although a great deal has been done to rid the area of its women of the night—not so long ago one-third of all its houses were brothels—it is only recently that the authorities have begun to stem the tide of sex shops and peep shows that blossomed in their place. Soho is not a no-go. It may not appeal to your taste, but, compared with most other sin centers of the world, it is relatively tame. In any case, irrespective of whether it has cleaned up its act, Soho cannot be ignored. To do so would be to turn your back on the highest density of good dining to be found in the whole of London.

The area runs diagonally across Leicester Square, and is bordered by **Charing Cross Road** (still famous for its bookstores—Foyle's, Zwemmer's, Collet's, and others) and the shopping thoroughfares of Oxford and Regent streets. Stand in the middle of Leicester Square and you may or may not be in Soho. Depending on exactly where you are, you might even find you have one foot in Soho and the other in the West End. No matter. **Leicester Square** is a good place to begin a Soho saunter. It is difficult to imagine, despite the grass underfoot and the towering plane trees, that in Henry VIII's time the area was at the heart of a royal hunting ground, surrounded by open country and rural villages, with the City of London still a few miles off to the east. (The very name Soho is derived from an old hunting cry, the contemporary equivalent being "tallyho.")

The actual square, known originally as Leicester Fields, was named after the earl of Leicester, who built its first town house on what is now the site of the Angus Steak House, on the northern side of the square. Soon other houses went up, in what was one of the country's earliest spates of property speculation. Once commoners moved in to occupy them, however, the earl moved out. Today the square is a bright-lights mecca that mainly entices out-of-towners in search of a newly released movie (there's also a ticket booth selling seats for same-day theater performances at half price; but keep an open mind, and don't expect tickets for smash hits—the system works best for second-rank shows and plays).

Soho's social history is colorfully cosmopolitan. French Huguenots fleeing the consequences of the revocation of the Edict of Nantes, Greeks escaping the Turks, Swiss, Italians, Germans, Jews, and other refugees have all immigrated to Soho in large numbers, most sharing a background of persecution in their home countries. By 1914, for example, one-third of the houses here were occupied by Jews, a figure that will come as a surprise to people who think of the East End as the traditional Jewish district in London.

The cosmopolitan mix today is best seen in the enormous number of ethnic restaurants. Stand, for example, on the corner of Leicester Street (just north of the square) and Lisle Street, and you'll see Poon's Chinese restaurant virtually next door to Manzi's Italian fish restaurant, which, just to add to the confusion, used to be a

German hotel whose visitors' book recorded Karl Marx and his wife and children as onetime guests.

Among the many echoes of the French accent in Soho is **The French House** at 49 Dean Street, a regular pub but one as close as you're likely to come to a French bar in London (although its owner, Gaston, recently retired). The walls are lined with with photos of French boxers, and the atmosphere is heavy with not-too-distant memories of Charles de Gaulle, who, during the war, patronized the bar along with other members of the Free French movement. There's also the delightfully bohemian **Pâtisserie Valerie** on Old Compton Street and **Maison Bertaux** on Greek Street, perfect places to rest weary feet while having a coffee and croissant or *gâteau*.

If Londoners had to pick a single street that summed up the essence of Soho, the honors would go to **Old Compton Street**. No more than 300 yards long, it contains an Algerian coffee store, a French restaurant, a Spanish deli, an Italian pizzeria, a Malaysian restaurant, a Vietnamese restaurant, and, one of the most recent arrivals, an American diner called Ed's. The area's diversity is well summed up by the newsagent called A. Moroni & Son, who sells just about every newspaper in the world (though not, surprisingly, *The New York Times*). One of the most cheerful streets in Soho is **Berwick Street**, the site of a market since the 1840s. Although it deals mainly in fruit and vegetables, you'll find some clothes and fabrics here as well.

The most recent ethnic group to move into Soho in significant numbers are Chinese from Hong Kong. In fact, it wasn't until 1981 that the area in which they settled, centered on the now pedestrianized **Gerrard Street**, was officially recognized as **Chinatown**. The Chinese have totally revitalized the area, which used to be a run-down, inner-city slum. Although London's Chinatown is far smaller than its counterparts in, say, New York City or San Francisco, the area's shops, restaurants, and overall atmosphere are almost completely Chinese—and, yes, there are telephone boxes shaped like pagodas (though they are just as likely to be out of order as any other public telephone in London). There is a large Chinese supermarket, too, on Gerrard Street, and while you are unlikely to need bags of frozen prawns or packets of bean shoots (unless you are staying in an apartment with a kitchen), you will find useful between-meals snacks and cold drinks here at prices much lower than what you'll pay in kiosk and fast-food outlets around Piccadilly and Leicester Square.

Soho has numerous blue plaques commemorating the famous and red lights announcing the presence of the infamous. No matter where you walk in Soho and no matter what ethnic stamp is currently on the street, evidences of its history abound. William Blake was born here, Hazlitt died here. On Gerrard Street you'll spot a plaque that describes the time that the writer John Dryden spent here. Just a few doors along the road, in the house now occupied by the Loon Fung restaurant, the writer and statesman Edmund Burke resided. On the opposite side of the street you'll spot an original 18th-century building with a portico, now the Loon Moon supermarket, that is famous for a former occupant, the Turk's Head Tavern. The Turk, mentioned by Dickens and by Boswell in his biography of Johnson, was the great literary hangout of the day (interestingly, the current media hangout is Groucho's, a private club just around the corner on Dean Street).

The parish of Soho was once far grander in scale than it is now, and boasted the Church of St. Martin-in-the-Fields (on Trafalgar Square) as its parish church. As the area grew in popularity as a residential section of town, the scale became unmanageable, and the parish was split in two. St. Anne's was built as the new parish church—but, since the war, all that remains is a tower with a unique barrel-shaped clock, the only one in London. It is best seen from the spot where Romilly Street meets Dean Street, although at present it is surrounded by building construction that eventually will spawn a community center, representing the spirit of a newer, cleaner Soho, a phoenix rising from an image-poor past.

But back to the blue plaques. Casanova lived on Frith Street and also on nearby Meard Street, which still contains a row of mid-18th-century brick houses, among the oldest in the area. (Chopin gave a recital in one.) Jean-Paul Marat lived on Romilly Street in a house with a distinctive bay-window overhang, or "jetty." He came to London not as a revolutionary but as a doctor, and labored over a treatise on eye diseases while he lived here.

Another unifying Soho theme, apart from its history, sexual notoriety, and good eating, is music. In the 1950s it was famous for its coffeehouses, which spawned the U.K.'s first superstars of pop. Though all of the original venues are gone, Soho is still the place to hear music.

Ronnie Scott's is the jazz epicenter, located, coinciden-
tally, opposite a brick building where Mozart came to
entertain at the age of eight. Just a few yards away, on the
same side of the road, yet another blue plaque marks the
spot where, at an embryonic stage in the development of
another branch of entertainment, John Baird demonstrated the very first television set.

To most people, **Soho Square**, in Soho's northeast corner near the intersection of Charing Cross and Oxford
Street, is the heart of the area. It is certainly its greenest
core, with a statue of King Charles II standing among the
trees holding what looks like a spout in one hand. It *is* a
spout; the king used to be a fountain "powered" by a row
of windmills along what is now Oxford Street. The square
was once a garden for the exclusive use of residents, but
they departed and the park became public. Today it's a
popular summer retreat for lunchtime sandwich-eaters
and more than a scattering of winos. A close inspection of
the building that looks like a Tudor hunting lodge in the
center of the square will reveal that it is mock Tudor. Built
in the 1930s, it was modeled after the type of hunting
lodge that used to keep the royal heads dry in the event of
rain. It is now a tool shed.

If you literally want to get a taste of the real Soho
without going through the increasingly tame neon city,
try the famous **Gay Hussar**, a few yards off Soho Square
along Greek Street: It is Hungarian food at its most authentic and filling.

The West End

Although visitors may find the nomenclature to be
rather confusing—it's in central, not western, London—
Londoners never think twice about the West End's location. To them the West End means central shopping (and
the theater). If you want to immerse yourself in the
commercial heart of town, just mingle with the lunchtime office workers or weekend pilgrims from the suburbs who come to shop here.

Two miles of crowded pavement line **Oxford Street**,
the West End's main artery, which is trampled daily from
Marble Arch at its western end to Centrepoint skyscraper
at Tottenham Court Road. Its reputation has been carried
to all corners of the globe, yet its days as London's premier shopping street seem numbered. There was a time
when no self-respecting chain of stores would fail to

open a branch on Oxford Street; without the address, a concern would hold little credibility in the retail hierarchy. But nowadays a disloyal shopping public, hungry for more fashionable styles and ever watchful of the avant-garde, has tended to give the street a wide berth and is taking its credit cards to more fashionable, polished rivals along Kensington High Street, in Covent Garden, and on Fulham Road in Chelsea.

Commercially, at least, it is still viable for a retail outlet to have at least one branch on Oxford Street—Saturday crowds justifying police with megaphones to move people out of the way of oncoming buses cannot be bad for business. (There's even a regular shuttle-bus service that ferries shoplifters to the police station.) But the traditional Oxford Street names would probably be far happier if the tacky discount stores, furiously trying to unload cheap sweatshirts, plastic watches, tasteless imitations, and gimmicky paraphernalia, weren't their neighbors. Even offshoot Carnaby Street, a West End high spot during the swinging 1960s, is now surviving on its reputation alone; in reality, its veneer is more than a trifle faded.

Largely it's the quality department stores (Selfridge's, John Lewis, Marks and Spencer, C and A, Debenhams, and British Home Stores) that keep the lunchtime, Saturday, and late-night Thursday shopping crowds flowing down Oxford Street. They are the last great British shopping institutions, giant magnets without which Oxford Street would have died long ago.

Marking the street's Park Lane (western) extremity, **Marble Arch** deserves a brief mention. Built by George IV to celebrate England's victory over Napoleon, it originally stood outside Buckingham Palace. But state coaches couldn't pass between its chubby, Portland stone piers, or "legs," and in 1851 it was moved to the West End, near the old site of the Tyburn Gallows. If Marble Arch figures high on the tourist's list of London sights, to native motorists it signifies little more than bumper-to-bumper traffic jams.

St. Christopher's Place, an alley so narrow you could easily miss it, leads off the north side of Oxford Street almost opposite Bond Street and is lined with high-fashion, one-off boutiques, stores that sell just one example of a particular design. The Warehouse clothing store and the home-furnishing frippery store, The Reject Shop, are doing a roaring trade in the Plaza shopping mall. And running at a tangent to the mainstream traffic off the

south side of the Bond Street tube station is super-chic
South Molton Street, which is closed to vehicular traffic.

Manchester Square, north of Oxford Street behind
Selfridge's, contains the **Wallace Collection**. When the
first marquis of Hertford started amassing 18th-century
paintings and French furniture and artworks, the collection was housed in Paris, but by the time it had passed
into the hands of Richard Wallace, five generations later, it
was in England, where it was opened to the public in
1900. (For the interesting area around the Wallace Collection, see Marylebone Road in the London North section.)

Take a sharp turn to the south at Oxford Circus, step
down **Regent Street**, and you take a giant stride up the
elegance scale. The street, laid out by John Nash in the
early 19th century, was originally planned to run straight
from the prince regent's home, Carlton House, north to
the new Regent's Park, but Nash interrupted the tedium
of the endless avenue approach with his unmistakable,
lavishly expensive curves. Immediately attractive to the
rich and famous (Nash himself lived at number 14; Lady
Hamilton, Admiral Nelson's renowned mistress, resided
down the road at number 25), Regent Street soon became
an attractive proposition for shopkeepers as well.

Although large chunks have been reconstructed over
the years, Regent Street, now controlled by the Crown
Estates Commissioners, is enjoying a revival. The mock-
Tudor-style Liberty's and the Dickins & Jones department
stores, and the racks of trenchcoats at Burberry's on Lower
Regent Street, for example, are still here, and the grim
airline offices and fusty one-off stores are being gradually
nudged out by a brigade of parquet-floored, marble-
pillared designer newcomers like the U.S.–imported Gap,
the middle-of-the-road Next, and the popular Laura Ashley
fabric outlets. The world's biggest toyshop, **Hamley's**, is to
be found on six floors in Regent Street. It's a paradise for
children of all ages, with any and every toy you could
possibly want, plus dozens you've never even heard of; all
those working models you can see through the window
are bound to lure you in. It opened as Noah's Ark in 1760 at
Holborn, but moved to Regent Street in 1881.

Window-shop, if nothing else, on **Bond Street** (Old
Bond Street to the south, running up from Piccadilly, and
New Bond Street at the northern end up to Oxford
Street). A jewelers' lair for decades, the street has re-
tained its sumptuous image, with sky-high rents and retail
prices to match. The same applies to **Jermyn Street**, just

south of Piccadilly, in the direction of the Thames, where you must be rich *and* male because a large proportion of shops here (Bates, Harvie & Hudson, and Astleys, for example) cater exclusively to men with a whim for a jar of mustache wax or a badger-hair shaving brush.

Two of the West End's biggest shopping attractions are on Piccadilly: **Burlington Arcade**, built in 1819 as Britain's first covered shopping mall, for fine woollens, linens, jewelry, and the like; and the upscale **Fortnum & Mason** emporium. Even the royal family stocks up on groceries in the latter's frogs'-legs-to-*fines-herbes* food hall. While you are here, stop for a moment to notice the clock on the shop front, where the polite figures of the original Mr. Fortnum and Mr. Mason appear on the hour, turn, and bow to each other to a tune played by 17 bells. Weary shoppers who wander off in search of sustenance in the area can choose between two of London's most palatial afternoon tea haunts—the Soda Fountain in Fortnum & Mason and, a scone's throw away, down Piccadilly to the west, the Palm Court Room in the Ritz hotel. If they're both full, cross the road and listen to the harpist in the lounge of the Hotel Meridien.

Follow such heavenly delights with a visit to the **Royal Academy of Arts** in Burlington House, nearby on Piccadilly. The grand courtyard, filled with snaking lines at peak visiting times (especially on Sunday mornings during the annual Summer Exhibition), fronts a Renaissance-style building. Inside is a grand, sweeping staircase and galleries of treasures, including Michelangelo's *Madonna and Child*. The Royal Academy is such a London institution that most visitors don't realize it is devoted mainly to temporary exhibitions.

At the back of Burlington House is the more modest, though equally Italianate-looking, **Museum of Mankind** (6 Burlington Gardens), whose exhibitions always focus on non-Western cultures. Within the same building is the British Museum's ethnographic collection, including a skull carved from a single piece of Mexican crystal.

Savile Row, also north of Burlington House, is famous throughout the world for having the finest tailors in London. Gieves & Hawkes at number 1, and Hardy Amies at number 14, are among the better-known names. Number 3 was the headquarters of the Beatles' company, Apple Corps.

London is at her most gaudy and flirtatious with tourists in **Piccadilly Circus**. (Piccadilly got its name from a large house built in the early 1600s on what is now Great Windmill Street. The owner, Robert Baker, made his money selling "picadils," stiff collars worn at Court— hence his house became known as Piccadilly Hall.) Walls of neon flicker day and night here, captured by a million cameras. As part of the Circus's general face-lift, the aluminum statue of Eros (officially the Angel of Charity), once marooned in the tawdry center of the Circus, has been renovated and is now back in the limelight on the south side. Approval of his new good looks is welcome: When Eros was unveiled in 1893, *The Times* described him as the "ugliest monument in any European capital, more suited to the musical hall," while many simply frowned on his nakedness.

Piccadilly's newest entertainment venue is the **Trocadero Centre** on Coventry Street, which has a Brass Rubbing Centre, a Guinness World of Records exhibit, and a multivisual show, *The London Experience*. The complex, with its shops and restaurants, is open seven days a week.

The back doors of the Trocadero open onto **Shaftesbury Avenue**, the West End's evening breadwinner. More than 100 years old (its centenary was in 1987), the heart of London's theater district boasts six theaters and two cinemas. Shaftesbury Avenue was named after the the earl of Shaftesbury, the 19th-century philanthropist who carried out much of his alms-giving work in this area; its construction actually resulted in the demolition of several squalid Dickensian slums. The first theater to go up along the new avenue was the Lyric, in 1888. The Royal English Opera House on Cambridge Circus followed, but demand for fine singing was slack, as the music hall was in fashion, and the theater was renamed the Palace. Musicals are still the staple diet of London's theater, particularly if they're written by Andrew Lloyd Webber and Tim Rice. The Palace, in fact, is now owned by Lloyd Webber, and once housed his *Jesus Christ Superstar,* the second-longest-running musical in the history of British theater.

The Apollo, the Globe, the Queen's, and the Shaftesbury complete the six. Originally the New Prince's theater, the Shaftesbury is most famous for its misfortune: A gas explosion interrupted Fred and Adele Astaire's dancing in Gershwin's *Funny Face,* while later the musical *Hair* literally brought the house down when part of the ceiling collapsed. If your theater-going plans are thwarted because the blockbuster shows are full, you'll usually be able to get a ticket to Agatha Christie's *The*

Mousetrap, which opened at the Ambassadors Theatre in 1952 and is still running (it moved to St. Martin's Theatre, just off St. Martin's Lane, in 1974), making it the longest-running show in the world.

Mayfair

Between the West End and, to the west, Hyde Park you'll find Mayfair, which owes its name to a disorderly fair that was held every May between 1686 and 1764 where Curzon Street and Shepherd Market now are. The small, appealing parts of Mayfair are the rows of elegant brown-stones that were the original *Upstairs, Downstairs* houses of London's upper (and lower) echelons. Concentrated chiefly on Mayfair's two most famous squares, Grosvenor and Berkeley, these brownstones boast former servants' quarters that today command some of the highest rents in town, while the mews houses, once the stable yards for the coach and horses (with upper-floor living accommodations for the driver), sell for small fortunes. **Grosvenor Square** also houses the embassy of the United States of America, the largest embassy in Great Britain, which covers one whole side of the square and is watched over by an American eagle with a wingspan of 35 feet.

The essence of Mayfair is its elegant shops and squares, though working Londoners are also aware that the city's most prestigious office buildings tower above it. Window shoppers and those with plenty of disposable income should head for Brook Street, South Molton Street (one of the city's most elite pedestrianized precincts), New and Old Bond streets, and Savile Row (all discussed above). Smaller showrooms and galleries are to be found on Dover Street, also home to **Brown's Hotel** at number 22, London's renowned "gentleman's" hotel, founded by a former butler to Lord Byron and now owned by Trust-house Forte. The hotel has worked hard to preserve its atmosphere of quietude and privacy, and it still attracts some of the city's most gentrified visitors. It also serves an excellent traditional tea.

In Charles Street is the **Chesterfield**, whose rooms are cheaper than—and as comfortable as—many in the grander international hotels along the more famous Park Lane, and whose two restaurants and bar (for the price of a gin and tonic you can browse through the day's newspapers and the week's magazines) are comfortable rendezvous. Curzon Street, part residential (number 19 marks the spot where Disraeli died in 1881) and part commercial, backs onto **Shepherd Market** (the name belies its wealth), a delightful "village" of narrow streets, period houses, and pubs like Ye Grapes, cafés geared for alfresco dining, and tiny courtyards—the whole linked by a series of archways. The area is also noted for its prostitutes.

Thanks to the heavy traffic and plethora of motorcycle messengers in central London, a quiet stroll around **Berkeley Square** is possible only on a Sunday. Nevertheless, it's not difficult to appreciate the grandeur of its 200-year-old plane trees (all that remain of Berkeley Woods), which shelter some of the city's most beautiful architecture. Two buildings to look out for are number 45, the former home of Clive of India, and number 50, where **Maggs**, the antiquarian book specialists, delights book lovers.

Westminster

Westminster is London wearing its most royal plumage and governmental robes. On the map, the area officially defined as the City of Westminster is vast, bordered by Camden to the north and the Thames to the south, but even Londoners rarely relate the name to its full territorial stake. Westminster really connotes the government buildings of Whitehall, the Houses of Parliament, Westminster Abbey, the Prime Minister's official residence at 10 Downing Street, and St. James's Park. And while it is a residential borough, its palaces and government offices, including the bulk of the ministry headquarters, overshadow the lives of its ordinary citizens.

Buckingham Palace, built for a duke in 1703 and bought by King George III in 1762, is Westminster's prize showpiece. John Nash, to whom London's present-day appearance owes so much, played a significant part in the building's restructuring in 1825, although many of the trimmings that you see today were the result of a face-lift in 1913 by Sir Aston Webb. Today's palace is yesterday's Buckingham House, a beautiful pillared and porticoed mansion house of white Portland stone overlooking a semicircular arc of manicured gardens. The grandeur continues inside, from the bedchambers to the state rooms; even the stable block is magnificent. Until the 19th century the royal family used Buckingham House as its personal residence, as it was only minutes down the road

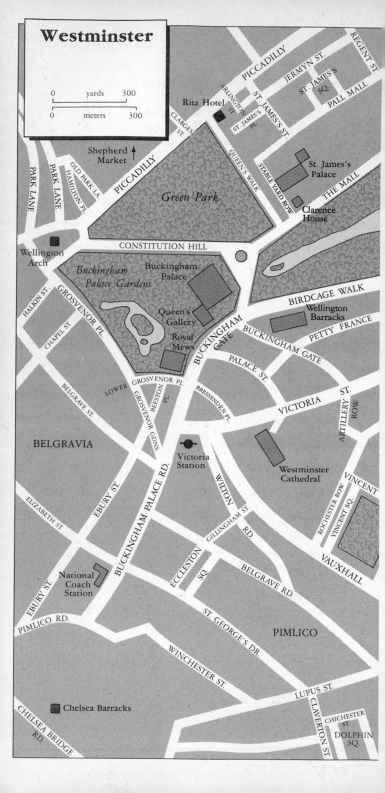

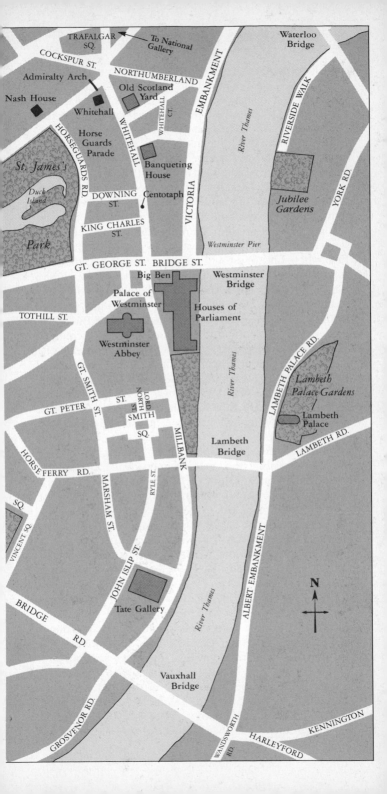

from its official home, **St. James's Palace**, in Pall Mall at the foot of St. James's Street (south from Piccadilly). The red-jacketed and shakoed guards in front of the palace at the foot of St. James's Street are much photographed. (See below for the Changing of the Guard ceremony.)

It wasn't until 1837, when Queen Victoria spread her bustle on the throne, that the role of Buckingham Palace became official. St. James's Palace, Henry VIII's turreted gift to Anne Boleyn when they were married, is now virtually redundant, though any announcement of a change of ruler is traditionally made from its Friary Court balcony.

Londoners' interest in **Clarence House**, between St. James's Palace and the Mall, was greatly enhanced during 1990 when, on August 4, the Queen Mother became 90. For many years this most popular member of the royal family (or "the firm," as the duke of Edinburgh refers to it) has appeared at the gate of the palace to greet well-wishers, rather than remotely from a balcony. But it is always to the balcony that the Queen waves discreetly (and usually unobserved) on her way to the ceremony of Trooping the Colour. Clarence House (Stable Yard Road, St. James's Palace) dates from 1828, and was designed by John Nash. During World War II it was the headquarters of the Red Cross and St. John Ambulance, and between 1947 and 1950, prior to her accession, it was the home of Princess Elizabeth.

If the gold Royal Standard flag is flying high above Buckingham Palace, the Queen is in residence. Occasionally, you may catch a glimpse of one or another of the royal family sitting rather anonymously in the back of a sleek black Daimler. The Queen Victoria Memorial right outside Buckingham Palace was not just erected for people to climb on to watch processions and ceremonials, though it is useful for that. The principal figure, of Queen Victoria, was unveiled in 1911; its creator, Thomas Brock, was knighted on the spot.

The palace is not open to run-of-the-mill sightseers. Two or three times a year, however, a few thousand members of a more select public—aristocrats, sporting personalities, the higher echelons of local government, and the like—are invited within this inner sanctum to one of the Queen's summer garden parties. The even luckier, if that is the right word, are invited here to investitures, in which knighthood and other honors are bestowed. But there are compromises. The **Queen's Gallery**, just around the corner in Buckingham Gate, is open every day except Mondays for exhibitions of paintings from the royal collection. In the **Royal Mews,** on Buckingham Palace Road, open on Wednesday and Thursday afternoons, are the family's Cinderella-like coaches, including the cherub-covered Gold State Coach, which carried Queen Elizabeth II from the palace to Westminster Abbey for her coronation. The Glass Coach, which transports royal brides, is also on show, as are some vintage royal cars, such as the 1901 Daimler built for Edward VII.

Westminster is London's venue for pomp and circumstance. The **Changing of the Guard** at Buckingham Palace, a military pageant of horse guards and infantrymen dressed in black bearskins and red tunics, is the familiar image most often chosen to depict London on postcards and travel posters. At 11:00 every morning between April and July (alternate days, August to March), the St. James's Palace detachment of the Old Guard is inspected in Friary Court. Carrying the Colour (the regimental flag), it then marches off via the Mall, the wide formal boulevard between Trafalgar Square and Buckingham Palace designed by Charles II. At Buckingham Palace the palace detachment is lined up and inspected. The St. James's detachment enters by the South Gate and, together with the Buckingham detachment, awaits the arrival of the New Guard (at 11:30). Led by a regimental band, the New Guard marches into the palace forecourt via the North Centre Gate, having earlier assembled at Wellington Barracks on Birdcage Walk along the southern side of St. James's Park. By 12:05 it's all over for another day (except for the duties of the street cleaner).

The **Institute of Contemporary Arts**, with often obscure and controversial items featured among its contemporary exhibitions, is in Nash House on the Mall. It offers three galleries, as well as a cinema, a theater, and a restaurant.

For such a central city borough, Westminster has a surprising amount of greenery. Running along the south side of the Mall, with its fashionable promenades, lanes, and walkways, **St. James's Park**, the oldest royal park in London, has been compared to the grounds at Versailles. James I, a passionate lover of wildlife, stocked it with deer; Birdcage Walk, which runs along the park's southern flank, was named after a string of aviaries established by Charles II. Nowadays the fauna is limited to birds and lunchtime office workers enjoying an alfresco sandwich. Duck Island, in the middle of the park's elongated lake (another Nash creation), is a private sanctuary for several species of birds. There's even a lodge on the lake's island, a whimsical gesture from Nash. Stand on the small bridge that hoops over the lake and look across the water at the turrets and minarets of tree-fringed St. James's Palace and you might even feel as if you're in the middle of a Hans Christian Andersen story.

After a turn around St. James's Park, Charles II would habitually stroll up Constitution Hill, which cuts through neighboring **Green Park** north of Buckingham Palace. Although only the Queen Victoria Memorial separates them and both border on the Buckingham Palace grounds, Green Park has a completely different feel than St. James's. It's much smaller (53 acres in contrast to St. James's 93) and has rejected any attempts at floral trimmings, opting for just an ample rash of trees and grass. As its name suggests, it remains an expanse of simple, unadulterated green and is the ideal place to walk off a breakfast or a grander feast from the nearby Ritz hotel up on Piccadilly— Green Park's northern boundary.

The quarter of **St. James's**, east of Green Park and north of St. James's Park and including St. James's Square, is an almost exclusively male preserve, its domain defined by the presence of a number of gentlemen's clubs, the most famous being Brooks's, Boodle's, White's, and the stuffy like. Walk down Lord North Street late at night, for example, and you could be back in Georgian London. Step inside these inner sanctums of conservatism (subject to invitation, of course, and your sex), and the only event likely to disturb the status quo is the creak of a chubby leather-backed chair, the tinkle of ice against crystal, the rustle of the pink pages of the *Financial Times,* and the slow ticking of a grandfather clock. You can occasionally peek through the windows at such scenes, but only at that time of day when the inside lights have been fired and the curtains have yet to be drawn on the outside world.

Pall Mall, which runs from St. James's Palace east to Trafalgar Square, was also conceived by Charles I, in this case so that he could play *pallemaille,* a newfangled game he had discovered across the Channel that is roughly equivalent to English bowls. He leased a house here to Nell Gwynn, who poutingly insisted that she should own the freehold of the house—after all, her "services" to the Crown were given freely. Charles agreed, and 79 Pall Mall is still the only privately owned property on the broad avenue.

The top (east end) of Pall Mall opens up into **Trafalgar Square**. Laid out by John Nash in 1820 as part of his grand design, it's rather a hodgepodge of architectural styles. The focal point of the square is its central area, with fountains by Sir Edwin Lutyens and the granite Nelson's Column by William Railton (with the statue of Lord Nelson on top by Baily—contrary to common fallacy there is no eye patch—and four bronze lions by Landseer forming the base plinth). Four cylindrical stone plinths stand at the corners of the square, each with a bronze octagonal lamp. The door on the one at the southeast corner is a recent addition; a clue to its purpose can be seen in the observation slits. In the late 19th century it was used as a secret observation post, just big enough to accommodate a man and a telephone. Adolf Hitler was one of those aware of the importance of Nelson's Column—he intended to move it to Berlin, after conquering Britain, as a symbol of world domination. Today, the square is home to flocks of pigeons, as well as a huge spruce Christmas tree donated every year by Norway in gratitude for Britain's help during World War II. On December 31 New Year's revellers in a generally harmless alcoholic haze cheer Big Ben's midnight chimes here: not a bad place to be if you are alone in London then. Trafalgar Square is always the terminus of political rallies and demonstrations as well, the anti-establishment shade of which Nelson would no doubt disapprove.

The **National Gallery**, by far the most beautiful building on Trafalgar Square, is backed by the National Portrait Gallery. Climb the steps to the National Gallery, a grande dame built in the Neoclassical style, and look back for a sweeping view of the square. Then get on with your exploration of the art inside. The gallery was opened in 1838 to house the nation's many art treasures (at the time the gallery shared its premises with the Royal Academy, but for reasons of space the latter has since moved to Burlington House, Piccadilly). Today all the great periods of European painting are represented here—works by Botticelli and Bellini hang in the Italian rooms alongside Leonardo da Vinci's *Virgin and Child with St. Anne and St. John the Baptist*. Constable's *Haywain* and Gainsborough's *Mr. and Mrs. Andrews* are also here, as are a great many Dutch and Flemish paintings.

The original aim of the **National Portrait Gallery**, around the corner in St. Martin's Place, was to portray Britain's history through paintings, sculptures, miniatures, and photographs of the country's historical person-alities. With so many famous people now represented here, it has become a visual *Who's Who*. Start at the top and work your way down in chronological order. The majority of people you'll see (apart from other visitors) are no longer alive, with the notable exception of the current royal family.

At the northeast corner of Trafalgar Square is the church of **St. Martin-in-the-Fields**, the parish church of the sovereign and the best-loved work of Scottish archi-tect James Gibbs. The first mention of it dates back to 1222, when it was a chapel serving Westminster Abbey, and it was later called St.-Martin-near-the-Cross (Charing Cross). The present church was built in 1722–1724 and was originally designed as a round church. (Although this design was rejected, it was later adopted for a church in Connecticut.) The tower, rebuilt in 1824, was very contro-versial at the time, rising centrally from behind the huge Classical portico, but this design was soon used in many churches, particularly in the United States. Francis Bacon and Charles II were christened, John Constable was mar-ried, and Nell Gwynn was buried here. The church pro-vided the venue for the now world-famous St. Martin-in-the-Fields Orchestra, and still hosts regular lunchtime concerts.

From the square, a stroll down **Whitehall** takes you past some of England's most prestigious civil-service depart-ments, including the Treasury, the gigantic headquarters of the Home Office and the Foreign Office, and the stark new Ministry of Defence building. On the left is the **Banqueting House**, a superb example of Palladian-style architecture built by Inigo Jones for James I in 1619, and still used for official receptions. Its ceilings are decorated with nine remarkable paintings by Rubens (they brought £3,000 and a knighthood to the artist). Thirty years after the hall was built, Charles I stepped from one of its windows onto the waiting scaffold where he was executed.

Old Scotland Yard (the former office of the Metropoli-tan Police, as seen in a thousand B-movies) is also on Whitehall, though the headquarters have since shifted to Victoria Street, also within the boundaries of Westminster. A military presence in the form of two Household Cavalry sentries who sit motionless, immune to the persistent flash of cameras (though they do change shifts every so often), is maintained at **Horse Guards Parade**, and a cere-monial guard is mounted daily at 11:00 A.M. (Sundays at

10:00 A.M.). A few yards farther down Whitehall is the Cenotaph, the stunted Lutyens monument to the soldiers who fell during the two world wars.

Located some 70 feet below Whitehall, **Winston Churchill's bunker**, the Cabinet's secret bombproof headquarters during World War II, opened its 16-foot-thick walls to visitors as a museum a few years ago. Nothing has changed in this six-acre maze of rooms and corridors since the Blitz: According to the map room and various notices around the place, the war is still going on. Sir Winston's bed and the telephone cabinet (disguised as a lavatory) from which he would phone President Roosevelt are just as they were.

Britain's prime ministers have never had to walk far to work. Behind the famous black door and lion-shaped brass knocker of **10 Downing Street** is an eight-room top-floor apartment; state rooms used for official receptions and banquets on the middle level; and Cabinet room, anterooms, and offices opening onto private gardens on the ground floor. Even when he attends sessions in Parliament, John Major has only to walk down Parliament Street, the name given to the lower portion of Whitehall. Downing Street is currently closed to the general public, so no one walks on it much at present.

The **Palace of Westminster** is an extravagant example of Gothic style. Its lean clock tower has four clock faces, each measuring 23 feet across, and its 13.5-ton bell, Big Ben, chimes each quarter-hour. The palace is another one of London's most photographed sights; the familiar view is taken from across the river. Although visitors to Britain can always line up outside for tickets to the visitors' (or "Strangers' ") gallery, for a closer inspection of the Houses of Parliament you have to take an organized tour. British residents can apply to their Member of Parliament; foreigners must apply well in advance for tickets from their embassy or contact the Know Where Agency (P.O. Box 38, Sevenoaks, Kent TN13 3LN; Tel: 732-45-79-02), which will arrange a tour with an M.P. (or, more often, a retired employee of the House supplementing a pension). A few yards away, in Victoria Tower Gardens, the bronze statue of Emmeline Pankhurst honors the leader of Britain's suffragette movement, who was on her deathbed in 1928 when the House of Lords first saw the bill for equal suffrage.

The typical tour of Parliament begins in Westminster Hall, the oldest and most historic part of the parliamentary complex and home to the original law courts before they moved farther north to their present site around Chancery Lane. These courts witnessed the kinds of state trials that have made history, including that of Guy Fawkes, the man who attempted to blow up the Houses of Parliament with kegs of gunpowder in 1605 and whose effigy now sits atop thousands of bonfires every November 5. From Westminster Hall the tour moves on to the Royal Gallery, the Prince's Chamber, the Lords' Chamber (where every bill passed by the Commons or initiated in the Lords has to receive the Peers' assent before becoming law), the Members' Lobby, and the royal throne in the Peers' Chamber. The stationary figures in the Central Lobby are prime ministers Churchill, Lloyd George, Arthur James Balfour, Herbert Asquith, and Clement Attlee.

The highlight of any tour is the **House of Commons**, the arguments and debates of which are broadcast and now televised into every British home. This room full of green leather benches (in contrast to the red of the House of Lords) seats 437 M.P.s plus 15 Commons officials at any one time. (There are fewer seats than M.P.s entitled to them; this is a deliberate policy—instigated by Winston Churchill—with the intent of heightening the sense of occasion when the House is full.)

In the Norman Porch, you can see a collection of some two million parliamentary records, including the original copies of all acts of Parliament, some dating back to the Middle Ages.

Across the street from Parliament stands **Westminster Abbey**, the second most famous church in England. It is the royal church, where monarchs are crowned on the ancient coronation chair, a piece of furniture that has served this regal purpose since William the Conqueror became king on Christmas Day, 1066.

The abbey was originally owned by a Benedictine monastery, one of the few that managed to escape Henry VIII's anticlerical wrath, which accounted for the destruction of much of ecclesiastical England. Today some five million people visit the abbey each year, so if you come in search of spiritual peace and sanctuary you'll be a shade disappointed. Even the burial space is overpopulated with kings and queens, from Edward the Confessor, who founded the abbey in 1065, to Elizabeth I, as well as such historic literary figures as Chaucer, Tennyson, Dickens, Kipling, Hardy, and Browning. The top seed are buried in the Poets' Corner; Ben Jonson was actually buried upright—by choice, as it happens, but it certainly made a contribution toward alleviating the space problem.

Westminster School, founded at the beginning of the 13th century for clerks of the abbey, is one of the oldest surviving schools in London. Adjoining the abbey are its oldest parts, which were part of the monastic dormitory, built about 1100.

Next to Westminster Abbey is **St. Margaret's**, the parish church of the House of Commons. Founded by Edward the Confessor in the 11th century, it was rebuilt in the 14th century, and that part is the core of the present building, with details dating from the 18th and 19th centuries. (In 1539 an attempt was made to raze the church and use its stones for the construction of the duke of Somerset's new house in the Strand, but the duke's men were fought off by parishioners.) The east window contains London's most important early-16th-century stained glass, and the marriages of Samuel Pepys, John Milton, and Winston Churchill were performed here.

If you walk along the river from **Westminster Pier**, adjacent to Westminster Bridge and very close to the Houses of Parliament, as far as Charing Cross Pier, you'll come in sight of another landmark: Cleopatra's Needle, the twin of the one that stands in New York's Central Park. Both originally stood beside the Temple of Heliopolis in Alexandria, but the bronze sphinxes at the base of the granite monolith are of a much more recent date. The statue is across the street from part of the **Embankment Gardens**, which in the warm weather that seems increasingly to be a summertime occurrence in London pick up any stray breeze from the river. At certain times there are open-air musical performances in the bandstand. The gardens are also a haunt of homeless "dossers," the men and women who inhabit London's cardboard city, but they usually only appear at night and are generally harmless.

One can only praise the Classical-style **Tate Gallery**, built near the Pimlico tube station on Millbank, a section of the river's north shore upriver from Parliament between Lambeth and Vauxhall bridges. The gallery's origins date back to 1897, when the country was looking for a home for a national collection of British art. Sugar magnate Sir Henry Tate put forward the money, plus his personal collection of 64 paintings. Many a Londoner's Sunday afternoon is spent browsing its galleries—the original 64 paintings have been joined by continually changing exhibitions as well as a permanent collection of British works from the 16th to the early 20th centuries, a vast collection of Impressionist works, and, since 1916—when it was decided the Tate would not just be an extension of the National Gallery—many works of modern art from abroad. Matisse, Braque, Chagall, and Picasso share space with Jackson Pollock, Henry Moore, Barbara Hepworth, and Alberto Giacometti. In its Clore Gallery, the Turner Bequest contains more than 300 oil paintings. The entire collection has recently been rehung and rearranged in chronological order, tracing the development of British art to the present day. The results are impressive. The Tate also has a good restaurant (lunches only) famed for its wine list, as well as a self-service cafeteria.

A minor detour across the Thames (at this point the "south" bank is to the east) will bring you to **Lambeth Palace**, a Medieval building and the London residence of the Archbishop of Canterbury for more than seven centuries. It's open to groups by prior arrangement (apply to the Palace Secretary; Tel: 928-8282) from 10:00 A.M. to 5:00 P.M., Mondays through Fridays.

Though it is only a twelve-minute train ride south across the Thames from Victoria station and then a ten-minute walk (ask to be pointed in the right direction at the station), **Dulwich Village** is more like a leafy, well-preserved enclave in stockbroker-country than a London suburb. It really would not be too surprising to see post-chaises scooting along the mostly 18th-century main street through the village, past houses set back from the road behind wide grass verges, enhanced by white fence posts and fences. (Half close your eyes, and parts of it are likely to remind you of Colonial Williamsburg.)

Opposite what was once known as The College of God's Gift, founded in 1613, stands the extremely attractive and welcoming **Dulwich College Picture Gallery**, designed by Sir John Soane and opened in 1814. Its collection of Old Masters is impressive, and it is also famous for having been robbed more than its share of times, with pictures mysteriously reappearing a year or two after their theft in the back of taxis or on park benches. The gallery, the grandiose 19th-century buildings, and the impressive playing fields of Dulwich College are another ten-minute walk from the village. The college itself is sometimes open to the public by prior application in writing to the Master, Dulwich College, London, SE21.

LONDON WEST
Knightsbridge—Belgravia

Think of Knightsbridge, and you inevitably think of **Harrods**. The two names seem to reinforce each other in a fragrant blend of high income and refined taste. No matter where in the world you normally do your shopping, Harrods, on Brompton Road, warrants a pilgrimage and at least a small spree.

They say a customer once went into the Harrods pet department and asked for an elephant. "Certainly, sir," replied the assistant. "African or Indian?" Your own needs might be rather more basic, but whether you go to Harrods to buy or to browse, you can't fail to be bowled over by the sheer weight of its style, let alone its contents.

Harrods is the largest store in Europe. It has its own bank, its own power station, and its own water supply (it draws its water from three wells—the deepest of which is 489 feet below the store). Just to reel off a few of its stock statistics, it offers 150 types of pianos, 9,000 ties, 450 kinds of cheese, 130 kinds of bread, 85 different brands of malt whisky, and more or less anything else that is made on the planet. No wonder its telegraphic address still is "Everything London." If you want just a taste, head for the Food Hall, a palatial, beautifully tiled, magnificently stocked emporium. The store's own-brand items, often packed in distinctive green tins with the Harrods label, make easy and popular presents.

Harvey Nichols, nearby at Knightsbridge—the street as distinct from the area—and Sloane Street, the main intersection west of Buckingham Palace and the Palace Gardens, past where Piccadilly ends in a vast traffic interchange, is London's "other" department store. Harrods may have its special Queen's entrance, but Harvey Nichols is the store where you're more likely to come across Princess Di casting an eye over the designer labels. Apart from the main shopping arteries of Brompton Road and Knightsbridge proper, another shopping mecca that caters to the wealthy is **Sloane Street**, which runs south from Knightsbridge and the Knightsbridge tube station. In fact, the very name has spawned its own London social

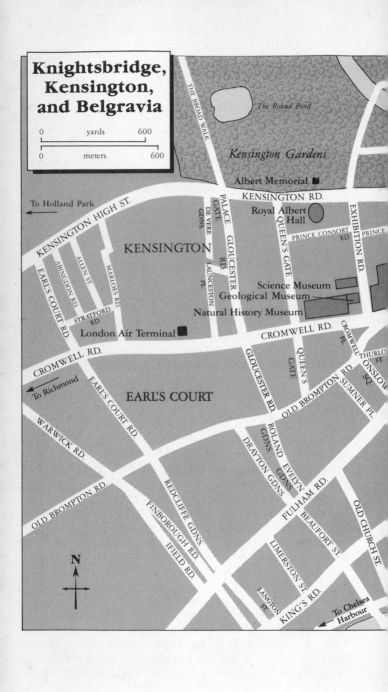

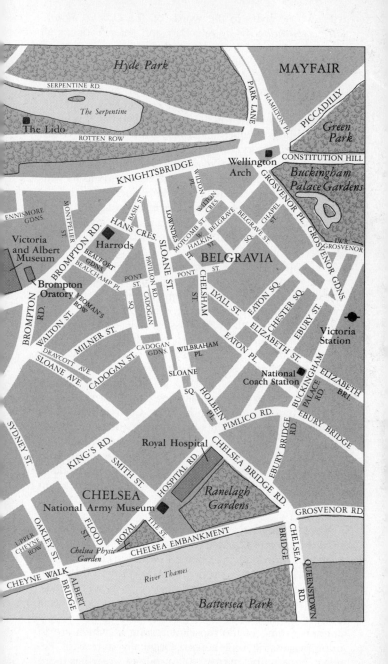

type, whose style, in the words of *The Official Sloane Ranger Handbook* (by Ann Barr and Peter York), is all about "quality, conservatism, and classicism." And that's exactly what you can expect from the majority of stores on Sloane Street.

The tiny streets that lie in the elbow formed by Knightsbridge and Sloane Street constitute a neighborhood of expensive town houses and small, exclusive stores selling antiques, paintings, haute-couture gowns, and pretty frippery. Cross Sloane Street, and Belgravia's **Halkin Arcade**, in particular, which spans Motcomb and West Halkin streets, has more priceless items in its windows than you'd come across in a sheikh's palace—which is, indeed, the ultimate destination of many of the items on sale here. This entire area is also home to many of London's finest small hotels; see the Accommodations chapter below.

Those in search of **Belgravia** won't find a sign, but they've found it once they're in Wilton Crescent, Belgrave Square, Eaton Place, or Eaton Square. Belgravia, lying just east of Sloane Street, was a neat, early-19th-century development later rebuilt in Neoclassical style. Surprisingly, it is not the generously proportioned 18th-century Grosvenor Square, the Mayfair home of the U.S. embassy, but Belgravia's Chester Square that has earned the nickname "American Square in Mayfair," on account of its high proportion of ex-pats in residence. In recent times they have included Henry Fonda, Tony Curtis, and Robert Wagner. Today's residents are likely to be seen in the area's top Italian restaurant, **Mimmo d'Ischia** (on Elizabeth Street), presided over by the flamboyant Mimmo and his lively team of waiters, or on the opposite side of the street in the **Ebury Wine Bar**, which specializes in steaks grilled before your eyes (if you sit at the counter, that is).

Knightsbridge (the name recalls the time when French nobles took up residence in Knightsbridge to escape the egalitarian consequences of the Revolution) is also home to **Beauchamp Place** (pronounced *Beecham*), off Brompton Road east of Harrods. Contrary to recent trends, Beauchamp has remained a refreshingly anachronistic oasis of small, independently owned boutiques and restaurants (some of the most interesting of which are in unprepossessing basements). Originally a row of Regency houses, this narrow 400-yard-long street has more variety than many shopping streets ten times its length.

Knightsbridge is not only an elegant place to shop but an elegant place to live as well. After all, the Queen lives just around the corner. The sweeping crescents, anonymous mews, and manicured squares—with their smart Rollers, Jags, Bentleys, and Daimlers patiently waiting like faithful retainers at curbside—all lie within an easy stroll of both the high-quality shops and, to the north, **Hyde Park**, that vast, pool-table expanse of greenery, at 360 acres the largest in London, and the setting of Kensington Palace, the home of Prince Charles and Princess Diana.

Kensington Gardens, the royal gardens of Kensington Palace, are worth a visit. See the bronze statue of Peter Pan, the Sunken Garden (to remind you of the formality of the original 1728 gardens), the monuments to William III and Victoria, and, for the children among us, daily puppet shows in the summer. The palace's State Apartments are also open to the public.

Hyde Park, along with Kensington Gardens, is the London equivalent of New York's Central Park, a place to let off pent-up steam by jogging, hiring a rowboat, or renting a horse from Lilo Blum's stables. If you opt for the latter, you can follow the hoofprints of the palace guards, who canter around a mile-long sandy track known as Rotten Row in the wee hours every morning. In addition to its before-work, after-work, and weekend activity, the park still lives up to its popular image—nannies wheeling perambulators along the Broad Walk, children throwing crusts of bread to the ducks, model boats making their way sedately across Round Pond, Sunday brass-band concerts, small-time politicos expounding on a soapbox at Speakers' Corner (Britain's symbol of democracy, where anyone can express whatever opinion he or she may hold dear) in the northeast corner near Marble Arch, and Spartan swimmers plunging from the Lido into the Serpentine at 5:30 A.M., often breaking a layer of ice to do so.

Notting Hill

The broad Bayswater Road, which forms the northern boundary of Hyde Park, begins its westward journey at Marble Arch. Once past the western edge of the park, it almost immediately becomes the southern boundary of Notting Hill, where a large percentage of the city's West Indian immigrants have settled. Increasingly, they've been joined by professionals who find the combination of eth-

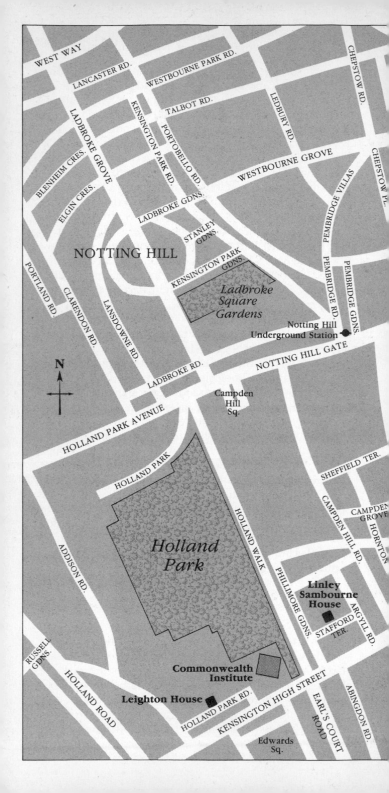

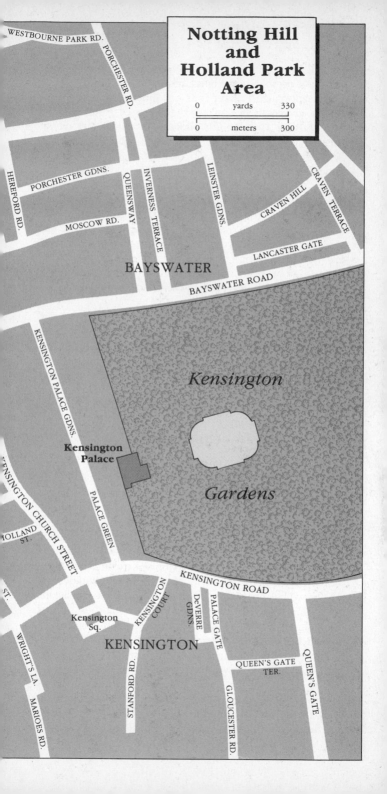

Notting Hill and Holland Park Area

0   yards   330

0   meters   300

WESTBOURNE PARK RD.

PORCHESTER RD.

HEREFORD RD.

PORCHESTER GDNS.

QUEENSWAY

INVERNESS TERRACE

MOSCOW RD.

LEINSTER GDNS.

CRAVEN HILL

CRAVEN TERRACE

LANCASTER GATE

BAYSWATER

BAYSWATER ROAD

Kensington

KENSINGTON PALACE GDNS.

Kensington Palace

Gardens

KENSINGTON CHURCH STREET

HOLLAND ST.

PALACE GREEN

ST.

KENSINGTON ROAD

KENSINGTON COURT

STANFORD RD.

DeVERE GDNS.

PALACE GATE

Kensington Sq.

WRIGHT'S LA.

KENSINGTON

MARLOES RD.

QUEEN'S GATE TER.

GLOUCESTER RD.

QUEEN'S GATE

nic color and the gentility of five-story houses on tree-lined avenues such as Elgin Crescent irresistible.

Sensationalized newspaper headlines of riots and robberies invariably follow in the wake of Notting Hill's August Bank Holiday Caribbean Carnival, but don't let them put you off going, either to the carnival itself—Westbourne Grove and Ladbroke Grove in particular are jam-packed with stalls, floats, and people dancing in the streets to reggae steel bands—or at any other time of the year, especially weekends.

Saturdays at the **Portobello Road Market**, where you will find antiques, Victoriana, and a variety of junk, are already on the tourist circuit. What you don't want to miss are the many small, specialized art and photographic galleries that have recently opened along Kensington Park Road, parallel to Portobello, as well as down various side streets.

If you'd like an American-style breakfast, start the day relaxing over your newspaper in the multilevel **Gate Diner**, also on Kensington Park Road. More serious eating takes place at **Monsieur Thompson's** nearby at number 29, or at **Leith's** at number 92. **Julie's Wine Bar and Restaurant**, opposite David Black Oriental Carpets on Portland Road, also attracts the smart set.

Chelsea

Like the Roman Empire, ancient Greece, and the Weimar Republic, Chelsea has already wallowed in its golden era. Unlike the other three, however, its place in the annals of history is not rooted in its military supremacy or imperialistic acquisitiveness but rather in the ephemeral world of fashion. The Chelsea that attracted the attention of the world in the early 1960s was symbolized by the scantiest of all emblems: the miniskirt. Chelsea earned that attention by virtue of the creativity of its highly talented designers, as well as the scores of artists, writers, and musicians who came to live within its geographical and emotional boundaries. It was the birthplace of "Swinging London," a notion born of an alchemy of coincidences—an enormously attractive environment, proximity to central London, and the then-low rents.

The decade of the 1960s was not a unique period of creativity for Chelsea. Scores of famous people, particularly in the arts and literature, had lived in the village previously, among them Charles Kingsley, Dante Gabriel

Rossetti, T. S. Eliot, Henry James, Oscar Wilde, and the so-called sage of Chelsea, Thomas Carlyle, whose Queen Anne house on Cheyne Row is open to the public during the summer. Other famous residents included Mark Twain (Samuel Clemens), who lived at 23 Tedworth Square, Chelsea, while in London in 1896. His visit was made during an extended tour of Europe, and it was here (in mourning for his daughter Susy, and because he shunned company) that reports of his death began to circulate; reports that he later called "greatly exaggerated." At Chelsea Harbour, off Lots Road, you can also catch one of the **Thames Line Riverbuses**, which run daily from here downriver through central London to London City Airport, with seven stops in between. No traffic jams here, just great views! Get your tickets from dispensing machines before you board.

Chelsea, between Knightsbridge and Kensington (Kensington is the area just to the west of Knightsbridge, farther out along the southern side of Hyde Park) and, to the south, the Thames, still merits a visit today, and not just to mourn its passing glory. Chelsea is a delightful environment in which to live or, as a compromise, to visit. Its terraces and squares, studded with trees and lined by rows of pretty, pastel-painted town houses that look like overgrown dolls' houses, seem more in keeping with a rural than an urban context. Chelsea's main drag, **King's Road**, supposedly named after the path that Charles II took to visit Nell Gwynn—who then lived in the neighboring borough of Fulham—is still one of the best shopping streets in London; in many ways the street is better than ever, as the retail action now stretches from Sloane Square in the east along the New King's Road continuation and on into Fulham Road, which parallels King's Road to the north.

There's no longer any need to groan at how the punks have added a stamp of mockery to Chelsea's fashion pedigree. Although it's only a few years since this was their territory, today there's hardly a safety pin, mohawk, or studded jacket to be seen; instead, the Saturday crowds sport checkered Paul Smith suits, tartan kilts, wedge haircuts, and sensible shoes, and spend small fortunes in interior-decor stores like Habitat and luncheon spots like the Habitat Café.

Clothing stores still predominate, but there are also plenty of antiques arcades and art galleries. If you happen to be partial to Victorian and Edwardian lighting, find your way to **Christopher Wray's** period light emporium at 600 King's Road. He stocks hundreds of models, mostly quality reproductions, some originals. The street is also heavily endowed with lighting stores of the modern-design type. **Antiquarius** is a covered 200-stall antiques market selling Art Deco and Art Nouveau designs, English porcelain, watercolors, and period jewelry and clothing.

In between is a generous sprinkling of pubs and restaurants, many occupying the same site for more than two decades now. The most famous include **The Man in the Moon** and the **Markham Arms**; plant-filled and patioed, the latter hosts throngs of lager drinkers in summer. The Pheasantry, a popular 1960s meeting place with an unusual arched entrance and guild plaques, now houses a complex of several Spanish restaurants. And **Dominic's Bistro** still attracts aficionados of dining in front of candles in Chianti bottles.

Perhaps the busiest eatery of them all, on account of its minute proportions, is **The Chelsea Bun Diner**, tucked down a side road on Limerston Street. Arrive anytime between 7:00 A.M. and 11:30 P.M. and you can be served a foaming cappuccino, a traditional English breakfast, a sandwich, or a burger. Everything's homemade, but the owners have no liquor license, so bring your own bottle.

Places of historical interest in the neighborhood include the **Chelsea Physic Garden**, 66 Royal Hospital Road on the bank of the Thames, established by the Society of Apothecaries in 1673, making it the second oldest botanic garden in England (after Oxford's, 1623). Its 5,000 plant species include—as the name suggests—the medicinal variety as well as Britain's biggest olive tree (there used to be cannabis, too, until 1982, when a dedicated home botanist jumped over the wall in the middle of the night and took the specimen home). Short courses for gardeners and conducted garden tours can be arranged. The **National Army Museum**, which records the history of the British military and exhibits, along with medals, military badges, uniforms, and military paintings, themes showing the human side of "The Story of the Army," is also in Chelsea, as is the **Royal Hospital**, home of the much photographed Chelsea Pensioners, originally founded by Charles II "for the support and relief of maimed and superannuated soldiers." After Mary Quant designed the miniskirt, originally sold on King's Road in her store Bazaar, uniformed pensioners sharing the frame with pretty girls with dead-straight hair, heavily made-up eyes, and lots of leg were the photographic cliché of London.

Don't miss the lovely 18th-century houses on riverside **Cheyne Walk**, and look for the blue plaques that tell you about former famous residents: George Eliot (pen name of Mary Anne Evans, 1819–80) lived briefly at number 4; the Pre-Raphaelite painter Dante Gabriel Rossetti took number 16 with Algernon Charles Swinburne and George Meredith in 1862. Rossetti's pets included a bull, raccoon, wombat, kangaroos, armadillos, and peacocks. The noisy peacocks so upset the neighbors that a clause (still in existence) forbidding the keeping of peacocks was forced into future Cheyne Walk leases. Numbers 19–26 stand on the site of the former Chelsea Manor, where Queen Elizabeth I grew up and reputedly planted the mulberry trees over the wall by number 24. Rolling Stone Mick Jagger also had a house on Cheyne Walk in the 1960s.

South Kensington

You may feel that Chelsea falls short on serious culture, but neighboring (to the north) South Kensington more than compensates for it. **Exhibition Road**, running north off Cromwell Road, was Prince Albert's special project. As Queen Victoria's consort he was able to wield enough power to open the Great Exhibition in Hyde Park in 1851. It was such an immense success that in 1856 all profits were used to buy the Gore Estate, on which, he demanded, a collection of educational establishments should be built. Judging by the hordes of schoolchildren filing into the estate's grand collection of museums, which spill down the Cromwell Road west of Harrod's and the Brompton Road, his wishes have been well respected.

Queen of them all is the **Victoria and Albert Museum**, home to a vast collection of fine and applied art. It's the sort of museum best tackled by studying the plan, picking your favorite handful of "theme" rooms, and ignoring the rest. In fact, those who decide to "do" all the galleries would be wise to invest in a pair of hiking boots, as they stretch a total of seven miles. At least the abundance keeps people coming back, discovering something new each visit. Don't miss the collection of Chippendale furniture, John Constable's landscapes on the first floor, or the Jones Collection, a riveting display of French interior decoration, painting, furniture, ceramics, and other deco-

rative arts, including examples of Marie Antoinette's lavish tastes. The costume court contains one of the greatest
clothing collections in the world, popular with pencil-
wielding fashion students. The rest of the museum's collections can only be hinted at: Japanese, Islamic, and
British art and music; Raphael cartoons. . . .

Just west on the Cromwell Road is the **Natural History
Museum** and its more specialized adjunct, the **Geological
Museum**. From the outside the Natural History Museum
resembles a grand sandstone church; the massive interior
can be divided into five main departments: botany, ento-
mology, mineralogy, paleontology, and zoology. It's also
one of the city's most popular museums; most Londoners,
even if they haven't visited, have at least seen pictures of
the skeletons of the *Brontosaurus, Tyrannosaurus rex,*
and other dinosaurs in the magnificent central hall. After
that, it's a question of which awe-inspiring sight to look
for first. The ceiling of the Whale Hall in the west wing
has to be seen to be believed: Skeletons and models of
several species of mammals hang from it like spiders
from their webs. There are also fossil collections, bird
galleries, underwater creatures and coral, plants and min-
erals, plus a gallery devoted to simple ecology.

For fans of interactive displays, the **Science Museum,**
just north of the Geological Museum on Exhibition Road,
is unbeatable, with knobs to twiddle, lights that flash, and
plenty of bleeping sound effects. Children make up a
generous proportion of the museum's devotees—there's
even a Children's Gallery on the lower ground floor
devoted to teaching simple scientific ideas using diora-
mas and working models. Older visitors, having been
mesmerized by the Foucault pendulum that hangs near
the entrance on the ground floor (its slow deviation
proves that the earth does indeed rotate), usually head
straight for the Apollo 10 space capsule and simulated
moon base in the new Exploration of Space Gallery. But
the museum also caters to steam engine buffs (Puffing
Billy, the world's first locomotive, is in the road and rail
transport wing) as well as lovers of astronomy, nuclear
physics, modern technology (see the Challenge of the
Chip display), photography, electronics, and navigation.

The **Royal Albert Hall** is north of the Science Museum
on the Kensington Road, just across from Kensington
Gardens. If it were in Spain you'd swear the hall was a
bullring. A multipurpose venue, it hosts everything from
Rolling Stones concerts to political conventions, gradua-

tion ceremonies of the University of London to boxing matches, but is perhaps best known as the site of the summer Promenade concerts, or "the Proms." The hall, which seats about 8,000 people, was built as a memorial to Prince Albert and inspired by the Roman works in Provence. Guided tours are available from June to mid-September, and include the Royal Box.

One final sight is number 14 Princes Gate, South Kensington, where John Fitzgerald Kennedy lived with his father, Joe, when the latter was American ambassador to Britain after 1937.

Richmond

Identifying Richmond on any map of London has never been difficult. At the region's heart lies a gigantic green expanse, usually located near the map's bottom left-hand corner. If you fly into Heathrow from the east, this expanse appears as a sea of green floating below the left-hand windows. Richmond is a prosperous borough that not only has more open spaces than any other in London but also has hundreds of listed buildings—even the trees have preservation orders slapped on them. Should circumstances not allow you to live in Richmond, there's no excuse for omitting it from a London visit.

Richmond upon Thames, to give the borough its full name and pertinent location, spans the banks of the river upstream from central London between Hammersmith Bridge and Hampton Court. Despite its proximity to central London (30 minutes by tube), it's actually a collection of small "villages": Barnes, Ham, Kew, Teddington, Twickenham, and Mortlake, all of which have managed to cling to significant shows of antiquity.

The name Richmond was inherited from a palace rebuilt by Henry VII, who in turn had borrowed the name from his Yorkshire earldom. All that remains today of the original building is the **Gatehouse**, just off Richmond Green. During the 15th century Richmond Palace, originally called Shene, was a favorite Tudor retreat. Later, Shakespeare staged performances of his plays here, while the wardrobe that Queen Elizabeth I stored in the palace—it contained well over 2,000 dresses—would put Joan Collins to shame. Both Henry VIII and Elizabeth I died here, and the palace's importance gradually declined until it was finally demolished in 1660, after the Restoration.

Despite its distinctive character, Richmond is just a half-hour Underground trip on the District Line from central London. From Richmond station it is a two-minute walk to the Green. You can also travel by British Rail from Waterloo Station in about 20 minutes. But the most scenic way to approach Richmond is aboard one of the boats that chug up from Westminster Pier in central London during the summer. Once you step ashore you'll find yourself in the middle of a completely self-contained village. There's likely to be a cricket match in mellow swing on the Green, the locals (anyone from barristers and bankers to writers and actors) toing and froing with liquid refreshments in hand between their patch of grass and the beery interior of the Cricketers pub.

Different styles of architecture jostle for position—Georgian, Palladian, Tudor, and Victorian—but the last definitely predominates. Minutes away are the Richmond Theatre and aging, narrow walkways and streets such as Old Palace Lane, which runs from Trumpeters' Court to the river, and **Maids of Honour Row**. The latter is a famous row of four tall 18th-century houses, complete with wrought-iron gates and railings, built in 1724 for the companions of Caroline, wife of the future King George II. But the name is now more synonymous with the **Maids of Honour Tearoom** on Kew Road. At the latter, you can either line up for a table and wallow in the cottagey ambience, or take out a bag of scones, cakes, and Maids of Honour curd tarts (made from a secret recipe) and eat them at your leisure down by the river.

Summer is the best time for a **riverside walk** (in spring and autumn, heavy tides have been known to flood the walkway). Low tide in hot, dry weather reveals the river's steep, sandy banks. Low-slung trees trail their leaves in the water, and ducks, swans, and moorhens rock along on the wash left by motorboats revving past. The most hectic time for the Thames here (not to mention its wildlife) is March, when the **Oxford and Cambridge Boat Race** is held. Cutting through the waters from Putney to Mortlake, this is an amateur race for rowing "eights" and an important competition for the two universities, whose teams practice for months beforehand. It lasts about an hour and a half, and the best viewing points are on the Surrey bank above Chiswick Bridge, Mortlake, close to the finish line, or anywhere else along the towpath. Be sure to wear either light blue (Cambridge) or dark blue (Oxford) to show your allegiance.

Richmond's stretch of river is also active during **Swan Upping**, an ancient and rather curious pageant held every July. The Worshipful Companies of Vintners and Dyers, along with representatives of the Queen, spend one week rowing their half-dozen Thames skiffs upstream from Sunbury to Pangbourne, ceremoniously catching swans, counting them, and nicking the beaks of the year's new batch of cygnets. The tradition dates back to the Middle Ages; its original purpose was to establish the ownership of these then-profitable, prestigious, and tasty birds. The Crown can still lay claim to any unmarked swans, a right that is today administered by the Lord Chamberlain's office and implemented on the spot by Captain Turk, the Queen's official Swan Master. At present only some 200 swans are to be seen in the entire Lower Thames, and the Swan Upping ceremony has become a crucial census for ecological reasons.

The least urban of London's boroughs, Richmond contains three royal parks as well as the Royal Botanic Gardens at Kew. All four are popular weekend haunts. **Richmond Park**, the largest of the royal parks, covers 2,500 acres and was first enclosed by Charles I as a deer park. In fact, it's still worth your trouble to pack a pair of binoculars so you can examine the large herds of fallow and red deer that roam freely here.

The park's woodland gardens and Isabella Plantation are at their best from mid-April to the end of May, when the azaleas and the rhododendron dell are in full bloom. Historic buildings here include the King's Observatory; the White Lodge, built in 1727 as a hunting lodge for King George II (open only in August); and Princess Alexandra's home, the Thatched House Lodge. Stop for tea at **Pembroke Lodge**, a restaurant and café with its own garden and terrace, found on the west side of Richmond Park, down the road through the park heading south from Richmond Gate. This place, ideal for pensive reflection, was the childhood home of the philosopher Bertrand Russell.

Ham House, in Richmond, has been well restored by the National Trust to show what life was like for a 17th-century aristocrat. It has all its original furniture, as well as displays of costumes and paintings, including the famous miniature of Queen Elizabeth I by Nicholas Hilliard. The formal garden has been replanted as it was 300 years ago.

For years it cost only two pennies to pass through the turnstiles of Kew's **Royal Botanic Gardens**. The fee has now risen, but it's still a bargain. Take the District Line to Kew Gardens station, and follow the posted directions from there for the entrance. From May to September you can also take a riverboat from Westminster Pier. The 300 acres of landscaped gardens originally were made up from the combined estates of Richmond Lodge (now demolished) and **Kew Palace**. This small Jacobean mansion is the last of a group of royal residences, and was formerly known as the Dutch House. (The original Kew Palace was demolished in the early 18th century.) The three-story palace is open to the public daily from 11:00 A.M. to 5:30 P.M., April to September.

The Royal Botanic Gardens, also known as Kew Gardens, contain more than 25,000 species of plants from all over the world. A cry went up throughout the land at the havoc that the hurricane of October 16, 1987, wreaked on Kew, toppling 800 trees and destroying in one night 150 years' worth of careful nurturing. Though the worst-hit areas are now open again, restoration work continues, especially on river and lakeside areas. The magnificent Palm House reopened in the spring of 1990 after extensive renovation. This remarkable piece of architecture, built in 1844–1848, is a fantasy in glass inspired by the classic Victorian greenhouse, and contains about 3,000 species of palms.

Aircraft heading to or leaving from Heathrow Airport fly overhead at the peak rate of one a minute, creating an incongruous din as visitors wander through groves, woodlands, and rock gardens, stopping to visit the Orangery, the four temples, the tall red Pagoda, or one of the plant houses. These fine Victorian conservatories, with such names as Alpine House, Water Lily House, Temperate House, and the new Princess of Wales conservatory, are an architectural mélange of cast iron and glass. The 17th-century Dutch House, a sturdy red-brick and gabled building, is one of the exceptions, and is all that remains of the original Kew Palace.

The Temperate House, one of the biggest hothouses, is dominated by a single giant palm whose towering leaves brush the ceiling. Visitors can walk along an upper balcony for aerial views of fountains and ponds full of ornamental fish. When visiting the houses be prepared for abrupt climatic changes—within the space of a few paces you can be transported from the tropical rain forests of South America to the arid desert of Arizona.

For the most delightful river walk to be had in these

parts, head for the Hammersmith Bridge (a two-minute walk from either of Hammersmith's two Underground stations—one of which is served by the Metropolitan Line, the other by the District and Piccadilly lines) and walk along the north bank toward Chiswick. The best time for such a walk is early on a summer's eve, when you can buy a glass of "bitter" (ale) in any (or each) of four charming pubs—the **Blue Anchor**, the **Rutland Arms**, the **Ship**, and the **Dove**—and sit and sup in the open with a friendly crowd, idly watching the scullers whose boat-houses line the banks below the bridge. **Hammersmith Terrace** is a delightful row of Georgian houses (several with their tiny gardens right above the river) separated from the houses by the towpath. William Morris used to live in Kelmscott House here.

Just before you reach Chiswick Square, step into the churchyard of St. Nicholas, where the painters James Whistler and William Hogarth are buried. Beyond lies **Syon House**—famous for Robert Adam's Great Hall—the London residence of the duke of Northumberland. The house is open to the public, although Syon's biggest draw is its gardens, the 18th-century handiwork of Capability Brown, who included a lake, conservatory, aviary, and aquarium in his designs. He had nothing, however, to do with the Heritage Motor Museum, which is also on the grounds and houses a collection of British cars from 1895 to the present day, nor with the London Butterfly House, which displays numerous species fluttering madly about in a tropical greenhouse. More energetic walkers can cross Hammersmith Bridge and follow the south bank as far south as the **Bull's Head** pub in Barnes, their faces held toward the setting sun.

Hampton Court

When Henry VIII made Richmond Park the place to hunt, outsiders built hunting lodges nearby, and it became, at the same time, a popular stopping-off place for boats on their way upriver to Hampton Court Palace after Henry became its owner. Unlike other palaces that have stood empty as museums, Hampton Court has been lived in continuously since it was built by Cardinal Wolsey, the Lord Chancellor of England, in 1515. George III was the last sovereign in residence; today it is partly occupied by pensioners of the Crown, the "Grace and Favour" tenants. The palace is unique in that it represents the very best examples of English architecture of both the 16th and early 18th centuries. And the location, hard on the Thames, is stunning.

In March of 1986 a fire caused severe damage to Hampton Court. Amazingly, although many works of art were destroyed or damaged, most of the palace's valuable contents, including an outstanding collection of 500 Renaissance paintings, were saved. The building itself, however, suffered enormously. The fire gutted the King's Audience Chamber, the Cartoon Gallery (named for the Raphael cartoons bought by Charles I and moved to the Victoria and Albert Museum more than a century ago), and State Apartments designed by Sir Christopher Wren for King William and Queen Mary. Restoration work will almost certainly stretch into the middle of the decade, but most of the palace was open to the public a week after the fire.

Although inhabited by a succession of kings and queens, Hampton Court is probably best known for its associations with Henry VIII, who, after he became its owner, extended the palace in earnest, including building the Chapel Court as a nursery for Prince Edward, his son and presumed heir. But by the time William and Mary came to the throne, the Tudor style was considered rather passé, and they commissioned Wren, the architect of St. Paul's Cathedral, to demolish the entire palace and build a new, more symmetrical and spacious residence on a scale that would rival Versailles. Because the palace was fully inhabited, Wren could only work on a portion of it at a time, and, mercifully for posterity, the money ran out before he could implement his grand designs. Hence the uniqueness of Hampton Court: One of the most complete examples of a Tudor palace coexists harmoniously alongside buildings by England's greatest architect.

The most popular element of Hampton's horticultural displays is its **maze**, first planted in 1714. It may not look too challenging from the outside, but it can take up to an hour to get out of the half-mile labyrinth of yew-hedge. So don't leave finding the way out till the main gates are about to close. Some visitors from abroad, it is said, have seen their homebound aircraft pass overhead, their having missed a Heathrow departure just down the road.

Hampton Court is easy to get to from central London. It is less than half an hour on British Rail from Waterloo Station, but you can also pick up that BR line at the Wimbledon station on the District Line of the Underground. Most people get on the District Line to Wimbledon at Earl's Court station. You can also get there by riverboat from Westminster Pier and other locations.

LONDON NORTH
Camden Town

The charm of Camden Town, the lively district bang in the center of north London about a ten-minute Underground ride due north of Tottenham Court Road, lies mainly in its social and cultural mishmash. Along its core arteries (Camden High Street, Chalk Farm Road, and Parkway), plant-filled wine bars and bistros, antiques shops, and smart clothing boutiques rub shoulders with disheveled discount stores, secondhand music retailers, and the pulpy droppings from the fruit and vegetable market on Inverness Street. Harmless down-and-outs, occupants of the Arlington Road shelter for the homeless, are deep in inebriated conference on most street corners.

The slightly seedy, hippie ambience of **Camden Lock's weekend market** is famous throughout London. Its scale is generous, spilling from the cobbled lockside area surrounding the stagnant basin waters to Chalk Farm Road, almost as far as the former Roundhouse Theatre (located in an old brick-built railway locomotive shed). The blue-canopied stalls are surrounded by trendy shops and renovated haylofts and warehouses.

Anyone wishing to sell his or her wares to the battalions of yuppies and punks lines up at nine in the morning and, if lucky, is allocated a stall. The market has everything from potted palms to pine furniture, handmade jewelry to Hawaiian shirts, posters to pure-wool sweaters, antiques and bric-a-brac to high-tech gift items.

In the middle of this friendly chaos, two French-inspired restaurants are doing a roaring trade. Camden Brasserie and Le Bistroquet stare in quasi-hostility at each other across Camden High Street just south of the bridge over the Regent's Canal. **Camden Brasserie** is the cheaper of the two. Like the black-and-white photos of the market's punk habitués that line the walls, the menu rarely changes, but that doesn't deter the arts-and-media clientele, many of whom saunter over from the futuristic-looking TV-AM building just around the corner. **Le Bistroquet** is more chic, more expensive, and more imaginative. Ceiling fans rotate overhead, spiky-haired waiters and waitresses whiz among the tables, dishes such as fish *en papillote* are

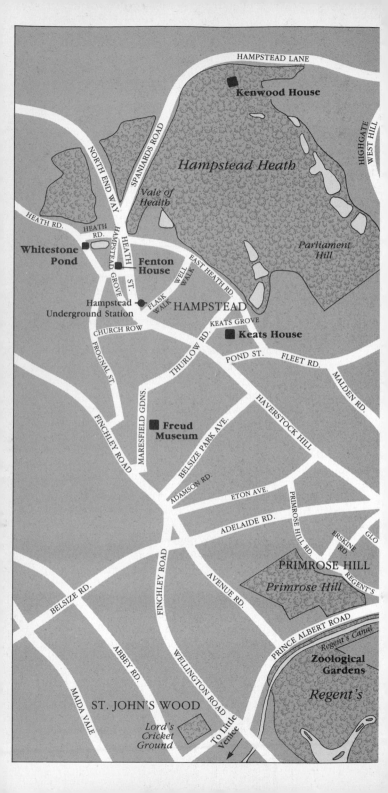

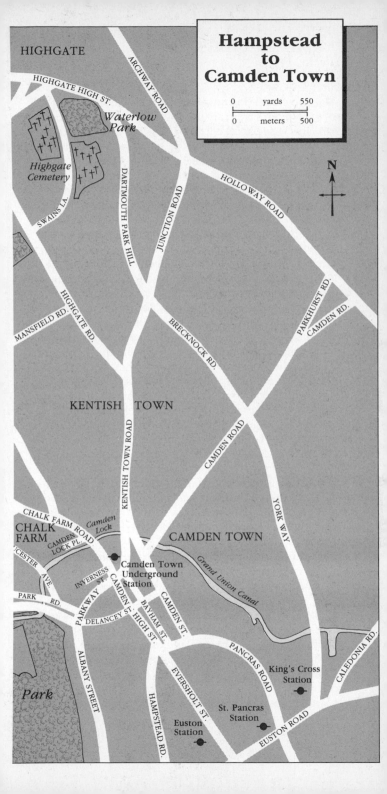

unveiled, redolent of capers and fresh fennel, and the smart talk flows.

The 50 acres of **Primrose Hill**, an offshoot of Regent's Park to Camden's west, are a voluptuous green hummock on an otherwise pancake-flat horizon. This area earned its name from its wildflowers, although in the 18th century the area blossomed with as many derelicts as blooms, and only the foolhardy would dare cross its boundaries once night had fallen. Today Primrose Hill's Regency terraces rank among the most salubrious and expensive in north London. On Sunday afternoons the grassy mound is busy with kite-flyers and walkers who climb to its summit to enjoy one of the best panoramas of London.

The function of the most prominent structure on the southern horizon would be impossible for most visitors to guess. It is an aviary, designed by Lord Snowdon and, standing within the **London Zoo** in Regent's Park, one of the city's biggest tourist attractions. Open seven days a week, the zoo was founded by Sir Stamford Raffles (a name more immediately associated with the hotel in Singapore, the British trading colony he founded).

Apart from the aviary, other highlights of the menagerie, which is home to more than 5,000 animals, include a tropical house where hummingbirds freely commute between thick foliage and your head; an "open-plan" lion house; an insect and arachnid house (not for the spiderphobic); and a tigers' den, where only a pane of glass separates you from the beasts' sharp canines. There's also a rich-smelling elephant house, where the public can witness regular teeth-cleaning and toe-filing sessions; several high-octane monkey houses; and the Moonlight World, where nocturnal fauna are deceived into activity at hours that suit visitors.

Chalk Farm, the area tightly bordered by Primrose Hill, Regent's Park Road, and a main railway line, had been a fairly run-down precinct until gentrification occurred in the 1970s. The main thoroughfare here is Regent's Park Road; its lower portion is now a neighborhood of shops that seem to sell a blend of everything—wine and kitchen equipment included—that an affluent community could possibly need. There's also a smattering of restaurants, including the refined **Odettes** and **Lemonia**, a stylish Greek eatery.

A large proportion of Camden is made up of parklands. During the British civil wars of the 17th century the future of **Regent's Park**, arguably London's most urban park, looked gloomy, as most of its trees were razed to be used as firewood for the needy. It was John Nash, backed by the prince regent, who at the end of the 18th century engineered today's triumph. Today, within the manicured hedges that line the Outer Circle road lie 500 acres of gardens, shrubbery, and bird life, all in a basic Victorian format, right down to an old-fashioned bandstand where tubas and trumpets entertain lunchtime and Sunday-afternoon picnickers. (It suffered catastrophically in a recent terrorist-bomb explosion, but is back in action.)

More modern trappings include a boating lake (formed by damming the River Tyburn), a children's boating pond, the zoo, and ornamental bridges. There's also an open-air theater, where the New Shakespeare Company performs a program of three or four plays throughout the summer. The glades and woods provide the perfect setting, and the audience, sitting on tiered seats exposed to the elements, can move around with the scenes when necessary, clutching their plates and glasses of wine as they go.

Once you are inside the Queen Mary's Gardens, within the Inner Circle road, the sounds of London are reduced to that of an occasional airplane. This fragrant enclave is a mass of 20,000 perfumed rose bushes grouped around a landscaped rock pool on the site where Nash originally planned to build a royal palace for the prince regent.

The Outer Circle road is lined with **Nash terraces**—smart, cream-colored, porticoed and pillared buildings that nowadays function as fashionable offices as well as private homes. The houses were originally built to raise money for the Crown and attracted the well-known and well-to-do—Hugh Walpole lived at 10 York Terrace, for example; King Edward VIII's lover, Mrs. Simpson, was ensconced at 7 Hanover Terrace; and H. G. Wells lived at 13 Hanover Terrace.

The only significant dwelling *within* the park is Winfield House, once the mansion of Woolworth heiress Barbara Hutton. It's now the official London residence of the U.S. ambassador, and can be viewed only through the closely guarded gates at the bottom of the drive on the Outer Circle road. Almost opposite, straddling the south end of St. John's Wood High Street, is the Central Mosque, copper-domed and minareted, one of the most incongruous sights in the vicinity. At sunset it can be mistaken for the sun setting behind the trees.

The **Regent's Canal**, part of the Grand Union Canal

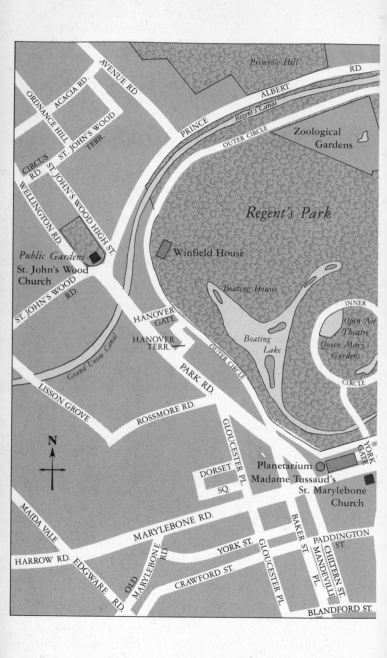

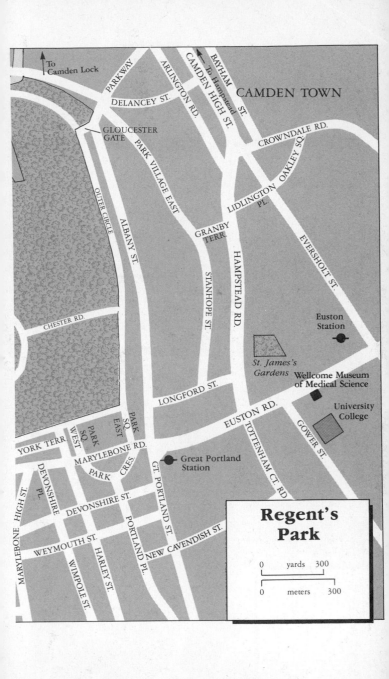

Regent's Park

```
0        yards      300
0        meters     300
```

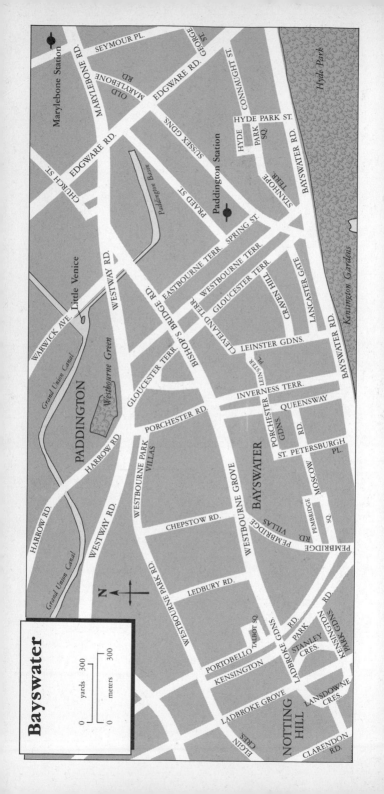

Bayswater

yards 300

meters 300

0

N

Marylebone Station

SEYMOUR PL.

MARYLEBONE RD.

OLD MARYLEBONE RD.

EDGWARE RD.

GEORGE ST.

CONNAUGHT ST.

HYDE PARK ST.

HYDE PARK SQ.

BAYSWATER RD.

Hyde Park

EDGWARE RD.

CHURCH ST.

SUSSEX GDNS.

PRAED ST.

Paddington Station

Paddington Basin

STANHOPE TERR.

Kensington Gardens

EASTBOURNE TERR.

SPRING ST.

WESTBOURNE TERR.

GLOUCESTER TERR.

CRAVEN HILL

LANCASTER GATE

WESTWAY RD.

BISHOP'S BRIDGE RD.

CLEVELAND TERR.

GLOUCESTER TERR.

LEINSTER GDNS.

BAYSWATER RD.

Little Venice

WARWICK AVE.

Grand Union Canal

PADDINGTON

Westbourne Green

GLOUCESTER TERR.

LEINSTER TER.

INVERNESS TERR.

PORCHESTER RD.

QUEENSWAY

PORCHESTER GDNS.

HARROW RD.

WESTWAY RD.

WESTBOURNE PARK VILLAS

ST. PETERSBURGH PL.

HARROW RD.

WESTBOURNE PARK RD.

CHEPSTOW RD.

WESTBOURNE GROVE

PEMBRIDGE VILLAS

MOSCOW RD.

BAYSWATER

PEMBRIDGE SQ.

PEMBRIDGE RD.

LEDBURY RD.

PORTOBELLO RD.

TALBOT SQ.

LADBROKE GDNS.

PARK

LADBROKE RD.

STANLEY CRES.

KENSINGTON PARK RD.

KENSINGTON PARK GDNS.

KENSINGTON

LADBROKE GROVE

NOTTING HILL

ELGIN CRES.

LANSDOWNE CRES.

CLARENDON RD.

network, flows around the northern perimeter of the park (you can see some of the zoo animals from the water) before taking a dogleg up to Camden Lock. Its total length runs to eight miles, from the pretty core of **Little Venice** west of the park near Paddington Station to Limehouse in the Docklands to the east. Several longboats operate regularly in summer between Camden and Little Venice, including the *Jenny Wren* and *Jason's Trip.* The boat ride takes you along the still waters past rows of Georgian houses to Little Venice, where you can break your journey with a jar of ale in the tiny, low-ceilinged **Warwick Castle** pub (especially vital if, as an alternative, you cover the one and a half miles on foot). The London Waterbus Company operates regular service on the Zoo Waterbus between Camden Lock and the zoo. *My Fair Lady* serves lunch and dinner; nondining passage is not offered. You can catch these boats near either the Warwick Avenue (near Little Venice) or Camden Town Underground stations.

Little Venice is north of **Bayswater Road,** the northern boundary of Hyde Park; **Queensway,** a main neighborhood shopping and dining street, runs north off Bayswater.

Marylebone Road

When Madame Tussaud, a French sculptress and one of King Louis XVI's tutors, arrived in London with her bizarre collection of wax facsimiles of heads that had rolled during the French Revolution, she could not have dreamed that **Madame Tussaud's,** the exhibition she established on the southern fringes of Regent's Park on the Marylebone Road in 1835, would eventually become London's most-visited attraction. Today visitors line up far down the street to see lifelike figures of historical, political, royal, and show-business personalities. Some exhibits are remarkable, but by no means could all be confused with their originals. In the **Planetarium** next door there are permanent constellation exhibitions as well as, every evening from Wednesday through Sunday, laser shows accompanied by rock and classical music. Try to avoid the lines by going early and skipping Saturdays altogether, when the ranks of tourists are swelled by British out-of-towners.

Marylebone Road (originally St. Mary-le-bourne; *bourne* meant "river" in the 18th century) is long and busy. It is also the location of St. Marylebone Church, most famous for its tiered tower and cupola. The church is wedged into the opening of Regent's Park's York Gate, one of the main entrances to the park, built in 1817. Marylebone Road's offshoots, stretching almost as far as Regent's Park in the north and Oxford Street to the south, include Harley Street, where the country's top physicians have clinics, and Wimpole Street, where Robert Browning courted Elizabeth Barrett.

Baker Street, the biggest and longest of these offshoots, is most famous for being the fictional address of detective Sherlock Holmes. In his day, that part of Baker Street was known as York Place. Today, thanks to the renumbering of the street in 1930, the house at 221b is inhabited by the Abbey National Building Society, whose employees must every day reply politely to "Dear Sherlock Holmes" letters. For those determined to pursue the famous detective, he can be found at the **Sherlock Holmes public house** (formerly the Northumberland Arms Hotel) on Northumberland Street in Westminster. Upstairs, you will find a complete reconstruction of his study, and in the pub itself there are posters and photographs of various actors who have played the immortal detective.

The more interesting and prettier Marylebone High Street, parallel to Baker Street, is lined with shops and small cafés. **Maison Sagne**, at number 105, is one such refreshment stop. This Swiss pâtisserie and bakery, established in 1921, is still baking pastries and cakes on the premises. Antiquities can be found in **Blunderbuss**, on Thayer Street (the southern continuation of the High Street), an eclectic shop full of pistols, helmets, swords, and other military bric-a-brac. The Wallace Collection (see the West End, above) is just west of Thayer.

Chiltern Street, parallel to and east of Baker Street, is interesting for its fashionable boutiques, its antiques stores and fabric shops, and its music and musical instrument shops stocking oboes, flutes, early-music instruments, and musical scores.

Islington

One of the first of London's "villages" to be gentrified by an influx of middle-class residents, Islington—east of Regent's Park and north of the City—suffers from a proliferation of real-estate agents whose windows advertise "bijoux" properties with quarter-of-a-million-pound price tags. Well-connected by subway (Highbury & Islington stop on the Victoria Line, the Angel on the Northern Line, a 15-minute trip from central London), Islington has come a long way since its days as one of London's seediest working-class boroughs.

The Domesday Book records Islington as a small settlement within the Great Forest of Middlesex, a largely rural, dairy-producing district supplying London. In the 17th century, when plague and fire caused a mass exodus from central London, Islington became a fashionable residence for the nobility and otherwise well-heeled (Charles and Mary Lamb lived here), who were attracted by its rejuvenating spas. By the 19th century Islington was a curious mixture—the construction of better roads and the introduction of railways resulted in the development of fine terraces and squares—but the central core had declined and was awash in grime, poverty, and working-class slums (although George Orwell, Walter Sickert, and Evelyn Waugh all made their homes here).

Today Islington is the undisputed territory of the intelligent socialist. Ruled by a council of liberal tendency, it's a borough that survives on meager finances but doles out welcome bowls of sympathy. Such a reputation has made it a place of refuge for struggling minority groups and has spawned countless voluntary self-help associations, among them the Islington Voluntary Action Council, designed to help those who would doubtless suffer discrimination elsewhere.

However, as is often the case with economically depressed areas (Islington is the eighth-poorest borough in London), its low property prices have attracted an influx of the upwardly mobile. Rubbing shoulders with those relying on state support, the newcomers are buying the last of the borough's decaying properties and converting them into smart residences. And they buy all their fixtures and fittings in **Upper Street**. Aptly named, not only for its clientele but also for its contents, Islington's main thoroughfare is chockablock with wine bars, restaurants, designer kitchen-accessories shops, and all manner of other late-20th-century paraphernalia.

Of course there are antiques stores. Islingtonians frequent **Camden Passage**, north of the Angel tube station, a narrow, flagstoned, pedestrians-only street behind the miniature Islington Green, where wrought-iron shop signs advertise numerous emporiums: Franco's, The Furniture Vault, Gordon Gridley, Ark Angel, and Laurence Mitchell, to name a few, not to mention **The Angel Arcade**, a Gothic-style precinct of 20 shops selling silver, porcelain, rare

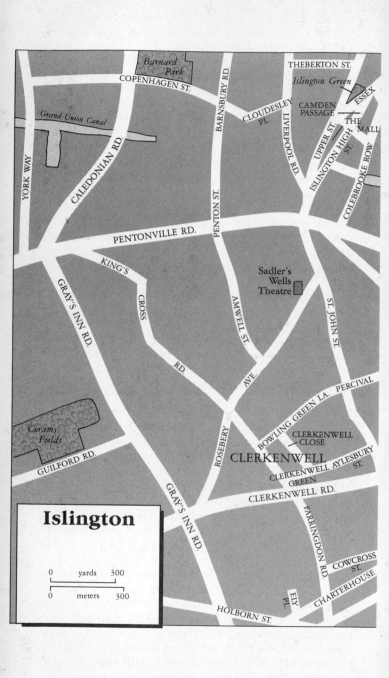

Barnard Park

COPENHAGEN ST.

THEBERTON ST.

Islington Green

CAMDEN PASSAGE

ESSEX

Grand Union Canal

BARNSBURY RD.

CLOUDESLEY PL.

LIVERPOOL RD.

UPPER ST.

THE MALL

YORK WAY

CALEDONIAN RD.

ISLINGTON HIGH ST.

COLEBROOKE ROW

PENTON ST.

PENTONVILLE RD.

KING'S

CROSS

RD.

GRAY'S INN RD.

Sadler's Wells Theatre

AMWELL ST.

ST. JOHN ST.

Corams Fields

AVE.

BOWLING GREEN LA.

PERCIVAL

CLERKENWELL CLOSE

GUILFORD RD.

ROSEBERY

CLERKENWELL

CLERKENWELL GREEN

AYLESBURY ST.

CLERKENWELL RD.

GRAY'S INN RD.

FARRINGDON RD.

COWCROSS ST.

Islington

CHARTERHOUSE

ELY PL.

0   yards   300

0   meters   300

HOLBORN ST.

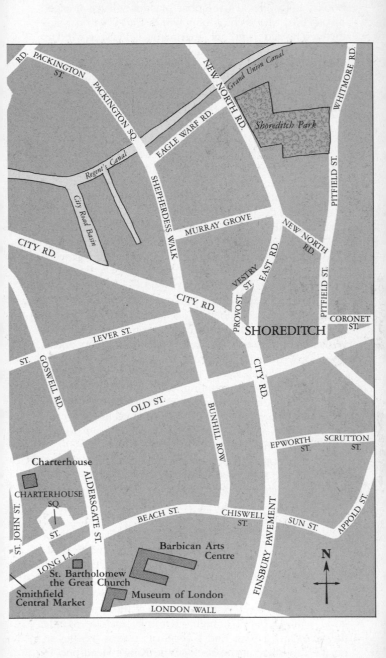

books, and objets d'art. Finbar Macdonnell has a caged
mynah bird whose chirruping will distract your browsing
through his old prints and engravings. And if you wind up
in **The Mall**, on neighboring Islington High Street, you
may never come out—it contains a bewildering 35 galleries filled with antiques and decorative arts. On Wednesday
mornings and all day Saturdays there are also rows of
antiques stalls set up in Camden Passage.

A large part of the borough of Islington is dominated
by a district to the south called **Clerkenwell**, named after
the Clerks' Well, which was discovered in 1924 in what is
now the *New Statesman/Society* building. The well was
christened after the Medieval parish clerks of the City of
London (south of this area), who performed miracle
plays near here on the banks of the River Fleet. The
Charterhouse, a beautiful, towered building near the
Aldgate Underground stop and Smithfield market (see
below), owes its construction in 1371 to Sir Walter de
Manney, who recognized its potential as a center of
prayer and place of refuge for plague victims. Since then
the Charterhouse has been home to Carthusian monks, a
palace visited by Elizabeth I, and a famous boys' school.
Large parts of it were destroyed during the Blitz; what
remains is home to the Charterhouse Pensioners and is
open on Wednesdays for guided tours.

The fertile meadowland on which Clerkenwell was
founded is alive with spouting wells. Some are still quite
productive, like the one under the **Sadler's Wells Theatre**
(home to Opera London) on Rosebery Avenue. The pu-
rity of the local well water attracted beverage makers
such as Gordon's, famous for its gin distillery, and Samuel
Whitbread; both still occupy their original sites. In fact,
the Whitbread Brewery Shire Horses still clop along their
morning delivery rounds to pubs in the City to the south
and southeast and also turn out for the Lord Mayor's
Show and other ceremonial occasions.

No wonder Islington's wine bars are so well stocked.
Serendipity, in the Mall, is a cool, conservatory-like cocktail bar. **The Dome**, on Islington High Street, has a
Parisian ambience, particularly when the windows are
opened wide in summer and the smell of croissants
drifts into the street. A glass of wine at these places is a
good way to begin a night that may include a little
theater: Many a West End box-office success has begun
on the tiny stage at the back of the **King's Head** pub in
Upper Street. Performances are held nearly every night.

When the show ends, live music in the bar begins. The pub's old decor and gentrified spit-and-sawdust feeling is complemented by the staff's quaint habit of using a cash till that dates back to the days before the decimal system went into effect, so keep your currency converter handy or be prepared to trust the change.

After the theater you can squeeze into **Minogues** on Theberton Street, one of London's few Irish pub/ restaurants, for flowers on the table and traditional dishes ordered from a blackboard menu. **Young's Chinese** is a short distance away on Upper Street; the nearby **Upper Street Fish Shop** is bright, breezy, and a bit upscale, at least for a fish-and-chips shop.

You'll have to get up early to catch the market traders at **Smithfield Market**. This wholesale meat, poultry, and game market in the southern portion of Clerkenwell near the Barbican Underground stop, though of little initial attraction to the visitor, has been a London tradition since the 12th century. Located on the site of Islington's old Caledonian livestock market (in those days the cattle were alive), it extends over eight acres, has 15 miles of rails, is capable of hanging 60,000 sides of beef, and is active Monday to Friday.

The Norman **St. Bartholomew the Great Church**, one of the oldest in London, lies a few minutes' walk to the east, and contains the only pre-Reformation font in the city. There is also a restaurant here called **Café du Marché** that looks as if it belongs somewhere on Paris's Left Bank. It's hard to find, though: Stand on Charterhouse Square, look north, and you'll see it tucked down a tiny alleyway.

Hampstead

Hampstead is London at its most rural. Drop strangers in the heart of the 800 acres of leafy, luscious **Hampstead Heath**, north of Regent's Park and Camden, and they will swear that they have been abandoned in some remote English shire, a verdant, bushy-tailed wilderness far from the madding crowds. Only when their ears turn away from birdsong to the distant hum of metropolitan traffic will they accept the heath's urban coordinates. Stuff them into a taxi and they can be in central London in 20 minutes.

As a place to live, Hampstead's tree-lined lanes and twisting alleys have long been favored by the wealthy and well known. Residents have included Robert Louis Stevenson, D. H. Lawrence, John Keats, John Galsworthy, George

Orwell, William Blake, and John Constable. By the early 1900s Hampstead had become London's Montmartre, full of painters, their entourages, and hangers on. Wander around the streets today and you'll see many of the distinctive blue plaques that mark the residence of a famous previous tenant.

Hampstead Heath is also one of the "lungs of London." Tranquillity and clean air (at least by city standards) are its stock in trade, and the lichen grows thick. Judging by the real-estate prices, which rank among the highest in the city, such virtues have much appeal today. Among its rich and famous residents are Jeremy Irons, John Le Carré, and Boy George. Hampstead being what it is, no one appears to spare a second glance when one of these mortals is spotted buying out-of-season asparagus at a local greengrocer, taking tea at the Louis pâtisserie, or sipping a cappuccino at the Dôme Café.

Despite the massive Heath, the appeal of Hampstead is all too easy for the London visitor to miss. Emerge from the Hampstead Underground station—London's deepest, at 192 feet below ground level—into a busy intersection lined with unexciting shops and you'll immediately wonder what the fuss is all about. Turn down Hampstead High Street, and take a left into **Flask Walk**, and the neighborhood takes a turn for the best.

The very name Flask puts things into immediate historical context. It is derived from the bottles of medicinal waters that once were filled from nearby chalybeate springs and sold here. The shops now go in for Perrier and other variations on the *eau* theme, but several are well worth a browse. One of Hampstead's many pleasant pubs, **The Flask**, is also on the Walk.

Hampstead is the one place in London where a map and compass are as useful to the tourist as a handful of currency. To experience the best of the greenery you need to walk in, around, and through the Heath, and, with luck, return to the point where you started. Take heart in the knowledge that even locals go astray.

Follow Flask Walk into Well Walk, another place with watery associations, and pause at number 40, once the home of John Constable, England's finest landscape painter. From his house, after a few more minutes, you should come face-to-face with the Heath. The point to head for, out of sight but likely to be known to passing strollers, joggers, dog walkers, bird watchers, and the like, is **Kenwood House**.

A very large and very white house situated on the far side of the Heath northeast from where you are standing, Kenwood is a classic example of the 18th-century species of gentleman's country home. First owned by Lord Chief Justice William Murray, who employed Robert Adam to enlarge and embellish the property, Kenwood is now a bequest to the nation, and it contains a fine collection of paintings by Rembrandt, Vermeer, Rubens, and others. During the summer there is a series of open-air concerts on the grounds.

From Kenwood, walk through the rhododendron gardens, littered with the occasional piece of weathered sculpture, along the linden-shaded gravel path, and ask to be pointed toward the Spaniards Inn, where both Charles Dickens and Dick Turpin, the highwayman, drank. From there, slip through the still narrow gap between the inn and the tollhouse, both 18th century and famous for the part played by the landlord in 1780 in saving Kenwood House from the mob during the Gordon riots (the U.K.'s worst-ever riots, provoked by anger over the repeal of anti-Catholic legislation). Then head south along Spaniards Road (or, better still, follow a more rural course parallel to the busy thoroughfare) toward Whitestone Pond, whose dark waters mark the highest point in London (437 feet). Just before you reach the road you will catch a glimpse of the distant city skyline rising out of the Thames valley, an especially spectacular sight when the afternoon sun is low on the horizon, striking gold against the city structures.

As this is the high point of the walking tour, you might like to take time out at **Jack Straw's Castle**, a white wooden eyesore of a pub named after one of the leaders of Wat Tyler's Peasants' Revolt of 1381 who was caught while trying to seek refuge near here and later hanged on the site where the pub now stands. The current pub was rebuilt in the 1960s after the original was destroyed in World War II. Or you can follow North End Way to the popular **Bull and Bush Tavern**, built on the site of a 17th-century farmhouse that was briefly home to Hogarth and was later made famous in 19th-century music halls. A still-popular song has the rousing refrain "Down at the old Bull and Bush."

Also, don't miss the **Vale of Health**, the only village *on* Hampstead Heath. It is likely that there were inhabitants here as early as a thousand years ago, but it wasn't developed in earnest until the late 18th century. In the hope of

attracting new people to the village, it adopted its charming name. One such person was D. H. Lawrence; look for
blue plaques. **Parliament Hill,** near South End Green,
covers 270 acres and rises to 319 feet. From here the
panoramic view takes in the whole city. The hill owes its
name to the 1605 Gunpowder Plotters, who intended to
meet here to watch the Houses of Parliament burn on
November 5. These days it's a favorite haunt of kite-flyers.
If you get too hot on the Heath, you can always cool off
with a dip in the Hampstead Mixed Bathing Pond, open
May to September. There is also the men-only Highgate
Pond (for competent swimmers) and the female (over 8)
Kenwood Pond, all natural ponds, quite basic but rather
British.

Hampstead has a few other landmarks well worth a
detour before you return to more central parts of town.
One is **Keats' House** on Keats Grove (open to the public),
set in the delightful garden where the poet composed
"Ode to a Nightingale." Another is the 17th-century **Fenton House** on Hampstead Grove, with an interesting collection of paintings, furniture, and ceramics, as well as a
highly regarded collection of early keyboard instruments.
A third landmark is the remarkable 18th-century terrace
of "brownstones" along **Church Row**. Planted with trees,
and with the Church of St. John's (where John Constable
is buried) at the end of the row, the scene is quintessentially English. Imagine it with a dusting of snow and you
have the makings of a classic Christmas card. Look for
number 99 Frognal, where General de Gaulle lived during much of World War II. In **The Freud Museum,** 20
Maresfield Gardens, six rooms remain as they were when
Freud died here. In addition to the famous couch, you
can see manuscripts, antiquities, books, and the original
Viennese furnishings he brought with him when he es-
caped Nazi-occupied Austria in 1938.

Head now for **Highgate**, another London hilltop village, which meets Hampstead on Hampstead Heath.
Close to another **Flask** pub (this one, with its large courtyard and outside summer tables, looking extremely rural), a onetime haunt of Karl Marx and William Hogarth,
where the latter would work depicting scenes of drunken-
ness, and where Dick Turpin is once supposed to have
hidden, lies **Highgate Cemetery**. It is divided into two
sections: The section to the east of Swains Lane is the
newer half, and contains the grave and bold bronze bust
of Karl Marx; the section to the west is a tangled, over-

grown, rather bizarre yet beautiful world of vaults and other monumental masonry. George Eliot and Sir Ralph Richardson are also to be found in Highgate Cemetery.

In adjacent Waterlow Park stands **Lauderdale House**, which Nell Gwynn, mistress of Charles II, is said to have used as a summer residence. Now open to the public, it offers exhibitions of work by local art college students as well as recitals. Among the 17th- and 18th-century houses in the Grove you will find number 3, where Coleridge lived for a short time.

Finally, of particular note on Highgate Hill (don't miss the views while you're looking for it) is the Whittington Stone, on the spot where Dick Whittington, the boy who ran away to London in search of his fortune and became Lord Mayor, is supposed to have heard Bow Bells summon him to "Turn again Whittington, thrice Lord Mayor of London." (Incidentally, Whittington was mayor *four* times. And the position of *Lord* Mayor was only created many years later.) His legendary companion, the cat, who sits on the stone, was added in 1964.

LONDON EAST
East End

London's East End is not an obvious destination for visitors. It is far from refined, short on interesting shops, relatively light on historic buildings, and lacking in greenery. But for anyone interested in London as a sociological phenomenon, the East End—located at the eastern end of the city, from about the Tower area onward, and hugging the northern bank of the Thames—is an essential detour.

Although London has nowhere near the same melting-pot alchemy that, say, New York City does, it has certainly welcomed its fair share of huddled masses. The first to stake a claim were the Huguenots in the 16th century. Close on their heels came Sephardic Jews, Irish Catholics who excavated the city's docks, Polish and Russian Jews escaping the pogroms, and later, though less concentrated as a group in this particular section of town, thousands of Central European Jews fleeing Nazi persecution.

In 1887 a sociological study described Whitechapel as simply the "dwelling place of the Jews," a place where they practiced tailoring and other traditional skills. Today the East End is still steeped in Jewish history. For example, Bevis Marks, near Aldgate Underground station, is Britain's oldest surviving synagogue, built for the Sephardic community in 1701. Jewry Street is nearby, and there is even a Jewish soup kitchen on Brune Street. Cable Street is famous for the "battle" in which Jewish resistance to a march by Oswald Mosley and his Black Shirts stemmed the rising tide of fascism in Britain in the 1930s.

In recent years there has been a shift in the ethnic makeup of the East End. Many Jews have moved out, upgrading their properties and buying in more desirable parts of town (particularly in the northwest London suburbs of Golders Green and Hendon; most of the Orthodox have moved to Stamford Hill). Even the Great Synagogue of Duke's Place closed in 1978, and so have ten others in the neighborhood, as the Jewish population has declined from 125,000 in 1900 to around 12,000 today.

Their places have been filled by a fresh wave of immigrants from the Indian subcontinent, notably Bengal and Bangladesh, who have taken over the lower-priced real estate as well as the traditional sweatshops. There are now as many *halal* butchers in the main shopping streets as there are kosher. On one street corner, where Fournier Street meets Brick Lane, there is a structure that was built as a Huguenot chapel, later became a synagogue, and is now a mosque.

The East End has always been on the "other" side of the tracks, a tough, working-class district of terraced houses, outside lavatories, and communal baths. At the end of the last century its slums were notorious. They inspired, among others, the American philanthropist George Peabody to finance the building of apartment blocks in an effort to alleviate the worst areas of overcrowding. Crime and prostitution flourished here, and the area was the setting of the macabre deeds of Jack the Ripper.

To locate this famous and still slightly raw and intriguing corner of London, walk about half a mile north of the Tower of London or due east from the Bank of London. But before you venture east, try to catch at least one episode of Britain's most successful soap, "Eastenders." Like all soaps, it pays only lip service to the truth, but it will at least familiarize you with the Cockney dialect. Anyone born within the sound of Bow Bells, it is said, is a true Cockney, and most of the East End's places of interest lie within earshot of their chimes.

If your itinerary allows, save the East End for a Sunday morning. Do this not so much for any religious resonances—though many beautiful churches designed by Christopher Wren and Nicholas Hawksmoor (including Christ Church, Hawksmoor's masterpiece, which overshadows Spitalfields fruit and vegetable market) are found in this part of town—but for its **Petticoat Lane market**. You won't find that name on a map, though; just take the tube to Aldgate and follow the crowds. If you prefer to trust a map, look for Middlesex Street and you'll find yourself in the heart of the action.

There are a few antiques and bric-a-brac stalls but nothing to compare with, say, Portobello Road or Camden Lock. In fact, the market's name hails from the days when it was predominantly a clothes market. Today's wares, on the other hand, are as much a celebration of plastic and fly-by-night manufacturing as anything remotely tied to nostalgia. The real pleasure of Petticoat Lane is all about listening to the patter of the stall holders, barrow boys, costermongers, and fly-boys, the unlicensed traders always ready to flee at the first sign of a bobby. You should simply drift along with the crowd, soaking up the sheer vitality of the scene. This is an extremely popular market, almost an institution among local residents, so you'll find yourself mingling with just about all the Cockneys in London.

Petticoat Lane is one of those classic markets where, wags say, you can find whatever was stolen from you the week before. Don't trust the irresistible prices, explained away by an unfortunate accident whereby the merchandise just happened to fall off the back of a lorry. Be equally wary, despite the temptations, of Club Row, where they sell pleading dogs of dubious pedigree and caged birds whose vocabulary usually turns out to be as extensive as that of their canine neighbors, again contrary to the vendors' promises.

There are other interesting sights in the East End worthy of higher cultural esteem. The **Whitechapel Art Gallery** is one of the best in London (the Tate recently recruited a new chief curator from its ranks), and specializes in exhibitions devoted mainly to contemporary European artists, while opposite the Whitechapel Underground is the London Hospital, most famously the home of Joseph Merrick, better known as the Elephant Man. Cinema devotees will want to check out the Coronet on Mile End Road, not for its current screen presentations but to pay respects to the site of the music hall where Charlie Chaplin made his debut. And a great favorite for a family outing is the **Bethnal**

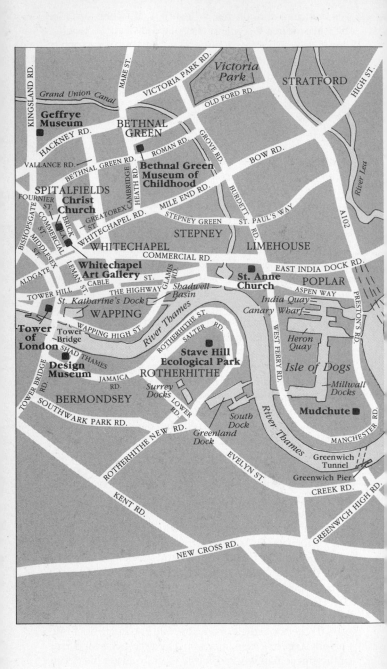

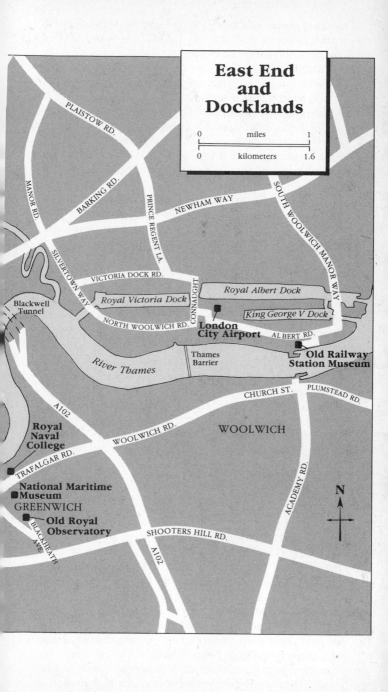

Green Museum of Childhood on Cambridge Heath Road, with collections not only of children's toys but also of costumes and furniture.

With all its ethnic character, you won't go hungry in the East End, but you may have to leave your food prejudices behind. **Tubby Isaacs' seafood stall** on Greatorex Street is an East End institution, and the place to buy small plates of jellied eels, whelks, cockles, and winkles. Or you might like to risk your palate on the hot to very hot dishes at the Indian restaurants on Brick Lane, basic in price but with burning consequences—though if you order *korma,* or *kurma,* you'll still retain the power of speech. **Bloom's,** on Whitechapel Road, the East End's main artery, is London's best kosher restaurant. Takeout sandwiches and borscht followed by pastrami are the order of the day here.

Two less obvious attractions in the East End are the Geffrye Museum and **Wesley's Chapel.** The latter, at 47 City Road, is very much a place of pilgrimage for Methodists. The first stone in this, "the mother church of Methodism," was laid by John Wesley in 1777, and the great man preached here during the last years of his life, living in the house next door until his death in 1791. (He is buried in the graveyard behind the chapel.) The **Geffrye Museum,** Kingsland Road, has an unusual, altogether charming atmosphere. Contained within almshouses shaded by plane trees, and founded by a local benefactor, Sir Robert Geffrye, is a small but perfect collection of fine furniture dating from the 1600s to 1939. During school holidays and on Saturdays special activities are arranged for local children.

Docklands

Visitors to London beware. The capital is changing faster than any other city in the world except perhaps Paris, Hong Kong, and Tokyo. But if you stick to the familiar haunts of the City and the West End, visiting only such popular landmarks as Westminster Abbey, the Houses of Parliament, St. Paul's Cathedral, and Buckingham Palace, you won't notice a thing. Even many Londoners are none the wiser—their typical reaction, when shown what's happening on their very doorstep, is amazement at just how much has already been altered.

Venture just five minutes or so east from the Tower of London and you'll discover a London that is undergoing redevelopment on a scale seen only on two previous occasions—after the Great Fire and during the 1950s, when London was busy repairing the ravages of war. Although work began only in the early 1980s, the Docklands has already become the most important and exciting inner-city development in Europe.

The Docklands is a vast area of basins, locks, and canals where, during the peak of the country's imperial power, raw materials were unloaded from the colonies and manufactured goods were exported to the rest of the world. But with the gradual loss of empire and the undermining of England's commercial supremacy, coupled with the growth of containerized traffic, the docks gradually dwindled in importance. Decline led to decay, and over time the area became a giant urban wasteland.

In a location as big as central London itself (a land area equivalent to that stretching from Marble Arch to the Tower of London and from Waterloo to Euston), old warehouses—some still smelling of the spices they once stored—are being slowly transformed into chic stores, wine bars, restaurants, exhibition centers, craft workshops, art galleries, museums, and hotels.

Within a five-minute walk east of Tower Bridge is **St. Katherine's Dock**, built in 1825–1828 despite 11,000 protesting inhabitants, and at one time providing warehousing for valuable commodities such as carpets, cigars, French perfume, spices, and ivory. (Hence Ivory House, which, at its peak, handled a grisly 22,000 tusks a year.) These docks now house England's historic ships collection, full of old Thames sailing barges. Nearby, modern yachts anchor in a basin surrounded by arcaded warehouses constructed by Scottish engineer Thomas Telford. The **Dickens Inn**, a wooden warehouse now converted into a pub with a sawdust floor and two restaurants, is also nearby.

On the south side of the river, a short but breezy walk across the Tower Bridge, is the new **Design Museum**, housed in Butlers Wharf (see below). Established by the Conran Foundation, it features mass-produced consumer goods from all over the world, such as early vacuum cleaners, radios, and Coca-Cola bottles.

Ecology has not been ignored in these grandiose schemes. On the Isle of Dogs, **Mudchute** was created in the late 19th century from the residue of mud and silt excavated during the building of Millwall Docks. This gooey sludge was literally shot across the road through a chute, and grass has since grown over it. Today Mudchute is a 32-acre working farm that even raises sheep for slaughter, and the Stave Hill Ecological Park, in the heart of the Surrey Docks, contains 400 species of flora.

Canals in the Docklands that were filled in during the 1960s, having ceased to function as commercial arteries, are now being dug out for purely aesthetic considerations. With its eight miles of River Thames and 460 acres of retained water, the Docklands has already been compared to Amsterdam and Venice—which is also where several architects have looked for inspiration.

In fact, top names in architecture, both British and foreign, have been recruited to renovate the area's warehouses, some of which survive from the 1790s (although most are from the 19th century), as well as to design new residential and commercial buildings. Sir Terence Conran, fresh from revitalizing the high streets of Britain, has done a similar job on **Butlers Wharf**, an outstanding remnant of original 19th-century riverside warehouses, turning it into shops, restaurants, offices, and the above-mentioned Design Museum.

A transformation is also planned for the pumping station on **Shadwell Basin** a bit east of the Tower in Wapping, built by the London Hydraulic Power Company in 1890 as one of five stations of its kind, and designed to provide power not only to the surrounding docks but also to all of central London (for everything from raising the curtains at Drury Lane to lighting Joseph Kennedy's South Kensington house when he was the U.S. ambassador to Britain). Plans are not settled at this writing.

The **Docklands Light Railway** (DLR) is for the new residents, workers, and visitors. Quite unlike the Underground, this high-tech system runs on a raised track some 20 feet above street level, using many of the original Victorian viaducts, from the Tower of London to the tip of the Isle of Dogs (see Island Gardens below) and east along the Thames to Stratford. Tickets are available from automatic ticket-dispensing machines, and should be purchased before boarding.

In October of 1987, the London City Airport was opened. This mile-long runway, sandwiched between the Royal Albert and George V docks, accommodates 50-seater DeHavilland Dash-7 aircraft that link the Docklands with Jersey, as well as cities on the Continent within a 400-mile radius of London. As we go to press it looks as if the Dash-7s will be replaced by more versatile BAe 746 jets, resulting in a much wider range throughout Europe and possibly transforming the future of this airport. Among those who *do* use it, however, it is proving its worth: Just 15 to 20 minutes after collecting their baggage—less than half the time it takes to journey into central London from Heathrow—arriving travellers can be in the heart of the City, making the airport an ideal gateway for financiers and other businesspeople. There is also a Thames Line Riverbus stop at the City Airport Pier here. The Docklands has, in other words, come full circle: It was because of the commercial importance of the Thames and the dock system that London was able to become the financial capital of the world, and it is here that its success may once again be ensured.

You can take the DLR up to Stratford and transfer to the London Link Railway, to reach, at the end of the line (just past the City Airport), the North Woolwich **Old Station Museum**. Restored to its period glory, the Old Station, with its lovely old flagstone floors, exhibits railroad memorabilia from the Great Eastern Railway and the North Eastern Railway in the Booking Hall, the Ticket & Parcels Office, and the Ladies and General Waiting rooms. The pride and joy of the museum, however, is the lovingly restored "Coffee Pot" saddle-tank engine, the only survivor of a class of engines regularly used to shunt goods about the area.

From the visitor's point of view the most exciting aspect of the Docklands is not what's new but what's old. Historic watering holes such as the **Prospect of Whitby** on Wapping Wall, the **Town of Ramsgate** on Wapping High Street, the **Angel** on Rotherhithe, the **Hoop and Grapes** on Aldgate High Street (one of the oldest pubs in Britain, installed in a a timber-framed building built before 1660), and the aptly named **House They Left Behind** on Glamis Road are all part of the Docklands fabric. Several of these places back onto the Thames; on a fine summer evening you won't find a more absorbing sight than the view across the drift of the tide to the Surrey Docks from the tiny balcony at the back of the Grapes.

There are more than 100 listed buildings in the area, including half a dozen early-18th-century Hawksmoor churches (favorites are Christ Church, Spitalfields, and St. Anne, Limehouse). Many properties, including old churches, are being spruced up and their courtyards cleared of years of matted vegetation.

A large chunk of Britain's maritime history was spawned

by London's docks. Most 18th-century Royal Navy vessels were built here, as was the *Great Eastern,* the largest ship built in the 19th century. Some are now permanently berthed in the docks as tourist attractions; the *John W. Mackay,* probably the oldest steam-driven cable ship in the world, is among them, berthed in the West India docks.

The Docklands is also Charles Dickens country. The Quilp residence in *The Old Curiosity Shop* was at Tower Hill, and Quilp's Wharf was across the river at Shad Thames. Just behind Hawksmoor's St. George's-in-the-East in Wapping is the site thought to be the opium den Dickens visited shortly before he died. Lizzie Hexam lived in Limehouse, and so did Miss Abbey Potterson, the proprietress of the Six Jolly Fellowship Porters (alias the Grapes) in *Our Mutual Friend.* Jacob's Island (which Dickens called Folly Ditch) was the home of Bill Sikes (not to mention where he was hanged) in *Oliver Twist.* The **George Inn**—still a pub—in Southwark's High Street appeared in *The Pickwick Papers* and *Little Dorrit.* The George has been preserved and is now owned by the National Trust.

What's best about the Docklands is that this is a living environment, not an artificial stage set manicured for tourists. When the Docklands really was docks, high walls kept Londoners from seeing, let alone enjoying, their backyard acres of water. Today, with the building of scores of promenades along the Thames and the canals, an entire waterscape is opening up before their eyes.

Greenwich

Greenwich, the historic maritime heart of London, lies some five miles east of the center of town on the southern bank of the Thames. Because its maritime traditions still shape its present-day appeal, it is especially fitting to arrive in Greenwich by boat from Westminster Pier or from Charing Cross Pier (behind Charing Cross Station). Step off the pier and, within a few paces, you can be mounting the gangplank of the *Cutty Sark,* a magnificent clipper that plied 19th-century trade routes carrying cargoes of tea, the brew that oiled the cogs of an empire. Beautifully restored and resting in its own dry dock, it is an important piece of nautical history, and houses a fine collection of figureheads and scale replicas of ship's cabins of the period.

Just a few yards away, dwarfed by the soaring masts of

the *Cutty Sark,* is the comparatively tiny *Gipsy Moth IV,* the yacht that carried Sir Francis Chichester on the first solo circumnavigation of the globe in 1966–1967. Nearby is the Royal Naval College, inspired by Wren, Hawksmoor, and Sir John Vanbrugh, and, just across the main road, the **National Maritime Museum**, which brings Britain's rich seafaring heritage vividly alive. Housed in a grouping of some of the country's finest 17th-century buildings, the museum displays paintings, models, and real-life boats, as well as exhibits that evoke some of the country's great naval battles and the voyages of discovery by Captain Cook and other adventurers. Inigo Jones's **Queen's House**, restored by the National Maritime Museum and opened by the Queen in May of 1990, is also nearby. It was once home to Queen Henrietta Maria, the wife of Charles I.

After exploring these sights, hike to the top of Greenwich Park, where, from the ankles of the statue of General Wolfe, you'll enjoy a grand view of the river. Try to time your climb so you reach the summit by 1:00 P.M., when the famous ball drops from the top of the **Old Royal Observatory**. The moment marks the correct Greenwich Mean Time. The observatory, part of the Maritime Museum, houses the largest refracting telescope in the U.K. as well as an extensive collection of historical timepieces and astronomical instruments. A plaque marks the Greenwich Meridian, the spot that defines the zero line of longitude—stand astride it and you'll have one foot in the Eastern Hemisphere, the other in the Western.

Farther downstream, and included on many riverboat trips, is the new **Thames Barrier**, one of the most remarkable works of engineering in modern times. Built between 1975 and 1982, it consists of steel plates that lie flat on the riverbed, but pivot up to a vertical position when a flood threatens, reaching as high as a five-story house. There are six gates, between which are huge piers that house the operating machinery. There is an excellent visitors' center, with audiovisual displays and scale models explaining how it all works, plus cruises around the Barrier. (Access is via the south bank only.)

An interesting alternative return route to central London is to follow the foot tunnel beneath the Thames from Greenwich to the (really a peninsula), **Isle of Dogs**, so called because the Royal Kennels were situated here as early as the reign of Henry VIII. Charles II used to exercise his spaniels in these then-rural parts. Also here, on the Tower side of the river, are the Island Gardens, the last (or first) stop on the Isle of Dogs part of the Docklands Light Railway, and claimed by some to have the best view in London. After admiring the view of Greenwich (painted by Canaletto in 1755), you can catch the Light Railway back to Tower Bridge.

London Area Tracks

Sports-minded visitors to London, or those who like to rub shoulders with a slightly raffish element, should consider a visit to a horse-race meeting at Kempton Park, Sandown Park, or Windsor (all of which have summer evening meetings with a very pleasant, easygoing atmosphere of their own, and are easy to get to). If the greyhounds are more your thing, try Hackney, Walthamstow, or White City, among other tracks.

You don't have to bet to enjoy the considerable spectacle of thoroughbred horses or highly strung dogs racing to the wire, and you can be as comfortable—good restaurants, well-run bars in all cases—or as down to earth as you wish. Buy a copy of the daily *Sporting Life* (which, incidentally, is the Queen Mother's favorite newspaper) for a mass of background information, including "how to get there" details and a complete listing of greyhound tracks.

LONDON MUSEUMS

"If a man is tired of London he is tired of life," said Samuel Johnson. The same can be said of the museums that grace the present-day metropolis; in a lifetime of museum-going you will not tire of the riches to be enjoyed behind their doors.

The nearest Underground stop follows each address in parentheses. Regular closing days, if any, follow each entry. For special exhibitions, consult listings in current periodicals.

Apsley House: The Wellington Museum, 149 Piccadilly (Hyde Park Corner). Fine porcelain and silverplate, batons and swords, and paintings by British and Continental masters now fill the duke of Wellington's aristocratic residence, designed by Robert Adam in the 1770s and remodeled by Benjamin Wyatt in the 1820s. Closed Mondays and Fridays.

Bear Gardens Museum and Arts Centre, 1 Bear Gardens, Bankside (London Bridge). Exhibits re-create the theaters, such as the ones Shakespeare knew, that were concentrated in this area until the 18th century. Closed Mondays and Tuesdays; open Wednesdays and Thursdays by appointment only.

Bethnal Green Museum of Childhood, Cambridge Heath Road (Bethnal Green). The old toys, games, and dollhouses are not the only attraction here; the upper floor is given over to historic costumes of the rich and poor. Closed Fridays.

British Museum, Great Russell Street (Russell Square). The Elgin Marbles and the Rosetta Stone are but two of the treasures in the world's largest collection of antiquities. The vast and diverse inventory also includes Chinese porcelains, European drawings, Medieval timepieces, and the holdings of the British Library, whose 25 miles of shelves house editions of every book ever printed in England.

Cabinet War Rooms, Whitehall (Westminster). The Cabinet's bomb-proof World War II headquarters, including Winston Churchill's bunker, have been authentically restored. (Tel: 930-6961).

Carlyle's House, 24 Cheyne Row (Sloane Square). The Scottish historian and essayist moved into this house in 1834 and lived here until his death in 1881; manuscripts, books, and furniture—and the sense of the comfortable life Carlyle led here—are perfectly preserved. Closed Mondays and Tuesdays, and from November through March.

Commonwealth Institute, 230 Kensington High Street (Kensington High Street). A colorful collection of arts and crafts—many for sale—from 40 Commonwealth countries fills this dramatic circular building.

Coram Foundation (Foundling Hospital Art Museum), 40 Brunswick Square (Russell Square). Thomas Coram, a retired sea captain, established a home for destitute children in 1739. Hogarth, Gainsborough, and other artists donated their works to raise funds, and many of these materpieces have been bequeathed to the museum. Closed Saturdays and Sundays.

Courtauld Institute Galleries, Somerset House, The Strand (Aldwych). The mainstays of this sumptuous collection are the Impressionist paintings acquired by Samuel Courtauld—Manet, Degas, Bonnard, Gauguin, Cézanne, van Gogh. Here, too, are 30 paintings by Rubens, canvases by Tiepolo and Breughel, and works by Roger Frye and other members of the Bloomsbury Group.

Design Museum, Butler's Wharf, Docklands (Tower Hill). Salt shakers, typewriters, roller skates, and other trappings of everyday life are displayed as works of art in sleek galleries overlooking the Thames. Closed Mondays.

Dickens' House, 48 Doughty Street (Russell Square). The novelist was well-to-do by the time he bought this house, in 1837; little of the original furnishings remain, but there is a fine collection of manuscripts, portraits, and other Dickens memorabilia. Closed Sundays.

Dr. Johnson's House, 17 Gough Square (St. Paul's). Dr. Johnson and his assistants compiled the *Dictionary* in the garret of this house; a first edition is displayed in the memento-filled rooms below. Closed Sundays.

Dulwich College and Picture Gallery, Dulwich (train from Victoria Station). Edward Alleyn, the realm's greatest actor in the 16th century, commissioned an elegant manor in what is now a south London suburb and filled it with paintings of his fellow thespians. The collection has grown over the years to include works by Rembrandt, Poussin, Reynolds, and Gainsborough, and is housed in a splendid Neoclassical gallery designed by Sir John Soane, completed in 1814. Closed Mondays.

Fenton House, Hampstead Grove (Hampstead). The oldest, largest, and finest house in Hampstead is furnished with exquisite period pieces, porcelain, and an outstanding collection of musical instruments.

Freud Museum, 20 Maresfield Gardens (Finchley Road). The famous couch and other personal belongings fill the house where the father of psychoanalysis lived after he fled Vienna in 1938. Closed Mondays and Tuesdays.

Geffrye Museum, Kingsland Road (Old Street). Authentically furnished period rooms honor centuries' worth of British furniture-making. Closed Mondays.

Geological Museum, Exhibition Road (South Kensington). Vast and well-designed exhibits trace the geological history of the British Isles and the rest of the earth; the gemstone collection is arguably the world's best.

Ham House, Ham Street, Richmond (Richmond). In this elegant mansion on the Thames near Hampton Court, furniture, paintings, and architectural detail evoke all the grandeur of the Baroque. Closed Mondays.

Hampton Court (train from Waterloo Station). Henry VIII began the painting collection—which now includes

Titians, Holbeins, and Breughels—that graces this palace just outside London.

Hayward Gallery, South Bank Arts Centre (Waterloo). This vast space overlooking the Thames hosts temporary exhibitions organized by the National Arts Council.

Hogarth's House, Hogarth Lane (Chiswick Park). This exceptionally perceptive artist, who captured the essence of 18th-century British life in his engravings (many hanging here), called his summer home his "box on the Thames." Closed Tuesdays and Thursdays during the winter months.

Imperial War Museum, Lambeth Road (Lambeth North). Weaponry and military equipment, decorations, and uniforms from the two world wars; the newest addition is an eight-minute-long "theatrical experience" in which visitors endure a vivid re-creation of a World War II air raid.

Institute of Contemporary Arts, The Mall (Green Park). The well-executed temporary exhibitions here provide a glimpse of the latest from the British avant-garde.

Jewish Museum, Woburn House, Tavistock Square (Eusten and Russell Square). A small but fascinating collection of scrolls and ritual objects. Closed Saturdays and Mondays.

Keats' House, Keats Grove (Hampstead). The Romantic poet wrote "Ode to a Nightingale" in the garden of this small house, whose rooms are filled with his diaries and other memorabilia.

Kenwood House, Hampstead Lane (Highgate). The hand of man intrudes gently into the natural splendor of Hampstead Heath: Robert Adam designed the Classical 18th-century façade of this Stuart-period mansion, which houses one of London's best picture collections, including works by Rembrandt, Turner, and others.

Leighton House, 12 Holland Park Road (Kensington High Street). Lord Leighton, the Victorian painter, built this house in 1866 to suit his tastes, which—as displayed in the tiled Arab Hall and in his paintings—were charmingly excessive. Closed Sundays.

Linley Sambourne House. 18 Stafford Terrace (Kensington High Street). Original William Morris decoration, as well as the bell pulls, greenhouses, and other trappings of Victorian life, remain beautifully intact. Open Wednesdays and Sundays, March to October.

London Transport Museum, Covent Garden (Covent

Garden). The old flower market of Eliza Doolittle fame now houses a vast collection of the vehicles Londoners have used to get around their great city over the years.

Madame Tussaud's, Marylebone Road (Baker Street). The wax figures made by this Frenchwoman, who learned her craft fashioning death masks during the French Revolution, are one of London's biggest draws. You can turn your sights to the stars at London's **Planetarium**, next door.

Museum of London, 150 London Wall (Barbican). The latest technology depicts London from its Stone Age beginnings to the present—re-creations of the first Thames settlements; a dramatically lit view into a remnant of the wall that surrounded Roman London; a model that shows the progression of the Great Fire; and entire 19th-century streets. Closed Mondays.

Museum of Mankind, 6 Burlington Gardens (Piccadilly Circus). Arts from the Americas, Africa, and Asia fill this Victorian building, which serves as the ethnographical division of the British Museum; for lack of space, exhibits change on a regular basis.

Museum of the Moving Image, South Bank Arts Centre (Waterloo). Fred Astaire's top hat and tails and Marilyn Monroe's shimmy dress are here, along with hundreds of other artifacts of the silver screen.

Museum of the Worshipful Guild of Clockmakers, Guildhall, Aldermanbury (Bank). There are 700 timepieces here, all extraordinary, among them a watch in the shape of a silver skull that belonged to Mary Queen of Scots. Closed Saturdays and Sundays.

National Army Museum, Royal Hospital Road (Sloane Square). A comprehensive history of the British army, with weaponry, campaign maps, and uniforms, all handsomely displayed.

National Gallery, Trafalgar Square (Trafalgar Square). What is considered by many to be the world's finest collection of Western art hangs in what are probably the best-designed galleries anywhere. Rembrandt, Rubens, Botticelli, and other masters form the foundation of a collection that now includes some 2,000 paintings.

National Maritime Museum, Greenwich (by boat; see Getting Around). Royal riverboats, maritime paintings, ships' logs, and other relics pay homage to the era when Britannia ruled the waves. Closed Mondays.

National Portrait Gallery, 2 St. Martin's Place (Trafalgar Square). Portraits—be they paintings, photographs, drawings, even caricatures—capture famous Britons from the Middle Ages to the present.

Natural History Museum, Cromwell Road (South Kensington). The number of specimens here, including whales, dinosaurs, gemstones, Stone Age artifacts, and insects, is close to 40 million, and the remarkable collection is growing at the rate of about 350,000 objects a year.

Old Royal Observatory, Greenwich (by boat; see Getting Around). Telescopes, clocks, and other astronomical equipment are on display in a fine Wren-designed building. Closed Mondays. (Tel: 081-858-4422).

Old Railway Station Museum, Pier Road, North Woolwich, Docklands (last stop on Docklands Light Rail System). A lovingly restored 19th-century Italianate station recalls the heyday of rail travel

Percival David Foundation of Chinese Art, University of London, 53 Gordon Square (Euston). The Western world's finest collection of Chinese porcelains. Closed Sundays.

Pollock's Toy Museum, 1 Scala Street (Russell Square). This collection of 19th- and 20th-century toys is sheer delight. Closed Sundays.

Public Records Office Museum, Chancery Lane (Chancery Lane). The Domesday Book, Shakespeare's will, Guy Fawkes's confession, and some of the other most remarkable documents of British history can be found here. Closed Saturdays and Sundays.

Queen's Gallery, Buckingham Gate (Victoria, Hyde Park Corner). There isn't room in this former chapel to display more than a fraction of the superb royal collection of art; exhibits change frequently. The **Royal Mews**, just down Buckingham Palace Road, houses state coaches. Both closed Mondays.

Royal Academy of Arts, Burlington House, Piccadilly (Piccadilly Circus). Reynolds, Constable, and many of England's other great artists have been members of this august institution. The great works of art the academy has accumulated over the years are on display only as part of the society's numerous and ambitious public exhibitions. Hours vary with exhibitions.

Royal Air Force Museum, Grahame Park Way, Hendon (Hendon Central). The trip out to this northern suburb is mandatory for aviation enthusiasts; this is one of the world's best collections of aircraft.

Science Museum, Exhibition Road (South Kensington). Seven acres of galleries chronicle man's mastery of scientific principle and technological achievement: Foucault's Pendulum, behemoth steam machinery from the 19th century, space craft, and countless other exhibits.

Sir John Soane's Museum, 13 Lincoln's Inn Fields (Holborn). A wonderful jumble of artifacts—sarcophagi, paintings by Canaletto and Turner, Piranesi drawings—runs riot in the home of this prominent 18th- to 19th-century architect; the house is as much an attraction as the collections. Closed Mondays.

Somerset House, The Strand (Aldwych). Sleuths in detective fiction came here to dig when this 18th-century riverside palace housed the Registry of Births, Deaths, and Records. Now the building is the headquarters of Inland Revenue, and its state rooms house temporary exhibitions. Hours vary with exhibitions.

Tate Gallery, Millbank (Pimlico). London's foremost collection of modern art begins with the Impressionists and runs through Pollock, Hockney, and other contemporary artists. The latest addition to the formidable British collection is the Clore Gallery, a temple to the paintings of Turner.

Theatre Museum, Russell Street, (Covent Garden). Richly decorated displays capture several centuries of the British stage; good show. Closed Mondays.

Tower of London: the Crown Jewels (Tower Hill). The glittering prizes here include the Koh-i-Noor diamond (109 carats); Charles II's crown; and the Royal Sceptre (containing a 530-carat diamond, the largest ever cut). Closed Sundays from November through February.

Victoria and Albert Museum, Cromwell Road (South Kensington). Once characterized as "England's attic," the V & A is a vast storehouse of decorative arts: French interiors, Chinese jades, Spanish altarpieces, Persian carpets—seven miles of galleries in all, devoted to textiles, costumes, jewelry, glass, ceramics, and all other manner of craftsmanship. Closed Fridays.

Wallace Collection, Hertford House, Manchester Square (Bond Street). The Marquises of Hertford accumulated what is perhaps the largest collection of French paintings and *objets d'art* outside of France, as well as works by Titian, Rubens, and other European masters. The Hertford mansion is now one of London's richest galleries.

Wellcome Museum of Medical Science, 183 Euston Road (Euston). The general public can venture no farther than the entrance hall, where historic pharmacies from different countries have been faithfully reconstructed. Closed Saturdays and Sundays.

Whitechapel Art Gallery, 80 Whitechapel High Street (Aldgate East). The building, put up in 1897 by C. Harrison Townsend, a follower of the Arts and Crafts movement, is an attraction itself; the temporary exhibitions of modern art are much attended. Closed Mondays.

—Stephen Brewer

GETTING AROUND IN LONDON

The telephone area code for inner London (roughly anywhere within a four-mile radius of Trafalgar Square) is, with one or two exceptions, (071). The area code for outer London is (081). Throughout this chapter we have given the area code only if it is (081); if it does not appear, you can assume that the area code is (071).

Airports

Heathrow (Tel: 081-759-4321; British Airways, 081-897-4000) is 15 miles west of the city and can be reached in 45 minutes on the Piccadilly Underground line from central London (one stop before the last for Terminal 4; last stop for Terminals 1, 2, and 3); trains run every five minutes, 20 hours a day. Airbuses pick up at several points throughout the main hotel areas of central London. **Gatwick** (Tel: 081-668-4211) is 30 minutes from Victoria Station by British Rail Gatwick Express (every 15 minutes from 5:30 A.M. to 11:00 P.M.; hourly service throughout the night). Combined Gatwick Express/Underground tickets are available at any Underground station.

British Rail

London is served by several railway stations whose lines fan out like spokes on a wheel to various destinations of day-trip interest to the visitor. The best single source of information is the **British Travel Centre** at 12 Regent Street; open Mondays through Fridays, 9:00 to 6:30; Saturdays, 9:00 to 5:00; and Sundays, 10:00 to 4:00; Tel: 730-3400 Mondays to Saturdays. Inquiries about specific services can be directed to the various stations: Charing Cross (Tel: 928-5100); Euston (Tel: 387-7070); Holborn Viaduct (Tel: 928-5100); King's Cross (Tel: 278-2477); Liverpool Street (Tel: 283-7171); London Bridge (Tel: 928-5100); Marylebone (Tel: 262-6767); Paddington (Tel: 262-6767); Victoria (Tel: 928-5100); and Waterloo (Tel: 928-5100). (For all of these numbers, a central stacking system ensures that phone calls are answered in strict rotation, so be patient and wait for a reply.) For information on the area of England each station serves, see the Useful Facts section at the front of this book.

Visitor Information

The most detailed sources of information for visitors to London are the weeklies *Time Out* and *City Limits,* which come out on Wednesdays and are sold at all newsstands. *The Standard,* London's weekday evening newspaper, is also a useful source of information, particularly on entertainment. Major tourist-information centers include:

London Tourist Board and Convention Bureau, 26 Grosvenor Gardens, London SW1W 0DU, open Mondays through Fridays, 9:00 to 6:00 (Tel: 730-3488); **London Tourist Information Centre** at the following locations: Victoria Station Forecourt, open daily, 9:00 to 7:00, later in July and August; Selfridge's department store (basement), Oxford Street, open 9:30 to 6:00, Mondays through Fridays, 9:30 to 8:00, Thursdays; Harrods department store (fourth floor), Knightsbridge, open Mondays through Saturdays, 9:00 to 6:00, Wednesdays, 9:30 to 7:00, Saturdays, 9:00 to 6:00; Heathrow Terminals 1, 2, and 3 Underground Station, open daily, 8:00 to 6:30; Tower of London (west gate), open Mondays through Saturdays, 9:30 to 6:00, Sundays, 10:00 to 6:00; **British Travel Centre**, 12 Regent Street, near Piccadilly Circus, open Mondays through Fridays, 9:00 to 6:30, Saturdays, 9:00 to 5:00, Sundays, 10:00 to 4:00 (Tel: 730-3400 Mondays through Saturdays). There are also Tourist Information Centres in Clerkenwell, Croydon, Greenwich, Harrow, Hillingdon, Kingston-upon-Thames, Lewisham, Richmond, Tower Hamlets, and Twickenham as well as in St. Paul's Churchyard in the City of London.

The two that carry the most comprehensive selection of booklets, maps, and the like are those in the Victoria Station Forecourt and on Regent Street near Piccadilly.

Moreover, the hall porter of your hotel probably knows as much as anyone at the information centers.

Guided Tours

London Transport (Tel: 222-1234) operates half- and full-day tours from Victoria Coach Station, Buckingham Palace Road. For information, maps, and brochures contact the British Travel Centre, 12 Regent Street, Piccadilly Circus (Tel: 730-3400). Other tours are operated by **Cityrama** (Tel: 720-6663) and **Harrods** (Tel: 581-3603). Both *Time*

Out and *City Limits* give details of the numerous independent lecturers and walking-tours available. There are also taxi guide services; details are available from Tourist Information Centres.

You can take a one-hour helicopter flight over London for £500 (for up to four people); Cabair, Tel: (081) 953-4411.

Underground (Tube) and Buses

London Transport has a 24-hour travel-information telephone service (Tel: 222-1234; English only), and also operates **Travel Information Centres** at the following stations: Charing Cross, Euston, King's Cross, Oxford Circus, Piccadilly Circus, St. James's Park, and Victoria.

For the first-time visitor the Underground presents a challenge, but in fact it is quite simple and much the quickest way to move around London, as there are nine lines and over 200 stations, all interconnected. Just consult the London Underground map—a masterpiece of simple design—buy your ticket (which you must hand in to the ticket collector at the *end* of your journey), and board the train on the platform indicated by the line's last stop *in the direction you intend to go.*

The first trains run from 6:00 or 6:30 A.M. (later on Sundays) and the last stop at approximately midnight. Children under five ride for free, and those under 14 ride at reduced fares, as do 14- and 15-year-olds with a Child Rate Photocard (available from post offices in the London area; be sure the child has a passport-size photo and proof of age). Free maps of tube and bus routes and a huge number of ever-changing leaflets describing various fares and special passes are available at Underground and bus stations. The map of the city bus network is posted on tube station platforms, bus shelters, and main bus stations. Individual bus routes are detailed at bus shelters.

Travelling by bus means you can window-shop as you sit in traffic jams, but of course it is much slower. The system is more complicated than the Underground, as there are 129 central London bus routes. But with the aid of a bus map, and by looking at the relevant details posted on bus shelters, you will soon work it out. To stop a bus, hold your arm out horizontally when standing at a bus stop.

Fares on both tube and bus are computed according to stages and zones; therefore, a relatively short bus ride crossing three fare zones will cost the same or more than a much longer ride in a single zone.

Tourist Passes

The **London Explorer** pass allows unlimited travel on all London red buses (except structured sightseeing tours) and almost all Underground routes (including Heathrow by Airbus or tube) for one, three, four, or seven days. Children under 16 receive reduced rates. The **Capitalcard** offers unlimited off-peak travel (after 9:30 A.M., Mondays through Fridays) throughout London by train, Underground, or bus for one day; both passes are available at British Rail and Underground stations.

A Visitor Travelcard, available through a travel agent before you leave home, offers more or less unlimited use of the tube, buses, the Docklands Light Railway, and British Rail within London and suburban zones for up to seven days—along with discount vouchers for a number of tourist attractions, such as Madame Tussaud's.

Taxis

London's black cabs (a few are maroon or some other color) are rated the best in the world. Any cab with its yellow "For Hire" sign lit should stop if you flag it, and provided your journey is under six miles and within the borders of London, the cab must take you where you want to go. (A taxi-share scheme has also been recently introduced.) Tip 10 to 15 percent. You may telephone the following companies to arrange for a taxi: **Radio Taxis** (Tel: 272-0272, 272-3030, or 253-5000; 24 hours); **Addison Lee** (Tel: 720-2161); or **Abbey Car Hire** (Tel: 727-2637).

Driving in London

Do not use your car in London unless it is absolutely necessary: Traffic is extremely dense, traffic jams are the rule of thumb, and parking places—if you can find one—are expensive. **National Car Parks** has several locations throughout London; two of the more central ones are on Cavendish Square (Tel: 629-6968) and on Brewer Street near Piccadilly Circus (Tel: 734-9497). The NCP at the National Theatre, Southbank (Tel: 928-3940), is less expensive. A free list of locations is available from NCP, 21 Bryanston Street (Tel: 499-7050). The North and South Circular ringroads of London are easily accessible from the city center and link up to all major motorways around London.

Rental Cars

Budget: Central reservations (Tel: 0800-181-181; toll

free); King's Cross Station (Tel: 837-9877); NCP car park, Semley Place, near Victoria Station (Tel: 730-5233). **Avis:** 68 North Row, near Marble Arch (Tel: 629-7811); Gatwick Airport (Tel: 0293-297-21); Heathrow Airport, Hounslow, Middlesex (Tel: 081-897-9321). **Godfrey Davis Europ Car:** Central reservations (Tel: 081-950-5050); King's Cross (Tel: 387-2276); Heathrow Airport (Tel: 081-897-0811). **Hertz:** Central reservations (Tel: 081-679-1799); near Victoria Coach Station (Tel: 730-8323). It is best to pick up a car at one of the London airports, which has the added advantage of allowing you to become familiar with driving on the left before you hit the traffic in central London.

Boat Excursions

Boats leave from Westminster Pier and travel up the Thames to Kew every 30 minutes from 10:30 A.M. to 3:30 P.M.. Trips upstream to Hampton Court leave at 10:00, 10:30, 11:30, and noon (Tel: 730-4812). **Zoo Waterbus** departs from Little Venice, near the Warwick Avenue/Camden Town tubes, for trips on the Regent's Canal (Tel: 482-2550); **Jason's Trip** also offers cruises along the canal from Camden Town tube (Tel: 286-3428). Riverboat Information Service, a recorded message giving the times and routes of river trips, can be reached at 730-4812.

There is a new **Riverbus** service, the Thames Line, operating high-speed catamarans every 20 minutes from Chelsea Harbour to Greenwich via Charing Cross Festival Pier, Swan Lane Pier, London Bridge Pier, and West India Dock Pier. Boats operate from 7:00 A.M. to 8:00 P.M. weekdays only (weekend service is planned). Fares depend on the length of your journey; Tel: 512-0555.

Excursions

Green Line/London Country buses leave from Marble Arch, Hyde Park Corner, Oxford Circus, and Victoria Coach Station for various towns of interest in the surrounding area. For information on routes and fares (including the Diamond Rover tickets, valid for one to three day's unlimited travel on the network) call 081-668-7261. Several companies also offer one-day tours, including **Harrods** (Tel: 581-3603), **Frames Rickards** (Tel: 837-3111), and **Evan Evans** (Tel: 930-2377).

—David Wickers with Katie Lucas

ACCOMMO-DATIONS

By Katie Lucas

Katie Lucas, the author of a best-selling book on walking tours of London, runs a specialized London-based British tours company.

Part of the pleasure of visiting London is staying in a hotel that is typically and eccentrically British. London is rich in just such places. Many London hotels occupy converted town houses full of hidden corners and great charm. Others are refurbished Victorian and Edwardian hostelries in which no two rooms are alike. Even new hotels in London often try to make each room different from the next.

The following list is far from comprehensive, but it includes some of the best ones in different price ranges. As prices are always subject to change, and individual accommodations within each hotel vary in size, quality, and location, we indicate only the general range you can expect to pay. An inexpensive double among *our* recommendations would be around £40; moderate, roughly £60 to £110. Expensive will be around £160 and, of course, on up. Keep in mind that as London is crowded with visitors year-round, it is always best to book well in advance. Also, because London is such a huge city, you should decide upon the area in which you wish to stay before you make your booking; there is no point in saving money on a hotel only to spend it on travelling to and from the places you wish to visit.

The telephone area code for inner London, including all accommodations listed here, is (071).

Tower/City

The Tower Thistle Hotel. Despite its ugly modern exterior and out-of-the-way location on the edge of the City, just east of the Tower of London, this moderately priced hotel does have its pluses: a most wonderful position on St. Katharine's Dock, unmatched views, and attractive rooms.

St. Katharine's Way, E1 9LD. Tel: 481-2575; Telex: 885934; Fax: 488-4106; in U.S. (212) 689-9284 or (800) 847-4358; Telex: 6718291; Fax: (212) 779-0732; in Canada, (800) 268-1133 or, in Ontario and Quebec, (800) 387-8842; in Australia, (008) 22-1176 or (02) 223-7351.

Whitehall/Strand

Royal Horseguards Thistle Hotel. Large but cozy, this pleasant, moderately priced hotel has taken over most of the elegant buildings of the old National Liberal Club, with its long political history. Magnificently situated on the Embankment overlooking the River Thames, it is shielded from the noise of both river and road traffic by leafy gardens, and is within easy walking distance of most of Westminster's historical sights as well as the theaters and clubland of St. James's. Because of its proximity to Parliament there is a Division bell in **Granby's Restaurant** to summon Members of Parliament to vote. The coffee shop serves light meals all day, and the cocktail bar also serves a selection of inexpensive food at lunchtime. There is a business-services center, which includes the use of a personal computer, and, of course, 24-hour room service.

2 Whitehall Court, SW1A 2EJ. Tel: 839-3400; Telex: 917096; Fax: 925-2263; in U.S., (212) 689-9284 or (800) 847-4358; Telex: 6718291; Fax: (212) 779-0732; in Canada, (800) 268-1133 or, in Ontario and Quebec, (800) 387-8842; in Australia, (008) 22-1176 or (02) 223-7351.

The Savoy Hotel. Built on the site of the Medieval palace of Savoy, this is probably London's best-known luxury hotel and is doubtless the one with the most fascinating history. It was built by the brilliant impresario Richard D'Oyly Carte out of the profits he made on his productions of the operettas of Gilbert and Sullivan, which were performed at his Savoy Theatre next door. When he took his productions of Gilbert and Sullivan to America he was so impressed by the standards of the luxury hotels there that he decided to build a comparable one in London. He certainly succeeded: The Savoy was the first hotel in the world to be lit by electricity and the first hotel in London to have elevators. Another brilliant advance in civilized life, but nothing to do with Mr. D'Oyly Carte, was the invention of the martini in the **American Bar**. Next to this popular gathering spot is the **Savoy Grill**, a favorite place for after-theater suppers.

The Strand, WC2R 0EU. Tel: 836-4343; Telex: 24234; Fax: 240-6040; in U.S. and Canada, (800) 223-6800; in New York State, (212) 838-3110; in Sydney, (02) 233-8422; in the rest of Australia, (008) 222-033.

Bloomsbury

Hotel Crichton. This 19th-century house across from the British Museum in Bloomsbury is a well-run and inexpensive hotel, and is understandably popular. The large breakfast (included in the price) is a good start to a day of sightseeing.

36 Bedford Place, WC1B 5JR. Tel: 637-3955; Telex: 22353; in U.S., (800) MIN-OTEL.

Grays Hotel. An elegant Victorian townhouse opened as a hotel in 1987, in an area on the edge of Bloomsbury where there are very few hotels, Grays has great style, with a luxurious, intimate atmosphere enhanced by sumptuous furnishings and flower-filled rooms. There are just eight double bedrooms, but if you want to be pampered in this corner of London at moderate rates, this hotel is for you.

109 Guilford Street, WC1 N1DP. Tel: 833-2474; Telex: 25335; Fax: 439-0820.

The Kenilworth Hotel. This recently refurbished hotel on the edge of Bloomsbury close to the British Museum caters to business meetings and small conferences. Even so, it's well equipped for tourists, and is a good value.

97 Great Russell Street, WC1B 3LB. Tel: 637-3477; Telex: 25842; Fax: 631-3133; in U.S., (800) 447-7011 or (800) 44-UTELL; in Ontario/Quebec, (800) 268-7041; in Toronto, (800) 387-1338; in Vancouver, (800) 663-9582; in Australia, (008) 22-11-76.

Covent Garden/Soho

Fielding Hotel. If you are visiting London to wallow in opera or the ballet, this is the hotel for you, as it is situated in a quiet, gas-lit alley one minute from the Royal Opera House. Even if the delights of the opera are not for you, the Fielding is still a delightful place to stay: being in the center of Covent Garden is like stepping onto a set for *My Fair Lady*. The hotel is shielded from the noise of this exciting area of London by the bulk of Bow Street Magistrates Court, which is famous as the site of the first police station in the world, as well as the home of the Bow Street Runners. The hotel is small, with lots of stairs and no elevators, modest-size rooms, and plenty of character. Best of all, it's inexpensive. There is a breakfast room and bar.

4 Broad Court, Bow Street, WC2B 5QZ. Tel: 836-8305; Fax: 497-0064.

Hazlitt's. Soho has always been renowned as the red-light district of London: raffish, sleazy, but also fun and crammed with restaurants of all types, good and bad, cheap and expensive. Over the last few years things have changed, and Soho has become more respectable. Created from three Georgian houses, one of which was the home of William Hazlitt, the great essayist whose father founded the Unitarian church in Boston, Massachusetts, Hazlitt's, on Frith Street, in the heart of Soho, is a rather higgledy-piggledy kind of place, with lots of corners, stairs, potted plants, and great charm. Breakfast is served in your room, but for other meals there are all the restaurants of Soho to choose from. There are no porters and no elevators here, and although there are direct-dial telephones in the rooms, the switchboard is closed to incoming calls between 11:30 P.M. and 7:30 A.M.

6 Frith Street, W1V 5TZ. Tel: 434-1771; Fax: 439-1524.

North of Oxford Street

Dorset Square Hotel. This small, attractive hotel occupies several 19th-century town houses on the corner of two-and-a-half-acre Dorset Square, just to the southwest of Regent's Park (the square was the original site of Lord's Cricket Ground, created by Thomas Lord in 1787 and moved a few blocks north to its present location in 1811). Despite the discreet town-house atmosphere and its very moderate price, the Dorset Square offers all the most up-to-date amenities: state-of-the-art security systems, 24-hour room service, and secretarial services.

39-40 Dorset Square, NW1 6QN. Tel: 723-7874; Telex: 263964; Fax: 724-3328; in U.S., (800) 543-4138.

Durrants Hotel. This is one of the oldest hotels in London, having been built in 1789. Therefore it is hardly surprising that the service is efficient and discreet; the management has had plenty of time to get it right. The atmosphere is dignified yet cozy, with wood-paneled walls and leather-covered wing chairs in the many sitting areas. It has a very clubby atmosphere, and a loyal following.

Although most of the hotel has been refurbished, it is
essential to specify exactly what you require when you
make your booking, as not all rooms have private facilities.
The rooms also vary widely in size, quality, and comfort.
Durrants is situated around the corner from Marylebone
High Street, with its excellent shopping opportunities.
There are also several very good restaurants in the area if
you don't wish to dine in the hotel restaurant, and the tiny
bar is one of the most charming and Dickensian in London.
If all else fails, 24-hour room service is available, as are fax,
telex and photocopying services. Moderate.

26–32 George Street, W1H 6BJ. Tel: 935-8131; Telex:
894919; Fax: 487-3510.

Mandeville Hotel. Tucked away in Marylebone north of
Oxford Street near Wigmore Hall and the Wallace Collection, this attractive and reasonably priced hotel is a favorite
of busy executives who make use of its restaurant, coffee
house, two bars, and comprehensive business services.

Mandeville Place, W1M 6BE. Tel: 935-5599; Telex:
269487; Fax: 935-9588; in U.S., (402) 493-4747 or (800)
44-UTELL; in Canada, (416) 967-3442; in Australia, (02)
235-1111.

Merryfield House. This small hotel is perfect for people who do not have much money to spend but want a
comfortable, quiet, and convenient place to lay their
heads. Each room has its own sparkingly clean bathroom,
with plenty of towels. Located on a quiet side street in
Marylebone, it is close to Baker Street, Madame Tussaud's, the London Planetarium, and the Wallace Collection. A full English breakfast is served in your room.

42 York Street, W1H 1FN. Tel: 935-8326.

The Montcalm. Although close to the noise and bustle
of the department stores and shops of Oxford Street, the
Montcalm is situated on a quiet tree-lined Georgian
crescent close to Marble Arch. Unlike many of the better
London hotels it is not decorated in the English Country-
House style, but rather a plush Mid-Atlantic one: It
exudes a discreet, understated elegance. The leather-
and-suede-decorated bar is a popular meeting place, and
the restaurant lives up to the hotel's French name. There
is 24-hour room service available, as well as secretarial
and valet services. Unusual for London, the rooms are
also air-conditioned. Expensive.

Great Cumberland Place, W1A 2LF. Tel: 402-4288; Telex:
28710; Fax: 724-9180; in U.S., (800) 645-5687.

Mostyn Hotel. Relaxing comfort, a welcome relief from the bustle of Marble Arch and Oxford Street, is what the Mostyn is all about. In 1740 Lady Black of George II's court commissioned John Adam to build her a grand house. Her home, which is now listed by the Historic Buildings and Monuments Commission, has been skillfully incorporated into the rest of the present building, but you can see part of the original structure as you enter the restaurant and cocktail bar. The grand staircase, superbly molded ceilings, wall paneling, and handsome fireplaces all exhibit the airy spaciousness of 18th-century design. Moderate.

Bryanston Street, W1H 0DE. Tel: 935-2361; Telex: 27656; Fax: 487-2759.

Ramada Hotel. This large and lavishly decorated Victorian hotel, once the Berners Hotel and recently upgraded as part of the moderately priced Ramada chain, is situated in the heart of rag-trade land, just north of Oxford Street and close to Soho. Its splendid marble entrance hall is a popular meeting place for Londoners.

10 Berners Street, W1A 3BE. Tel: 636-1629; Telex: 25759; Fax: 580-3972; in U.S., (800) 228-9898 or (800) 228-2828; in Toronto, (416) 485-2610; elsewhere in Canada, (800) 268-8998; in Australia, (008) 22-24-31 or (02) 251-8888.

The Savoy Court Hotel. In a quiet mews just moments from the noise and bustle of Oxford Street sits this small, reasonably priced, and unpretentious hotel. Maybe its greatest asset is that it is almost next door to one of the biggest Marks and Spencer stores in Europe, as well as being one minute from Selfridge's. For those intent on shopping it is a wonderful location, and the hotel has a cocktail bar and restaurant to revive you when you return exhausted with your purchases.

19–25 Granville Place, W1H 0EH. Tel: 408-0130; Telex: 8955515; Fax: 493-2070.

Seaford Lodge. This stately Victorian house in Chalk Farm recently has been refurbished and converted into a small, pleasant, and moderately priced family-run hotel, with two ground-floor rooms fully equipped for disabled visitors. It also boasts a perfect location from which to stroll to the weekend market at Camden Lock and the antiques shops in the same area. The hotel does not have a liquor license, but it does serve breakfast; other meals can be arranged.

2 Fellows Road, NW3 3LP. Tel: 722-5032.

Mayfair

Brown's Hotel. In 1830 James Brown, a gentleman's gentleman who was married to Sarah, the lady's maid to Lady Byron, bought the first of the large Mayfair houses that make up this most understated but elegant hotel. Over the next 150 years another 11 houses in Dover Street and Albemarle Street were acquired, making the hotel a veritable rabbit warren but in no way detracting from the impeccable service that makes this one of the most civilized places to stay in London. The cozy, paneled public rooms are crammed every afternoon as people enjoy the delicious afternoon tea for which Brown's is famous. It was in this hotel, in 1876, that the first successful telephone call was made in Britain—between the youthful inventor Alexander Graham Bell and the young son of the landlord, Henry Ford. It was also from this hotel that Theodore Roosevelt walked to his wedding at St. George's Church in Hanover Square, and just a few years later that Franklin and Eleanor Roosevelt spent several days of their honeymoon in the same suite. Expensive.

Albemarle and Dover streets, W1A 4SW. Tel: 493-6020; Telex: 28686; Fax: 493-9381; in U.S. and Canada, (800) 225-5843; Telex: 6852554; in Australia, (02) 267-2144 or (008) 222-446.

The Chesterfield. Created from a town house in the heart of Mayfair, close to Berkeley Square and Curzon Street, the Chesterfield is a gracious hotel. Named after the fourth earl of Chesterfield, who was a local landowner, this hotel is affiliated with the English Speaking Union, whose headquarters, Dartmouth House, are next door. The interior is warm and inviting, and the staff is very friendly and helpful. The rates are moderate, and members of the English Speaking Union receive a 20 percent discount.

35 Charles Street, W1X 8LX. Tel: 491-2622; Telex: 269394; Fax: 491-4793; in U.S., (800) 223-9868; in Toronto, (800) 268-7041; in Vancouver, (800) 663-9582; in Australia, (008) 22-11-76.

Claridge's. This wonderful hotel in the heart of Mayfair, near New Bond Street, may remind you of the great transatlantic liners, and the service is comparable, too. Quite simply, Claridge's is the ultimate in luxury and discreet service, which is probably why guests of the royal family are frequently put up here. The rooms are among the most comfortable and best equipped anywhere, yet they still retain the grace and style of a bygone era. During World War II Claridge's became a haven for exiled royalty and heads of state. An amusing story is told of a diplomat who telephoned Claridge's and, asking to speak to the King, received the reply, "Which king?"

Brook Street, W1A 2JQ. Tel: 629-8860; Telex: 21872; Fax: 499-2210; in U.S., (212) 838-3110 or (800) 223-6800; in Canada, (800) 223-6800; in Australia, (008) 22-20-33 or (02) 233-8422.

The Connaught. This very expensive establishment near the U.S. embassy is more like a very select club than a hotel; most of the guests have been staying here—and eating at the renowned **Connaught Grill**—for years. The high standards the hotel maintains are all the more appreciated these days, when they are so rare. Most of the staff has been here for years, providing impeccable service. Both the hotel and the grill are hard to get into.

16 Carlos Place, W1Y 6AL. Tel: 499-7070; Fax: 495-3262; in U.S., (212) 838-3110 or (800) 223-6800; in Canada, (800) 223-6800; in Australia, (008) 22-20-33 or (02) 233-8422.

The Delmere Hotel. Close to Paddington Station and Bayswater, this former town house is the best choice on a street of small hotels. With 40 attractive rooms, it caters not only to the vacationer but also to the business traveller, offering all the usual support services, including fax machines. Moderate.

130 Sussex Gardens, W2 1UB. Tel: 706-3344; Telex: 8953857; Fax: 262-1863.

The London–London Hotel. This newly opened hotel is inexpensive but has high standards, as well as all the usual amenities. Converted from several large houses on a quiet London square, it is close to Paddington Station, which serves the west of England as well as some of the nearer tourist destinations such as Windsor. The hotel is also close to the Bayswater district north of Hyde Park, and, for those who like to shop, Oxford Street is within walking distance. Thatchers, the hotel restaurant, specializes in meat-free food.

2–14 Talbot Square, W2 1TS. Tel: 262-6699; Fax: 723-3233.

Le Meridien. This fashionable hotel is once again the ultimate in opulence. Built in 1908 to serve the luxury end of the market, it gradually went downhill, becoming seedy and shabby. Happily, it has been rescued, and an immense amount of money has been spent on turning it into one of the best hotels in London. The Edwardian building not only survives, it glories in its own magnificence. The **Oak Room** is one of the best—and most expensive—restaurants in London, while the **Terrace Garden Restaurant** is less expensive, very pretty, and one of the few places open after the theater for supper. The health club also has a restaurant, as well as exceptional health facilities such as a 12-meter swimming pool, squash court, sauna, and much more. The public rooms are what you would expect from a hotel of this quality, and the bedrooms are lovely—and air-conditioned. Of course, there is 24-hour room service. And of course the hotel is expensive.

Piccadilly, W1V OBH. Tel: 734-8000; Telex: 25795; Fax: 437-3574; in U.S., (800) 543-4300.

Park Lane Hotel. This large, independently owned hotel opened its doors to the public in the 1920s, and the aura of that era still hangs over it. There are vast public rooms such as the Palm Court Lounge, which is an excellent meeting place, and the Art Deco Ballroom, which is often used for art and antiques fairs. Over the last few years a great deal of money has been spent on the hotel, and it shows, particularly in the 350 bedrooms (many air-conditioned) and bathrooms. The views from the top floors are spectacular, especially the rooms on Piccadilly, which have a wonderful view over Green Park to Parliament and Buckingham Palace. Unusual for London, the hotel has an 180-car garage, which is much appreciated in the crammed streets of Mayfair. It also has all the usual public rooms, 24-hour room service, a business center, and a fitness center. Expensive.

Piccadilly, W1Y 8BX. Tel: 499-6321; Telex: 21533; Fax: 499-1965.

St. James's

Dukes Hotel. This small and attractive hotel off St. James's Street is tucked away in a courtyard brimming with flowers. With service that matches its comfort, no wonder it is recommended by regulars who wouldn't think of staying anywhere else. Expensive.

35 St. James's Place, SW1A 1NY. Tel: 491-4840; Telex: 28283; Fax: 493-1264; in U.S., (800) 544-7570; in Australia, (02) 360-1666.

The Ritz. This is where the word "ritzy" originated, and everything about it is just that—from the service to the decor, from the opulent public rooms, the most beautiful in London, to the elegant guest rooms and suites. The **Palm Court** is the best place in London for afternoon tea;

the magnificent, gilded dining room looks out onto Green Park. The Marie Antoinette Suite, next to the dining room, is where Winston Churchill, General Eisenhower, and General de Gaulle planned the invasion of Normandy.

Piccadilly, W1V 9DG. Tel: 493-8181; Telex: 267200; Fax: 493-2687; in U.S., (800) 222-0939; in Canada, (416) 924-1711; in Australia, (02) 264-9966.

The Stafford Hotel. Reached from St. James's Street through a cobbled mews (although there is a more conventional entrance in the front of the hotel), this is one of London's hidden treasures. The smallish and expensive Stafford occupies two converted 19th-century town houses just to the east of Green Park. Public rooms are formal but welcoming, and attention to detail is in evidence everywhere—comfort even extends to a tunnel leading from the hotel beneath nearby buildings into the park. The restaurant is likewise excellent and expensive. In the cellars, hidden away among the bottles of wine, is a small, private, and fascinating museum of wartime memorabilia, complete with sandbags and posters of the period; during World War II this was a bomb shelter for the American and Canadian officers who used the hotel as a club.

16–18 St. James's Place, SW1A 1NJ. Tel: 493-0111; Telex: 28602; Fax: 493-7121; in U.S., (800) 544-7570; in Canada, (800) 468-7745; in Australia, (02) 360-1666, (02) 264-9966, or (008) 25-1664.

Sloane Square/Victoria Station

Eccleston Hotel. Within easy walking distance of Victoria Station and its trains to Continental Europe and Gatwick Airport, and Victoria Coach Station and the Underground, both with their links to Heathrow, this large and efficiently run hotel has an ideal location for the business traveller or vacationer. Although inexpensive, the Eccleston offers most of the amenities you would expect to find in a more expensive hotel. Office facilities can be arranged.

82–83 Eccleston Square, SW1V 1PS. Tel: 834-8042; Telex: 8955775; Fax: 630-8942; in U.S., (617) 581-0844 or (800) 223-6764.

The Elizabeth Hotel. Situated only a few doors away from one of the former residences of Sir Winston Churchill on one of the many garden squares of London, this small and inexpensive hotel has a loyal following among travellers. A full English breakfast is included in the price, and residents may use the tennis court in the communal gardens.

37 Eccleston Square, SW1V 1PB. Tel: 828-6812.

Goring Hotel. Perhaps London's best small hotel, the Goring is still owned by the same family that built it in 1910. (The Goring was the first hotel in the world to have central heating and private bathrooms in every room.) Much-loved by regulars, it occupies a quiet location by the Royal Mews of Buckingham Palace and is close to Victoria Station. Many of the rooms, as well as the comfortable and pleasantly seedy lounge and bar, overlook a garden. The motto of the hotel is "There is no longer a Mr. Claridge at Claridge's, there is no longer a Mr. Brown at Brown's, but there will always be a Mr. Goring at Goring's!" Moderate.

15 Beeston Place, Grosvenor Gardens, SW1W 0JW. Tel: 834-8211; Telex: 919166; Fax: 834-4393; in U.S., (312) 251-4110 or (800) 323-5463.

Royal Court Hotel. Sloane Square, where the famous King's Road begins, is the heart of Chelsea. Here, punks can be seen next to film stars, artists, authors, and other habitués of one of London's most interesting villages. One of London's very best department stores, **Peter Jones**, which on Saturdays is more like a club than a store, is situated on the square, as is the Royal Court Theatre, renowned for producing avant-garde plays. Between these two bastions of Chelsea life sits the moderate to slightly expensive Royal Court Hotel. Despite its location it is surprisingly peaceful, and justly popular. The restaurant, **No. 12**, is very pretty, and offers good international cuisine. You'll also find the Old English Tavern and Court's Café Bar, both of which are very popular, on the premises. There is 24-hour room service in the attractive and newly decorated rooms.

Sloane Square, SW1W 8EG. Tel: 730-9191; Telex: 296818; Fax: 824-8381; in U.S., (800) 44-UTELL.

The Rubens Hotel. Built at the turn of the century to serve Victoria Station, this moderately priced hotel situated opposite the Royal Mews has recently been refurbished. Included in its many facilities are five meeting rooms that can be rented for conferences or social occasions. Located close to excellent Underground and bus services, as well as Victoria Station, the Rubens is particularly convenient.

39–41 Buckingham Palace Road, SW1W 0PS. Tel: 834-6600; Telex: 916577; Fax: 828-5401.

St. James's Court. Originally built at the turn of the century as grand apartments, by London standards this hotel is huge, with 390 bedrooms—but this does not mean it is without character; far from it. Recently upgraded, the St. James's is built around a landscaped central courtyard with a magnificent fountain. The building boasts the world's largest brick frieze, which depicts scenes from Shakespeare, but for more modern tastes the facilities also include three very good restaurants, a health and leisure center, and a large business center. Considering its location, south of Buckingham Palace and close to St. James's Park, the St. James's Court is very reasonable.

Buckingham Gate, Westminster, SW1E 6AF. Tel: 834-6655; Telex: 928225; Fax: 630-7587; in U.S., (212) 972-6830, (402) 498-4300, or (800) 44-UTELL.

The Wilbraham Hotel. This is another small, friendly, and relatively inexpensive hotel created from several converted town houses. The location, just off Sloane Street and Sloane Square in Chelsea, and close to many good restaurants, is excellent. Breakfast is served in your room, as is early morning tea if you wish it. Tastefully decorated, with a genteel air and genteel service to match, the Wilbraham is much recommended by London hotel aficionados.

1–5 Wilbraham Place, SW1X 9AE. Tel: 730-8296.

The Willett. You'll find this inexpensive hotel on a narrow street lined with large red-brick houses. It is close to Sloane Square in the heart of Chelsea, and so very close to many of the good shopping areas. A sumptuous English breakfast buffet is included in the price.

32 Sloane Gardens, SW1W 8DJ. Tel. and Fax: 824-8415; Telex: 926678.

Knightsbridge/Kensington

Alexander Hotel. Several of the large, terraced houses on this pleasant street in South Kensington have been converted into bed-and-breakfast hotels, but the Alexander is one of the best, albeit among the most expensive. Recently renovated, it offers attractive bedrooms with good-size bathrooms and an attractive restaurant leading onto the garden, which is perhaps its greatest asset, as tea can be taken there on those sunny London days rather than in the sitting rooms. Moderate.

9 Sumner Place, SW7 3EE. Tel: 581-1591; Telex: 917133; Fax: 581-0824.

Basil Street Hotel. This moderately priced and wonderfully old-fashioned hotel has a large clientele that wouldn't think of staying anywhere else. Its excellent location in Knightsbridge off Sloane Street is perfect for shoppers—which is probably why the large room to the left of the entrance is set aside for women from the country who come to London to shop. In fact, the whole hotel has a very clubby atmosphere and is furnished throughout with comfortable chairs and writing desks. The staff-client ratio is higher than it is anywhere else in London, and the staff tends to stay.

8 Basil Street, SW3 1AH. Tel: 581-3311; Telex: 28379; Fax: 581-3693; in U.S., (402) 493-4747 or (800) 44-UTELL.

The Beaufort. On a cul-de-sac of very large, terraced houses near Harrods, this small hotel is privately owned and attractively decorated in country-house style. Guests are given their own key to the front door when they arrive, and come and go as though the hotel were their own home in London. Continental breakfast is served in your room or in the small sitting room, and there is a complimentary 24-hour bar. Expensive.

33 Beaufort Gardens, SW3 1PP. Tel: 584-5252; Telex: 929200; Fax: 589-2834; in U.S., (800) 548-7764.

The Berkeley. This modern luxury establishment, close to Hyde Park and the shops of Knightsbridge, has all the old-fashioned qualities you expect from a great London hotel. Unusual for London, though, are its penthouse swimming pool, beauty and health center, and a basement garage (a great plus in a city where parking is such a problem). Secretarial and valet service; 24-hour room service.

Wilton Place, SW1X 7RL. Tel: 235-6000; Telex: 919252; Fax: 235-4330; in U.S., (212) 838-3110 or (800) 223-6800.

Blakes Hotel. Owned and decorated by the beautiful actress and designer Anouska Hempel, this hotel is like no other: It is completely original in every way. Each room is decorated in a different theme, and the public areas also show Ms. Hempel's flair for exotic decorations. The attractive restaurant is presided over by a Japanese chef, who produces some of the most imaginative food in town. Not surprisingly, given Ms. Hempel's connections, this expensive hotel in the deep fastness of South Kensington between Cromwell Road and King's Road is a home away from home for many show-business people.

33 Roland Gardens, SW7 3PF. Tel: 370-6701; Telex: 8813500; Fax: 373-0442.

Capital Hotel. Small, quiet, and beautifully decorated, not to mention just around the corner from Harrods and the bustle of Knightsbridge, this hotel is a gem, though expensive. The restaurant (one of the best in London) is a favorite of gourmets, but if you want to cook for yourself there are some private luxury apartments available in the house next door (see below).

22–24 Basil Street, SW3 1AT. Tel: 589-5171; Telex: 919042; Fax: 225-0011; in U.S., (914) 833-3303 or (800) 223-5695; in Canada, (416) 447-2335.

11 Cadogan Gardens. There is no sign on the door of this small, moderately priced hotel off Sloane Street south of Harrods to suggest that it is anything other than a private house. Nor is there a reception desk or a restaurant; just a visitor's book and room service. Ring the bell next to the front door and a manservant will let you in. Created from several Victorian houses, this hotel is much favored by diplomats and art dealers. Room service provides light meals, but for anything more substantial just venture down the road, where you'll find plenty of excellent restaurants.

11 Cadogan Gardens, SW3 2RJ. Tel: 730-3426; Telex: 8813318; Fax: 730-5217.

Gore Hotel. This pleasant and moderately priced small hotel across from Kensington Gardens, west of Royal Albert Hall, is very quiet yet close to all the activity of South Kensington. It has, in addition, a pleasant lounge and a restaurant that serves light meals.

189 Queen's Gate, SW7 5EX. Tel: 584-6601; Telex: 296244; Fax: 589-8127; in U.S. and Canada, (800) 528-1234; in Australia, (02) 212-6444.

L'Hotel. This delightful small hotel on the street behind Harrods has an air of the country about it, so it is no surprise that it is frequented by people who come up from the country to shop or attend meetings and who neither want nor need all the services of a larger hotel. The guest rooms are simple, as befits L'Hotel's moderate rates, but they are most attractive, with pine and brass fittings. There are no public rooms, but the bistro in the basement, **Le Metro**, is very popular with hotel guests and neighborhood residents alike. L'Hotel is a sister hotel of the Capital next door (see above).

28 Basil Street, SW3 1AT. Tel: 589-6286; Telex: 919042;

Fax: 225-0011; in U.S., (914) 833-3303 or (800) 223-5695; in Canada, (416) 447-2335.

Hyde Park Hotel. At 10:30 every morning you can see the Horse Guards riding past this stately hotel, one of London's oldest, on their way from the Horse Guards Barracks next door to the changing of the guard at Whitehall. With a lovely dining room overlooking Hyde Park, and several bars and lounges, this member of the Trusthouse Forte Group is a favorite meeting place for Londoners and visitors alike. All rooms have recently been redecorated and are partially furnished with antiques.

66 Knightsbridge, SW1Y 7LA. Tel: 235-2000; Telex: 262057; Fax: 235-4552; in U.S. and Canada, (800) 225-5843; Telex: 6852554; in Australia, (02) 267-2144 or (008) 22-2446.

Kensington Palace Hotel. This is another of the Thistle Hotels, and, as with many of their group, it is conveniently located for shopping, sightseeing, and good local restaurants. It also has unequaled views over Kensington Gardens and Palace. Quite large, with 320 rooms, it has a pub, restaurant, bar, and coffee shop, as well as 24-hour room service and same-day laundry. But, of course, being large and moderately priced, it also attracts tour groups.

De Vere Gardens, W8 5AF. Tel: 937-8121; Telex: 262422; Fax: 937-2816; in U.S., (212) 689-9284 or (800) 847-4358; Telex: 6718291; Fax: (212) 779-0732; in Canada, (800) 268-1133, or in Ontario and Quebec, (800) 387-8842.

The Knightsbridge. This is a small, cozy, unpretentious place, and one of the least expensive of several small hotels on this quiet cul-de-sac just west of Harrods, off Brompton Road. Don't expect much more than a bed, Continental breakfast, and a front-door key. Spend your money instead in the delightful restaurants on nearby Beauchamp Place.

10 Beaufort Gardens, SW3 1PT. Tel: 589-9271; Fax: 823-9692.

The Lowndes Hotel. The Thistle Hotels group has several good hotels in London, but the Lowndes is probably the most popular. With a wonderful location in Knightsbridge close to all the best shops and restaurants, this hotel has always had a loyal following. It is quiet, with attractive public rooms, but on the moderate side of expensive, and it has all the charm of a small hotel with the amenities of a large one, including business facilities and 24-hour room service.

21 Lowndes Street, SW1X 9ES. Tel: 235-6020; Telex: 919065; Fax: 235-1154, in U.S., (800) 233-1234.

Onslow Hotel. Once upon a time this hotel was so genteel that you were frightened to cough, because all the retired spinsters doing their knitting would look up and frown. Then, because of its location in buzzing South Kensington, someone had the bright idea of doing it up. Now it is very popular, at once moderately priced and well situated. Pleasant public rooms, including bar and brasserie; 24-hour room service.

109–113 Queen's Gate, SW7 5LR. Tel: 589-6300; Telex: 262180; Fax: 581-1492.

The Pelham Hotel. This hotel in South Kensington, a very popular corner of London that is close to many important museums as well as to the shops and restaurants of Knightsbridge, is a hidden treasure. Like numerous other London hotels, the Pelham comprises two very large converted houses, but the standard to which they have been converted is extraordinary. It is owned by Kit and Tim Kemp, who also own the Dorset Square Hotel, and the attention to detail is everywhere evident. Luxury exists here, but happily, not at luxury-hotel prices.

15 Cromwell Place, SW7 2LA. Tel: 589-8288; Telex: 8814714; Fax: 584-8444; in U.S., (800) 553-6671.

16 Sumner Place. Built in 1848, these four interconnected and charming town houses create an agreeable ambience for those who like pleasant surroundings but don't want to break the bank. And they're very well placed in South Kensington, too, south of the V & A and just south of the South Kensington Underground station. The hotel has two drawing rooms, in one of which tea and coffee are served throughout the day; the other is a delightful conservatory drawing room overlooking the very attractive walled garden.

16 Sumner Place, SW7 3EG. Tel: 589-5232; Telex: 266638; Fax: 584-8615.

Notting Hill and West of Hyde Park

The Abbey Court. Very elegantly converted from a large town house, this small hotel offers very personal and friendly service at moderate rates. Snacks and drinks are available around the clock, and a full English breakfast can be served in your room every morning. This area of London (Notting Hill; just west of Bayswater and north of Kensington Gardens) abounds with restaurants of every kind for other meals.

20 Pembridge Gardens, W2 4DU. Tel: 221-7518; Telex: 262167; Fax: 792-0858.

The Halcyon Hotel. Newly converted from two large houses on the corner of Holland Park (west of Hyde Park/ Kensington Gardens), the Halcyon, though expensive, is already popular with theater people. No doubt they are drawn here by the greenery beyond the front door and the tastefully decorated rooms, designed to make you feel like a guest in a country house. The restaurant is also highly regarded.

81 Holland Park, W11 3RZ. Tel: 727-7288; Telex: 266721; Fax: 229-8516; in U.S., (800) 323-7500.

Observatory House Hotel. Campden Hill is an attractive hilly area of 18th- and 19th-century houses that stretches from Kensington to Notting Hill. Almost at the top of the hill, and equidistant between the Underground stations of Notting Hill Gate and Kensington High Street, is the Observatory House Hotel. The air is cleaner than in central London, the surrounding area most attractive, and the walk will do you good. This small bed-and-breakfast hotel is in an interesting 19th-century building built on the site of the old observatory of the astronomer Sir James South. Staying in this recently refurbished hotel is like staying in an exclusive London club, but at very reasonable prices. Amenities include in-room safes and secretarial services.

37 Hornton Street, W8 7NR. Tel: 937-1577; Telex: 914972; Fax: 938-3585.

Pembridge Court Hotel. This small, privately owned hotel on a quiet tree-lined street has 26 comfortable rooms, as well as a cozy lounge, restaurant, and bar. The Pembridge Court is close to the fun of the Portobello Road antiques market, which takes over all the surrounding streets on Saturdays, and is also close to Notting Hill, with its many restaurants and pubs. The north side of Kensington Gardens is just a stroll away. A point worth noting is that the upper floors of this small hotel are served by an elevator.

34 Pembridge Gardens, W2 4DX. Tel: 229-9977; Telex: 298363; Fax: 727-4982.

Portobello Hotel. Media people tend to frequent this moderately priced hotel in a hard-to-find corner of Holland Park, within a stone's throw of Portobello Road market and all the fun shops and restaurants of this corner of town, west of Hyde Park/Kensington Gardens. The bar/restaurant is open to guests 24 hours a day, and the whole place has a very easygoing atmosphere. Rooms range in size from a ship's cabin to very large, but they all have the necessary amenities. The hotel also is equipped with a special clean-air system developed in Scandinavia.

22 Stanley Gardens, W11 2NG. Tel: 727-2777; Telex: 268349; Fax: 792-9641.

Bayswater

Henry VIII. For an inexpensive hotel, the Henry VIII has a lot to offer. Its position is just north of Hyde Park, on a quiet shopping street just off Bayswater and very close to Queensway, one of the liveliest late-night streets in London. A Continental breakfast is served in your room, or you can have a full English breakfast in the restaurant. Other features of this hotel include a heated indoor swimming pool, a sauna, and a gym. Full business facilities are also available.

19 Leinster Gardens, W2 3AN. Tel: 262-0117; Telex: 261365; Fax: 706-0472.

Whites Hotel. Looking like a beautiful white wedding cake, this recently restored, large, and expensive hotel boasts a wonderful location overlooking Kensington Gardens and Bayswater. On weekends the railings of the park become an open-air picture gallery where artists hang their paintings in the hopes of making a sale. The hotel's public rooms are most attractive, and the bedrooms have been decorated in an unusual and luxurious style, with all comforts included. Office facilities can be arranged.

90–92 Lancaster Gate, W2 3NR. Tel: 262-2711; Telex: 24771; Fax: 262-2147.

Other Areas

Hotel Conrad. There are no rooms at the Conrad, just suites, which is a totally new concept in Britain. Situated on the marina of fashionable Chelsea Harbour, just off the King's Road in Chelsea, with its exclusive shops and restaurants as well as luxury private residences, the location of this hotel is among the best in London. Although extremely expensive, the Conrad does have a lot to offer, with several restaurants, bars, and function rooms, as well as a health club with facilities such as steamrooms, saunas, and a lovely swimming pool. Each room has two telephone lines plus fax facilities, and individual air-conditioning and heating controls. There is also a business center with everything that a businessperson could need on the premises.

Chelsea Harbour, SW10 0XG. Tel: 823-3000; Fax: 351-6525; in U.S., (800) 445-8667.

Swiss Cottage Hotel. Swiss Cottage is an area of North London close to Regent's Park that has a strong Middle-European flavor to it. Many refugees from Central Europe have made their home here, and the main street, the Finchley Road, close to the Swiss Cottage tube station, reflects this with its wonderful Austrian and Hungarian pastry shops and cafés. This hotel, which from the outside looks like exactly what it is, namely four large converted London town houses, feels quite different once you step through the door. It is as though you have strayed into a Viennese sitting room. The hotel is family run, and it certainly has a distinctive decor, with its heavy overstuffed furniture and intrusive wallpapers. But it has a loyal clientele that appreciates its eccentricities and undoubted character. It also has 24-hour room service, a dining room, and a bar. Moderate.

4 Adamson Road, NW3 3HP. Tel: 722-2281; Telex: 297232; Fax: 483-4588.

Apartments

For those who'd rather look after themselves when they come to London, the answer is to rent a serviced apartment, of which there are many. Although they are not necessarily cheaper than hotels, you do get more space for your money. Here are some of the best.

Capital Apartments. These serviced luxury apartments are just next door to the Capital Hotel (see above, under Knightsbridge/Kensington) and its facilities, including its marvelous restaurant (just in case cooking for yourself doesn't fascinate).

26 Basil Street, SW3 1AT. Tel: 589-5171; Telex: 919042; Fax: 225-0011; in U.S., (914) 833-3303 or (800) 223-5695; in Canada, (416) 447-2335.

Dolphin Square. Not far from the Tate Gallery, this is the largest apartment complex in Europe and offers the widest range of apartments. They are perfectly adequate but definitely not in the luxury class, although the in-house facilities make up for this. There is a shopping arcade with baker, butcher, grocer, ticket agency, two licensed bars, squash and tennis courts, and a very good restaurant of the brasserie type that overlooks the large swimming pool. There is also a large central garden.

Chichester Street, Pimlico, SW1V 3LX. Tel: 834-9134; Telex: 913333; Fax: 798-8735.

Draycott House. Just off Sloane Square, these exceedingly well designed apartments—always very popular despite the high prices—are temptingly close to the shops and restaurants of Knightsbridge and the King's Road in Chelsea.

10 Draycott Avenue, SW3 3AA. Tel: 584-4659; Telex: 916266; Fax: 225-3694.

Durley House. Excellently situated on Sloane Street between Chelsea and Knightsbridge, these apartments were taken over in 1989 by the ubiquitous Kemps of Dorset Square and Pelham Hotel fame, who are fast becoming the leading entrepreneurs in the small-hotel world of London. Refurbished to the Kemps' usual high standards, the formerly ramshackle Durley House is no longer recognizable. The only drawback to this sort of makeover is that such excellent service and comfort don't come cheap: the price has more than doubled in the past year. (But included in these rates is the use of the tennis courts in Cadogan Square Gardens.)

115 Sloane Street, SW1X 9PG. Tel: 235-5537; Telex: 919235; Fax: 259-6977; in the U.S., (800) 553-6674.

47 Park Street. This is the place for those looking for unashamed luxury and privacy. Although Mayfair is synonymous with elegance, these sumptuous serviced apartments are the top of the tree. The entrance hall is commanded by a concierge who will look after you down to the smallest detail, and the in-house restaurant is none other than the Michelin-starred **Le Gavroche**. Even breakfast, served in your suite, is a gastronomic delight.

47 Park Street, Mayfair, W1Y 4EB. Tel: 491-7282; Telex: 22116; Fax: 491-7281.

In the English Manner. This firm offers over 50 luxurious apartments in various areas and price ranges, in and around London. All are attractively furnished, and on arrival fresh flowers and breakfast provisions will be waiting for you.

Lancych, Boncath, Pembrokeshire SA37 0LJ. Tel: (02) 397-7444; Fax: (02) 397-7686; in U.S., P.O. Box 936, Alamo, CA 94507; Tel: (415) 935-7065 or (800) 422-0799 outside California; Fax: (415) 934-9260.

DINING

By Susan Grossman

Susan Grossman was born in and lives in London. Formerly Travel Editor of The Telegraph Sunday Magazine *and research officer on* Holiday Which?, *she has presented a program on food for the BBC, was the editor of* What Hotel? *magazine, and is currently the editor of* Upbeat *magazine.*

There is no single gourmet dining area in London, although Soho, shedding its red-light image, is becoming increasingly well endowed with decent eateries. Covent Garden, on the other hand, has more than its share of mediocre establishments that have a fast turnover of tired shoppers and hungry theatergoers.

Some of Britain's best chefs are firmly ensconced in the top hotels; others move around, taking with them a steady band of dedicated followers to unlikely backwaters of London. And while London's ethnic restaurants have always been its most inexpensive eateries, a number of Indian, Japanese, Chinese, Thai, and Lebanese establishments now offer some of the best food in the capital in fashionable designer settings.

The following selection—and it is very much a personal selection—takes in London restaurants in all price ranges, serving all types of food.

ENGLISH

Although plenty of restaurants, particularly in hotels, serve traditional British food of the roast-beef-and-Yorkshire-pudding variety, there are an increasing number offering a more modern approach, imaginatively combining ingredients and flavors and using the best of British produce.

Although they are listed elsewhere under Eclectic or Brasseries, Alastair Little, Bibendum, and Kensington Place (all outstanding) also offer modern British dishes on their menus. The eponymous **Stephen Bull** does the same. Bull, one of London's most exciting chefs, changes his menu twice daily, and on it you will find some of the best examples of modern British cooking. Among outstanding dishes are fillets of John Dory (fresh from Cornwall) with a black olive butter; a twice-cooked goat's cheese soufflé; and a legendary "variations on a theme of chocolate." The simple decor—careful lighting and bare walls and floorboards—deliberately ensures there is no distraction from the food. 5–7 Blandford Street off Baker Street. Closed Saturday lunch and Sundays; dinner from 6:30 P.M. Tel: 486-9696.

Launceston Place (sister of Kensington Place: see Brasseries and Cafés), located on a quiet street of the same name behind Kensington High Street, achieves a candlelit intimacy in a couple of crowded rooms full of fine oil paintings and mirrors. The moderately priced menu here is decidedly British—roast beef and Yorkshire pudding on Sundays, and a groaning cheese board. Tel: 937-6912.

Leith's occupies three Victorian houses knocked into one at 92 Kensington Park Road in Notting Hill. Prue Leith, the talented principal of Leith's School of Food and Wine, owns this establishment, which has been expensively refurbished with French silver, English bone china, and Dartington glass. Swivel chairs make for relaxing dining, spotlights ensure that you can see how good the food is, and the Wagons Leith, trolleys for hors d'oeuvres and desserts, are outstanding. Dishes include charcoal-grilled rib of beef, ox tongue, and their unfussy like. There are also English cheeses, and herbs and vegetables from Prue's own farm in Gloucestershire. The prix-fixe menus (including VAT and service) are good value, and the interesting and extensive vegetarian menu is made up entirely of home-grown produce. Dinner only; Tel: 229-4481.

The **Tate Gallery restaurant** on Millbank, along the river near the north end of Vauxhall Bridge, is formal and rather expensive but well established. It serves lunch only (steak-and-kidney pie, roast beef, and various dishes made to old English recipes, such as trifle for dessert). Entrance is through the gallery (which is free); the restaurant is on the lower ground floor, with tables encircled by a Rex Whistler mural. The wine list has a fine reputation.

Tel: 834-6754. Closed evenings and Sundays. Also see the Museum Street Café (British Museum) under Brasseries and Cafés.

West London is not overpopulated by decent restaurants, so **Boucha's**, in a small row of shops at 3 North End Road just south of the Olympia, is worth knowing about. The tiny street-level dining room is yellow right down to the pleated chintz on the walls, the dried sunflowers, and the fortnightly changing menus (bubble and squeak or salmon fishcakes served with a peanut mayonnaise may be offered). Wines are "New World," and the two house wines American. Closed lunchtime and Sundays; Tel: 603-0613.

Roasts, bangers and mash, treacle tart, and spotted dick with custard are among the dishes to look for in the traditionally English establishments. No place does them better than the Connaught Hotel (part of the Savoy Group), on Carlos Place in Mayfair; see also the Savoy Grill in the Strand (both under Hotel Restaurants).

Simpson's-in-the-Strand (also part of the Savoy Group) has long been known—150 years—for its quintessentially English setting, club-like atmosphere, and traditional menu. There are several dining rooms with ornate ceilings, chandeliers, rich drapes, and original paintings, patronized by a host of civil servants. Roasts are carved from huge gleaming trolleys, and puddings include spotted dick and bread and butter. 100 The Strand, WC2. Tel: 836-9112.

Rules, 35 Maiden Lane, just north of the Strand, is a venerable institution dating back some 190 years, with signed portraits of celebrities on the walls. There is a good choice of game in season. Open from noon to midnight; Tel: 836-5314.

In St. James's, **Green's Restaurant and Oyster Bar** on Duke Street (Tel: 930-4566; closed Sunday evening) is famous for its nursery food (bangers and mash, steak-and-kidney pie, fishcakes, and treacle tart) as well as for its oysters. A newer sister, **Green's** on Marsham Street, Westminster, is popular with MPs because of its proximity to the Houses of Parliament. The menu is similar and typically English: shepherd's pie on Mondays, braised oxtail on Thursdays, and—unusual for London— a variety of simple dishes with prices to match. The staff won't mind at all if you just want an omelette and salad, or you can sit at the long curved bar and have a plate of oysters. Closed Saturdays and Sunday lunch; Tel: 834-9552. Both establishments also offer pre-theater suppers.

The chef at **The Greenhouse** (same ownership as The Capital Hotel), tucked away in a cobbled mews behind a privet hedge in London's West End, is Gary Rhodes, who won acclaim at The Castle hotel at Taunton in Somerset. The food is of the salmon fishcakes, smoked haddock, Welsh rarebit, beef stew, and sticky toffee pudding variety, cooked with flair, and dispatched by serving ladies in pinnies. Noisy, and popular with businesspeople for lunch. 27a Hay's Mews. Tel: 499-3331.

At 21 Romilly Street in Soho, **The Lindsay House** attempts to make you feel as if you are a guest in a private town house: You ring the bell to enter, drink an aperitif in front of an open fire in the downstairs sitting room, and eat upstairs amid drapes, flounces, and flowers from an elaborate and moderately priced 18th-century English menu that includes traditional English puddings. Even so, the place hasn't quite managed to exorcise the ghost of the Chinese restaurant that occupied these quarters before it. Open every day; dinner from 6:00 P.M. until midnight, 7:00 P.M. to 10:00 P.M. on Sundays. Tel: 439-0450.

The Lindsay House has three sister restaurants: **The English House** (on Milner Street, off Cadogan Square; Tel: 584-3002) uses 18th-century recipes, with the emphasis on game. **The English Garden** (on Lincoln Street, off the King's Road; Tel: 584-7272), in a terraced house on a residential street, with the main restaurant in a Victorian conservatory at the back, is somewhat less formal. **Waltons**, on Walton Street at Brompton Cross (Tel: 584-0204), is the flagship: an intimate, formal dining room, mirrored, draped, and filled with flowers.

HOTEL RESTAURANTS

Some London hotels have excellent, if pricey, restaurants—though most are a better value at lunchtime. The following is a selection of the best.

The **Four Seasons**, at the Inn on the Park Hotel, overlooking Hyde Park near the western end of Piccadilly, is a palm-filled, rather fussy room in which the young Bruno Loubet offers *cuisine du terroir* (classic bourgeois cooking with modern touches) like his mother made back home in Bordeaux. He also highlights dishes that are low in cholesterol and sodium. Although the meals are expensive, there is a reasonable *menu du jour* at lunch. Tel: 499-0888.

Next door at the Inter-Continental on Hamilton Place, Peter Kromberg presides over the surprisingly small and intimate **Le Soufflé** restaurant on the ground floor. The menu is based on cuisines from around the world, and the dessert soufflés must be ordered in advance. Again, the set lunches represent good value. Closed Saturday lunch; Tel: 409-3131.

Bernard Gaume, the resident chef at the Hyatt Carlton Tower, near Harvey Nichols at 2 Cadogan Place in Knights-bridge, is well respected for the French (but not nou-velle) cuisine he prepares for the **Chelsea Room**. The restaurant has a sunny conservatory overlooking the gar-dens of Cadogan Square, deep settees in an adjoining bar, and a moderate set lunch that includes half a bottle of wine (which is unusual for London). The **Rib Room** downstairs offers roasts and grills as well as a fine selec-tion of seafood. Tel: 235-5411.

The Oak Room in the Meridien Piccadilly is a spacious and gracious dining room, almost overwhelmingly sump-tuous in its decor, with huge gilt mirrors, chandeliers, and an accompanying pianist. Perhaps not the place for an intimate tête-à-tête, but the food is generally excellent (if pricey), and, again, at lunchtime there is an excellent *menu du jour*. Closed Saturday lunch and Sundays. Up-stairs, **The Terrace Garden**, a split-level conservatory with huge glass windows overlooking Piccadilly, is one of the prettiest dining rooms in London. Here the varied menu includes vegetarian choices and simple salads as well as more expensive dishes. Piano music. Open all day; Tel: 734-8000.

Probably the most consistently outstanding hotel din-ing room is the formal, wood-paneled, very English, and very expensive **Connaught** on Mayfair's Carlos Place. Tel: 499-7070. Over on the Strand, **The Savoy Grill** attracts businessmen at lunchtime with a menu that includes English specialties such as jugged hare or Irish stew as well as French dishes. A dinner jacket and tie are the expected attire on weekends. The hotel's **River Restau-rant** is rather more ornate, with elaborate decor, classical columns, and lovely river views during the day. A band plays at night. The Grill room is closed for Saturday lunch and on Sundays; Tel: 836-4343.

The more intimate **Claridge's** in Mayfair on Brook Street is popular with royalty. Here a Hungarian trio serenades waiting diners (take note if you hear "The Teddy Bear's Picnic"—it denotes the arrival of HRH The Princess Margaret). **The Causerie**, Claridge's other restau-rant, is a lot less expensive and more informal (though you're just as likely to spot the royals), and offers an early buffet supper from 5:30 P.M., as well as a lunchtime smorgasbord. Tel: 629-8860.

The French-Baroque Louis XVI dining room of the **Ritz Hotel** on Piccadilly at the northeastern edge of Green Park is an outstanding setting in which to dine, if rather formidable and expensive. It, too, has dancing, but only on Saturday nights. Tel: 493-8181.

On Park Lane at the eastern edge of Hyde Park, Trusthouse Forte's Grosvenor House Hotel boasts **Ninety Park Lane**, a luxurious dining room filled with paintings and antiques and offering French cuisine of the highest quality that all but justifies the high prices. Couples may feel more comfortable dining here in the evening, as women are scarce among the expense-account crowd at lunch. Closed Saturday lunch and Sundays. Tel: 499-6363.

The autumn of 1990 saw the reopening of the Dorchester Hotel next door, now owned by the Sultan of Brunei, who has spent many millions on the renovations. Anton Mosimann's sous chef (Anton now runs his own club/restaurant) is in charge of the **Terrace** (live band nightly except Sunday) and the **Grill Room**, and the hotel has a new restaurant serving Cantonese food. Tel: 629-8888.

The Halkin (Tel: 240-2200), just off Belgrave Square, in Belgravia, is scheduled to open early in 1991, with chef Paul Gaylor (formerly of Inigo Jones and Burt's) expected to achieve great things in this restaurant.

The **Capital**, near Harrods on Basil Street, has a small, highly thought of dining room with a set lunchtime menu that is a good value (Tel: 589-5171).

Of the rest, the Westbury's **Polo Room** on the corner of Bond Street and Conduit Street in Mayfair, is intimate and elegant, and good for people-watching, especially at lunch (Tel: 629-7755). The St. James's Court Hotel, south of Buckingham Palace on Buckingham Gate, has several restaurants, including the French **Auberge de Provençe**. Modeled after the Oustaù de Baumanière in France, the restaurant is unfortunately a somewhat drab re-creation (white-washed vaulted ceilings and tiles), but the food imaginatively captures the flavor of Provence. Popular with businessmen at lunchtime. Tel: 821-1899. In Hyde Park you can see Rotten Row from the elegant **Park Room** of the Hyde Park Hotel. The menu is Mediterranean; it also serves tea. Tel: 235-4552.

Over in Holland Park, the Halcyon Hotel has the **King-**

fisher, a small, airy, basement restaurant decorated like an indoor garden, with a York stone floor, a tiny courtyard, and excellent-value set menus. Tel: 727-7288.

The Conrad (a subsidiary of Hilton USA), London's first all-suite hotel, opened in 1989. On the river at Chelsea Harbour, it offers a good Champagne Sunday brunch buffet (with amplified live music) at which you can help yourself to anything from sausage and eggs to an excellent fish stew or roast beef and Yorkshire pudding. There are lovely harbor views, although unfortunately you have to sit indoors even on sunny days. Tel: 823-3000.

FISH

Restaurants that specialize in fish are becoming increasingly popular in London. A south-of-France atmosphere prevails in Pierre Martin's fish restaurants (he also has one in Villefranche on the Côte d'Azur). The simple, crowded **Le Suquet**, 104 Draycott Avenue at Brompton Cross in South Kensington, is popular with celebrities who don't mind rolling up their sleeves and tucking in to the vast *plateau de fruits de mer.* Tel: 581-1785.

La Croisette. 168 Ifield Road (north of the Fulham Road but nearer the Old Brompton Road—look for the awning), was the first of Martin's London restaurants to open. Ring and you will be ushered into a crowded basement where London's French come for the fixed menu and to socialize over the enormous cork platters loaded with crab, langoustines, winkles, oysters, and mussels. La Croisette is 100 percent French, down to the youthful staff in Cannes tee-shirts, the paintings of the Mediterranean, and the unsalted butter. Closed Mondays; Tel: 373-3694.

At Martin's **Le Quai St. Pierre**, 7 Stratford Road just off the Earl's Court Road, you can sit at the counter under a huge umbrella or at a table in the only slightly more formal dining room up the spiral staircase. What this place lacks in finesse it makes up for in atmosphere. Closed Sundays; Tel: 937-6388.

La Croisette is best for an intimate evening, Le Quai St. Pierre more fun if you're with a group, Le Suquet if you like star-spotting. All are excellent value for the money.

Manzi's, on Leicester Street on the north side of Leicester Square, is an old favorite that's always busy and always noisy. The fish is of the freshest, and arrives largely unadorned other than with tartar sauce and a basket full of chips. Dinner is served from 5:30 P.M. Tel: 734-0224.

With its long, narrow room reminiscent of a turn-of-the-century railway carriage, and its marble-topped oyster bar (popular at lunchtime) and discreet cushion-filled alcoves divided by etched-glass screens, the Savoy Group–owned **Wilton's**, on Jermyn Street opposite Hilditch & Key, is a London institution. About 500 oysters a day are consumed on the premises, either at lunch or as a pre-theater snack, and most are washed down with Champagne. Dishes are simply cooked and dispensed by matronly, rather awe-inspiring waitresses in long white overalls. It specializes in game in season and traditional English "savouries" such as anchovies on toast and Welsh rarebit. Tel: 629-9955.

Another famous oyster-and-Champagne bar is **Green's**, on Duke Street off Jermyn Street in St. James's, with a second branch in Marsham Court, Marsham Street, Westminster (see the English section above). **The Greenhouse** oyster-and-Champagne bar, 16 Royal Exchange (next to the Bank of England in the heart of the City), is a sibling of the two Green's restaurants. It is a tiny place, popular with bankers and the like, and is open weekdays only from 11:00 A.M. to 8:30 P.M.; Tel: 929-3131.

FRENCH

A few of London's restaurants regularly receive the highest accolades from the food critics. As well as several in hotels (see Hotel Restaurants), among the most outstanding are: **Le Gavroche**, 43 Upper Brook Street in Mayfair (Tel: 408-0881), owned by the famous Albert Roux (who also has the Waterside Inn in Bray) and very expensive, but with an affordable lunch menu; **La Tante Claire**, 68 Royal Hospital Road, in Chelsea (Tel: 352-6045), run by Pierre Koffmann (famous for his dish of pig's trotters), with a set lunch menu that's an outstanding value; and **Chez Nico**, 35 Great Portland Street, a stone's throw from Oxford Street, where owner/chef Nico Ladenis's largely classical French menu has been satisfying his discerning followers for years. The food here is simply outstanding and presented flawlessly. (The lack of salt shakers on the table is per Nico's orders: He claims many of his customers need educating. If you want to get as far as the stunning chocolate desserts, don't ask for the salt.) A meal here is an almost theatrical experience, and the prix-fixe lunch menu is an especially good value. (Tel: 436-8846).

All three of the above places are expensive, are closed weekends, and need booking well in advance.

Nico's old premises at 48a Rochester Row in Westminster are now called **Very Simply Nico** and offer an informal brasserie-style experience with a reasonably priced set menu. Open every day except Sundays, with dinner served from 6:00 P.M.; Tel: 630-8061.

Le Mazarin consists of a series of alcoves leading off a main dining area in an elegant pink basement at 30 Winchester Street, just beyond Victoria Coach Station. With his exquisite sauces and high-quality ingredients, chef-proprietor René Bajard delights gastronomes who don't want to spend a week's wages on a meal. The set menu, an excellent value, may include foie gras, game, and shellfish; the gastronomic menu is only a little more expensive. Closed Sundays and Mondays; Tel: 828-3366.

Le Boulestin, in the basement of 1a Henrietta Street, Covent Garden (south of the Piazza and opposite the Jubilee Market), opened in the 1920s. While the food is classic French, the decor is Edwardian country home, with banquette seating, heavy drapes, marbled pillars, and horsey paintings. Service is formal (the sommelier even makes a fuss over the mineral water), there is a minimum charge of £40 (unusual for London), and it stays open late for after-theater dining. Closed Sundays; Tel: 836-7061.

In Soho, **La Bastide**, 50 Greek Street just off Soho Square (Tel: 734-3300), is a small, fairly formal, street-level restaurant offering serious and sometimes unusual French-provincial dishes at reasonable prices. Not in the same league, but worth trying if you're in the Southwark area, is **La Petite Auberge de Saint Savin**, 29 Tooley Street, about as close to a simple, cheap, Parisian dining room as any place in London gets. Family-owned, with old-fashioned decor and dim lighting, it's on the South bank opposite the gruesome London Dungeon, near London Bridge, and a couple of doors down from **Hay's Galleria**, an exciting development of shops and restaurants overlooking the river. The set menus include French onion soup, snails, and excellent homemade foie gras, and are a good value. Alsatian snacks and wines at lunchtime only. Outside seating in summer. Closed weekends; Tel: 378-0621.

The St. Quentin restaurants in Knightsbridge are owned in part by the Savoy Group. The **St. Quentin**, a bustling, elegant French establishment on two floors at 243 Brompton Road (opposite the Brompton Oratory), serves a reasonable prix-fixe lunch. Tel: 589-8005. The **Grill St. Quentin**, 2 Yeoman's Row (past the Bunch of Grapes pub), occupies a huge, bright, and warmly lit basement reminiscent of La Coupole in Paris. Closed Sundays; Tel: 581-8377.

You can also eat inexpensive French food in London's numerous brasseries (see Brasseries and Cafés).

ITALIAN

Italian food is becoming increasingly fashionable in London, and as a consequence more expensive. Currently the Italian restaurants not only to be seen in, but also to experience authentic cooking in, are Cibo, the River Café, and Orso.

Cibo, in a backwater of Kensington west of Holland Park at 3 Russell Gardens, opened in September of 1989 and met with immediate success. Authentic peasant food (in enormous quantities) is served on colorful earthenware pottery against a backdrop of modern art, which includes a three-dimensional "Giorgioni" look-alike. Cibo is noisy, somewhat cramped, and fairly expensive. Try the *risotto* and the *zabaglione alla frutta*. Closed Sundays; Tel: 371-2085.

Orso, 27 Wellington Street in Covent Garden, a sister to Joe Allen's around the corner, is a dimly lit, noisy, cavernous basement, vaguely 1950s in design, that is popular with media people. Pizzas and pastas are served here along with dishes such as *risotto* and pig's trotters. The entrance is a dark doorway just north of the Aldwych. Open noon to midnight every day; Tel: 240-5269.

It is well worth the effort to find the **River Café**, on Thames Wharf, Rainville Road, between Putney and Hammersmith bridges. Part of a complex of converted warehouses, it overlooks a relatively undeveloped stretch of the Thames. Run by Rose Gray and Ruthie Rogers (wife of architect Richard, who has his offices in a neighboring warehouse), the kitchen is open to the dining area, the tables are black and square, and the chairs wicker and steel. The food is authentic regional Italian, with an emphasis on Tuscan cuisine. There are tables outside in summer. Open for dinner weekdays only, with last orders at 9:30 P.M. Also Saturday and Sunday lunch; Tel: 381-8824.

There are any number of old-school Italian trattoria in London. One of the most fashionable is **San Lorenzo**, around the corner from Harrods at 22 Beauchamp Place, popular with Princess Di and others, who eat pasta among the potted plants and exchange the sort of gossip that columns are made of; Tel: 584-1074. **Santini**, 29 Ebury Street near Victoria Station, attracts businessmen at lunchtime with its reasonably priced set menu. It is ultrasmart, quietish, and airy; the menu hovers around the Veneto. Tel:

730-4094. Santini's newer sister restaurant, **L'Incontro**, 87 Pimlico Road in Belgravia, also specializes in the cuisine of the Veneto. A pianist plays every evening except Sunday; Tel: 730-3663.

San Martino, on Chelsea's fashionable Walton Street, is unusual in that Martino grows his own vegetables and herbs (at home and in the restaurant's window boxes), including black cabbage for the minestrone and arugula for the salads. He also makes his own *bresaola* and specializes in his native Tuscan dishes as well as game in season. Tel: 589-1356.

Few London restaurants offer more than a couple of tables for eating outside in summer, but **La Famiglia**, opposite the World's End pub on Chelsea's Langton Street, has a large, plant-filled courtyard (seating 100) strung with lights. Alvaro, the owner, entertains many Chelsea residents ("Albert Finney says it's an extension of his dining room"). Everything is freshly cooked, and most of Alvaro's devoted staff have been with him since he opened 15 years ago. Last orders at 11:30 P.M.; Tel: 351-0761.

Bertorelli's, on Floral Street opposite the stage door of the Royal Opera House in Covent Garden, offers reasonably priced regional dishes, pasta, and light snacks in a café/wine bar downstairs. Open for lunch and dinner until 11:30 P.M. Closed Sundays; Tel: 836-1868.

Don't let the refined Edwardian atmosphere fool you: **Kettners**, around the corner at 29 Romilly Street, is actually a branch of Pizza Express. The Champagne bar is a fashionable Soho meeting place and is open until midnight. There is a cocktail pianist every evening and on Thursdays and Fridays at lunch. Tel: 734-6112.

The other members of the same chain, **Pizza Express** on Dean Street, Soho (Tel: 437-9595), and **Pizza on the Park** in Knightsbridge (Tel: 235-5550), both have live jazz.

AMERICAN
If you're in the mood for a hamburger, the place to go is the **Hard Rock Café**, at the Hyde Park Corner end of Old Park Lane—that is, if you can stand loud music and don't mind sharing a table or lining up to get in. In Soho, **Ed's Easy Diner**, a small, neon-lit café wedged into the corner of Old Compton Street and Moor Street, serves quick, 100 percent additive-free burgers and soda. In the jukeboxes on the counter, 5p buys 1950s rock and roll. There is also a branch on King's Road at number 362.

Joe Allen's, in a brick basement at 13 Exeter Street just behind Covent Garden, livens up with a theatrical crowd late at night.

The **Rock Island Diner** on the top floor of the London Pavilion at Piccadilly Circus is a huge 1950s-style eatery with a Chevy suspended over the bar. The DJ plays 1950s music, there's a roller-skating mâitre d', and food is of the meatloaf-and-steak-sandwich variety. Open seven days a week, 11:00 A.M. to 11:30 P.M. No need to reserve ahead, but you may have to stand in line. While you're here you might want to visit the Rock Circus, Madame Tussaud's newest animatronic homage to well-known stars of the rock-'n'-roll era, though you have to be well over 30 to really enjoy it.

Zuma, down the road from the Conran Shop in Chelsea Cloisters on Sloane Avenue, has modern art on its walls, contemporary decor, stripped wood flooring, chrome and wicker chairs, and dishes that may include spicy shellfish stew or crabcakes with blueberry and goat's cheese tart. Steak with eggs and hash browns are on the Sunday brunch menu; snacks at the bar. Tel: 225-1048. Equally fashionable is **Columbus**, which occupies a minimal-istically lit and decorated basement near Harrods at 8 Egerton Garden Mews (turn left at the Bunch of Grapes pub). The chef, Neal Grossman, is the brother of food critic Lloyd (who is part owner). Somewhat ironically, the food is only average, though that doesn't detract from the restaurant's popularity. Dishes are of the contemporary American school, with touches of the Far East and Southeast Asia thrown in, plus expensive B.L.T. pizzas. Tel: 589-8287.

BRASSERIES AND CAFÉS

Brasseries and cafés are usually cheaper than more formal restaurants, and many serve meals—which tend to lean toward French cuisine—from breakfast onward.

Currently popular with Londoners is **Kensington Place**, 201–205 Kensington Church Street, the noisy Continental sister of the more formal Launceston Place. Revolving doors lead to a high-tech glass-fronted brasserie that specializes in exciting and unfussy European dishes featuring the freshest of ingredients. It is reasonably priced and always crowded. Open every day from noon to midnight; Tel: 727-3184.

The Continental-style **Soho Brasserie** at 23 Old Compton Street offers typically French dishes such as fish soup, as well as snacks at the long bar (which is a popular drinking venue). On summer evenings when the restaurant gets crowded, the full-length doors are opened and patrons spill out onto the sidewalk. Open noon until 11:30 P.M.; closed Sundays. Tel: 439-9301.

Off Piccadilly, **Langan's Brasserie** on Stratton Street near Green Park is always crowded (but it's big so you can usually get in). The two floors (upstairs is quieter, but it doesn't serve its famous spinach soufflé up there) are jammed with splendid paintings, lots of large round tables, and a regular influx of conversation stoppers, including the occasional entertainers (Michael Caine is one of the owners). The extensive menu offers dishes, including daily specials, of variable quality, and the service can be interminably slow. But you shouldn't leave London without eating here at least once. Open Mondays through Fridays, 12:30 P.M. to 2:45 P.M. and 7:00 P.M. to 11:45 P.M.; Saturdays, 8:00 P.M. to 12:45 A.M. Live band after 9:00 P.M. Tel: 491-8822.

Le Caprice, on Arlington Street in Mayfair, is chic, stylish, and frequented by stars. Reserve well ahead, unless your name alone will get you in. The decor features lots of black, white, and chrome, with photos on the walls. Simple snacks and diet-conscious meals are served from 6:00 P.M. until midnight; brunch on Sundays until 3:00 P.M. Tel: 629-2239.

Joe's Café, on Draycott Avenue at Brompton Cross, opposite the Conran Shop, is very stylish and is about as far removed from an ordinary café as you can get. Waiters sport black waistcoats and white shirts that match the black-and-white decor and black-and-white tagliatelle. The lunch menu includes salads, bagels, and a few hot dishes. Evening meals are more formal, though still quite inexpensive. The bar is open weekdays from 6:00 P.M. to 9:00 P.M.; otherwise, you have to eat. It also serves Saturday breakfast and brunch on Sundays. Tel: 225-2217.

The **Emporio Armani Express**, 191 Brompton Road, a couple of blocks down from Harrods (Tel: 823-8818), is as smart as the clothes it sells. Armani worked closely with his architect on the design, hence the elegant bone-handled monogrammed cutlery and the Armani eagle on every table. Long and thin like a railway carriage, the restaurant serves modern Italian dishes, snacks such as *crostini* or *foccaccia,* as well as cakes, teas, and espresso during store hours: Mondays through Saturdays, 10:00 A.M. to 6:00 P.M. (7:00 P.M. Wednesdays).

Tall Orders 676 Fulham Road (the west end), is a gimmick that works. Modern European food is served (warm, not hot) in Chinese-style wicker *dim sum* baskets stacked high, dishes piled one on top of the other. Try the grilled swordfish with white beans in virgin olive oil, the salmon carpaccio with guacamole, and, of course, the lemon tart. If you can't decide, choose a "multi storey" selection, or, for children, a mini-sized "fairy storey." Reasonable prices and an animated, lively atmosphere. Open seven days a week from noon to midnight; Tel: 371-9673. A branch, **Tall Orders in Soho**, is on Dean Street at 2 St. Anne's Court (Tel: 494-4941).

The **Cafe Kensington** (Tel: 938-2211), on the site of the former barracks in Lancer Square at the bottom of Kensington Church Street, is a good stop for lunch. The head chef is from Clarke's up the road. Guitar, blues, or jazz background music, and a cruise-liner feel; there are tables outside for dining in fine weather. Open daily until midnight.

London, perhaps surprisingly, has few restaurants with good food *and* river views. The **New Serpentine Restaurant** in Hyde Park, a temporary construction alongside the old Serpentine restaurant (which is due to be rebuilt), has both. A conservatory-style structure, complete with trees and garden chairs, it is run by Prue Leith (see Leith's in the English section, above), who offers a good wine list, imaginative menus, and reasonable prices. Lovely views of ducks and boats and especially romantic at night. It also serves teas and morning coffee (Tel: 402-1142). Open daily from 10:30 A.M. to 10:30 P.M. (summer), 4:30 P.M. (winter). Near the Serpentine Gallery.

In St. James's, south of Piccadilly, **Fortnum & Mason's Fountain Restaurant** (entrance on Jermyn Street) has always been popular for tea. Frequented by elegant shoppers, the restaurant is open all day and also serves salads, ice cream, grills, and light meals until 11:00 P.M. (closed Sundays). There is also a more formal restaurant on the fourth floor that is open during store hours.

Visitors to the British Museum should search out the tiny, reasonably priced, but unlicensed **Museum Street Café**, a few hundred yards south of the museum. The menu is short and the dishes mostly char-grilled or roasted without sauces. It doesn't take credit cards, and isn't open on weekends. Tel: 405-3211.

The **Blueprint Cafe** on the first floor of the Design Museum at Bulters Wharf on the south bank of the Thames is too expensive to be a real café, though the atmosphere is stylishly informal. Owned by Conran (see

Bibendum), Blueprint has a menu that changes daily.
There are stunning views of Tower Bridge and the
Thames from the highly sought-after tables on the outside
terrace in summer. Lunchtimes are packed. Closed Sunday and Monday evening. Tel: 378-7031.

ECLECTIC
A growing number of London chefs take their inspiration
from several countries; on the same menu you may find
dishes from Europe, America, and the Far East.

One of London's most accomplished yet modest young
chefs is Alastair Little, who runs a stylized, simple, mono-
chrome café to which he's given his name on Soho's Frith
Street. With its black lacquered tables, bright lighting, and
unpretentious decor, at first glance **Alastair Little's** looks
like a Japanese restaurant. Actually, you might get something vaguely Chinese from the menu ... or French, or
Danish, or modern British—whatever captures the chef's
fancy. Little changes his menu twice daily, and his imaginative and moderately priced dishes are considered to be
some of the most exciting in London. Lunch from 12:30
P.M. to 2:30 P.M., dinner from 7:30 P.M. to 11:30 P.M. Closed
Saturday lunch and Sundays. There's also a small downstairs bar (no reservations accepted) where patrons can
order fish, including sushi, and cold dishes. No credit
cards. Tel: 734-5183.

Sutherlands, around the corner from Carnaby Street
on Lexington Street, is highly regarded for its stylish
design (a long, narrow, windowless room with "acid"-
treated mirrors and black menus) and its equally artistic
culinary creations impeccably presented on large white
plates. For a not unreasonable fixed price you can get two
courses as well as dishes such as steamed courgette (zuc-
chini) flower filled with lobster mousse, excellent bread
(parmesan, caraway), and breathtaking sorbets (try the
lavender). Dinner from 6:15 P.M. Closed Saturday lunch
and Sundays. Tel: 434-3401.

The Ivy, 1 West Street just off the Charing Cross Road
on the western edge of Covent Garden, is wedged into a
corner opposite the St. Martin's Theatre, where *The
Mousetrap* has been playing for 39 years. Reopened last
year (now a sister of the Caprice), it has found instant
fame with its varied menu: salads, oysters, black pudding,
braised oxtail, and bang bang chicken. Not expensive; last
orders are at midnight. Tel: 836-4751.

Clarke's, 124 Kensington Church Street, takes its name from its enterprising owner. You don't get a choice on the evening menu (you do at lunchtime), but don't let that put you off. Whatever comes out of the basement kitchen (which you can view from the dining room) is good. The menu offers dishes from Italy, France, and California, although Sally Clarke also regularly offers English cottage-made cheeses and home-grown vegetables and fruits. The menu changes nightly; closed weekends. Tel: 221-9225.

Renowned chef Simon Hopkinson, who has no patience for nouvelle cuisine, is at the helm of the spacious, bright dining room of **Bibendum**, on the first floor of the Michelin Building on the Fulham Road in Chelsea. Elegant and fashionable, Bibendum attracts serious food lovers and celebrities. The menu is mostly expensive (though lunch is more of a bargain—try the fish and chips), and spans the cuisines of France, Italy, and Britain. Tel: 581-5817.

One Ninety Queen's Gate, near the Albert Hall, was conceived as a restaurant/club for chefs and is now a gourmet club run by a committee of famous chefs. Open to the public, it is discreetly hidden behind an elegant stuccoed façade. Inside, there are cherubs on the ceiling in the entrance hall, a comfortable wood-paneled bar on the ground floor, and several intimate, slightly decadent boudoir-style dining rooms downstairs. The food is "gutsy" and the portions generous. Chef Anthony Worrall-Thompson may offer stuffed pig's trotters or tripe, as well as unusual combinations such as mullet served with white beans and duck foie gras. Prices are reasonable, and the ambience makes it ideal for a romantic dinner for two. The restaurant also offers a remarkably cheap executive lunch. Worrall-Thompson is also cooking for the cheaper Bistrot 190 on the ground floor of the newly revamped Gore Hotel next door (see Early and Late). Tel: 581-5666.

With the backing of thirteen shareholder friends, chef Bryan Webb bought **Hilaire's** on the Old Brompton Road, opposite Christie's of South Kensington, from Trusthouse Forte, and has installed highly imaginative modern British as well as European dishes on his menu. The upstairs street-level room is small and has cool green walls, paddle fans, and deferential service. The downstairs basement area is more intimate. The set menu is reasonably priced. Closed Saturday lunch and Sunday evening; Tel: 584-8993.

Also see the South of the River section below, and Stephen Bull in the English section above for other eclectic selections.

EARLY AND LATE

Apart from brasseries, which serve meals all day, most London restaurants don't start serving until 7:30 P.M. and stop at 11:00 P.M., so you have to make plans if you want to eat before or after the theater, unless you fancy Chinese and ethnic food. (Many of these restaurants often stay open very late.)

Some theaters and concert halls have their own restaurants (including the South Bank complex, the Mermaid, the Barbican, and the Palace Theatre). Many theaters have sandwiches and coffee available in the bar.

In Covent Garden, the French **Café du Jardin**, 28 Wellington Street, serves a pre- and post-theater supper from 5:30 P.M. to 11:30 P.M. Royal Opera House patrons, rather more formally attired than the rest of the clientele, wander in clutching their programs, and waiters wend their way between tables balancing trays of Cognac. Choose the ground floor to be seen, downstairs to get on with it. The food, though inexpensive, is as erratic as the service. Tel: 836-8769.

Magno's, around the corner on Long Acre, is rather more formal but also relatively inexpensive, and its pre-theater menu of simple, quick dishes that change weekly is an especially good buy. Tel: 836-6077. On nearby St. Martin's Lane, the enormous **Café Pelican** (Tel: 379-0309) stays open until after 1 A.M.. Almost next door, **Café Flo** has an excellent menu and attracts the early dining set. Tel: 836-8289.

Rules, 35 Maiden Lane, serves traditional English food in a decor to match, and is open from noon to midnight; Tel: 836-5314. **Le Borlestin** (see French), 1A Henrietta Street, also welcomes late diners; Tel: 836-7061.

The **Savoy Grill**, in the famous luxury hotel off the Strand, is within walking distance of the theaters and offers a pre-theater menu. After the show you can go back for dessert and coffee in the Thames Foyer. Jackets and ties are required in both places. Tel: 836-4343. If you don't meet the dress code, **Upstairs at the Savoy** will serve you relatively inexpensive snacks, oysters, Champagne, and vintage wines by the glass from noon to midnight weekdays, and 5:00 P.M. to midnight Saturdays (closed Sundays). You can sit at the marble counter or at one of the tables along a narrow corridor, from which you'll have a fascinating view of people arriving at the front entrance. It also offers a breakfast buffet on weekdays (8:00 A.M. to 10:00 A.M.). Also handy for theaters with early evening curtains are: **Alastair Little's** bar (Eclectic); **Sutherland's** (Eclectic); **Orso** (Italian); **Burt's** (Vegetarian, below), and **Manzi's** (Fish).

One of London's best-loved oyster-and-Champagne bars, **Green's**, 36 Duke Street in St. James's (near Jermyn Street), starts serving at 5:30 P.M. The atmosphere is formal (regulars include royalty), but some of the traditional English dishes, including kedgeree and bangers and mash, most certainly aren't. Tel: 930-4566.

Le Caprice, on Arlington Street in Mayfair, is open from 6:00 P.M. to midnight daily, as is Kensington Place (see Brasseries, above). **The Causerie** at Claridge's in Mayfair has an early buffet supper from 5:30 P.M. You can get reasonably priced snacks at **Fields**, a huge restaurant/coffee bar in the crypt of St. Martin-in-the-Fields Church (near Charing Cross Station) until 8:30 P.M.

The **Terrace Garden** at the Hotel Meridien is open every day from 7:00 A.M. to 11:30 P.M. for an inexpensive breakfast, lunch, or dinner, a light French snack, or tea. In this spectacular conservatory overlooking Piccadilly, a harpist plays at tea, a pianist most evenings.

The Limelight, previously a disco and nightclub on the site of a former church at 136 Shaftesbury Avenue (near Cambridge Circus), Tel: 434-1572, is now four separate dining, dancing, and drinking areas. The Late Supper Club has live music from 10:30 P.M. to 3:00 A.M. There is also the Gallery Bar serving cocktails and lighter dishes of the lobster–club-sandwich variety.

Brown's in Albemarle Street, behind Bond Street, is one of the Trusthouse Forte hotels. It serves tea or high tea from 4:15 P.M. to 5:45 P.M. (salmon fishcakes, griddles, and scones with clotted cream). Tel: 493-6020.

Bistrot 190, an elegant high-ceilinged room on the ground floor of the Gore Hotel on leafy Queens Gate, stays open until 5:30 A.M. Around the corner from the Albert Hall, the "Mediterranean"-style food (charcuterie with homemade pickles, *bollito misto,* Toulouse sausages with mashed potatoes) is prepared by chef Anthony Worrall-Thompson, who also owns the successful One Ninety Queen's Gate next door (see Eclectic). The room is bright, airy, and faintly colonial in style; there are vases of herbs and virgin olive oil on each table and you can help yourself to bread and olives. Tel: 581-5666.

Across Waterloo Bridge on the South Bank, **RSJ**, in a converted hayloft behind the National Theatre at 13a Coin Street, is a restaurant that offers imaginative French dishes. Fixed-price menu or à la carte. Open for lunch and from 6:00 P.M., with last orders at 11:00 P.M.; closed Sundays. Tel: 928-4554.

ETHNIC

Indian

Some of London's best Indian restaurants are also some of its most unpretentious, but those of the new school have turned up the lights, spruced up the decor, and begun to offer cocktails as well as beer with their curries. Heading the list of these upscale Indian restaurants are **The Last Days of the Raj** at 22 Drury Lane (Tel: 836-5705) and the **Red Fort** at 77 Dean Street (Tel: 437-2525), both in Soho; **Jamdani** at 34 Charlotte Street (Tel: 636-1178), which specializes in unusual dishes; and **Lal Qila** nearby at 117 Tottenham Court Road (Tel: 387-4570). All are moderately priced and offer North Indian cuisine.

At the **Bombay Brasserie** in Bailey's Hotel on Courtfield Close, 140 Gloucester Road in South Kensington, the decor is impressively colonial in style—chandeliers, ferns, a conservatory, paddle fans, and a white piano. You can sample food from all over India here, and as at many Indian restaurants, the buffet lunches are a good value. Tel: 370-4040.

Chinese

London's Chinatown, where you'll find most of the city's best Chinese restaurants, is found south of Shaftesbury Avenue in and around Gerrard Street, in Soho. **Fung Shing** on nearby Lisle Street, **Good Food** on Little Newport Street, and **Wong Kei** on Wardour Street are authentic old-school Cantonese establishments where you can eat cheaply and well.

You can get some of London's best wind-dried food (a Chinese process of hanging out food to dry naturally) at the ever-popular **Poons**, 4 Leicester Street, as well as at the vast **Chuen Cheng Ku**, 17 Wardour Street (it's been there 20 years or so), and **New World**, on Gerrard Place. **Yung's**, on Wardour Street, appeals to insomniacs, because it's open from 4:00 P.M. until 4:00 A.M.. No need to reserve a table at any of the above.

London's first formal Chinese restaurant was **Ken Lo's Memories of China**, on Ebury Street near Victoria Station. Tel: 730-7734. A second branch with the same name overlooks the boats in Chelsea Harbour and, unlike most other Chinese restaurants in the city, offers a varied menu, an inexpensive *dim sum* brasserie, and Sunday brunch. Celebrities, businesspeople, and royalty drop in by yacht, with and without bodyguards. You can arrive by riverboat (from the Embankment) or via Lots Road. Two floors, "Ming dynasty" gold-and-blue decor, and a pianist. Tel: 352-4953.

For beautifully presented Chinese food and a backdrop of cascading water, try **Zen** in Chelsea Cloisters on Sloane Avenue (Tel: 589-1781) or **Zen Central**, 20 Queen Street off Curzon Street in Mayfair (Tel: 629-8089). Both attract a fashionable clientele, including many Chinese. (There's a third branch in Hampstead; see below.)

Thai

It's well worth the journey out to the Fulham Broadway (south of Earl's Court on the District Underground Line) for a meal at the **Blue Elephant** restaurant, which is almost opposite the Underground station at 4–5 Fulham Broadway. Here, in an exotic setting of ferns and bamboo, an ever-smiling staff expertly presents moderately priced Thai dishes and beautifully sculpted fruit. Tel: 385-6595.

Popular Thai restaurants in Soho include **Chiang Mai** at 48 Frith Street (Tel: 437-7444); the rather gloomy **Bahn Thai**, where you can choose from hundreds of dishes, on the opposite side of the street (Tel: 437-8504); and **Sri Siam** at 14 Old Compton Street (Tel: 434-3544), a long, narrow, rather pricey establishment.

Japanese

Some of London's most expensive Japanese restaurants are found in the City near St. Paul's. **Miyama** on Godliman Street (Tel: 489-1937) caters to businesspeople on expense accounts and is closed on weekends. **Ginnan** on Cathedral Place serves up fast lunches for quite a bit less but is closed on Saturdays; both places close at 10:00 P.M.

Elsewhere in London, the expensive **Suntory** at 72–73 St. James's Street (south of Piccadilly) is popular among discerning Japanese (Tel: 409-0201); the **Miyama** at 38 Clarges Street (Tel: 499-2443; closed Sundays and Saturday lunch), off Piccadilly near Green Park, is much less expensive, especially at lunchtime; and the prix-fixe meals at **One Two Three**, 27 Davies Street in Mayfair (Tel: 409-0750), which is closed on weekends, are also a good value. The basement **Ikkyu**, 67 Tottenham Court Road near Goodge Street station, is handy for shoppers. Closed Sunday lunch; Tel: 636-9280.

Middle Eastern

The Lebanese **Al Hamra**, almost opposite the Curzon Cinema in Mayfair's Shepherd Market, is much more sophisticated than you might expect a restaurant specializing in Middle Eastern cooking would be. The tables are set close together, so if you're not sure what to eat you can follow the example of a neighboring diner. You'll be safe, however, if you stick with the hot and cold starters (wiped up with pita bread) and the salads, which come in huge baskets and include plenty of chunky raw vegetables. Open until midnight every day. Tel: 493-1954. Insomniacs can find Middle Eastern solace at **Maroush II**, 38 Beauchamp Place just south of Harrods, until 4:30 A.M. (Tel: 581-5434), as well as at the slightly less expensive **Maroush**, 21 Edgeware Road near Marble Arch, until 1:00 A.M. Tel: 723-0773. **Maroush III**, nearby at 62 Seymour Street, is open until 12:30 A.M.; Tel: 724-5024.

Greek

Greek restaurants aren't currently in vogue in London, but the old standbys do a brisk business. Among these is the **White Tower**, 1 Percy Street (off Tottenham Court Road), which has been offering Greek and Continental dishes since 1938. Closed weekends; Tel: 636-8141. The less expensive **Beotys**, 79 St. Martin's Lane (near the theaters), has been around for more than 40 years; it starts serving pre-theater dinners at 5:30 P.M. Tel: 836-8768. For a livelier atmosphere, you can watch plates being thrown around and dance on the tables in **Anemos** (now also owned by the White Tower), 32 Charlotte Street. Still lively but a bit less raucous is the cavernous, candlelit, and usually crowded **Kalamaras** on Inverness Mews, an alley behind Queensway in the Bayswater area just north of Hyde Park. The Greek owner often plays the bouzouki for diners. Open until midnight. Closed Sundays and at lunch; Tel: 727-9122.

Eastern European

For years, Socialist MPs and intellectuals have enjoyed Eastern European food of the sauerkraut and black-cherry soup variety at the **Gay Hussar**, 2 Greek Street (near Soho Square). The management has changed, but you can still sit in old-fashioned comfort and eat smoked goose with a bottle of Champagne. Dinner from 5:30 P.M.; closed Sundays. Tel: 437-0973. Waiters at **Bloom's**, 90 Whitechapel High Street in the East End, dispense chicken soup and gefilte fish to customers with minimal grace, as they have for years. The restaurant serves kosher food. Tel: 247-6001.

VEGETARIAN

London's strictly vegetarian restaurants are few and far between, but there are numerous restaurants that cater to non–meat eaters and most can produce a choice of suitable vegetarian dishes, especially the brasseries. Ethnic restaurants are usually the best bet, however. *The Vegetarian Good Food Guide,* available in bookshops, is useful.

Of the more formal restaurants, **Leith's**, 92 Kensington Park Road, has a vegetarian menu; many of the herbs and vegetables are grown by Prue Leith (she runs her own cooking school) on her farm in the Cotswolds. Tel: 229-4481. **Burt's**, 42 Dean Street (Tel: 734-3339), is a fashionable and formal Soho restaurant that takes its food and its presentation seriously (no brown rice and sandals here). Prices aren't cheap but the vegetarian and fish dishes are interesting enough to warrant the expense. Dinner from 5:30 P.M. Also in Soho, **Frith's**, on Frith Street, has a vegetarian café in its basement with a short menu that includes vegan (strict vegetarian dishes) as well as several Italian offerings. Closed Saturday lunch and Sundays; Tel: 734-7535.

Less expensive restaurants include **Cranks**, a chain that was among the first to offer "healthful" food in London. The various branches (including Marshall Street, near Oxford Circus, and The Market in Covent Garden) offer a selection of salads and hot dishes at very reasonable prices but they are café-like in design and don't encourage lingering. Also in Covent Garden, you can get vegan dishes, pastries, pizzas, and a few hot dishes at **Neal's Yard Bakery** (it closes at 6:30 P.M.), or try **Food for Thought** around the corner on Neal Street, which offers reasonable prices and high-quality food. It closes at 8:00 P.M. and on Sundays.

The Thai restaurant **Sri Siam**, on Old Compton Street in

Soho (Tel: 434-3544), is recognized by the Vegetarian Society. The **Dining Room** is a basement restaurant offering organic food with wine. Frequently changing dishes are written up on a blackboard. Located next to Southwark Cathedral on the corner of Cathedral Street (entrance on Winchester Walk) on the south side of London Bridge, it is open for lunch and until 10:00 P.M. in the evening (closed on Mondays and weekends). Tel: 407-0337.

London's oldest vegetarian restaurant is on Primrose Hill in North London. **Manna,** 4 Erskine Road, offers huge portions of home cooking to devout locals as well as intrepid visitors. Tel: 722-8028. Walkable from the Chalk Farm tube station.

FAMILIES

Most London restaurants don't take kindly to young children, but the few that do are worth knowing about. Apart from pizza places (Pizza Huts are possibly the best; they have high chairs and give kids coloring sheets and crayons) and the coffee shops in the smarter hotels, the following are worth considering:

TGI Friday's (Thank God It's), on Covent Garden's Bedford Street, is a noisy, fun place that specializes in pizzas, burgers, and "cocktails" for children—as well as the real thing for adults. Under-12s qualify for a very cheap menu before 7:00 P.M. Balloons on weekends. Tel: 379-0585.

There are two branches of **Smollensky's Balloon**, one in the Strand (Tel: 497-2101) that has a play area for children seven or under; the other, smaller, on Dover Street (Tel: 491-1199), up the road from the Ritz Hotel. Both are best for children on weekends (especially Sundays), when the balloons are at the ready and clowns and entertainers work the tables.

Just south of the John Lewis store on Oxford Street is the **Chicago Pizza Pie Factory** in Hanover Square, a good place to rest with youngsters if you're mid-shopping, though they don't put on anything special. Or try the **Chicago Meat Packers** (near Foyles Bookshop), 96 Charing Cross Road, which offers a children's menu until 8:00 P.M., as well as a model railway. Magicians do their tricks on Sundays at lunchtime. Tel: 379-3277.

OUTER LONDON:
THE NORTHERN SUBURBS

Camden Town

Camden Town is a bustling cosmopolitan area with lots of Greek restaurants (try **Nontas** on High Street, Tel: 387-4579, or **Daphne's** on Bayham Street, almost behind it, Tel: 267-7322) and several brasseries. Among the best of the latter is the **Café Delancy**, on the street of the same name near Camden Lock, a simple French café with bare floorboards and a noisy, smoky atmosphere. Good for breakfast, snacks, and meeting people, especially staff from the nearby TV AM studios. Tel: 387-1985.

Hampstead

Hampstead has many restaurants but few good ones. Among the best is the rather formal **Keats**, at the High Street end of Downshire Hill (one of Hampstead's most prestigious residential streets, around the corner from Keats's house). The contrived, library-like atmosphere demands whispered conversations, but the largely French dishes are imaginative and well executed. Tel: 435-3544.

Less formal is **Le Carapace**, up the hill on Heath Street (near Whitestone Pond), where they serve an enormous basket of crudités (hard-boiled eggs and artichokes among them) with peasant bread and garlic mayonnaise. Charcoal grills are the specialty, as are huge individual *tartes* for dessert. There is an open fire in winter, a few tables outside in summer, and a nonsmoking area. In addition, the set menus are a good value. Tel: 435-8000. Next to the post office you'll find **Zen W 3**, the designer Chinese restaurant (and sister of the two Zens in town). Water cascades down the bannister, and the large floor-to-ceiling windows overlook the bustle of High Street. Tel: 794-7863.

Islington

Camden Passage browsers (antiques) and City business-people frequent **Frederick's**, a much-loved, though somewhat inconsistent, French conservatory-style restaurant of long standing. Vegetarian dishes. Tel: 359-2888.

OUTER LONDON:
SOUTH OF THE RIVER

Some restaurants south of the river can be quite difficult to get to. Those listed below are well worth the effort.

Wandsworth

Harvey's, 2 Bellevue Road, is one of the very best restaurants in London, and its location, some miles from the center of town among a small parade of shops opposite Wandsworth Common, is no obstacle to serious food lovers. Marco Pierre White is an inspired cook, his bright street-level dining room an attractive blend of pastels. Each dish is a masterwork of creativity (some have up to 25 different components) to be savored slowly. Harvey's also offers set menus, and lunch, in particular, is an exceptional value. Closed Sundays and Mondays; Tel: 672-0114.

Battersea

The atmosphere at **L'Arlequin**, 123 Queenstown Road, just over Chelsea Bridge, is serious but understated; Christian Delteil, the chef/owner, has little time for pretension. Mme. Delteil looks after the restaurant's patrons, many of whom are journalists from *The Observer,* just up the road. Again the set lunch menu is reasonably priced, but evening meals are expensive. The restaurant is on the 137 bus route from Knightsbridge. Closed weekends; Tel: 622-0555.

Cavalier's, two doors up the road at 129 Queenstown Road, is well lit and spacious. Young David Cavalier keeps a watchful eye on his neighbor, but the food, which tends toward the modern British, is altogether different. Cavalier pays enormous attention to detail and likes to impress with three-dimensional dishes that stand up on the plate. Very reasonable lunch menu, and cheaper in the evening than L'Arlequin. Closed Sundays and Mondays; Tel: 720-6960.

Kew

Very near the famous gardens at Kew (and useful as a stopover en route for Heathrow) is **Chez Max**, 291 Sandycombe Road, Kew (Tel: 081-940-3590). Owned by two brothers, it is a somewhat cramped and noisy (read classic) French bistro serving excellent fresh bourgeois food (*poulet de bresse,* homemade terrines, French oysters). Large Art Deco windows open onto the street, and the decor is period 1920s and 1930s. Don't dress up. Closed Mondays.

INFORMATION

The Restaurant Switchboard (sponsored by London restaurants), Tel: (081) 888-8080, offers advice and suggestions, and can even be used to make reservations.

The Good Food Guide (edited by Tom Jaine) is the British foodies' bible, with restaurants recommended by its readers.

The Vegetarian Good Food Guide is an offshoot of *The Good Food Guide* (both are available in bookshops).

RESTAURANTS BY GEOGRAPHICAL AREA

Bloomsbury
Museum Street Café (Brasseries and Cafés)

Chelsea
Bibendum (Eclectic)
The Conrad (Hotel Restaurants)
La Croisette (Fish)
La Famiglia (Italian)
La Tante Claire (French)
San Martino (Italian)

The City and the East End
Bloom's (Eastern European)
Ginnan (Japanese)
Greenhouse (Fish)
Miyama (Japanese)

Covent Garden Area
Beoty's (Greek)
Bertorelli's (Italian)
Le Boulestin (French; Early and Late)
Café Flo (Brasseries and Cafés)
Café du Jardin (Early and Late)
Café Pelican (Early and Late)
Cranks (Vegetarian)
Fields (Early and Late)
Food for Thought (Vegetarian)
The Ivy (Eclectic)
Joe Allen's (American)
Magno's (Early and Late)
Neal's Yard Bakery (Vegetarian)
Orso (Italian; Early and Late)

River Restaurant (English)
Rules (English; Early and Late)
The Savoy Grill (English; Hotel Restaurants; Early
    and Late)
Simpson's-in-the-Strand (English)
Smollensky's Balloon (Families)
TGI Friday's (Families)
Upstairs at the Savoy (Early and Late)

Fulham/Hammersmith
Blue Elephant (Thai)
River Cafe (Italian)
Tall Orders (Brasseries and Cafés)

North and West of Hyde Park
Cibo (Italian)
Kalamaras (Greek)
Kingfisher (Hotel Restaurants)
Leith's (English; Vegetarian)
Manna (Vegetarian)
Stephen Bull (English; Eclectic)

Kensington
Bistrot 190 (Eclectic; Early and Late)
Bombay Brasserie (Indian)
Boucha's (English)
Cafe Kensington (Eclectic)
Clarke's (Eclectic)
Hilaire's (Eclectic)
Joe's Café (Brasseries and Cafés)
Kensington Place (Brasseries and Cafés; Early and
    Late)
Launceston Place (English)
New Serpentine Restaurant (Brasseries and Cafés)
One Ninety Queen's Gate (Eclectic)
Le Quai St. Pierre (Fish)
Le Suquet (Fish)

Knightsbridge
Capital (Hotel Restaurants)
Chelsea Room (Hotel Restaurants)
Columbus (American)
Emporio Armani Express (Brasseries and Cafés)
The English Garden (English)
The English House (English)
Grill St. Quentin (French)
Maroush (Middle Eastern)
Maroush II (Middle Eastern)

Maroush III (Middle Eastern)
Park Room (Hotel Restaurants)
Pizza Express (Italian)
The Rib Room (Hotel Restaurants)
St. Quentin (French)
San Lorenzo (Italian)
San Martino (Italian)
Waltons (English)
Zen (Chinese)
Zuma (American)

Mayfair and St. James's
Al Hamra (Middle Eastern)
Brown's (Early and Late)
Le Caprice (Brasseries and Cafés; Early and Late)
The Causerie (Hotel Restaurants; Early and Late)
Claridge's (Hotel Restaurants)
Connaught Hotel (English; Hotel Restaurants)
Fortnum & Mason's Fountain Restaurant
    (Brasseries and Cafés)
Four Seasons (Hotel Restaurants)
Le Gavroche (French)
The Greenhouse (English)
Green's Restaurant and Oyster Bar (English; Fish;
    Early and Late)
Grill Room (Hotel Restaurants)
Hard Rock Café (American)
Langan's Brasserie (Brasseries and Cafés)
Miyama (Japanese)
Ninety Park Lane (Hotel Restaurants)
The Oak Room (Hotel Restaurants)
One Two Three (Japanese)
Polo Room (Hotel Restaurants)
Ritz Hotel (Hotel Restaurants)
Smollensky's Balloon (Families)
Le Soufflé (Hotel Restaurants)
Suntory (Japanese)
Terrace (Hotel Restaurants)
The Terrace Garden (Hotel Restaurants; Early and
    Late)
Wiltons (Fish)
Zen Central (Chinese)

Soho
Alastair Little's (Eclectic; Early and Late)
Anemos (Greek)
Bahn Thai (Thai)

La Bastide (French)
Burt's (Vegetarian; Early and Late)
Chez Nico (French)
Chiang Mai (Thai)
Chicago Meat Packers (Families)
Chicago Pizza Pie Factory (Families)
Chuen Cheng Ku (Chinese)
Ed's Easy Diner (American)
The English Garden (English)
Frith's (Vegetarian)
Fung Shing (Chinese)
Gay Hussar (Eastern European)
Good Food (Chinese)
Ikkyu (Japanese)
Jamdani (Indian)
Kettners (Italian)
Lal Qila (Indian)
The Last Days of the Raj (Indian)
The Limelight (Early and Late)
The Lindsay House (English)
Manzi's (Fish; Early and Late)
New World (Chinese)
Pizza Express (Italian)
Poons (Chinese)
Red Fort (Indian)
Rock Island Diner (American)
Soho Brasserie (Brasseries and Cafés)
Sri Siam (Thai)
Sutherlands (Eclectic; Early and Late)
Tall Orders in Soho (Eclectic)
White Tower (Greek)
Wong Kei (Chinese)
Yung's (Chinese)

South of the Thames

L'Arlequin (Battersea)
The Blueprint Café (Brasseries and Cafés)
Cavalier's (Battersea)
Chez Max (Kew)
The Dining Room (Vegetarian)
Harvey's (Wandsworth)
La Petite Auberge de St. Savin (French)
RSJ (Early and Late)

Near Victoria Station

Auberge de Provence (Hotel Restaurants)
Green's (English; Fish)

The Halkin (Hotel Restaurants)
L'Incontro (Italian)
Ken Lo's Memories of China (Chinese)
Le Mazarin (French)
Santini (Italian)
Tate Gallery restaurant (English)
Very Simply Nico (French)

Outer London (North)
Café Delancy (Camden Town)
Le Carapace (Hampstead)
Daphne's (Camden Town)
Frederick's (Islington)
Keats (Hampstead)
Nontas (Camden Town)

PUBS, NIGHTLIFE, AND ENTER-TAINMENT

By Alex Hamilton

Alex Hamilton is the author of seven works of fiction—and a travel book on the Trans-Siberian railway. He is a winner of the Fitzgerald Award for travel writing, and is Travel Editor of the British national daily, The Guardian.

PUBS AND BARS

PUBS

Publicans, who may be addressed as "landlord" or, sometimes, "guv'nor" (but not often "friend," without giving offense), know a lot about beer, rather less about spirits, and hardly anything about wine. This probably reflects the amounts they sell of each. Distillers and winegrowers do not own pubs, but brewers do, with a consequent overwhelming influence on their stock, their appearance, and their staff. At least, brewers own the majority; pubs are known as "tied houses" when they principally sell beers from the brewer that owns them. The rest, which offer a fine miscellany, are known as "free houses." However officious a brewer may be, though, it is the personality and style of the publican—himself or herself—that make the vital difference. Though publicans are bound to observe the laws that protect the consumer and maintain the peace, they have one important freedom: They can bar whomever they wish, and without giving a reason.

Another, more recently acquired freedom—by no means universally popular—allows them to decide their own open hours, which must fall between 11:00 A.M. and 11:00 P.M. After a period of experimentation and uncertainty, the practical effect of this liberation is that most pubs feel obligated by their competition to stay open all that time, and the nonstop drinker can seem as much a fixture as the sign warning minors (under 18) off alcohol. The ritual shouts of "Last orders!" and "Time, gentlemen please—your glasses!" often emphasized by a ship's bell or a barking dog, with a 15-minute allowance of "drinking-up time," are still followed by "chucking-out time," which in rougher neighborhoods is not the most sensible moment to be sauntering along the sidewalks.

To read the catering trade weekly *The Morning Advertiser* on a Monday is to feel the whole pub network is under imminent threat of collapse. There are columns of vacant tenancies and pubs for sale. Stiff increases in rents and taxes and the many other entertainment options that have been created for a more affluent society have been a severe test. But some purging was needed; too many pubs were slovenly and dispiriting. And not to worry: There are still between 5,000 and 6,000 serving London. Their durability can be graphically demonstrated in the colossal development of the old Docklands area, where, in a great wasteland of demolition, dozens of pubs have been left as coping stones waiting for a new community to grow up around them.

Many old pubs have quaint names. The Ferret & Firkin, The Frog & Nightgown, and The Dog & Overdraft are journalistic fictions, but The Bag of Nails (derived from Bacchanales) and The Elephant & Castle (from Infanta of Castile) are real, and there are four called The Pig and Whistle. Indeed, the visitor should be aware that some popular pub names are adopted many times over. In London there are 25 pubs called The King's Head and 12 called The Queen's Head; there are 22 Railway Taverns; the ancient emblem of spring, The Green Man, is used 19 times, as is The George. The Coach and Horses, The

Crown, The Rising Sun, The Red Lion, and The Blue Posts
are each to be found in all sorts of incarnations, so in
asking directions or instructing a taxi it is wise not only to
give the name of the pub but also to specify the street.

It goes without saying that the discovery of London pubs
is an intoxicating experience, but it is also important to add
that the drinking-and-driving laws are now being enforced
with much greater severity, with the result that some patrons have shifted to low- and non-alcohol beers and
lagers (such as Swan Light and Kaliber). All pubs sell a
range of bottled beers, lagers, and stouts, chilled and of
varying strength. At the upper end are such as Worthington
White Shield, an unstable beer with a sediment that the
barman may leave you to pour for yourself; Gold Label;
Export Special; and what the Scots call "wee heavies," a
concentrated barley product. The most common foreign
beers are Danish Carlsberg lagers, the Australian Fosters,
and the American Budweiser. The quality of draft beers,
pumped from the cellar, has been saved by CAMRA, the
Campaign for Real Ale.

Draft beers are usually labeled on the pump handles,
including Irish Guinness and dry cider, and are ordered
in measures of pints and half pints. If you want a glass
with a handle, ask for your beer "in a jug" or "with a
handle." There are still a few pubs, though not in the
center of London, where habitués keep their own tan-
kards hanging on nails. As a very rough benchmark, £1.50
will buy a pint of bitter.

The earnest student of beer with a long swallow can
repair to **The Sun,** northwest of Gray's Inn and opposite
the children's hospital on Great Ormond Street in Holborn, which has the largest selection of cask-conditioned
ales in the world: 187 at last count (not, obviously, all on
tap simultaneously), with oddities such as Oy Vay, weiss-
bier (a grain), Merrie Monk, and Old Scrap Cyder. (An
early-evening tour of the 1688 cellar can be arranged by
calling the landlord; Tel: 405-8728.)

Pubs change, if slowly. Two very fine summers have
prompted tables and chairs to appear on the sidewalks,
Continental style. The big difference in London is the
disappearance in many pubs of the old divisions between
the plush saloon bar and the more basic and lower-
priced public bar. The printed notices you will see warning workmen not to come in with dirty boots and overalls
are an indication both of gentrification and of the amount
of construction work going on in London these days. But,

rejigged, upholstered, and smartened as many pubs may be, they adhere to the traditions of dark wood and paneling, heavy furniture, brass rails, and overcrowded gantries (shelves holding casks). The bric-a-brac that festoons the walls is reminiscent of the clutter of Victorian households: sporting prints, old advertisements, bellows and warming pans, pictures of thespians and royals, theater bills, cigarette cards, painted plates, Toby jugs, horse brasses, heavy double entendres burnt in wood, tea caddies, artificial flowers—the Rabelaisian profusion is a cleaner's nightmare, all reflected back through the smoke by huge etched mirrors.

In the current brewers' dispensation, the carpets are patterned and fitted, the lighting either dim or harsh, the toilets basic, the heating from gas-fired imitation coal grates, the cigarettes from vending machines, the Muzak from speakers, and the food from a lunch counter. That food tends to be starchy and filling, an unconscionable volume of pies, sausage and mash, steak and kidney, Cornish pasties, chips and beans, baked potatoes, cold meat and salads, and none of it expensive: £3.50's worth will anchor you to the seat.

All this is the norm. The pubs below score a notch or two higher.

Central London

By Central London we mean Soho, the West End, and Marylebone.

Just as time begins for the British at Greenwich, so distances are measured from Trafalgar Square. Appropriately, one of the pubs against which others measure themselves can be found at one of its corners, where St. Martin's Lane leaves it, a dart's throw from the statue of poor Edith Cavell. This is **The Chandos**—spacious, good beer, quick service, and a slightly more dashing menu than most that includes such items as beef olives, steak-and-pepper pie, and smoked mackerel. The pub is very much a meeting place, with six ground-floor cubicles, like little chapels with their stained-glass windows looking out onto the square, and the Opera Lounge upstairs (the English National Opera is housed a few doors up the road) with its deep leather armchairs and blessed freedom from Muzak.

Farther up St. Martin's Lane, past an eclectic shopping alley called **Cecil Court** (which travellers should note as the collectors' hub for original Baedeker guides, as well as for old prints, out-of-print books on music, collect-ibles, and golf, and more), are two unusual places. **The Green Man & French Horn** is very long and narrow, like a cul-de-sac with a ceiling, the result of joining two pubs together. Victorian prints on the walls here illustrate the gloomy story of the decline of a drunkard and his family. Opposite, **The Salisbury** is much more ample, an island bar set in an ocean of Rococo decoration and kitsch. The food is good, though the prices are a bit above average.

Among the plethora of pubs around Piccadilly Circus and the great shopping arteries nearby (the electronics stores of Tottenham Court Road, the rag trade and shoe leather stores of Oxford Street, and the travel, fashion, ceramics, and silver emporia of Regent Street) it is hard to finger many of real distinction. But there are a few shining exceptions. On Beak Street, on the Soho (east) side of Regent Street, **The Old Coffee House**, with its burnished brass and copper fittings, comfortable furni-ture, and crimson carpet, offers a relaxed ethos and an amiable staff serving a wide range of bottled and hand-pumped beers. By contrast, **The John Snow**, farther into Soho, has substituted varnish for its former lugubrious charm and is now a pathetic memorial to the great Victo-rian who discovered the source of cholera in the then-contaminated water conduits of Broadwick Street. Like-wise, **The Blue Posts** on Ganton Street suffers from the bane of tied houses: inattentive barmen.

Carnaby Street, that magnesium flare of the Swinging Sixties, offers **The Shakespeare's Head** at the corner of Great Marlborough Street, with wooden floors, good hot food, and an upstairs restaurant, but otherwise nothing to write home about. In Soho, choose **The Dog & Duck** on Bateman Street (a small street between Dean and Greek streets). Go not for the food but for the company of the flotsam and jetsam of bohemian society, a pleasant con-trast to the monogrammed gear of the staff. Small and rowdy, it has an upstairs snug (a small private room) with saucy cartoons and postcards and cozy casement tables from which to look down on the street action. **The French House** on Dean Street, with a somewhat raffish clientele and a staff that knows more about wine than most, has a reputation that dates from World War II, when it was the off-duty rendezvous of the Free French Army in Britain.

If you penetrate the hinterland north of Oxford Street into Marylebone, you will see an odd and exclusively summer phenomenon of recent times in the complex of streets beyond Selfridge's department store—great swarms of yuppies, men and women alike in uniform charcoal-gray suits, gathered like colonies of seals outside such places as **The Lamb & Flag** on the corner of James and Barrett streets.

But the year-round special in Marylebone is **The Prince Regent** on Marylebone High Street. The portrait of the prince himself is a complete fantasy, not the corpulent Prinny we think of but a handsome Young Lochinvar. The pub has a strong miscellany of regulars, drinking under cartoons, prints, and its celebrated collection of cheese plates. On the bar, many now-deceased regulars from the 1890s onward are commemorated with small brass plaques, and one who is still alive, Jimmy Green, has presented the establishment with a box now waiting on a high shelf to receive his ashes when Bacchus calls the final "Time, gentlemen please!" on him.

In cobbled Weymouth Mews, west of and parallel to Portland Place, you'll find one of the oldest pubs in London, **The Dover Castle**, a former coaching inn on the first stage from the City en route to Oxford. The current landlord has a dog called Tess that will fetch beer mats thrown for her like a gun dog bringing back partridge. The lounge and pleasant back room of this free house are crowded at lunch and in the early evening with media, design, and advertising people.

East of Tottenham Court Road and across Gower Street, **The Museum Tavern** stands opposite the British Museum on Great Russell Street. With so many scholars and literati restoring their parched gray cells here, plus the pub's eccentric practice of serving afternoon tea, it is not surprising that a neighboring publisher has issued a book on its history, which dates from 1723. Ceiling fans turn above the tables, and there are waitresses, professional bartenders, a well-stocked cellar (although prices are on the high side), and a generally good-natured crowd.

Heading north and east across Southampton Row, stop for a quick one at **The Queen's Larder** in the Cosmo Street alley leading into Queen Square (there are hospitals of all sorts in this area and therefore doctors and nurses, too) on the way to the always fashionable **Lamb** on Lamb's Conduit Street, where you'll find hospital people at midday and theater people at night. Brass rails around the tables stop the drinks from falling off, and the strange old pivoting panels at the bar were apparently installed to prevent the staff from hearing private conversations. An even rarer feature is a nonsmokers' cubbyhole. On the walls hang rows of faded pictures of theatrical divinities alongside Hogarth prints and *Vanity Fair* cartoons. Modern cartoons, including originals of some recently printed, can be bought opposite in **The Cartoon Gallery**, unique in Britain, and founded and run by the veteran cartoonist Mel Calman.

The City

A jungle by day, a desert by night, the City has always had different hours and rules for its pubs—and its own police force to see them observed. The tendency is to close by 8:00 P.M., and not to open at all on weekends. Still, the old, heavy-beamed pubs like **Olde Wine Shades** on Martin Lane (near the junction of Cannon and King William streets) and **Ye Olde Mitre** in Ely Place off Holborn Circus do a brisk enough business with the stockbrokers, financiers, and conveyancers (real estate lawyers) to compensate for the shorter hours. The beer fancier curious to know what happens when a pub brews its own stuff can try **The Market Porter** on Stoney Street, south of the Thames across London Bridge and off Borough High Street.

The name of the latter suggests the great wholesale food markets that once pulsed within the City precincts and provided special indulgences for thirsty early-morning traders. The last significant example of these markets, still operating on its original site, is the Central Meat Market, which has stood at Smithfield since the tenth century. The license to operate from 5:30 A.M. is still exercised by some pubs here; two in particular are recommended for their lively, humorous trader talk and hearty breakfasts with ale. The first, **The Cock Tavern**, is in a basement down steps from the second archway; the other, **The Fox & Anchor**, is adjacent to the entry to serene Charterhouse Square. Market porters critical of the beef served in cafés on Smithfield sometimes bring in their own steak to fry, but that isn't necessary in The Fox & Anchor. One of the historical curiosities of Smithfield is **The Castle** on Cowcross Street, where King William IV, pressed for cash, called in and left his watch as a pledge for a loan, later granting the pub a pawnbroker's license in perpetuity.

The southern neighbors of Smithfield are St. Bartholomew, London's busiest hospital, and the Old Bailey, the central criminal court. Opposite Bart's is **The White Hart**, a serviceable and friendly establishment; opposite The Bailey formerly stood **The Magpie & Stump**, a ferment of gossip and good low-life stories spun by a clientele composed largely of lawyers and journalists. Dissolved in redevelopment for three years, an embryonic new version is now in place and scheduled to open in 1991. Pending completion, some of its trade has been taken by **The Viaduct**, a free house. Police signs about handbags and thieves may explain the disagreeably harsh light here.

A find north of Smithfield is **The Crown**, a 17th-century inn on a small, attractive square called Clerkenwell Close. The square's great feature is the Marx Memorial Library, a storehouse of Socialist literature, from seething tracts and compassionate novels to stolid economic analyses, assembled to honor the author of *Das Kapital,* who labored on his seminal work at the British Library. Apparently apolitical, the pub nevertheless still separates the plusher saloon area from the public bar; it also has a back-room restaurant and an upstairs room where one-act plays today carry on the tradition of evening entertainment that once took the form of music-hall performances.

Chelsea

The pub crawl, an increasingly meandering walk punctuated by pints at a succession of pubs favored mainly by younger men, has a nearly perfect track in King's Road, where, between the Royal Court Theater on Sloane Square and the S-bend of The World's End, no fewer than 12 pubs await the crawler, not to mention several in adjacent streets, including **The Queen's Head** on Tryon Street, which has long attracted a gay clientele, and **The Front Page** on Old Church Street, perversely renamed after having been The Black Lion for 300 years (the same brewing company has renamed Whitechapel's Red Anchor, on Cameran Place, **The Sporting Page**).

Just around the corner from the Queen's Head on the main drag itself is **The Markham Arms**, a famous rendezvous for socialites during the 1960s. It still has a name, but some of its feel is gone, and the section of old photos labeled "Memory Lane" has the pathos of a lost estate. **The Chelsea Potter**, another great source for the gossip columnists, has held up better. Its very young clientele chatters like starlings, though the pub is so dark it looks closed from the outside even when it's not.

The Six Bells by the Town Hall (between Sloane Square and the King's Road) has been renamed **Henry J. Bean's**

("But his friends all call him Hank") and transformed into a cocktail zoo with heavy-metal sounds, fast food, and fancy drinks. The hundreds of customers in this grand old barn average age 19, but the big garden in the rear remains a great romantic asset. At **The Cadogan Arms** on the corner of Old Church Street you'll find another young and lively but less frantic crowd, a jeans-and-sweater bunch swarming over its split levels. From here on west the pubs have lately taken to offering breakfast from 9:00 A.M. and sometimes earlier—the full-scale bacon, eggs, sausage, tomato, toast, and marmalade meal. **The Man in the Moon**, at the corner of Church Walk, is a free house with heavy maroon drapes, caramel-colored lighting, throbbing music, and its own theater club upstairs (see Fringe Theater, below). Then, at the S-bend at the end of King's Road, comes a cluster: upholstered leather seating and Denise's Kitchen serving bubble and squeak and turkey-and-corn pie in **The Water Rat**; a bar-and-billiards saloon downstairs and early breakfasts in **The Magpie & Stump**; the impersonal modern brick of The Riley Arms (enough said); and, finally, the harshly lit saloon, high ceilings, and slot machines of The World's End Distillery. Its name is the best thing about it, and, indeed, you may as well make The Man in the Moon the last drink on the route; anyway, eight pints are a skinful. (But there are other attractive Chelsea pubs; see especially Dinner on the River, below.)

North of Hyde Park

This area covers the Paddington, Bayswater, Notting Hill, and Holland Park districts.

The visitor who on a fine day saunters about the great expanse of Hyde Park, watching the antics of the sunbathers and swimmers around the Serpentine Lido, dropping in on its art gallery, admiring the style of the wealthy horse riders along Rotten Row, and enjoying all those little dramatic cameos of the human comedy that evolve in a large green and public open space, may find himself or herself, as the sun sets, having walked much farther than seemed possible and feeling as dry as a newt in a curtain rod. It may then come as something of a shock to leave the park at, say, Lancaster Gate on the northern side, and realize that very little has been provided to refuel the poor human creature or let it put up its feet. In these circumstances, then, it is imperative not to stand on ceremony; one must be grateful for the discovery of any kind of hostelry, regardless of quality.

There stands—as it has for 200 years—on the Bayswater Road, which skirts the northern edge of the park, **The Swan on "the Water"** (the phrase has been used for decades by those who sink or swim in this melting pot of a district). Were it not for its longevity, seeing the pub pulsing with polyglot sing-alongs led by a sweating pianist you might say the Swan had been built solely for tourists.

Sharing the Swan's virtue of selling drink in an area that seems to favor weathered hotels that sport their stars and crowns and credit-card affiliations like campaign ribbons is **The Leinster**, reached by turning off "the Water" opposite Lancaster Gate into Leinster Terrace. (Before 5:30 P.M. the would-be drinker with the extra handicap of children can dump them around the corner on Craven Hill at the **Toy and Model Museum**.)

The situation eases somewhat in the bizarre hinterland of Bayswater and Paddington, though you are often liable to come across whole tracts where seemingly no brewer has ever been granted a visa. What is odd about this stretch west of the Edgware Road (the great artery that runs north out of London from Marble Arch and the Speakers' Corner of Hyde Park) is its residential mixture, sedate and even grand apartment terraces giving way to a hotel and bed-sitter land of long- and short-stay visitors, and of every conceivable provenance. With a few exceptions, pubs rarely thrive either in areas dominated by the very rich or, naturally, where most of the business is immigrant, and the housing here is largely occupied by people with Muslim, Hindu, or Chinese backgrounds. Together with African, Caribbean, and Asian presences, each having its own sphere of influence as you proceed west through Paddington, Bayswater, and Notting Hill, the variety of trading interests provides surprising juxtapositions, and the conventional British pub often appears to be the odd one out.

Typical of the busiest thoroughfares is **Queensway**, running north from Black Lion Gate out of Kensington Gardens, the western extension of Hyde Park, and connecting with another vital street, **Westbourne Grove**. On Queensway, where the first coin-operated launderette in Europe (1949) spins the wash among tax-free stores and pizzerias, and an exotic cocktail bar offers the "Mega

Fishbowl for four persons" near a shop specializing in videocassettes for Arabs, can be found the **Texas Lone Star Saloon**, a sort of honky-tonk 5,000 miles from home, and **The Prince Alfred**, unkempt and disheveled among the apartment-finding agencies, and flaunting its loaded ashtrays and cigarette-burned carpets cheek by jowl with Marco Polo's "Mongolian barbecue." At the junction of Queensway and Westbourne Grove, **The Redan**, commemorating the fall of Sebastopol to the British in 1855, is marginally better. Around the corner, the ebony frontage of Piers *looks* promising, but the interior, decorated with tired fake vegetables, is less than enchanting. Nevertheless, for the student of the British pub, these enduring places are important. The landlord may be as neurasthenic as Oblomov, his staff a band of terrorists *manqué,* the clientele as detached and motionless as if they were on opium, not beer, but in each case the pub is for some Londoners "the local," a comfort as deep as Mother.

And so, buoyed by this consideration, plod in a curve into the prosperous crescent of Pembridge Villas until, on the corner of Portobello Road, **The Sun in Splendour** rises into view—aptly named in the circumstances. In 1967 it was the *London Standard's* "Pub of the Year" and now, as a "vintage pub" with a beer garden, a Saturday barbecue, and a list of wines posted, the flavor of a Mayfair saloon still hangs about its pale green furnishings. With mindless music plonking out of its music machine, and a barmaid who has never heard of the label you call for, it will do—but no more than that—as a port of embarcation for the Portobello Road.

On that celebrated stretch of antiques merchants there is a pub on practically every corner, presumably as a restorative after strenuous discussion with an antiques dealer. **Portobello Gold**, facing Denbigh Terrace, is a hybrid of restaurant and pub, with a good selection of beers. The main recommendation for **The Earl of Lonsdale**, at Westbourne Grove, is its game room with bar billiards, while for those who really fancy the game in a genuinely scratched and dilapidated pub, **The Warwick Castle** on the corner of Westbourne Park Road is the place.

On the corner of Talbot Road, opposite Marc Saint's famous tattooing studio, is a very distinctive pub, plain as a canteen but with jazz every Saturday night, a Courage pub apparently without a name at the moment. The pleasantest of the Portobello Road pubs may be the paneled

and partitioned **Wellington** on the corner of Elgin Crescent (one of the Finch's chain, which in London generally
can be relied on for both the beer and some character).
But the one that tends to attract the business is **The
Market Trader** on the corner of Lancaster Road, despite
its unprepossessing exterior with rusted nameplate and
two Pan figures protruding like gargoyles from the outer
wall. Inside, iron-backed chairs stand on a wooden floor,
with illumination from a row of huge candlesticks on the
bar that have shed their wax until they look like mops.
Here you will find good beer and interesting company.

Leaving the markets behind again, and heading for the
Notting Hill Gate Underground station via Ladbroke Grove
and Holland Park Avenue, keep an eye out at the junction
of those two for a great sprawl of a place on two levels
called **The Raj**—big enough indeed to have prompted the
management to set up internal signposts pointing the way
to the food. A thoughtful addition is the bar stool in the rest
room.

By the Notting Hill hub itself there is **The Old Swan**, a
bit hearty with its photographs of "Old Swan Pissheads"
and the like; for something a little more genteel try **The
Macaulay Arms**, a short distance down Kensington
Church Street, or, a little farther on at the corner of
Campden Street, **The Churchill Arms**. The relationship of
both to the great men whose names they bear is minimal,
though Macaulay did live and work in the area, and
Mellor & Baxter, antiquarian booksellers, do display
Churchill's history of the Second World War in the window. As for the rest, under the aegis of Churchill there is
excellent East Asian cuisine with a Thai chef in the pub. In
the Macaulay Arms there are open bookshelves for patrons, full of works by authors whose main impact was
made over half a century ago, including John Buchan,
Michael Arlen, Van Loon, and A.E.W. Mason. The literary
aspirations of this comfortable lounge are emphasized by
a sententious quote from Mark Twain that hangs over the
bar: "What marriage is to morality a properly conducted
liquor traffic is to sobriety." What can he have meant?

WINE BARS

The closer association of Britain with Continental Europe
has not yet, from the wine drinker's point of view, had any
very noticeable effect on prices here, but the reductions
must surely come when the Common Market drops trade
barriers on New Year's Day, 1993. Knowledge and appre-

ciation of wines and places dedicated to their drinking have already improved, resulting in an increase in the number of wine bars, which have been taking some of the trade from the pubs.

The expansion has had two styles: The older is the *masculine* manner, leaning heavily on tradition and characterized by oak beams and rampart-like counters, clumsy, comfortable furniture—big casks often standing in for tables—a sprinkling of sawdust on the stone floors, a full-dress battalion of high-quality Champagnes such as Veuve Clicquot, and cumulus clouds of cigar smoke. Many of the best examples are to be found among the 40 owned by Davys, as well as among the chain run by Balls Brothers. There is, not surprisingly, a strong concentration in the City, among which **The Bottlescrue** in Bath House on High Holborn, **The Pulpit** on Worship Street (north of Liverpool Street Station), and **The Boot and Flogger** on Redcross Way (across London Bridge in Southwark) will wrap you in a dark and dignified ethos suitable to conversation about the bottom line.

The ancestor of them all is **Olde Wine Shades**, Martin Lane off Cannon Street, which opened in 1663 and was the only such establishment to survive the Great Fire three years later. Its owners have another, even more celebrated, place, **El Vino's**, on Fleet Street, which proffers a similar choice of fine wines, Ports, and Sherries drawn from a great parade of casks. Although the national newspapers are now scattered away from Fleet Street, something of the former mood persists, with old fire-brigade journalists reminiscing about the good old days. The rule here barring women has been abrogated, but it is still preferred that women sit at a table rather than stand at the bar, and wear skirts rather than trousers. The dress rule for men is particularly strict: In the absence of jacket or tie you will be asked to leave. (A few doors down, opposite the ancient and also vinous **Olde Cheshire Cheese** pub, is a Tie Rack shop.)

An entrepreneurial New Zealander, Don Hewitson, is now making a mark with a slightly lighter version of this style, putting French art posters on the walls, and white cloths on the tables, and offering tasty meals at around £10. His little empire comprises **Shampers**, on Soho's Kingly Street (parallel to Carnaby Street); **The Cork and Bottle**, in a cramped basement on Cranbourn Street off Leicester Square; and the much ampler flagship, the award-winning **Methuselah's** on Victoria Street, which is much liked by younger people (and not merely the trendies).

The other style of wine bar, which we will call the *contemporary* style, has had to adapt to designer-fashion currents, merging at the one end with restaurants, like the Soho Brasserie, or at the other with cocktail bars, such as The Long Island Iced Tea Bar on Cranbourn Street, or with tourist-oriented places that have exotic themes, such as the *tapas*-bar whirl of Brahms and Liszt in Covent Garden. Generally they do not serve beer, but instead offer a wide range of wines, among them French, Alsatian, German, Italian, Spanish, and, occasionally, Australian vintages, with prices starting at £6 a bottle and commonplace Champagnes at £17 to £20 a bottle.

There is no such phenomenon in London as the American singles' bar scene, but it is fair to say that some bars, like **Le Cochonnet** in outlying Maida Vale (northwest of Paddington), which has a wine list as long as a telephone directory, are chummier than others. Among a relaxed miscellany that stand out for their individual appeal and amiability are **Morgan's** on Soho's Ganton Street, which offers reasonably priced meals and a barman with both a genuine delight in wine lore and a wish to lead his patrons in the right direction; **Volkers**, handily sited off Trafalgar Square in the Haymarket, and the place to drink pink Champagne from a bottle clamped in a pewter cuirass while sitting at the bar on a copper milk churn filled with Champagne corks; and **The Metro**, by Clapham Common Underground station, a conservatory-style meeting place with a glass roof that is popular with neighborhood cats. The Metro sells no beer, but if one of your party is a beer-drinker and fetches in a crate of the stuff, nobody will mind.

COCKTAIL BARS

American bars and cocktail bars are as close to being synonymous in the British mind as Coke and Pepsi. An excellent choice with discretion and style, where a woman on her own may pause without discomfort, is the bar in **Brown's Hotel**, on Albemarle Street in Mayfair. On the same wavelength, with senior barmen who know what goes into a daiquiri or a Tom Collins, a whiskey sour or a planter's punch, are the nookeries of **Durrant's** on George Street in Marylebone, **The Connaught** on Carlos Place in

Mayfair, and, through a door on an inner courtyard off St. James's Street, **The Stafford** on St. James's Place—all have that pukka (first-class) tone.

The dazzling white counter and Art Deco of the **Savoy Bar** conjures up the spirit of the 1930s, when the creative barman Harry Craddock expanded the cocktail range way beyond the confines of its original definition—a concoction of any spirit with water, sugar, and bitters. The period decor persists, though the menu lacks imagination. Nevertheless, with its Champagne cocktails, sharp old-fashioneds, Moscow mules, and knockouts such as brandy Alexanders and black Russians for nightcaps, the Savoy keeps the faith. Expect to find similar standards prevailing in the **Ritz Bar** and **Claridge's Bar**. And, after a two-year overhaul of the hotel, the **American Bar** in the Dorchester Hotel can this year be expected to return to its former position as a watering hole for visiting celebrities.

The luxurious old favorites just mentioned have their counterparts in new branches of several chain hotels—the Hilton International, by the BBC on Portland Place (which has a fine opportunity in the acquisition of the old Langham Hotel); the Mayfair; and St. George's Hotel, opposite the new Hilton, with a bar on the 15th floor high above the spire of All Souls' Church—but the character of the bars in these newer establishments fluctuates with the changing tides of customers.

A cocktail lounge with a difference is that of **The Bombay Palace**, in a smart residential area on Connaught Street at the corner of Hyde Park Square. The special atmosphere may come from the mixtures of spices that go into the curries, which seem to suffuse the whole ethos.

Curiosities in vogue include the basement-art-gallery effect of **Freud's**, at the High Holborn end of Shaftesbury Avenue, and—a current phenomenon—the bar that suddenly changes its style on the whim of the owner, one example being **Efes II**, formerly The Manhattan, on Great Portland Street north of Oxford Circus. The bar now looks down on a kebab restaurant, but it still serves the cocktail that has lately been mandatory, and after which another busy house, on Cranbourn Street off Leicester Square, has renamed itself: **The Long Island Iced Tea Bar**.

ENTERTAINMENT AND NIGHTLIFE

DISCOS AND LIVE MUSIC

Believe no disco recommendation until you're in. Being admitted to a disco is generally a matter of matching its style and paying its admission price, but in the case of a few, whose attraction for an older set is their exclusivity, introduction by a member is needed and a hefty entrance fee is exacted. Remember, too, that as soon as a place makes it into print, one part of the crowd is ready to say it's history. **Annabel's**, on Berkeley Square, has lasted a few years and is entitled to be called semipermanent. It is notorious for its un-disco-like patrons, entry fee of £25, and annual membership of £500. **Stringfellow's**, on Upper St. Martin's Lane, is another place for the affluent, with a £300–£1,000 annual membership, and nonmembers granted admission at £15 per session.

Coming off this high plateau, the **Café de Paris** on Coventry Street (off Piccadilly Circus) and **The Hippodrome** on Charing Cross Road seem to get the most repeat business, and kind words for their music and pace. **The Hammersmith Palais** has been here forever, opening at least 20 years before Granddad came here to jive during World War II; now restyled, it is a good, modern disco near the Hammersmith Broadway tube station. **The Wag Club** on Soho's Wardour Street attracts a truly young crowd at the leading edge of streetwise.

But while **Gossips** on Dean Street in Soho, **Limelight** on Shaftesbury Avenue, and the cheerfully extroverted **Empire Ballroom** on Leicester Square all have their regulars and deserve them, some of the best disco action is a movable feast, like the crap game immortalized by Damon Runyon. Look for strangely dressed people on line buzzing with anxiety as they try to impress the men at the door with their street smarts and rightness for this evening's session.

Country-and-western music has its own special havens, most often arts centers or pubs like the **King's Head** out at Crouch End (in north London beyond Islington), the **White Horse** in Hampstead, and **The Swan** in Stockwell (south of the river and east of Clapham). Its temple, however, is the old Art Deco **Astoria Theatre** on Charing

Cross Road, where people can also dance on the two floors that once were the stalls and the dress circle.

JAZZ

London is not Copenhagen or Chicago when it comes to jazz. **Ronnie Scott** seems to have propped it up in his club on Soho's Frith Street since almost before the big band became obsolete, distributing the foreign strains through an unrivaled sequence of eminent player-guests (Tel: 439-0747). More recently arrived, but thoroughly established among aficionados for their nightly variety as well as quality, are **The Bass Clef** on Coronet Street, Islington, and the **100 Club** at 100 Oxford Street.

After **Pizza Express** on Dean Street and the **Dover Street Wine Bar**, the dilettante is left clutching at straws of the Sunday-Jazz-Brunch-at-the-Hotel-Russell kind, which must be a contradiction in terms, but farther out there are a couple of good jazz pubs, namely **The Bull's Head** in Barnes and **The Prince of Orange** on the Mile End Road. Some 25 years ago Philip Larkin suggested that as jazz increasingly became a composer's art, it would move from the club to the concert hall, but that transition has not yet been realized in London.

CLUBS, CABARET, AND CASINOS

The term "clubs" covers a multitude of sins and, no doubt, as many virtues. There are three main types, in addition to the residential kind that are run by the social, political, sporting, and artistic networks of the country and are joined only through introductions, and then generally for life, such as The Oxford & Cambridge, The Travellers, White's (Tory politics), The Garrick (publishers and literary intellectuals), and The Caledonian (Scottish regiments).

The first kind of club is of the same caliber as those mentioned above but is open to all, or has reciprocal arrangements with certain clubs overseas, such as The American Club in Piccadilly (Tel: 499-2303) or The Royal Overseas League (Tel: 408-0214) on St. James's Street. The Sloane Club (Tel: 730-9131) on Sloane Street, Knightsbridge, was founded as a ladies-only club but now accepts men as well. Peter de Savary's St. James's Club (Tel: 629-7688) is also unrestricted in its membership, but a night there can be as expensive as a life subscription to many other clubs.

The second kind of club is the nonresidential members' club, often with a restaurant and spacious bar, such as The Groucho Club, a media enclave on Dean Street, and the ad world's rendezvous, The Moscow Club on Frith Street. (If you want to join either of these you must be nominated by a member.)

The third kind usually switches on after nightfall. It may be quite demure, like **The Spanish Garden Club** off Maddox Street west of Regent Street, or somewhat raunchy like **The Pinstripe** on Beak Street, where drinks are served by topless French maids. Women accompanying men into cellar drinking clubs with topless entertainers such as are found in **The Gaslight Club** on Duke of York Street must be prepared for stony stares from the regulars.

Two clubs that depend on old-fashioned "glamour," with cabaret, sophisticated trappings, food and drink, and hostesses (but with an easy welcome for couples), are **Churchill's**, near the Royal Academy in Piccadilly, and **The Director's Lodge** in Mason's Yard off St. James's. Both offer erotic cabaret as a staple, but licensed striptease clubs with pretensions to Continental quality are few. Girls whose bodies seem to have been turned on a lathe show them off on the stage of Raymond's durable **Revuebar** on Brewer Street (a 30-year Festival of Erotica, but, thank goodness, with a changing cast). The same Raymond also runs the adjoining **Madame Jo Jo's**, a campier and more louche venue.

The Clubman's Club on Albemarle Street (Tel: 493-4292) offers membership to selected clubs all over Britain for an annual fee.

Casinos

The style of London gaming houses is quite unlike that found elsewhere. You must apply for membership 48 hours in advance, and the dress code of suit and tie for men is strictly enforced. There is no cabaret and no drinks or tips at the gaming tables. The settings, however, are generally grand, the meals good, and the level of play interesting to international gamblers. The picture cards, so to speak, are **Crockford's** (Tel: 493-7771) and **Aspinall's** (Tel: 629-4400), both on Curzon Street. Less exalted but still decent are **The London Park Tower Casino** (Tel: 235-6161) and the hotel casinos of the Ritz and the Hilton.

There are some 20 casinos in London, and the **British**

Casino Association (Tel: 437-0678) in Leicester House, Leicester Street, will provide callers with venues, rules, and regulations.

DINNER AND DANCING

Ballroom dancing has become more of a sport or a hobby these days than a social accomplishment, but the traditional dance rhythms are still to be heard accompanying diners in the great hotels, particularly at the **Savoy**, the **Ritz**, and the **Park Lane Hilton**. However, there are a number of ethnic restaurants—Greek, Italian, Spanish, Portuguese—with live music and small dance floors where couples who are a little rusty on the steps will not feel shamed by their performance. Among these are **Barbarella 2** (Italian) on Thurloe Street in South Kensington, **Costa Dorada** (Spanish) on Hanway Street in the West End, the **Grecian Taverna & Grill** on Percy Street in the West End, and **Os Aquanos** (Portuguese) on Porchester Road in Bayswater.

DINNER ON THE RIVER

By night, with the reflection of the city's lights on the river, the Thames takes on a different character, and many people like to take a dinner cruise or hitch up to one of the many pubs that give on to the water. The most frequently cruised stretch runs from Greenwich in the east to Kew Gardens in the west, with the departure point most often at Westminster Pier. Which direction the boat travels varies and is generally the decision of the captain of the day. **Catamaran Cruises** sails into (or away from) the sunset every evening except Saturdays (Tel: 839-3572). **Romance of London** operates three-hour cruises on Sundays only (Tel: 620-0474). **Tidal Cruises** offers a disco with supper (Tel: 839-2164).

There is no company as yet that sets passengers down at any of the river pubs; these have to be reached by road. Those that are particularly worth the effort are **The Doves** in West London's Chiswick; **The Samuel Pepys** in an old tea warehouse on Brooks Wharf, Upper Thames Road near Blackfriars Bridge; **The Anchor,** a creaking warren on the south bank of the Thames near Southwark Bridge (resonant with echoes of Dr. Johnson); and the Medieval **George**, off Borough High Street near London Bridge, whose cobbled yard is the set for Morris dancing and Shakespeare plays. (Take the Underground to the London Bridge Station for Brooks Wharf and Bankside.) **The Dick-**

ens Inn on St. Katharine's Dock is a lively and popular place in this burgeoning area.

THEATER

Periodic crises threaten to darken one theater or another as developers encroach or the art houses find their subsidy inadequate even when they are booked solid. Nonetheless, just over 50 commercial playhouses soldier on. **The National Theatre** in the South Bank complex comprises three separate stages; **The Royal Shakespeare Company** performs seasonally in the Barbican complex in the City; and that other stalwart of the classical repertory, **The Old Vic**, lies just south of Waterloo Bridge. The venue for much serious modern work, **The Royal Court**, dominates Sloane Square in Chelsea. In the summer, defying the vagaries of the weather, the **Open-Air Theatre** in Regent's Park mounts a season of Shakespeare. The citadels of popular entertainment are the **Drury Lane Theatre** (musicals) and the **London Palladium** in Soho (celebrity shows).

Newspaper listings are rarely comprehensive enough to satisfy either film buffs or theatergoers. The best service is provided by two weekly magazines: *Time Out* and *What's On* (both published on Wednesdays); these publications also include information on productions at outlying theaters.

The largest ticket-selling organization in Britain, for live events and sporting occasions as well as theater, is the **Keith Prowse** agency, which has many shops as well as booths in large hotels. For half-price tickets (plus booking fee) to same-day performances in West End theaters, apply to the **ticket booth in Leicester Square** between 2:30 P.M. and 6:30 P.M. Turning this idea on its head, a new charity venture with impeccable theatrical sponsorship, **West End Cares**, sells tickets at twice their face value for the best seats in the house at sold-out smash hits (Tel: 976-6751).

Fringe Theater

Innumerable elements make up the lively phenomenon of the London fringe theater: one-act plays, satirical revues, stand-up comedy, bravura solo acts, dramas that passionately argue political causes, expressionistic shows with no discernible argument, a local playwright working the parish pump, and a foreign import in translation for the first time. The fringe is a sprawling network that includes the by-products of established theaters near the middle of town, like **The Theatre Upstairs**, part of the Royal Court Theatre in Chelsea's Sloane Square, as well as very successful venues that, properly speaking, are not in London at all, like **The Warehouse** in Croydon.

Among the many fringe theaters, some of which have a transient, fitful career, half a dozen are worth mentioning. In Islington they are **The King's Head** and **The Old Red Lion**; in Hammersmith, **The Lyric Studio**; in Chelsea, at the opposite end of the King's Road from the Royal Court, **The Man in the Moon**; at Shepherd's Bush Green, **The Bush**; and in Notting Hill, **The Gate**.

This last is particularly loved by the critics for its habit of staging unknown foreign plays, but as a rule fringe managements do not have settled policies of commitment and prefer a varied diet. The fact that many are advertised as clubs is not often a bar to entry. Election to membership generally can be purchased at the door, and the fee—as low as 40 pence in the case of The Man in the Moon—is rarely a serious deterrent. Comfortable seating is not the strong point of such theaters; people like them for more important reasons that include an interest in discovering new talent and enjoying the camaraderie that can develop in their casual atmosphere. One of the most established fringe theaters, with consistently high standards, is **The New End** in Hampstead.

For advance bookings try the **Fringe Box Office** at the Duke of York's Theatre on St. Martin's Lane (Tel: 379-6002).

Children's Theater

Aside from the pre-Christmas season, when the playhouses break out in a rash of pantomimes, not a great deal is done on the London stage for children. However, there are a few specialists who fill their schedules with a range that runs from classics to mixed-media entertainments involving slides, film, modern rap, and music hall. The principal pillars are **The Unicorn Theatre** on Great Newport Street and **The Polka** on the Broadway, Wimbledon. **The Royal Britain Children's Theatre** is on Aldersgate Street in the City. **The Little Angel Marionette Theatre**, on Dagmar Passage off Cross Street in Islington, puts on performances for the very young as well as for older kids, and in the same vein there is the **Puppet Theatre Barge**, moored in Little Venice near Paddington Station. Some public libraries have also taken to putting on children's shows, notably Willesden Green Library.

Children's cinema, incidentally, can be found at the Barbican and the ICA on Pall Mall.

CLASSICAL MUSIC, BALLET, AND OPERA

From cinema to theater to concert hall to opera house, the prices rise in geometric progression, and at the top end patrons can feel pressure to make a commensurately heavy investment in their personal wardrobes. However, neither tickets nor clothes need be too extravagant in the "gods," or highest seats, of the showcase of opera, **The Royal Opera House**, Covent Garden (where demand always exceeds supply). The classic repertoire is sung in translation at the London Coliseum on St. Martin's Lane, home of the **English National Opera**. Both of these regularly include ballet in their schedules, but the heart of the balletomane lies in **Sadler's Wells Theatre**, at the northern end of Rosebery Avenue north of Farringdon Road, a cultural enclave as remote as a desert fort (it can be reached on the number 38 bus from Piccadilly; the nearest Underground stop is Angel).

The principal concert halls are those in the **South Bank Complex**: the Purcell Room, Queen Elizabeth Hall, and the Royal Festival Hall, which overlooks the River Thames. There is also **The Royal Albert Hall** in Kensington (where the annual Promenade Concerts are held) and **The Barbican Arts Centre** in the City. At the same level of intimacy as the Purcell, **Wigmore Hall** on Wigmore Street in Marylebone schedules recitals and chamber music.

In summer, open-air concerts, some with fireworks, are held by the lake on the grounds of **Kenwood House** on Hampstead Heath. Take a blanket, a thick sweater, and picnic (proper plates and glasses, please). No other advice on dress is needed for audiences of serious music; the majority of listeners at the great concert halls tend to dress formally but not competitively.

GOING HOME

The last Underground trains leave central London on weekdays at varying times between 11:30 P.M. and 1:00 A.M. (the Piccadilly Line), but midnight (and 11:30 P.M. on Sundays) is more the average. Night buses have Trafalgar Square as their hub—look for the prefix N on the route number and on the bus stop. About a third of London's

16,000 taxis are in action on the night shift, which is considered anything from 8:00 P.M. onward. The worst times for finding cabs are around 7:00 P.M. (when the day shift is going home, the night shift is not yet on the scene, and everyone else seems to be leaving the office or heading out to dinner and the theater) and at 11:00 P.M., when there is a general exodus from theaters, pubs, and restaurants. But at 1:00 A.M. there is often quite a fair supply, particularly near bridges where cabs are coming back into the center (such as Parliament Square or Aldwych). Oddly enough, though there is a small supplement after 8:00 P.M., the fare at night tends to be lower because of the relatively traffic-free streets. The first editions of the following day's newspapers begin to appear around 11:00 P.M. at the main railway terminals.

SHOPS AND SHOPPING

By Catherine Connelly

Catherine Connelly took up travel writing after a career in nursing. She has travelled extensively around the world but makes her home near London.

London's wide and colorful array of shopping areas—each with its special sightseeing and dining possibilities—offers a very enjoyable, if expensive, experience. The city remains one of the world's great trading centers and many of its stores can boast, without exaggeration, "You name it, we sell it." Finding it and buying it may be quite another story, however.

Credit cards are widely accepted everywhere here except in street markets, but travellers' checks are not always welcome at the smaller shops. Most large stores have a system for foreign visitors to combat that blight on shopping, the unpopular 15 percent Value Added Tax (VAT). Take your passport with you, fill in a form, get it stamped by Customs on departure, and mail it back to the store where you bought the goods. It will then send you a refund. You should be aware that some stores set a minimum price below which the plan doesn't operate, usually about £120 to £200 for visitors from countries in the European Community. Always ask before you buy whether the store will ship or mail items to your home address without the VAT. Some very expensive items such as motor vehicles and boats are outside the scope of these various schemes; in these cases you'll want to consult the supplier about separate arrangements.

Most shops give a receipt when you buy something. If not, simply ask for one. All reputable shops will either exchange the goods or give a cash refund or credit slip. Remember, you are entitled to ask for a cash refund instead of a credit slip.

The best bargains in London are to be found at the twice-yearly sales: from mid-June through August and from late December through late January.

If you are here only for a short stay and have a lot of specialized shopping to do, it might pay to engage the services of a resident expert. Most of the shopping-service organizations provide escorts. They know where to buy exactly what you want, at the right price. Charges vary according to the service required. Details can be obtained from Universal Aunts, 250 King's Road SW3 (Tel: 351-5767); Take-a-Guide, 85 Lower Sloane Street SW1 (Tel: 730-9144); or Undergraduate Tours, 6 South Molton Street W1 (Tel: 629-5267).

You need to be as careful in London as in any other major city. Avoid carrying large amounts of cash and beware of pickpockets. The best way to ensure that you are not ripped off is to stick to recognized markets and shopping areas and steer clear of casual street traders.

If you want something guaranteed "made in England," try the **Design Center Shop** at 28 Haymarket, just off Piccadilly Circus. The center has a permanent exhibition of the latest and best of British design, and all the merchandise is for sale.

In general, London shops are open from 9:00 A.M. to 5:30 P.M., Mondays through Saturdays, and closed on Sundays. Shops in the West End stay open until 8:00 P.M. on Thursdays. In Knightsbridge, Sloane Square, and on King's Road in Chelsea, the late shopping night is Wednesday. Suburban stores have similar hours, but some close one afternoon a week, usually Wednesday or Thursday, varying from area to area. Many shops in Covent Garden and other new malls are open until 8:00 P.M. most evenings.

London's shopping is extensive enough to fill a guidebook on its own (see the *Time Out* Directory to London's Shops and Services, which gives detailed listings of over 2,500 shops and services). The following is a roundup of the main shopping areas and recognized street markets.

Oxford Street

Although it has seen better days, Oxford Street is still the mecca for thousands of shoppers. Unable to afford the high rents, many small traders were forced out in the late 1980s. The empty shops, some occupied by squatters, create an air of tackiness, but there are many more still doing good business and offering the cheapest prices in London, although not necessarily the best quality.

It is on Oxford Street that you'll find the major department stores, as well as more than 30 different shoe shops. Buses stop at regular intervals along the street, which also has access to four Underground stations: from west to east, Marble Arch, Bond Street, Oxford Circus, and Tottenham Court Road. In addition, it has two branches of **Marks and Spencer** (the ubiquitous M & S), whose flagship store is at Marble Arch. Good-quality clothing at very reasonable prices is the hallmark of this chain, but until recently fitting rooms were not provided. Returning items here can be a chore as well, although company policy allows for ready exchange on production of a receipt. The Marble Arch M & S has fitting rooms (a new feature also of other leading branches) for clothing, and an excellent food hall.

Selfridge's imposing building, with flags flying, is an enduring landmark on Oxford Street. It is worth braving the inevitable crowds in the large food, kitchenware, and cosmetics departments for the sheer quantity and variety of goods. Moreover, Selfridge's guarantees to refund the difference if you find the same item cheaper elsewhere.

At 363 Oxford Street, near the Bond Street tube station, **HMV**, claiming to be the largest record store in the world, has a mega-selection of records, tapes, and compact discs suiting every conceivable taste to back up its boast. (Richard Branson's **Virgin Megastore** at the far end of Oxford Street near the Tottenham Court Road tube station retaliates by claiming to be the *best* record store in the world.)

Behind Bond Street and running diagonally south off Oxford, **South Molton Street** is reserved for pedestrians and is home to top hairdressers and expensive designer boutiques for men and women. For high fashion, **Browns** must be the first stop for labels such as Gaultier, Conran, Hamnet, Christian Lacroix, and Rifat Ozbek. Prices are very high, so if money is an issue, wait for the sales. **Butler & Wilson** has an enormous selection of fashion jewelry.

Back across Oxford Street, on the same side as Selfridge's, **St. Christopher's Place**, another traffic-free haven, is easy to miss but worth a visit for its affordable boutiques. **Whistles** stocks a combination of inexpensive and designer women's clothing, including maternity wear. Look for the labels of Lolita Lempica, Ghost, and knitwear by Artwork.

Continuing the detour north along **Thayer Street**, where an intriguing little shop called **Blunderbuss** sells all kinds of antique military uniforms, helmets, swords, and small arms, you'll come in a few steps to **Marylebone High Street**, which, although in the heart of the West End, could be the main street of any English country town— except that famous faces are twopence a dozen here (unlike the exotic fruits sold at the greengrocers). **Maison Sagne**, at number 105, sells (and serves at table) delectable Swiss pastries, while at number 183 there are several floors of antiquarian books, maps, and manuscripts collected and cataloged by **Francis Edwards**.

A few blocks west of Marylebone High Street is **Chiltern Street**, with interesting boutiques, antiques stores, fabric shops, and musical instrument makers and sellers.

Back on Oxford Street, the department store of **John Lewis** ("Never knowingly undersold") excels in reasonably priced and attractive household goods. The quality generally is excellent, but don't expect to find any innovations in fashion. Between John Lewis and Oxford Circus, a large branch of BHS (**British Home Stores**) specializes in inexpensive but fashionable clothing for men, women, and children. Household light fittings and fixtures are an especially good buy here.

From Oxford Circus east to Tottenham Court Road the sidewalks of Oxford Street are narrower and the crowds even more oppressive. There is little to attract the shopping visitor at this end of the street.

Regent Street

Regent Street still retains the curving Classical lines of the noble thoroughfare that John Nash designed and named for the Prince Regent in the early years of the 19th century. At Christmas its festive lights and decorations attract throngs of shoppers, and in summer its lampposts are adorned with hanging baskets of flowers. Most of the shops (as well as numerous large airline and tourism offices) are located on Regent Street between Oxford Circus and, to the south, Piccadilly Circus. These are also the names of the tube stations at either end, and there are a number of bus stops between the two "Circuses." The volume of traffic makes crossing the road an undertaking in itself.

At the junction of Regent and Oxford streets is the delightful **Wedgwood Gift Center**, selling the latest examples of the pottery that was created by Josiah Wedgwood in the 18th century, as well as fine porcelain and glassware. Export service is available on the premises. Heading south from Oxford Circus on the east side of the street you arrive almost immediately at **Laura Ashley**, with its wide range of distinctive and stylish ladies' and children's wear as well as fabrics. A step or two farther south and you can't miss the large mock-Tudor building first opened as a store in 1875 by Arthur Lassenby Liberty, an entrepreneur with a passion for the Orient. Inside, carved wood paneling adorns the elevators and galleries line the main shopping floor. **Liberty's** is justly famous for Tana Lawn and Varuna wool, silk scarves and neckties, clothes, fabrics, furnishings, fine crystal, and antiques, as well as for merchandise from the Far East.

Next up is **Hamley's**, "the biggest toy shop in the world"—although New York City's FAO Schwarz might dispute the claim. Six floors here are crammed with models and gadgets, toy boats, planes and trains, cuddly stuffed animals, electronic games, and all the latest trends of the toy world. To the left of Hamley's in the direction of Piccadilly, **Garrard**, the Queen's jeweler, makes it seem a privilege to be allowed through the door. The window displays alone are breathtaking. Garrard is noted especially for clocks of all descriptions. **Aquascutum**, that most British of fashion stores, is virtually next door on the opposite side of Glasshouse Street, and between that and the Quadrant Arcade the choices range from Mitsukiku's Japanese shop and Waterstones the booksellers to the Scotch House, which is jammed with woollens.

On the other side of the street, **Austin Reed** is the best known men's tailor this side of Savile Row (which is actually a back street just a few blocks to the west), without the astronomical prices. **Burberry's**, farther up on the left heading back toward Oxford Circus, will sell you one of its famous raincoats for around £300, as well as a brolly, a scarf, a hat, gloves, shoes, children's wear, and much else besides. It's a bargain hunter's paradise at sale time.

Piccadilly

Piccadilly originally took its name from a tailor who specialized in making *piccadills,* the frilly lace collars worn by fashionable Elizabethans, but today much of it is occupied by hotels, airline offices, and car showrooms. It still has plenty to offer the shopper, however, from great department stores like **Simpson's** for fashion and **Lilly-whites** in Piccadilly Circus, which has every type of sports equipment and clothing, to **Fortnum & Mason** farther west, which lends impeccable style to the world of groceries. Provision merchants by royal appointment and still going strong after two and a half centuries, it stocks everything and anything from bags of potato chips to a jar of the finest Sevruga caviar. The celebrated Fortnum's hamper, costing about £80 for four people, turns a picnic into a banquet—but you must telephone a day in advance to have one prepared for collection or delivery (Tel: 734-8040). Likewise, the Fountain restaurant at Fortnum's has long been a rendezvous for afternoon tea or a light pre-theater supper, and is open until 11:30 P.M.

On the opposite side of Piccadilly is **Airey & Wheeler**, a classy gents' outfitter famous for well-cut shirts. Indeed, this area of Mayfair is a haven for specialty shops, such as **James Lock**, 6 St. James's Street, where you can buy a hat molded to the exact shape of your head (which they measure with a strange contraption that was invented in Victorian times). Bowler hats were invented by Lock, and used to be the badge of the prosperous City businessman, but they are rarely seen today. **Crabtree & Evelyn**, also on St. James's Street, displays beautifully packaged preserves, soaps, and herbs on delightfully old-fashioned wooden counters. **Hatchard's** is a bookselling chain, and its premises on Piccadilly have one of the best and widest stock of books to be found anywhere, along with a knowledgeable and helpful staff. Even out-of-print books can be ordered here.

Among the arcades and covered shopping malls off Piccadilly, the early 19th-century **Burlington Arcade** is the most elegant, exclusive—and expensive. A full-time beadle is employed to make sure no one whistles or otherwise disturbs the peace in this Old World enclave. The Prince of Wales and his father, the duke of Edinburgh, get their Hammam Bouquet cologne from **Pen-haligons**, and the tiny **Irish Linen Company** shop sells beautiful household linens. Elsewhere in the arcade you will find jewelry and accessories, fine woollens and cashmere sweaters and scarves, leather goods, rare pipes, tobaccos, and cigars, and a range of other items suitable as gifts or souvenirs. But whatever you do, don't whistle.

The **Trocadero**, also on Piccadilly Circus, with access

from Coventry Street and Shaftesbury Avenue, is quite another cup of tea. Reopened in 1984 as an exhibition-cum-shopping center, cheap souvenir shops, boutiques, and restaurants now occupy this three-floor tower. **Fusion**, the futuristic steel-and-glass structure in the basement, is a showcase for the work of young and upcoming designers as well as established market leaders such as Katharine Hamnett.

Jermyn Street
This narrow thoroughfare running just south of and parallel to Piccadilly is the haunt of affluent shoppers who want only the best and know where to find it. **Tricksters** (at number 67) and **Turnbull & Asser** (number 71) may not be household names, but for the discerning customer they are *the* places to buy, respectively, shoes and shirts. Jermyn Street is also the home of **Floris** perfumes; **Dunhill** tobaccos, pipes, and leather goods; and the specialist cheesemonger **Paxton & Whitfield**.

Bond Street (Old and New)
There are in fact two Bond Streets, Old and New, which meet at the junction with Burlington Gardens. "New" in this case is something of a misnomer, as it was built around 1721 and contains some of London's most elegant and fashionable shops, a window-shopper's paradise. Old Bond Street, a short continuation of New Bond Street, stretches south from Burlington Gardens into Piccadilly.

Asprey doesn't boast, but with its glittering showcases of rare and beautiful jewelry, gold, silver, and antiques, it has to be one of the finest shops in the world. There's more of the same at Cartier, fine porcelain at Georg Jensen, high fashion at the houses of Chanel, Lagerfield, and St. Laurent, as well as magnificent leather goods at Gucci. If you're looking for distinctive notepaper, stop in at **Smythson**, suppliers of stationery to the Queen, and for any kind of musical instrument, try **Chappells**.

Fenwicks, the only department store on New Bond Street, offers an extensive range of lingerie and fashion wear, mostly for women and in all price brackets.

Admiral Lord Nelson once lived at 147 New Bond Street (which today houses **Wildensteins**, traders in fine paintings and drawings). The fine art gallery of **Arthur Ackermann & Son** deals in and publishes sporting prints spanning the past three centuries, but the flagship of the street is probably the auction house of **Sotheby's**. Viewing, usually for three days before a sale, is from 9:00 A.M. to 4:30 P.M. The actual sales take place at 11:00 A.M. Although bids running into millions attract the headlines, many of the sales are quite modest. (The other famous London auction houses are **Christie's** on King Street near the Green Park tube station, **Phillip's** on nearby Blenheim Street, and **Bonham's** on Montpelier Street over in Knightsbridge.)

Tottenham Court Road

Before (or perhaps instead of) heading west from the so-called West End to the lush pastures of Knightsbridge and Kensington, you might take a look at some of London's other lively central shopping areas. Tottenham Court Road can hardly be described as a shoppers' paradise (nor is it exactly pleasing to the eye), but it is the center for sound systems and electrical equipment of all kinds. **Lasky**, the leading dealer, has several branches along the road, supplying everything from the most obscure spare part to the last word in state-of-the-art systems. With so many shops selling similar items in such a small area it is easy to compare prices and shop for the best value.

Tottenham Court Road is also the place for stylish furniture in the showrooms of **Maples and Heals**, with **Habitat** specializing in the latest trends at everyday prices. **Paperchase** is a super shop in which to browse and buy wrapping paper, gift tags, unusual greeting cards, and many other paper items.

Charing Cross Road

Although it features in the title of a successful play, Charing Cross Road has none of the outward glitter and glamour of the West End, yet it remains a magnet for bookworms. **Foyles** here claims to stock every British book in print, but its staff doesn't always give the impression of being all that well informed about where to find what. **Waterstones**, nearby, is a newer bookstore, with a very helpful staff and wide-carpeted aisles between the shelves. It stays open late, too. **Zwemmer**, at number 76–80, is noted for books on art and architecture. The charm of Charing Cross Road for those with a nose for a rare book is the number of shops where it's still possible to browse among second-hand volumes, most long since out of print. For those with a nose for an unusual gift, **Smiths Snuff Shop** at number 74 offers 53 varieties, not to mention a wide range of smokers' requisites.

Soho

West of Charing Cross Road, Soho is one of the capital's older immigrant quarters, noted for its ethnic shops and restaurants and also as a favorite haunt of writers, artists, and show-business personalities. Various campaigns to "clean up" the area and rid it of its slums, prostitution, and sleazy sex clubs have almost, but not quite, succeeded. Berwick Street houses one of the best fruit and vegetable markets in London, and is noted for its many fabric shops, of which **Borovicks** is the best known. The latter is stacked with extravagant materials and boasts a gallery of signed photographs of the circus and theater stars who have worn costumes made from them. The staff is likewise animated and helpful.

Soho includes London's "Chinatown" on Lisle Street, Gerard Street, and part of Wardour Street, and the area is especially crowded on Sunday afternoons with Chinese families. **Loon Fung supermarket** here offers an excellent selection of pretty dishes and unusual cookware amid shelves piled with noodles, dried fish, sweets, and spices. Old Compton Street is full of exotic shops; one of them, the **Pâtisserie Valerie**, is worth a visit just to sample its heavenly chocolate truffle cake.

Covent Garden

East of Charing Cross Road lies Covent Garden, for 300 years the distribution center for fruit and vegetables brought into the capital from the rest of the country and the world. Then, in 1974, the wholesale fruit, vegetable, and flower market was moved to a new site south of the river, and after much controversy and local community action the abandoned warehouses were saved from demolition and turned into small galleries, workshops, studios, and offices.

The addition of cafés, boutiques, crafts shops, and market stalls of all kinds, and the revival of street theater and entertainment (much as it would have been in the 18th century), have created a draw for tourists as well as Londoners. You can buy affordable garments at the branches of many of London's best-known fashion shops here, or choose from an amazing variety of handicrafts and specialty items in the smaller shops that have sprung up in the surrounding streets.

Neal Street has more than its share, with the Copper Shop, the Tea House, and the Kite Store (names that speak for themselves) among the best. **Neal's Yard**, just off

Neal Street, caters to health-conscious shoppers with a whole-foods warehouse, farm shop, bakery, and Neal's Yard Apothecary, where old-fashioned remedies can be made up to suit individual requirements. **New Row** is worth looking into for **Naturally British**, which offers gifts, clothes, toys, and furniture of good quality, though the prices are rather high; and **Scottish Merchant** for knitwear, especially Fair Isle sweaters. If maps fascinate you, don't miss **Stanford's Map Shop** on Long Acre, another good street for strolling and window-shopping.

There is late-night shopping in Covent Garden six nights a week (until 8:00 P.M.), and there are open markets for antiques on Mondays, and crafts Tuesdays through Saturdays, from 9:00 A.M. to 5:00 P.M.

Knightsbridge

An improbable version of how this fashion-conscious area got its name is that two knights on their way to the Crusades fought to the death on a bridge that once stood here. Be that as it may, there is no doubt that Knightsbridge is where the fashionable people shop. In fact, if there is such a thing as a neighborhood shopping area for the royal family, this is it. The tall attractive blonde with the shy smile at the glove counter could be you-know-who, always escorted by a plainclothes detective.

The stylish shops extend into dozens of side streets and cul-de-sacs, but it is **Harrods**, of course, that dominates the scene. *The* Knightsbridge store is not actually in Knightsbridge at all but on the Brompton Road, but who is arguing? There is only one Harrods, famous throughout the world. No matter what you're looking for it has it, or can do it: Arrange your travel, rent a house, send anything anywhere. (It once dispatched a baby elephant to Ronald Reagan.) Throughout its many departments retailing every conceivable kind of merchandise, quality and service are of the highest, although the same, happily, cannot be said of its prices. There are bargains to be had at Harrods, especially during the legendary sales, when long queues form at the doors well in advance of opening.

Harrods apart, at sale time one favorite Knightsbridge store is the nearby **Harvey Nichols**, known to its devotees as Harvey Nicks. If you have seen what you want in a glossy magazine, this is the most likely place to find it, among racks packed with high-fashion names such as Helen Storey, Byblos, and Nichole Farrhi. The range of fashion accessories here is just as wide, and it is fun to visit the store's fashion shows. (Top cosmetics houses often give demonstrations with "free gifts" to tempt buyers.)

Knightsbridge is packed with fashion and shoe shops, Rayne, Bally, and Charles Jourdan among them. **The Scotch House** on the corner displays fine woollens, including cashmere, and (naturally) tartans of all clans, while famous names in jewelry are represented in the area by **Kutchinsky** and **Mappin & Webb**.

On Sloane Street, running south into Chelsea and "Sloane Ranger" country, you will find much sought after machine-knitted sweaters and skirts and hand-knitted sweaters with tiger motifs for around £300 at **Joseph Tricot**. Nearby, **Katharine Hamnett's** shop—with an aquarium in the window—offers everything from quietly understated fashions for men and women to dramatic creations studded with leather.

Beauchamp (pronounced Beecham) **Place**, off the Brompton Road a bit west of Harrods, is an enclave of smart fashion houses and restaurants in what used to be residential terraces. The windows lining the narrow street have displays to dazzle young female followers of fashion under such names as Janet Reger, Caroline Charles, Whistles, and Bruce Oldfield. Appealing antiques shops are interspersed with the street's boutiques; the **Map House** is the place to go if you are looking for genuine antique or reproduction maps and prints.

The Brompton Road continues into the Fulham Road, less aristocratic than Knightsbridge but with a growing reputation for both antiques and fashion. The former Michelin Tire Company building overshadowing the intersection known as Brompton Cross houses the **Conran** shop with its range of reasonably priced designer furnishings and fabrics, books, Italian cookware, English preserves, teas, and much more. If you are feeling drained and need a rest, under the same roof is a Champagne-and-oyster bar and the **Bibendum** restaurant.

King's Road, Chelsea

The king after whom this street is named was Charles II. One theory holds that it was the quickest route from Whitehall Palace to the house of his mistress Nell Gwyn in Fulham. Much more recently, Mary Quant invented the miniskirt and sold it on King's Road, which went on to achieve a reputation as the heart of the swinging London of the sixties. This faded as fashions changed—but not totally, as was unfortunately the case of Carnaby Street, now merely a tacky backwater off Regent Street. Especially on Saturdays, King's Road still attracts the young and fashion-conscious across a broad spectrum, from smart to eccentric and even bizarre. Boutiques and antiques shops of every kind abound.

Designers Sale Studio, at number 14, concentrates on famous labels' end of lines and canceled orders, so you can pick up Byblos, Krizia, or Ralph Lauren women's wear here at unbelievably low prices. **Antiquarius Antique Market**, opposite the cinema, has 200 stalls displaying fine arts, silver, antique jewelry, Edwardian silk blouses, period furniture, and all kinds of bric-a-brac.

West of the World's End pub, where King's Road leaves Chelsea and enters Fulham, there are fewer fashionable boutiques and bistros, but still more antiques shops. One of the best known is Christopher Wray's period lighting emporium at number 600, with its huge stock of Victorian and Edwardian lampshades and fittings. The **London and Provincial Antique Dealers Association** has its headquarters at 535 King's Road, where it represents 225 dealers in the London area. Its directory, *Buying Antiques in Britain,* is a useful guide, and the association will arbitrate on any complaints that cannot be settled directly with the individual trader.

Kensington High Street

As on any other High Street, you will find on Kensington High the branches of such well-known British chains as Marks & Spencer, British Home Stores, Next, and C & A. But this street runs through one of the most expensive residential districts of the capital, and the stock of these stores reflects this. You can step off the Underground train at High Street Kensington directly into a shopping arcade dominated by M & S.

Aside from the chain stores, upscale outlets of Benetton and Laura Ashley can be found alongside Kensington Market, which has seen better days but still offers the occasional bargain in denim or leather as well as second-hand clothes. **Marvalette** specializes in forties- and fifties-style clothes, and, on the other side of the street, behind the large white statues, **Hyper-Hyper** displays the work of 70 young British fashion designers. If you have children in mind or in tow, walk farther west to the Early Learning Center, the Young World Toy and Children's Book Center, and the Tree House for gifts.

Kensington Church Street, heading north from the High Street by St. Mary Abbots Church, is lined with dozens of antiques shops all the way up to Notting Hill Gate. Notable among these are **Robert Hales** for swords and other militaria, **Pamela Teignmouth** for 18th-century furniture, and **Rafferty** for clocks and watches.

One stop east from Notting Hill Gate on the Central Line brings you to Queensway, a lesser-known shopping area that stays open late. The star attraction here is **Whiteleys**, whose Edwardian building has been renovated and redeveloped into a precinct with numerous shops, restaurants, cafés, and a multi-screen cinema. It is a relatively calm place to shop under one roof, and is just dying to be rediscovered.

Street Markets

New shopping precincts and malls have killed off many of the street markets that were once such a feature of London, but some still survive. If you visit one and—sadly—don't find a bargain, at least you will get some free entertainment listening to the patter of the stallholders. Also watch out for the antics of the fly-boys, those unlicensed traders who work out of suitcases and are ready to snap them shut and run at the sight of a policeman.

Middlesex Street (better known as Petticoat Lane), between the Aldgate and Aldgate East Underground stations, is the most famous (or notorious) of the Sunday markets in the East End. Its stalls are filled with fun junk, fashions, household goods, and an impressive array of leather goods. There is little hope of understanding the fast-talking market traders' spiel, but in any case beware of goods offered at ridiculously low prices. They have probably "fallen off the back of a lorry."

On Saturdays from 8:00 A.M. to 5:00 P.M. **Portobello Road**, in an unfashionable part of London near the Notting Hill Gate and Ladbroke Grove tube stations, is crammed with antiques dealers lying in wait for innocent tourists, although it *is* possible to pick up interesting pieces here at fair prices. The numerous small galleries in the side streets are a better bet for a bargain. At all costs avoid the booths exchanging foreign currency.

North London's premier weekend market is **Camden Lock**. The variety of merchandise here and the characters who sell it attract large crowds. Anyone wishing to trade lines up in the morning and, if lucky, is allocated a stall. Alongside the market there are several crafts shops in converted canal warehouses. **Camden Passage**, off Islington High Street, is another good open market for bric-a-brac and antiques and is open on Wednesdays as well as Saturdays (when trading is at its peak). The nearest Underground station for both is Camden Town.

Greenwich isn't on the tube but can be reached by overground train, bus, or riverboat; if you happen to be visiting this center of Britain's maritime history on a weekend don't miss the open-air market. Open from 7:00 A.M. to 5:30 P.M. on Saturdays and Sundays, it is the best market south of the river or, according to some, in the whole of London. Look for the wonderful hat stall (as there is only one small mirror you might get jostled while you're trying on the merchandise). Oriental china and pottery are sold here at very reasonable prices. The bookstalls are a delight, too, especially for old poetry.

The best advice if you are visiting markets is to get there early. Not only are the best bargains still available, but the traders will be in a better humor.

DAY TRIPS
FROM
LONDON

*By Frank Dawes, Bryn Frank, Anthony Burton,
Angela Murphy, and David Wickers*

*Frank Dawes, the author of the South of London and
Windsor sections, also wrote the Overview and is the
editorial consultant for this book. Bryn Frank, who contributed the West of London sections, co-wrote the London
chapter. Anthony Burton, the author of the Oxford and
Cambridge sections, also contributed the Bibliography
and Chronology. He has written several books about the
industrial heritage of England and has written and presented several television series on the subject for the BBC.
Angela Murphy, the author of the Stratford-upon-Avon
and Warwick sections, is a free-lance journalist who has
contributed to several guidebooks, including the* Shell
Weekend Guide Book *to England and* Hachette's Guide
to Britain. *David Wickers, who contributed the day trips to
France and Belgium, co-wrote the London chapter.*

Practically any place in all of the southern half of England can be a day trip from London, by car if not by train
or bus. We have selected 20 destinations from the area—
including the nearby coasts of France and Belgium—as
being of the most general interest, and we discuss each in
enough detail to help you choose the one or ones that
appeal to you, and get the best out of the destination in a
day.

At the end of each section (south of London; west;
northwest; north; and the French–Belgian coast) we dis-

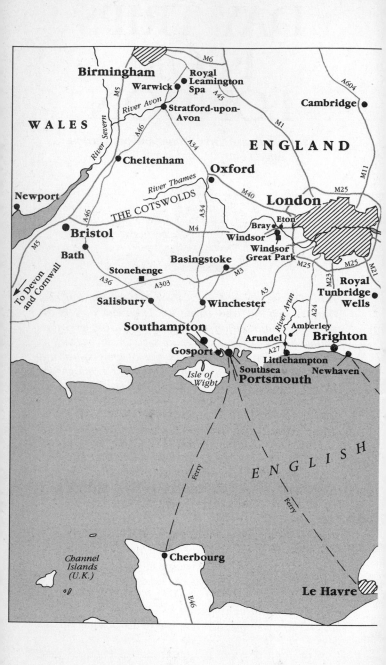

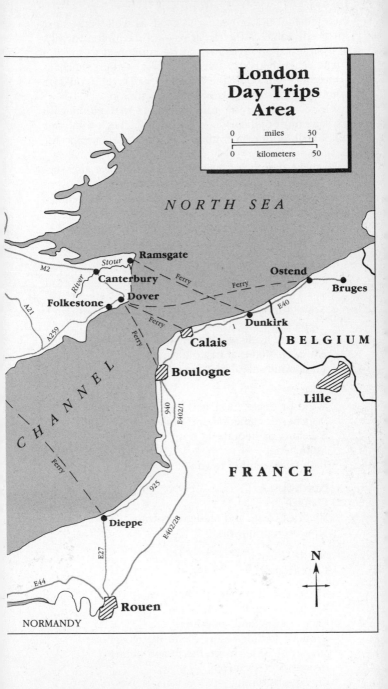

London Day Trips Area

0   miles   30

0   kilometers   50

NORTH SEA

M2

Stour River

Ramsgate

Canterbury

Ferry

Ferry

Ostend

Bruges

A21

Folkestone

Dover

Ferry

E40

A259

Ferry

Ferry

1

Dunkirk

Calais

B E L G I U M

C H A N N E L

1

Boulogne

940

E402/1

Lille

Ferry

925

F R A N C E

E402/28

Dieppe

E27

N

E44

Rouen

NORMANDY

cuss the logistics of getting to each, as well as the time involved. Some of the day trips—for example, Warwick and Stratford-upon-Avon—can be combined to make a single, if rushed, day out of London. Others, such as Canterbury and Boulogne or Calais (via Dover), could be combined for a two-day/one-night excursion.

There are plenty of tour operators in London who package most of these day trips, as well; check with your hotel hall porter or with a London travel agency for details.

To make these trips even more leisurely, we also suggest one or a few overnight accommodations in most of these destinations; for booking details see the Accommodations Reference section at the end of each section.

MAJOR INTEREST

South
Canterbury: cathedral and other Medieval historical sites
Royal Tunbridge Wells: 18th-century and Victorian spa town
Brighton: lively seaside ambience and shopping
Arundel: Medieval castle town
Portsmouth naval museums and historic ships

West
Windsor castle, Eton, and Runnymede
Winchester cathedral and College
Salisbury cathedral
Stonehenge
Bath: 18th-century town

Northwest
Oxford
Warwick castle and Medieval town
Stratford-upon-Avon

North
Cambridge

The Coast of France and Belgium
Boulogne: Medieval old town
Calais dining and shopping
Dunkirk seaside resort, Flemish atmosphere
Dieppe seaside resort: beach and dining
Bruges: Medieval city
Cherbourg dining

SOUTH

CANTERBURY

Although a large portion of this world-famous city about 58 miles east-southeast of central London in Kent, on the way to Dover, was razed in the German firebomb attacks of 1942 and later rebuilt in unromantic 20th-century style, Medieval Canterbury survives within stretches of Roman and Norman town wall and is easy to explore on foot. A visitor from a bygone age would instantly recognize, for example, the High Street, because instead of fighting a gradually losing battle against motor traffic Canterbury banished it entirely from the heart of the city. Canterbury may be a place of great antiquity, but it is also home to one of Britain's newest centers of higher education: The University of Kent stands on a hill named for Wat Tyler, who led the Peasants' Revolt of 1381.

MAJOR INTEREST

Canterbury Pilgrims Way exhibition
The cathedral
The King's School
Old Weaver's House
Canterbury Heritage Museum
City walls and castle
St. Augustine's Abbey
Roman pavement

Canterbury Pilgrims Way Exhibition

Geoffrey Chaucer wrote *"from every shires end of Engelond, to Caunterbury they wende,"* and the permanent Pilgrim's Way exhibition on St. Margaret's Street near the Tourist Information Center, an easy walk from either the east or west railway stations and parking lots, transports the present-day pilgrim back in time to the "Tabard Inn" in London's Southwark. From there a guide in period costume leads the way through representations of Medieval Kent. The "journey" is enlivened by the tales of Chaucer's "verray parfit gentil knight," the bawdy miller, the blowsy wife of Bath, the nun's priest, and the pardoner. At journey's end is a replica of Trinity Chapel and Becket's fabulous gold tomb—which was pillaged by Henry VIII when he broke with Rome over his divorce.

The Cathedral

The exhibition serves as an introduction to the heritage of centuries behind Christchurch Gate, just a few blocks away, whose carved oak doors are shut every night at 9:00 P.M. following the ringing of the curfew bell, safeguarding the security of the mother church of England. The cathedral was begun in 1070, and rebuilt after a fire a century later with stone shipped from Caen in Normandy. The 235-foot-high "Bell Harry" rises above the four other towers. A single bell at the top tolls only for the death of a monarch or an archbishop of Canterbury, who is primate of all England.

The first view of the interior is breathtaking, with a fan-vaulted ceiling soaring over 150 feet, hundreds of paintings and sculptures, and richly colorful stained-glass windows known as the "Poor Man's Bible."

On December 29, 1170, four knights who had overheard their king Henry III call out in despair "Who will deliver me from this turbulent priest?" waylaid Archbishop Thomas à Becket in the cathedral and murdered him. He was recognized as a martyr by the Church, and canonized as St. Thomas; the spot where he was cut down became a shrine. Everyone asks: "Where was Becket murdered?" A 1986 metal sculpture, with the single word THOMAS carved into the stone paving beneath it, marks the spot in the northwest transept.

As mentioned above, Becket's tomb itself is no more, but near where it stood in the mosaic-paved Trinity Chapel is the tomb of Edward, the Black Prince, with a superb brass effigy of the hero of Crécy and Poitiers in full battle armor. Opposite is the only tomb of a king to be found in the cathedral, that of Henry IV, who lies beside his wife, Joan of Navarre. Surveying the presbytery and choir, the crossing of the nave and transepts under the central tower, and the full perpendicular sweep of the nave is St. Augustine's Chair, carved from Purbeck marble in the 13th century and used for the enthronement of every new archbishop.

The Norman crypt beneath the nave and transepts is vast—230 feet long and 130 feet wide—with daylight streaming in on columns that bear the distinctive marks made by the masons who carved them 900 years ago. The heraldic shields of more than 800 families are displayed in the intricate vaulting of the cloisters, and the chapter house has a barrel-vaulted roof of Irish bog oak. It was here that Prime Minister Margaret Thatcher and President Mitterand of France signed the treaty to build the Channel Tunnel.

The King's School

North of the cathedral cloisters is Green Court, which lies at the heart of the King's School. Founded in 1541, the school is older than Eton. Its former pupils include the Elizabethan dramatist Christopher Marlowe, son of a Canterbury shoemaker, and, more recently, Somerset Maugham, who bequeathed his library to the school in 1961 and whose ashes were scattered on the roses outside. The rosebushes face an external staircase that leads to the oldest schoolroom; this staircase is a gem of Norman architecture. Palace Street, on the far side of Green Court through Mint Yard Gate, is full of interesting shops selling antiques, sports and country wear, period postcards, toys and posters, china, and jewelry.

From Palace Street it's a short walk to the **West Gate** via St. Peter's Street. Those who climb the spiral staircase to the battlements of this Norman tower (rebuilt in the 14th century) are rewarded with a fine view of the city. Through this gate Chaucer's pilgrims plodded and Henry V rode after his victory against the French at Agincourt. Ports for ancient cannon survive. Until Victorian times the tower served as a jail, but today it's a museum of arms and armor.

The Old Weaver's House

The black-and-white gables of this old house overhang the River Stour, a narrow stream flowing through the city and under St. Peter's Street. The house took its name from the Protestant weavers who settled in Medieval Canterbury, having fled from religious persecution in Europe. The jetty where their wool was unloaded from barges is today crowded with tourists embarking in boats and taking photographs of the ducking stool formerly used to silence nagging wives. The house itself is now a coffee shop and souvenir store, and stocks good local craftware.

Canterbury Heritage Museum

Holograms and computers are used here in the 13th-century Poor Priests' Hospital on Stour Street, near the junction of the High Street and St. Peter's Street, to create a "time-walk" from Roman times to the Blitz of 1942. The treasures on display include silver spoons used by the Romans, the original Canterbury Cross—a symbol of Christianity recognized throughout the world—a fully threaded loom tended by a model of a Huguenot silk weaver, and the writing desk of Joseph Conrad, who spent the last years of his life at Bishopsbourne nearby and is buried at Canterbury. But the prize exhibit is the "Invicta," the steam engine that hauled what locals claim was the world's first regular passenger train from Canterbury to its port of Whitstable in the 1830s.

The City Walls and the Castle

A walk reached by a ramp near the castle (southeast of the Museum on Castle Street) runs along the parapet of the city walls, which were begun by the Romans and extended and strengthened by the Normans. The walk encircles Dane John Gardens, which probably takes its name from the Norman "donjon," or castle.

The keep of the castle, whose 11-foot-thick walls have survived, overlooks the gardens, which are themselves surrounded by houses of the period. This little park is dominated by a grassy mound and has a charming monument to Shakespeare's rival, Christopher Marlowe. The Marlowe Theatre near the cathedral stages a varied program of opera, ballet, drama, and classical music, as well as light entertainment.

What little remains of **St. Augustine's abbey**, which Saint Augustine (the *other* Saint Augustine, the first archbishop of Canterbury) founded in 602, lies outside the city wall on the opposite side of the busy Upper and Lower Bridge Street and Broad Street loop, on the east side of the city. Its most impressive feature is the 14th-century Fyndon Gate at the top of Lady Wootton's Green.

Roman Tessellated Pavement

Hitler's bombs may have destroyed many historic buildings, but they also revealed the remains of even earlier settlements, such as this fine example of mosaic and

under-floor heating (hypocaust) from a Roman villa of
A.D. 100. It is to be found eight feet beneath the new
Longmarket shopping precinct, off Burgate between the
abbey ruins and the cathedral. During 1990 it underwent
extensive restoration and, together with a collection of
coins, pottery, jewelry, and other finds from Durovernum
(the Roman name for Canterbury) is well worth visiting.
The contrast with the late-20th-century shopping mall
above, where street musicians and buskers entertain
throngs of visitors, is intriguing.

Canterbury is accustomed to coping with two million
visitors every year—all of them packing into the Medieval
heart of the city where everything is located. As well as
shops to suit every taste and pocketbook—from the secondhand shops of Northgate to the **Chaucer Bookshop**
on Beer Cart Lane and **Canterbury Pottery** in the But-
termarket opposite the cathedral—there are numerous
teashops and taverns. The **Tea Pot** in Northgate is a good
place for a relaxing cuppa, while **Waterfield's** on Best
Lane serves something more substantial at moderate
prices. **Morelli's** ice cream parlors are dotted around the
city. Antiques and collectors' markets are held on Saturdays in the **Sidney Cooper Center** on St. Peter's Street
and at **Latimer's** on Ivy Lane during the week. The
Kingsmead Road Market takes place on Wednesdays.
    For those who decide to stay overnight so as to get a
leg up on the crowds, the **County Hotel** is in the most
central of locations on the High Street and has an excellent restaurant called **Sully's**. **The Falstaff**, which has
stood on St. Dunstan's Street since the days of Chaucer's
pilgrims, has been modernized without sacrificing its
character. All the sights mentioned above are within easy
walking distance of each other, and most are accessible to
wheelchairs.

ROYAL TUNBRIDGE WELLS

The natural setting amid the green hills of the High Weald
of Kent, with outcrops of sandstone such as Toad Rock
and High Rocks, and 250 acres of gorse-covered common
adjoining the town center, gives Tunbridge Wells, 36
miles southeast of London, its distinctive style. The wells,
fed by an iron-impregnated chalybeate spring discovered
by Lord North while out riding in 1606, soon became

famous as the English answer to the Belgian spa waters. Queen Henrietta-Maria gave them the stamp of royal approval when she took the waters during her pregnancy in 1629, and two centuries later Victoria, as a young princess, referred to the town as her "*Dear* Tunbridge Wells." But it was left to her son, when he became King Edward VII, to bestow the "Royal" prefix on the town in 1909.

During the Victorian era, when the prosperous middle class made Tunbridge Wells its own, the town acquired a reputation for snobbery and starchiness that has been a long time dying. Its archetypal residents were retired colonels of the Indian Army who wrote letters to *The Times* signed "Disgusted, Tunbridge Wells." Only now is it coming to terms with newer lifestyles, and development goes on apace.

MAJOR INTEREST

The Pantiles
Church of King Charles the Martyr
The Common
Trinity Arts Center
Calverley Park

Virtually every English country town today boasts its pedestrianized shopping precinct, but only Tunbridge Wells has one laid out three centuries ago during the reign of Queen Anne. By then many houses, shops, and taverns had been built around the common and on the surrounding hills, named Mount Ephraim, Mount Sion, and Mount Pleasant by the austere Dissenters. This group of settlements formed a new town, one that developed coffee houses, lottery and hazard rooms, apothecaries, and bowling greens during the Restoration period.

The Pantiles

The town square called the Pantiles is just a short walk from the train station. It took its name from the square clay tiles with which it was originally paved (15 of them can still be seen at the foot of the steps leading to Fox Brothers), which were replaced after almost a century by the large flagstones we see today. In one corner of the square, under a canopy supported by iron columns, is the original Chalybeate Spring, with the "dipper" traditionally used to dispense medicinal sips of the water on hand from Easter to September. Victoria took the waters every day during her visit in 1834, and walked with her mother, the duchess of Kent, in the Pantiles afterward. The square leads on to the colonnaded Upper Walk and then the Lower Walk, which is paved with red bricks and shaded by a row of lime trees. The Bandstand is used for regular evening performances, ranging from military and Kentish town bands to New Orleans jazz and old-time music hall entertainment.

The former Corn Exchange, one of the fine old buildings lining the Pantiles, houses "A Day at the Wells," a heritage center opened in 1990. It re-creates with sights and sounds the Georgian elegance of the Tunbridge Wells where Beau Nash, as master of ceremonies, decreed in the early 1700s that "All should learn—according to my Rule—to live in Society." It was a town of sedan chairs and coffee houses, grand balls and gaming halls, where the fashionable took the waters and strolled among the Tuscan columns in order to see and be seen.

By the mid-1980s, however, the Pantiles was beginning to look rather shabby, and a much-needed restoration has made over not only the Corn Exchange but also the Assembly Rooms, formerly used for weekly auction sales, and the Royal Victoria Inn, where Queen Victoria stayed. The face-lift has preserved historic façades while providing modern facilities for leisure, entertainment, high-quality shopping, and restaurants. **Todd's Vintry**, which has been in the Pantiles since 1768, sells a staggering variety of wines, cheeses, and confectioneries, while **Binns** is *the* place for afternoon tea in Tunbridge Wells. The **Duke of York pub**, occupying converted stables, serves good lunches with cask ales.

In Chapel Place, just off the Pantiles, is the **church of King Charles the Martyr**, the first church built in Tunbridge Wells, completed in 1696. It is a pretty sight with its white weatherboarded belfry and clock, but it is chiefly noted for the ornately decorated plaster ceiling inside, said to be the finest example of its kind in any church outside London.

The Common

It is possible to step from the Pantiles into a rural scene simply by going through a passageway beside the Swan Hotel and crossing Eridge Road. A steep 200-yard path up through the woods leads to the Old Race Course, where young Victoria and her mother would watch the races from a carriage protected by a special awning. The grassy track is still traceable, although no longer used for horse racing. A little farther on is the Higher Cricket Ground and, to the right, Wellington Rocks, a favorite place for children's games.

Before the first large houses in Tunbridge Wells were built on these heights, royalty and aristocracy had to camp on the common while they took the waters. Some of those first mansions are still in use as hotels, alongside other, newer buildings. **The Spa** is probably the most comfortable, and provides its guests with an indoor heated swimming pool, tennis courts, and a children's play area. The **Royal Wells Inn**, dating from the 1830s, boasts a vast coat of arms on its parapet, and its glass-enclosed balcony is a good place to have a drink while admiring the grandstand view of Tunbridge Wells.

Trinity Arts Center

Another steep footpath leads down across the common to Church Road, where the former Holy Trinity Church, whose foundation stone was laid by the duchess of Kent on her birthday in 1827, now serves as an arts center. In the late 1970s the church commissioners were, mercifully, thwarted in their plans to demolish the Gothic-style Trinity to make way for further development. The finely carved faces at the dripstone terminations of the roof are one of its most intriguing features. The center provides a venue for plays, concerts, dance, and exhibitions—a welcome complement to the town center complex just across Mount Pleasant Road, which houses the Tourist Information Center, museum, art gallery, and library, as well as the Assembly Hall on Crescent Road, which is the major theater and concert hall for the High Weald.

Calverley Park

Holy Trinity Church was in fact the first building of the "new town" that the great Georgian architect Decimus Burton was commissioned to design (in 1828) to rival the Pantiles. The style he chose was Greek Revival, and he used blocks of Wealden sandstone for his colonnades, pavilions, and pilasters. Calverley Parade and Calverley Terrace opposite the church were demolished in the

1930s to make way for the Civic Center buildings mentioned above, but **Calverley Park Crescent**, just up the road, rivals anything in Bath or around Regent's Park in London, while the villas in Calverley Park still conform to the self-contained village plan of the original design. No two structures are the same, but their bow windows and towers are in perfect harmony. Much of the surrounding park is open to the public, with tennis courts and a bowling green, a children's paddling pool, and a cafeteria. Calverley Park is near the train station, with the Pantiles and the common a short walk away. But Tunbridge Wells is very hilly, and so not the most ideal destination for the not-so-fit.

Tunbridge Wells is a major shopping area, able to fulfill almost any requirement from a lobster pick to a lawn mower. There are, in addition, ten parking garages, some multi-story. The major chain stores are to be found in the pedestrians-only Calverley Precinct between Calverley Road and Mount Ephraim. Behind it, **Monson Road**, with its curving, balustraded row of storefronts, has good shops for china, ornaments, and jewelry, as well as many varieties of tea and coffee at **Importers**. Nearby Camden Road has numerous antiques shops, including **Sawdust and Lace**, which sells dolls and dollhouses, rocking horses, and teddy bears.

Along Mount Pleasant Road and the High Street running from Calverley Precinct to the Pantiles are shops of every description. The **Great Hall** here is an attractively restored glass-roofed arcade with furniture shops, boutiques, and a branch of Hatchard's bookshop. Antiquarian bookshops, art galleries, and antiques dealers are concentrated on Chapel Place and Nevill Street. Tunbridge Ware, a type of inlaid woodwork, is much sought after.

Tunbridge Wells also has its associations with literary figures. E.M. Forster grew up here. A Regency house in London Road that was for a time the home of William Makepeace Thackeray is now a good restaurant called—simply enough—**Thackeray's House**. It has built a reputation for serving high-quality English fare at moderate prices, but is closed on Sundays and Mondays.

BRIGHTON

Queen Victoria was not amused by Brighton; on the other hand, George IV, as Prince of Wales ("Prinny" to fashionable Regency society), adored the place, which he first visited one Sunday in September 1783 when it was just a small fishing town called Brighthelmston.

Although it was known as early as the mid-18th century, when a local doctor published a pamphlet recommending the "oceanic fluid" as a curative, to be taken both by bathing and by drinking, Brighton, situated 53 miles due south of central London, is a town built on misbehavior. Prinny installed his morganatic wife, Mrs. Maria Fitzherbert, here in a house at the center of town. (Today the house is a YMCA hostel.) In less permissive times it was an open secret that unmarried couples, or at least couples who were not married to each other, slipped down to Brighton for an illicit weekend of pleasure.

Fifty years ago Graham Greene used the resort as the backdrop for *Brighton Rock,* a novel about sleazy crime, day-trippers, and the racecourse in the hills above the town. The "rock" of the title is not a geographical feature but a stick of rainbow-hued candy, very hard on the teeth, with "Brighton" spelled out in red sugar all the way through its white core. Greene's boy-gangster, Pinkie, would have no difficulty recognizing Brighton—and its rock—today.

Less than an hour from London by train, which puts it within easy commuting distance, Brighton is a smart place to live, much favored by creative people such as the late Lord Olivier. Not so long ago kippers could be had for breakfast on the Pullman service to town but, alas, the *Brighton Belle* is no more. Frankly, the steeply shelved beach of large round pebbles is nothing to write home about, except that a section of it just west of the marina is reserved for nudists. But Brighton still *revels* in naughtiness and is always fun to visit, even for a day—though it has enough to keep you entertained and occupied for much longer. It is a longish walk from the train station to the places of major interest listed below; better to take a cab or hop on a bus.

MAJOR INTEREST

The Lanes (antiques shopping)

Royal Pavilion and The Dome
Palace Pier views of the coast
The Aquarium
Volk's beachside railway

Trim suburbs climbing inland up the grassy slopes of the
Downs, manicured public lawns, and bright ribbons of
flowers give no hint of the centerpiece that, when revealed, hits the visitor smack in the eye. It is a palace
seemingly from the hills of northern India, complete with
minarets and onion domes, magically transported and set
down in the midst of an English garden. The **Royal Pavilion** was built not by a Mogul emperor but by the extravagant, debauched, lecherous, eccentric George IV. About
the time of his father's terminal bout with madness,
George hit upon the idea of transforming the mansion he
had built in Brighton into an Eastern fantasy palace. His
architect was John Nash, who laid out London's Regent's
Park and Regent Street and redesigned Buckingham Palace. No expense was spared. The result, the Royal Pavilion,
convinced some people that insanity ran in the royal family. Among some of the more polite remarks was this: "This
pot-bellied palace, this minaret mushroom. This gilded
dirt pie, this congeries of bulbous excrescences. . . ."

The interior was no less exotic than the exterior, satisfying the prince's taste for chinoiserie, which can still be
viewed today, together with marvelous Regency furniture,
porcelain, glass, silver, and gold plate. Many of the pieces
are on loan from Queen Elizabeth II. The Music Room, in
which a 70-strong royal orchestra would play while
Prinny sang to his guests, is a Nash masterpiece. Gutted
by a fire in 1975, the room was restored, then wrecked
again when a three-ton minaret crashed through the roof
during the great windstorm of 1987 (which also devastated the lovely central parks of Brighton). Once again,
however, the Music Room has been restored to its original spendor.

By the time the Pavilion was completed, the prince
regent had become king and lost interest in it. But the
fashion he had started rolled on. **Regency Square**, just
across the promenade from West Pier and planned as the
Royal Pavilion neared completion, provides the grandest
examples of the bay windows, balconies, and wrought-
iron tracery that graced the houses of the period.

Before he built the Pavilion, George commissioned
William Porden to build stables and a riding school in the

style of a Muslim mosque. Today **The Dome** is the home of the Brighton Philharmonic Orchestra and is also used for events as varied as rock concerts, trade-union conferences, and the degree-conferring ceremonies of Sussex University, whose campus, designed by Sir Basil Spence in the 1960s, is situated high on the Downs outside of town. The adjoining stables fronting Church Street serve as Brighton's public library, art gallery, and museum.

The Lanes

Nowhere is the atmosphere of Brighton, a heady mixture of colorful history and present glamour, more in evidence than it is in what remains of Brighthelmston, a square mile of small weatherboarded houses and twisting alleyways called The Lanes, close to the Royal Pavilion and The Dome. Book and antiques shops, jewelers and junk dealers, pubs and restaurants are crammed into these pedestrians-only byways, the entrances to which are clearly marked in the wider streets surrounding them.

At the center of this Medieval enclave is **Brighton Square**, a traffic-free 20th-century shopping precinct; the open-air cafés lend it a Continental atmosphere. Certainly you will hear a variety of European tongues here, and not only from tourists—Brighton is a busy center for English-language schools.

There is no need to confine your shopping to The Lanes, of course—Brighton has more than its share of stylish emporia, which have earned it a reputation as "London by the sea." Among the many fine stores on North Street, the department store **Hannington's**, the oldest (1808), prides itself on its knowledgeable and courteous staff. **Wyn Gillett**, 34 Upper North Street, sells antique linen and lace in pristine condition. **Graham and Jo Webb**, 59 Ship Street, specializes in antique music boxes, some of which play whole operatic overtures. Even farther off the well-beaten tourist track, in a narrow lane off Gloucester Road near the railway station, is **Pyramid**, which has a wide range of Art Deco pieces, from tea services and lampshades to telephones and mahogany-cased radios. The address is 9a Kensington Gardens.

The best-known seafood restaurants in Brighton are **English's** and **Wheeler's**. Lesser known, and less expensive, is **D'Arcy's** on Market Street, where the plaice and other fish are fresh from the Channel. The **Eaton Garden Restaurant** in Eaton Gardens, Hove (which adjoins Brighton to the west), also serves excellent fish and good old-fashioned English fare such as steak, kidney, and mushroom pie. For those seeking a traditional English tea, the **Mock Turtle Restaurant** at 4 Pool Valley serves a good pot of tea with lashings of homemade cakes and jams on Wood's blue-and-white willow china. Brighton has numerous first-rate French restaurants, too, among them **La Marinade** in Kemp Town and **Le Grandgousier** on Western Street, where rich sauces, garlic, and *l'escargot* provide a whiff of the land just across the Channel. Of course, new restaurants are always opening even as others fade away.

Between The Lanes and the sea is the newly built **Hospitality Inn Brighton**, boasting a four-story plant-filled atrium, two restaurants, and a fully equipped health club and swimming pool. It sits in stark contrast to its neighbor, the **Old Ship Hotel**, which is more than four centuries old. Thackeray stayed at the Old Ship while writing *Vanity Fair,* Charles Dickens gave public readings of his works in the ballroom, and Paganini gave a recital here in 1831. More recently the late poet laureate Sir John Betjeman was an habitué. Locally caught seafood is an Old Ship specialty, and the cellars are extensive.

Just a short walk westward along King's Road, facing the sea, are Brighton's finest hotels: the **Brighton Metropole** and the **Grand**. Stately neighbors, they have been extensively renovated, and both feature indoor swimming pools. Accommodation in either one includes well-appointed suites as well as rooms with all the modern amenities.

The Esplanade and Piers

It would be unthinkable to visit Brighton without taking a sniff of sea air and a stroll along "the front," which is as gaudy a promenade as you'll find at any other popular seaside resort. Between Brighton's two piers are fast-food joints, fish-and-chip cafés, cockles-and-whelks stalls, amusement arcades, bumper cars, paddling pools, putting greens, and sleazy shops selling a range of especially awful kitsch. Among the crowds taking the air are the inevitable dropouts, eccentrics, and punks, whose purple hair and safety-pin adornments have become as much a part of the tourist scene as the Beefeaters at the Tower of London.

The view from the end of **Palace Pier**, stretching a third of a mile into the sea from Grand Junction Road and

Marine Parade, takes in a wide section of English Channel coast, including the start of the white cliffs to the east. This is the younger of the two Victorian piers. The **West Pier**, recently saved from demolition by local enthusiasts, once again offers to visitors the slot machines that were shown in Richard Attenborough's film *Oh, What a Lovely War.* (Incidentally, Brighton and adjoining Hove were centers for movie-making before Hollywood set eyes on its first hand-cranked camera.)

Brighton's **Aquarium**, next to Palace Pier, is well past its centennial and still displays sea lions, seals, and turtles, as well as thousands of fish. In addition, dolphins perform daily in the 1,000-seat Dolphinarium. Also at hand is Britain's first public **electric railway**, Volk's. Opened in 1883 and travelling for a mile along the edge of the beaches (including the one for nudists), it carries passengers in little yellow wooden cars with open sides. The service runs from Easter to October and is inexpensive. At the farthest end of Brighton is one of the town's newer attractions, the largest yachting marina in Europe, opened by the Queen in 1979.

The Brighton Festival

In 1967, Lord Olivier brought this festival to his home town. Held every year in May, it is now one of Europe's liveliest, rivaling the more famous one in Edinburgh, and encompasses theater, jazz, classical music, big bands, opera, rock, cabaret, poetry, fireworks, and such eccentric experiments as a conducted tour of the sewers and the world's smallest theater—an actor on a motorbike with an audience of one in the sidecar. On the first Sunday in November fans turn out for the London-to-Brighton Veteran Car Run.

ARUNDEL

This small country town, set between the South Downs and the Channel coast, just 20 miles west of Brighton and 58 miles south of London, is a perfectly preserved piece of old England. It takes its name from that most famous of Sussex rivers, the Arun, which flows through a gap in the Downs at this point and on down to the sea at Littlehampton four miles to the south. The Downs are at their most glorious around **Amberley**, a thatched village dating back to the Saxons that is located just before Arundel on the railway from London.

Arundel boasts not only a magnificent castle—ancestral home of England's foremost Roman Catholic family, the Fitzalan Howards, dukes of Norfolk and earls Marshal— but also the cathedral, which they built in honor of their faith and which survived the Reformation and centuries of anti-Catholic discrimination. Apart from sightseeing, this area has much to offer artists and photographers, bird watchers and botanists, anglers and hikers. Tour boats ply the Arun among Littlehampton, Arundel, and Amberley (Tel: 0234-82-26-34). Arundel itself is a town of steep ascents and descents, and a cab from the train station to the castle or cathedral is recommended.

MAJOR INTEREST

Arundel Castle
Cathedral of Our Lady & St. Philip Howard
Wildfowl reserve
Amberley Castle
Amberley Chalk Pits Museum

The Castle

The massive battlemented towers and keep overshadow the little town and valley of the Arun—which they were of course built to defend. Although the castle's origins are Norman, most of the present building is Victorian mock-baronial. Its story is entwined with that of the dukes of Norfolk, whose home it has been for 500 years, but goes back much further, to 1067, when Roger de Montgomery was created earl of Arundel and given a third of Sussex for taking care of things back home while William of Normandy was busy conquering England. It was Roger who built the original motte-and-bailey castle of timber, replaced in the 12th century by the round keep of Caen stone, which survives, open to the sky, atop a grassy mound at the heart of the much extended castle you see today.

The Lower Lodge, through which the visitor enters the castle precincts, was part of the late 19th-century reconstruction by the fifteenth duke. A drive leads up through the wooded park (decimated during the great storm of October 1987) flanked by a turreted curtain wall; the castle is entered over a wooden drawbridge and through a barbican dating from 1295. Above the archway can be seen the marks of cannonballs fired by Cromwell's artillery during the siege of 1643. The inner gateway is original 11th-century and the quadrangle, with its expanse of striped emerald lawn, occupies what was once the lower bailey. From the gatehouse in one corner a stairway leads up the walls of the keep, which commands views over the town to the coast as well as the gap in the hills through which the River Arun winds its way. When the duke is in residence a banner flies from the top of this tower.

The buildings around the quadrangle contain much of interest, and include a Victorian private chapel with columns of polished Purbeck marble, the Barons' Hall with a soaring hammerbeam roof of oak harvested from the estate, the **picture gallery** with its chronologically ordered portraits of the dukes and duchesses of Norfolk as well as some of the earls of Arundel, and the **library**, fitted out in carved Honduras mahogany and containing 10,000 books, a collection particularly rich in Catholic history. These and other rooms are packed with priceless treasures: Medieval armor and swords, heraldic insignia, fine tapestries, and furniture (including the elaborate gilt bed made specially for Queen Victoria and Prince Albert when they visited Arundel castle in 1846). Paintings by Van Dyck, Gainsborough, and Reynolds hang beside recent photographs and mementoes of the family—to whom the castle is still home.

The tombs and monuments of the earls of Arundel and the dukes of Norfolk may be seen in the **Fitzalan Chapel**, partitioned from the rest of the parish church and accessible only from the castle grounds.

The Cathedral

The pinnacles of the cathedral soar above the London Road car park, between it and the castle. Despite its impressive Gothic lines, a pleasing counterpoint to the battlements dominating town and river, it was built only in the 1870s by none other than Joseph Hansom, inventor of the Victorian horse-drawn cab of that name. It became a cathedral even more recently, with the formation in 1965 of the Roman Catholic Diocese of Arundel and Brighton.

The cathedral would have been more dominating still, but the original plan to build a spire 280 feet high came to nothing. Its chief attraction is the shrine, in the north transept, of the thirteenth earl of Arundel, Philip Howard, who steadfastly refused to renounce his faith despite being incarcerated for eleven years during the Tudor period. He was canonized in 1970, almost four centuries after his death in the Tower of London. His behavior was in stark contrast to that of his kinsman, the third duke of Norfolk, who survived at court by ruthlessly sacrificing two of his nieces—Anne Boleyn and Katherine Howard—to the executioner's block when Henry VIII wanted to be rid of them as wives.

The Catholic feast day of Corpus Christi is celebrated in the cathedral every June with a unique carpet of blooming flowers covering the long central aisle.

Arundel Town

Attractive and well-preserved old buildings such as the **Norfolk Arms**, a former coaching inn that still welcomes visitors and looks after them with style, grace the streets of the town clustered below the castle walls.

An interesting **Toy and Military Museum** at 23 High Street (Tel: 0903-88-31-01) is open most days from Easter to October, but the Georgian building itself is little bigger than a dollhouse, and with anything more than half a dozen visitors at one time it is overcrowded. It contains the Henderson family's private collection of teddy bears, dolls, toy soldiers, puppets, models, rocking horses, money boxes, games, and novelties gathered over several generations.

In complete contrast to its Old World surroundings, **Pogey's**, on Tarrant Street, serves an inventive menu in an Art Deco setting.

Wildfowl Reserve

North of town the River Arun swings across a wide, flat plain, part meadow and part marshland, that often floods. The Wildfowl and Wetlands Trust leases 64 acres from the duke of Norfolk that comprise the habitat of a great variety of flora and fauna, including Bewick swans (which fly in from Siberia every winter), sandpipers, snipe, kingfishers, and reed buntings. There are seven hikes, all of them suitable for physically impaired visitors, and wheelchairs can be borrowed without charge.

The reserve's Visitor Reception Center (Tel: 0903-88-33-55) is on Mill Road less than a mile north of the castle;

look for the signs. The facilities include a gift and book shop, cinema, exhibition area, viewing gallery, and licensed restaurant. Dogs are not allowed into the reserve, which is open year-round except Christmas Day.

Amberley Castle

The wetlands are overlooked by another historic castle four miles to the north of Arundel in the village of Amberley, which can be reached by cab or bus from Arundel. For 900 years this castle has stood hidden from outsiders on the South Downs facing the flat plains of the Wildbrooks. Then, in 1989, it became a country-house hotel, also called **Amberley Castle**. Its great walls, battlements, and oak portcullis are intact, yet every room (each named after a different Sussex castle) has its own Jacuzzi. Amberley Castle was attacked by Cromwell and twice visited by King Charles II. A mural of the latter, with Queen Catherine of Braganza, is a notable feature of the hotel's 12th-century barrel-vaulted restaurant, the **Queen's Room**, together with lancet windows and French cuisine.

Amberley Town

No two cottages are the same in this village that invites you to linger (the **Black Horse pub** is a further inducement). Extinct rural industries are recalled here in building names such as the Old Brewhouse, the Old Malthouse, and the Old Bakehouse. More formally, some 36 acres of idled chalk pits have been turned into an open-air museum with its own narrow-gauge railway and a collection of industrial steam and diesel engines dating from the 1880s. The **Chalk Pits Museum** (Tel: 0798-83-13-70) also has a collection of vintage Southdown buses as well as a working blacksmith, boatbuilder, printer, and potter. Open Wednesdays through Sundays, Easter to October, it brings to life the sights, sounds, and smells of all those smoky, roaring workshops of the past, and has even managed to give an eight-ton, 1925-vintage steamroller a new lease on life crushing aluminum beverage cans brought by visitors. Funds raised by selling them to a scrap-metal dealer for recycling are plowed back into the museum.

PORTSMOUTH

Portsmouth, whose harbor has been the home base and fortress of British sea power since the 15th century, has been known as "Pompey" to generations of sailors. Today, with Britannia ruling the waves no longer, there are fewer warships on active service than ever before, and Pompey has at last fallen to an invasion of tourists. And why not? With its restored ships and maritime museums (not least the one commemorating the D-Day invasion that was launched from here in 1944), as well as the adjoining seaside resort of Southsea, there is something to interest almost everyone in this historic haven only 71 miles south and west of central London.

MAJOR INTEREST

Old Portsmouth
Her Majesty's Dockyard: *Mary Rose, Victory,* and
   Warrior
Royal Navy Submarine Museum
Southsea Castle
D-Day Museum (including the Overlord Embroi-
   dery)
Birthplace of Charles Dickens

Old Portsmouth

The huddle of little streets on the east side of the harbor mouth in the vicinity of the **Round Tower**, built by King Henry V to guard the narrow entrance to the harbor from Spithead, the stretch of water just offshore, is best explored on foot. (There are convenient car parks at Clarence Pier and King's Terrace, and Portsmouth Harbor train station is within easy walking distance of all points of interest in the old town.) Seagulls wheel and cry overhead, and there's a salty tang to the air. Broad Street, which runs past the Round Tower and Sally Port Gate (where naval officers came ashore or embarked), used to be filled with pubs and brothels and was nicknamed "Spice Island." The pubs remain, many with colorful names such as the Lively Lady, the Still and West, and the Seagull. The first fleet to the convict colony of Australia sailed from Portsmouth in 1788; today's voyages from the ferry terminal are to the nearer destinations of Le Havre and Cherbourg, Caen and St. Malo, Guernsey and Jersey. The best place to watch the maritime traffic is from the tip of Portsmouth Point at the bottom of Broad Street.

Charles Dickens's Birthplace

Even the modest terrace house in which Charles Dickens was born in 1812 has a military connection appropriate to the Portsmouth area: his father was a navy pay clerk. The house is in Landport, a northern suburb of the city that has been largely redeveloped since World War II, when heavy bombing destroyed much of it. Originally number 1 Mile End Terrace, its address is now 393 Old Commercial Road, and it is preserved as a museum (signposted off the A 3 highway, or take a cab from Old Portsmouth) and furnished in period style. The mementoes on display include the novelist's inkwell and the couch on which he died at Gads Hill. (The family moved to another house only a few months after his birth.)

Her Majesty's Dockyard

Victory Gate, a mile from the High Street down St. George's Road and a five-minute walk from the Portsmouth Harbor railway station and the Hard, as the ferry terminal is called, gives access to the Dockyard and the finest evocation of British seapower from the 16th to the 20th centuries. The story begins with Henry VIII's warship **Mary Rose**, raised from the waters of the Solent in 1982 in a remarkable salvage operation led by Prince Charles, himself a former naval officer. The ship is far from fully restored, but many of its Tudor timbers are preserved for inspection in a fine spray of water inside a special hall. Many of the artifacts carried on board, from bronze cannon to cooking utensils, a pewter tankard, and a pocket sundial, are displayed in the exhibit next door.

The masts of Admiral Nelson's flagship, **Victory**, still dominate the Dockyard. Visitors are guided through the reverently preserved vessel by modern successors of the "Jack Tars" who lived and died cheek by jowl below decks. They will point out the spot where Nelson fell fatally wounded in 1805 after bringing the Battle of Trafalgar against Napoleon's navy to a decisive conclusion. *Victory* represents the end of the era of the man-o'-war, wooden ships under sail firing their cannon at each other broadside on.

The trio of historic ships is completed by the **Warrior**, berthed at the quay just inside Victory Gate, the world's first ironclad, her sails supplemented by a Penn steam engine and her guns breech-loaded with rifled bores. The ship has been restored to her former glory as the showpiece of Queen Victoria's navy. Quartermasters in 1860s uniforms are on hand to answer questions, and visitors are encouraged to sit at a mess deck table, handle a Colt .45 revolver, climb in a hammock, and examine a cat-o'-nine-tails. Many other relics of the days of sail and steam are on display in the **Royal Naval Museum**, which is housed in one of the 18th-century dockyard buildings.

Refreshments are available in the heritage area of the Dockyard, but for an authentic taste of "Pompey" fare it is worth stepping outside the gates to the **George Tavern**, dating from 1781, on Queen Street. The bar food here is good and the dessert puddings are a specialty of the house.

Despite the growth in the numbers of visitors, Portsmouth is not well endowed with good hotels. One of the best bets is the **Holiday Inn**, but it's beside North Harbour at Cosham, nearly four miles north of Old Portsmouth.

Royal Navy Submarine Museum

A four-minute ferry ride from the Hard to Gosport, on the opposite, west, side of the harbor (13 miles from Portsmouth by road), brings you to a more recent piece of naval history. The museum's centerpiece is the submarine *Alliance,* completed in 1947, but it traces the story of underwater weapons, from a replica of the *Turtle,* the one-man sub built to attack the British fleet off New York in 1776, to today's roomier nuclear vessels.

Southsea Castle

On the east side of Old Portsmouth, the seaside resort of **Southsea** has long esplanades backed by green commonland and many of the handsome terraces built when the town became a watering place in the 19th century. (Take a cab or bus unless you are a dedicated walker.) Its dominating feature is the castle built by Henry VIII to improve his coastal defenses. On a fine summer's day in 1545 the king stood with his entourage on these newly constructed battlements watching his fleet sail out to engage a French invasion force off the Isle of Wight. The watchers recoiled in horror as the pride of the fleet, the *Mary Rose,* suddenly keeled over for no apparent reason and went down with all 700 hands.

The castle is today open to visitors year-round and houses yet another **museum of military history**. High on the walls where Henry VIII stood a swivel-mounted cannon points across the Solent.

Southsea "prom" has its piers and lifeguards and lots of diversions, including the Sea Life Center with a special ocean reef display behind walls of toughened glass. The **Crest** is one of the newest and best hotels along the front here, and apart from sea views offers an indoor swimming pool. Some of its rooms are reserved for nonsmokers.

The D-Day Museum

An important attraction along Clarence Esplanade in Southsea is the D-Day Museum, which includes reconstructions and film of the invasion in which a million and a half Americans, British, and Canadians were transported across the Channel, as well as numerous exhibits and a gallery containing the **Overlord Embroidery**. It took 20 needlewomen five years to reconstruct this saga of our times in 34 panels, 41 feet longer in total than the famous tapestry at Bayeux.

Portsmouth's military history doesn't end at Southsea, however. On its outskirts, a mile or two farther east along the coast, is the suburb of Eastney, which was developed in the 19th century, and the Royal Marines' barracks. The splendidly ornate Victorian officers' mess is now the **Royal Marines' Museum**. The corps was instituted in 1664 as a force for fighting at sea as well as on land, and also has a strong musical tradition. Silver memorial drums and trumpets commemorate the Marine bandsmen who died in two world wars.

GETTING AROUND

Canterbury
Canterbury, 58 miles southeast of London, has two railway stations, East and West, reached respectively from Victoria (1 hour, 20 minutes) and Charing Cross (1 hour, 30 minutes) with a train approximately every hour from each. By road it is via the A 2 and M 2.

Royal Tunbridge Wells

Tunbridge Wells, 36 miles southeast of London, is reached by train from Charing Cross in 48 minutes, with a train every hour, and more at peak commuter times. By car, use the A 21.

Brighton

Brighton, 53 miles south of London, is reached in a mere 51 minutes by express trains, which run hourly from Victoria Station. Gatwick Airport lies midway between London and Brighton. By car, use the A 23.

Arundel

Arundel, 56 miles south of London, is reached by train from Victoria (Amberley Station, before you reach Arundel, is on the same line) in around 1 hour, 15 minutes. It's an hourly service and stops at Gatwick Airport midway. There are also connections from Brighton, but these usually involve changing trains. By car, use the A 24, A 29, and A 284.

Portsmouth

Trains to Portsmouth, 71 miles southwest of London, leave Victoria Station at 20 minutes past the hour and arrive at Portsmouth Harbor Station 2 hours, 15 minutes later. By car, use the A 3.

ACCOMMODATIONS REFERENCE

Canterbury

▶ **County Hotel.** High Street, **Canterbury** CT1 2RX. Tel: (0227) 76-62-66; Telex: 965076; Fax: (0227) 45-15-12.

▶ **Falstaff.** 8–12 St. Dunstan's Street, **Canterbury** CT2 8AF1 Tel: (0227) 66-21-38; Telex: 96394; Fax: (0227) 46-35-25.

Royal Tunbridge Wells

▶ **Royal Wells Inn.** Mount Ephraim, **Royal Tunbridge Wells** TN4 8BE. Tel: (0892) 51-11-88; Fax: (0892) 51-19-08.

▶ **The Spa.** Mount Ephraim, **Royal Tunbridge Wells** TN4 8XJ. Tel: (0892) 203-31; Telex: 957188; Fax: (0892) 51-05-75.

Brighton

▶ **Brighton Metropole.** King's Road, **Brighton** BN1 2FU.

Tel: (0273) 77-54-32; Telex: 877245; Fax: (0273) 20-77-64; in U.S., (402) 493-4747 or (800) 44-UTELL.

▶ **Grand Hotel.** King's Road, **Brighton** BN1 2FW. Tel: (0273) 211-88; Telex: 877410; Fax: (0273) 20-26-94.

▶ **Hospitality Inn Brighton.** King's Road, **Brighton** BN1 2GS. Tel: (0273) 20-67-00; Telex: 878555; Fax: (0273) 82-06-92; in U.S., (213) 937-2530, (201) 587-1555, or (800) 228-9898.

▶ **Old Ship Hotel.** King's Road, **Brighton** BN1 1NR. Tel: (0273) 290-01; Telex: 877101; Fax: (0273) 82-07-18.

Arundel

▶ **Amberley Castle. Amberley** (near Arundel) BN18 9ND. Tel: (0798) 83-19-92; Fax: (0798) 83-19-98.

▶ **Norfolk Arms.** High Street, **Arundel** BN18 9AD. Tel: (0903) 88-21-01; Telex: 9878436; Fax: (0903) 88-42-75.

Portsmouth

▶ **Crest Hotel.** Pembroke Road, **Southsea** PO1 2TA. Tel: (0705) 82-76-51; Telex: 86397; Fax: (0705) 75-67-15.

▶ **Holiday Inn.** North Harbour, Cosham, **Portsmouth** PO6 4SH. Tel: (0705) 38-31-51; Telex: 86611; Fax: (0705) 38-87-01.

WEST

WINDSOR

From a plane approaching London's Heathrow Airport, or across the fields from a car on the M 4, the crenellated walls of Windsor Castle and its one big, round, hollow tower look like a child's dream of a heavenly sand castle.

Closer, from the three-mile-long avenue of trees called Long Walk, it seems to belong in Camelot rather than in this world of airports and freeways. Yet Windsor Castle, just 21 miles west of London, is uniquely a part of both: the home and fortress of nine centuries of English monarchy and of the present helicopter-hopping, polo-playing royal family.

MAJOR INTEREST

Windsor
The Guildhall (Wren, royal portraits)
Madame Tussaud's Royalty and Empire Exhibition

The Castle
St. George's Chapel (Chapel of the Order of the
   Garter)
The State Apartments
Queen Mary's dollhouse

Windsor Great Park
The Royal Mausoleum at Frogmore House
Windsor Safari Park

Around Windsor
Eton College
Runnymede

When Queen Elizabeth I commanded William Shakespeare to write a play for her court, this town of red-
roofed houses became the setting for *The Merry Wives of
Windsor*. The **Garter Inn** pub stands on the site of the
Harte and Garter, where Sir John Falstaff and his cronies
roistered.

At the Victorian (1849) Central Railway Station, **Madame Tussaud's** 130 life-size models evoke a later period:
the precise moment on June 19, 1897, when Queen
Victoria stepped off the train with her entourage in readi-
ness for the celebration of her Diamond Jubilee the
following day.

The **Guildhall** is a handsome colonnaded building
erected in the 17th century after plans by Sir Christopher
Wren. It houses a small museum of local history, but its
main attraction is its collection of royal portraits.

A good place to dine in Windsor is **The Castle**, a
Georgian coach inn opposite its namesake that offers a
plain à la carte menu. However, to escape the crowds it is
worth taking a half-mile walk across the pedestrians-only
bridge to the town of Eton (see below). **Christopher**, on
Eton's High Street (closed Saturday lunchtimes and at
Christmas), is fashionable and not terribly expensive. If
you want to splurge and sample some of the finest food in
Britain, head six miles upriver to Bray for a meal at the
Waterside Inn. The restaurant, run by the celebrated

Roux brothers of France, has views of smooth lawns and summerhouses, weeping willows, boats, and swans on the river. Book in advance; Tel: 0628-206-91.

The royal borough is overshadowed by the huge castle, which is perched on a chalk ridge above the River Thames and dominates the approaches from London.

The Castle

It is not difficult to picture Henry VIII, bloated with excess and age, dragging his ulcerated leg through the cloisters of Windsor, where courtiers plotted and whispered of heresy and treachery. It's even said that his halting steps can still be heard here. It was to Windsor that Henry fled in August 1517, when the "sweating sickness" struck the capital. But the epidemic followed the King, carrying off some of the royal pages who slept in His Majesty's chamber. The arms of Henry, along with the Tudor rose and the pomegranate of his first wife, Catherine of Aragon, are engraved in stone above the entrance gate named after the king. But Henry is only one of 41 monarchs who have added to and altered the castle that William of Normandy began just four years after he defeated Harold at the Battle of Hastings.

The original Norman round tower, which surveys the Thames as it winds through its green valley, is surrounded by other towers, walls, courts, lodges, and chapels built by successive royal dynasties. Plantagenets, Tudors, Stuarts, and Hanovers have added to the castle over the years. (The only interruption in the near millennium of royal residence at Windsor was the bitter decade of the Civil War in the 1640s.) The most recent occupants, the Windsors, so renamed their House of Saxe-Coburg and Gotha in 1917, when anti-German feeling was high. A new addition to the grounds is the Tudor-style mansion that the duke and duchess of York built for themselves.

Tradition rules here at Windsor, the heart of the system that from an island of warring barons created a nation and an empire upon which, it was later said, "the sun never set." British tradition is glorified every morning from Mondays through Saturdays at 11:00 with the elaborate rituals of the changing of the guard. Soldiers in their red tunics and black bearskin helmets stamp their boots and make the ancient walls ring. The same troops, in flak jackets rather than scarlet, embarked for the Falklands War in the summer of 1982. At Combermere Barracks on

St. Leonard's Road, just a few blocks from the castle, is the **Museum of the Household Cavalry.** (The Household Cavalry can also be seen mounting the guard daily at the Horse Guards opposite Whitehall in London.) The museum tells the story of the Blues (who, confusingly, wear red plumes in their helmets) and the Life Guards (white plumes) from 1685 to the present.

The **Chapel of the Order of the Garter**—St. George's Chapel—is the first building you see when you pass through the Henry VIII Gate. Carved choir stalls in the chapel include those of the Knights of the Garter, an order that, according to romantic legend, Edward III founded in 1348 after he picked up a garter the countess of Salisbury dropped while they were dancing. He rebuked the tittering courtiers with the words *"Honi soit qui mal y pense"* ("Evil be to him who evil of it thinks"), and this is the motto inscribed in gold letters on the dark blue velvet garter that to this day members wear beneath the left knee.

Edward IV began building the present chapel where the processings and ceremonies of the Knights of the Garter are enacted. (Their banners are hung in the choir.) The chapel was completed by Henry VIII, who shares a tomb here with Jane Seymour, his favorite among his many wives. The body of Charles I, beheaded in the Civil War and brought secretly to Windsor, was found nearby in the chapel vault when it was opened by George IV in the early part of the 19th century. Apart from Henry and Charles, eight other kings of England, including three from the present century, rest in peace beneath the chapel's fan-vaulted ceiling.

When, in 1820, George IV came to the throne late in life (he was prince regent for years during his father's madness), he transferred the family apartments from the dank north wing to the southern and eastern sides of the castle. He then had the Grand Corridor built to connect them with the **State Apartments.** The richly furnished State Apartments are used for royal ceremonies and receptions but are otherwise open to the public. The Queen's Presence Room is still as Charles II decorated it; the Neapolitan artist Antonio Verrio was commissioned to paint the ceiling. The walls are adorned with late-18th-century Gobelins, other tapestries, and royal portraits. In the sequence of rooms with majestic titles there are carvings by Grinling Gibbons, etchings by great masters, priceless porcelain and furniture, and paintings by Rubens, Rembrandt, Van Dyck, Canaletto, Dürer, Holbein, Reynolds, and others. The aptly named Grand Staircase is dominated by a vast, gleaming suit of armor made to measure in 1540 for a gouty Henry VIII. The Waterloo Chamber, created by George IV as a memorial to those who brought down Napoleon, has a seamless carpet 80 feet long and 40 feet wide. It was made in India for Queen Victoria and is probably the largest example of its kind in the world.

Everything in Windsor Castle is on a regal scale—everything, that is, except the **dollhouse** that was presented to Queen Mary in 1923 by the architect Sir Edwin Lutyens. It is built on a scale of 12:1, and so is everything in it, including works of writers such as Chesterton and Kipling and paintings by Orpen and Munnings, down to the electrical and plumbing fixtures of Lilliputian proportions. Like the State Apartments nearby, it is open to inspection.

Windsor Great Park

The 4,800-acre park, lying on the far side of the castle on a wide loop of the River Thames, was a hunting ground for William the Conqueror. And in fact, herds of deer roam here still. At the farthest end of Long Walk is an equestrian statue of George III dressed as a Roman emperor—a suitably sardonic memorial to the king who lost the American colonies.

On the grounds of Frogmore House, a royal residence in a quiet corner of the park dating from 1697, is the **mausoleum**. A masterpiece of mosaic and monumental masonry, it is a reminder of the Victorian way of death. Victoria, the Widow of Windsor, had it built for her beloved consort, Albert, whom she mourned for 40 years before she joined him. In the burial ground outside lie the remains of the king of the briefest reign, Edward VIII, and of the woman for whom he gave up the throne of England, Wallis Simpson.

A one-mile motor route takes visitors around **Windsor Safari Park**, two miles southwest of Windsor on B 3022, through an improbable reserve of lions and tigers, elephants and camels, zebras, bears, wolves, and baboons living wild in the green English countryside. The white turrets and battlements of the mansion overlooking the park, built half a century ago by an American automobile tycoon, are a pastiche of the real thing just down the road.

Eton and Runnymede

Eton College, that oldest of old schools which molded no fewer than 20 British prime ministers, stands modestly beside the High Street of the little town from which it takes its name, just across the river from Windsor. Some of the buildings, including the exquisitely painted chapel, date from the school's founding by Henry VI in 1440. A tower completed by Roger Lupton in 1520 looks down on the cobbled schoolyard and the playing fields beyond, on which the Battle of Waterloo was supposedly won. The younger boys still wear the inimitable Eton jacket and stiff collar, and the "Eton Boating Song" is still sung.

One fine summer's morning in 1215 King John and his entourage rode out from Windsor Castle to meet the king's disaffected barons, assembled on the open field of Runney Mede. Here King John was compelled to sign a charter curbing royal power by insuring the feudal rights of barons, the freedom of the church, and the customs of towns. This document—the first in British constitutional history—later became known as the Magna Carta, or great charter. The water-meadows of **Runnymede**, two miles northwest of Egham on the A 308, remain virtually untouched by the passing centuries. A small Classical-style temple was erected in 1957 by the American Bar Association, and nearby a memorial to President John F. Kennedy stands at the foot of Cooper's Hill. At the summit is another memorial, commemorating the 20,456 Allied airmen who died in World War II and have no known graves. Their names are recorded in the cloister.

Royal Windsor Horse Show

The Royal Windsor Horse Show is held in Home Park in mid-May. Members of the royal family play an active part, whether it be show jumping or driving. The best way to see the show, which is done while drinking Champagne and eating smoked-salmon sandwiches, is to become a member. Write to The Secretary, Mews, Windsor Castle, Berkshire. For those who would rather listen to Baroque music than compare the finer points of horseflesh, the **Windsor Festival** runs from late September through October.

WINCHESTER

Winchester is very much on the day-trip agenda for many visitors, though no commercial long-distance bus company includes it on conducted day tours. Perhaps this is because the city is well within commuting distance from London; if you take one of the sometimes cramped commuter trains in the afternoon you'll rub shoulders with office workers coming back from the capital.

As so often happens, the walk from the train station to the city center is unexciting and promises little—which makes your arrival in partly traffic-free High Street all the more enjoyable. But do make your way directly to this, the heart of the ancient city and the site of the great public school, the castle, and the riverside walks, as quickly as possible.

MAJOR INTEREST

Winchester castle
Winchester cathedral
Winchester College

Winchester Castle

At the western end of the agreeably compact city center is the 700-year-old **Castle Hall**. Built by Henry III on the site of a Norman fortress, it runs like a thread through English history. Henry V received the French ambassador here in 1415, before launching the campaign that ended in the English victory at Agincourt. Sir Walter Raleigh was sentenced to death here in 1603, Oliver Cromwell destroyed part of the building during the Civil War in 1645, and Judge Jeffreys held one of his "Bloody Assizes" here following the Monmouth Rebellion in 1655.

All this is much more historically reliable than the supposed association with King Arthur. The first thing you see on entering the great echoing Castle Hall is the famous Round Table on the west wall, supposedly dating back to 1152. But the romantic appeal is not a 20th-century phenomenon: The table was repainted and restored in 1522, when Henry VIII entertained Emperor Charles V in Winchester.

If the castle is missed by many visitors, the unusual **Westgate Museum** is probably seen by only one in a hundred. Housed in the 13th-century Westgate, literally the city's west gate, it is really just one room housing Tudor and Elizabethan armor and weapons. You can reach out and touch the history here.

Winchester Cathedral

Many people know before they even get as far as the spacious lawns that set it off so effectively that at 556 feet Winchester cathedral is the longest in Europe. They may also know that St. Swithin is buried in the churchyard, and that the manner of his burial made St. Swithin's Day part of English folklore. When Swithin, a humble man who was bishop of Winchester, died in 862 he was buried at his own request in the churchyard, where the rain would fall on him. On July 15 of that year, however, his remains were reburied inside the cathedral, and legend says this angered the saint so much that if it rains on July 15 it will rain every day for 40 days.

Among the many cathedral treasures that can be seen even in a short visit are the illuminated 12th-century Winchester Bible, and, in the transept, two wooden benches thought to be Norman; they are certainly the oldest pieces of oak furniture in the nation. There are, in addition, chests said to contain the bones of Saxon kings, including Canute and Ethelwulf. Jane Austen's grave is marked by a stone, but, curiously, no reference is made to her as a novelist. Another curiosity is that some windows contain 13th-century stained glass that was originally in Salisbury cathedral.

Winchester College

The cathedral is very impressive, but probably the favorite corner of Winchester is to be found to its south, in the quiet and comparatively little-frequented lanes that lead to and around Winchester College, one of several public schools—which are anything but public, of course—that claims to be the oldest in the country. The atmosphere here (visitors are allowed) is a cross between that of a monastery and an Oxford or Cambridge college. Pupils at the school, which was founded in 1382 for poor scholars, are known as Wykehamists, after founder Bishop William of Wykeham. If you only have time to explore one of the streets behind the cathedral, make it Kingsgate Street, which takes its name from one of the Medieval gateways to the old walled town.

The River Itchen runs close to the grounds of the school, and it is easy to find paths to stroll alongside. These paths are extremely pleasant when Winchester is crowded and hot; as always in major tourist destinations, try to avoid summer Saturdays, especially if you do not have a hotel in which to escape the melee.

If you really want to get close to history, you can still call at the **Hospital of St. Cross**, founded in 1137 by a grandson of William the Conqueror, for "the Wayfarer's Dole" of a token amount of bread and ale. In so doing you will be part of an 800-year-old tradition.

Should the Wayfarer's Dole give you a taste for something more substantial, try a lunchtime snack or bar meal in one of Winchester's ancient pubs, which tend to be tucked away down the back lanes. One of these, the **Royal Oak**, off Royal Oak Passage, is a contender for the oldest pub in the country. The **Eclipse**, in the Square, is a very pleasant place to sit outside on a summer day, with sidewalk benches under the pub's jettied black-and-white half-timbered upper stories. Originally the rectory for the little church of St. Lawrence, the building predates the cathedral itself. The Eclipse offers traditional English food such as toad-in-the-hole (sausage cooked in batter) and kedgeree (fish, rice, eggs, and condiments). Both the Square and Royal Oak Passage are near the northwest corner of the cathedral. For Itchen trout or pork in cream and cider sauce, with a better-than-average glass of pub wine, look for the **Wykeham Arms** on the corner of Canon Street, which is a westerly extension of College Street, running between the cathedral and Winchester College.

Even if you are in Winchester without a car, it is worth taking a taxi out to the city outskirts to **Lainston House Hotel**, which offers a good-value *table d'hôte* lunch on weekdays.

A number of other, lesser points of interest are worth looking out for if you are on foot, places that are sometimes missed by the car-bound visitor who takes in only the cathedral and perhaps a couple of Winchester's several interesting bookshops (among which are **Wells**, in Market Place, and **Blanchards**, on Jewry Street, though you'll find other bookshops—for used and antiquarian volumes—around Kingsgate Street). For example, search out the bronze statue of King Alfred, erected in 1901, that gazes down from the High Street in the direction of Westgate. Also look for the Gothic High Cross, on the High Street, and, a few yards away, close to the cathedral precinct, the **city museum**. It is particularly strong in Roman remains (including glass and mosaics), and its Victorian shops—real, not reconstructed—are very popular.

SALISBURY AND STONEHENGE

Neither the train journey to Salisbury nor the walk from the station, past small, functional shops and snack bars, are very inspiring. But do not despair, for this small city with a very impressive cathedral indeed, as well as lots of history that often gets overlooked because of the cathedral, is always worth the trip.

This is a rare case of a tourist attraction that may be best seen as part of an organized day out by bus from London. Evan Evans, for example, will take you to Stonehenge as well as Salisbury, saving you a lot of bother in the process. However, Stonehenge can also be seen during a day trip by rail to Salisbury; see Getting Around at the end of this section.

A recent major fire has spoiled an unusually attractive approach from a huge car park into the city center—what was a fine riverside arrangement of shops and a few offices; there may be some interesting renovations. But if the approach from the train station is dull and the approach from the car park is ravaged, the city itself has an immediate charm, and there is much to see even in a short space of time.

MAJOR INTEREST

Salisbury cathedral
Well-preserved shops and houses
Stonehenge

Around in Salisbury

The River Avon does not dominate Salisbury, but its presence is definitely felt: A good and popular place to get oriented early in the day is beside the County Hotel, where swans bob on the Avon and friends meet to go off for lunch in one of several local hostelries—and sometimes in the good fish-and-chips shop called **Stoby's**.

Note that this is *not* Shakespeare's Avon, the one that flows (also with swans) through Stratford-upon-Avon, but the one that rises north of Salisbury Plain, runs close to Stonehenge, and reaches the sea near Bournemouth, due south of Salisbury. John Constable painted Salisbury cathedral most memorably from the river's banks near Harnham—and even in the course of a day trip you can walk to the mill there, which doubles as an unpretentious restaurant; see below.

Salisbury's original symmetrical Medieval layout, which is roughly intact, has been compared with that of American cities, and makes orientation easy for visitors. A good point at which to begin a tour of the city, which even on a day trip can easily be coupled with a thorough inspection of the world-famous cathedral, is the parish church of St. Thomas Becket, which has a rare 500-year-old carved roof and a most impressive painting called *Doom*—a kind of day of judgment study—probably given by a parishioner who had made a pilgrimage to Canterbury.

A very well known bakery called **Snells**—also known for its take-out coffee and chocolate—may provide the makings of a memorable picnic within sight of the cathedral. Just around the corner is the public library, which stands on the site of the Cheese Cross (where cheese was traded) that once stood here. Of all the Medieval market crosses where trade was carried out in Salisbury only one, Poultry Cross, tucked away behind one corner of the marketplace, still exists.

If you visit Salisbury on a Tuesday or Saturday you'll find the lively open-air market in progress. A charter drawn up in 1227 permitted a daily market, but objections from local towns reduced these to twice-weekly affairs. Among other things, the marketplace is still associated with the great feast held for the coronation of Edward VII in 1902, when four thousand people sat down to an open-air meal of roast beef.

On the opposite side of the market from the library and St. Thomas's lies **Cross Keys Chequer**, a small precinct of interesting shops, including a good bookshop. The "chequer" is based on a Medieval layout of about 1225. Close by is the John A'Port House, officially a shop selling china and glass—quality souvenirs here—but equally well known for having been the home of a six-time mayor of Salisbury in the 15th century.

Behind the marketplace you will find Fish Row (no need to explain its origin) and Salisbury's tourist information center. Walk along Fish Row and you'll come to Butcher Row and then to Poultry Cross. There's a good pub, **The Haunch of Venison,** close to Poultry Cross, with better-than-average bar food and a restaurant, too.

Pick up New Canal Street and then Milford Street, where you'll find the **Red Lion Hotel,** an ancient inn whose heyday was probably in the early 18th century, when stage-coaches left for London at 10:00 every night. They don't serve the best food in the world, but the restaurant and, particularly, the bar offer lots of atmosphere.

On Catherine Street (via Milford Street) you'll find another, slightly more genteel, more comfortable hotel that also serves good hot bar meals. This is the **White Hart,** whose handsome sign was put up in 1827 in response to a sign erected by a rival establishment. On October 9, 1780, on his way to negotiate a treaty with the Dutch during the American War of Independence, Henry Laurens, a former president of the Continental Congress, was captured at sea and kept overnight at the hotel before being taken to London and incarcerated in the Tower. (He was exchanged for General Cornwallis in 1782.) The **Rose and Crown** on Harnham Road also has good bar food and a restaurant. (See below for these last two places as accommodations.)

Here you are on the edge of a particularly interesting, quiet, and architecturally appealing quarter of the city. First is St. Ann Street; note the impressive carved exterior of Joiner's Hall. From the end of St. Ann Street cross St. John Street and walk through St. Ann's Gate, perhaps the nicest approach to the **cathedral close**; it is much less touristy than the more frequently used High Street Gate. Built in 1333, when the close was first laid out around the almost 100-year-old cathedral, the gate still has traces of late-Norman carving.

The houses in the close itself are full of interest. Near St. Ann's Gate, at number 14, is where Henry Fielding wrote *Tom Jones,* and, on the far side of the cathedral, Myles Place was the home of the distinguished historian Sir Arthur Bryant, whose ashes are interred in the cathedral. On the same side of the close, in the King's House, is the impressive **Salisbury and South Wiltshire Museum** (which includes in its varied collections a reconstructed country doctor's surgery and a giant figure that used to be carried at the head of parades in Salisbury) and a building known as The Wardrobe, which houses the Museum of the Berkshire and Wiltshire Regiment. Facing the cathedral from another side of the close, though near these museums, is lovely **Mompesson House**, a National Trust property. It is a fine 18th-century building, with period furniture, *objets d'art,* and an unusual lived-in atmosphere.

Though it is not open to the public, look at the exterior of the College of Matrons, just inside the close near the High Street Gate. It was built in 1682 to house "twelve poor widows," and it still does, though the original means test is no longer applied.

It is said, by the way, that Trollope modeled his Barchester on Exeter, but it was while sitting in Salisbury's cathedral close that he conceived the idea of an intricate "cathedral society."

On the High Street do not miss one of provincial England's biggest and most interesting secondhand (and antiquarian) bookshops, **Beach's**, where the assistants wear uniforms. From High Street turn into Crane Street and walk as far as Queen Elizabeth Gardens, from where you can follow the Town Path—so marked—to **Harnham Mill**. The mill, mentioned above, dates from 1135, and was used to house cathedral artifacts during the move from the Old Sarum cathedral site to the new one.

The Cathedral

Old Sarum had grown up around the ancient church of St. Osmund and a castle on a hillside site, but it was later deemed unsuitable because it was affected by "too much wind and too little water," and the population was beginning to move south onto the more fertile plain. The move was made official by Papal sanction to build a new cathedral. Tradition holds that the bishop declared a new cathedral would be built a shot-arrow's distance from the old cathedral. Some arrow: Salisbury cathedral is about three miles away.

Many people are surprised by how light and spacious the cathedral (which was consecrated in 1258, only 38 years after the first stone was laid) seems inside. It belongs to a very distinctive period of cathedral construction; those of Lincoln and Amiens date from the same period. The nave is the longest in England after Winchester's, and there is much in the cathedral that is outstanding: the oldest piece of working machinery in Britain, and possibly the world, for one thing, in the form of a clock dating from 1386. The cathedral is also the repository of one of only four contemporary copies of the Magna Carta of 1215. This treasure has been kept in the cathedral continuously since 1225, except when it was hidden in a nearby quarry between 1940 and 1945 to protect it from German bombing. The spire was erected in about 1330, as it had not been part of the original plan.

Do not miss the cathedral's **cloisters**, which are the largest in area of any English cathedral, and a place of calm even when the cathedral is thronged with visitors—which does seem to be almost all the time. That last fact is an argument for visiting Salisbury during poor weather or during the winter months, especially now that there is central heating (the place was once well known for the number of people who brought hot water bottles to carol services).

Even within a one-day trip it is possible to visit Stonehenge from Salisbury. Buses leave the Salisbury train station three times a day, and the fare for the almost two-hour round trip is about £2. Further details are available from the tourist information center; Tel: (0722) 33-49-56.

If you decide to spend the night in Salisbury, the **White Hart Hotel** on St. John Street has an imposing façade and pleasant and spacious public rooms. It is also the favorite rendezvous of Salisbury's well-heeled citizens. For atmosphere, try the **Rose & Crown Hotel** on Harnham Road, which overlooks the river and has a well-known rose garden. Part of the building dates from the 14th century.

Stonehenge

Stonehenge, at the southern edge of Salisbury plain, just eight miles north of Salisbury, probably looms larger in your imagination than it does in actual fact. As has often been pointed out, its 162 stone blocks—unadorned, undressed, and only about 35 steps from one side to the other—would fit into the Library of Congress rotunda or within the dome of St. Paul's Cathedral. This most famous of all Britain's stone circles is one of Europe's greatest enigmas: Each year it inspires approximately three quarters of a million people to make a pilgrimage. These numbers are swollen by modern-day Druids, pop fans, and latter-day hippies who crowd onto Salisbury Plain for the summer solstice (as well as for the officially illegal rock festivals held to coincide with it). It is mainly on account of these celebrants that access to Stonehenge is today more restricted than it has ever been. Barbed-wire barricades have turned this into a look-but-don't-touch monument—no more KILROY WAS HERE engraved into the stones with penknives.

A thousand years before the Egyptians built the pyramids, Neolithic farmers lived on the windswept chalk plateau of Salisbury. There was little wood and less stone, but they nevertheless built burial chambers around which Stonehenge eventually grew—first as a cemetery, then as a temple. Over the years it was put to many uses, which is one of the reasons Stonehenge has so puzzled later generations.

As trade routes became busier and the population increased, Stonehenge and similar burial grounds took on the role of meeting places, not only for traders but also for participants in seasonal fertility rituals. Stonehenge was almost certainly not constructed because of any astronomical significance.

In 1130 Henry of Huntingdon, a dean at Lincoln Cathedral, was commissioned to write a history of England, and he included Stonehenge. He borrowed from an even earlier chronicle—largely fictitious—that claimed Merlin, seer and prophet to King Arthur, had the stones removed from Ireland and reconstructed on Salisbury Plain. James I was utterly intrigued by Stonehenge, and commissioned John Aubrey, best known for his *Brief Lives,* to produce a thorough survey. But Aubrey was much more impressed with nearby Avebury Stone Circle, and his work at Stonehenge was skimpy. Among all the dross was the correct suggestion that this was a residential site of early British tribes.

Charles II was among the "great and good" to be fascinated by Stonehenge, and he commissioned Inigo Jones, the superb architect of St. Paul's, Covent Garden, and the Banqueting Hall in London, to solve the mystery. Jones concluded that as "those ancient times had no knowledge of public works, either sacred or secular, for their own use or honour of their deities, they could not be responsible for such an impressive structure." It must, ergo, have been Roman in origin.

People seem to have great difficulty counting the stones. A legend from Elizabethan times has it that no ordinary mortal can count the stones twice and arrive at the same figure. *Gulliver's Travels* author Jonathan Swift and Celia Fiennes, the 17th-century traveller and diarist, were among those who made a stab at it. Each came up with a different number, and Swift hedged his bets— "either 92 or 93."

Samuel Pepys took a day trip from Salisbury to Stonehenge but found the cost of his party's saddle horses rather high. Of the site itself he was characteristically blunt: "Worth going to see. God knows what their use was."

Among the earliest of all visitors to Stonehedge were the Druids, Celtic priests who came over from the Continent about 300 B.C., by which point Stonehenge already had lain abandoned and unused for more than 1,000 years. They took it over for ceremonial purposes (though not, as fancifully used to be supposed, for ritual slaughter).

The Layout of Stonehenge

As you approach Stonehenge, you first come upon a ditch and a bank about 100 feet from the first stones. Inside this are the 56 Aubrey holes, found to contain remains of cremated human beings, and what is effectively a gateway to the site known as the Slaughter Stone, now fallen. The Heel Stone, a so-called sarsen stone, stands outside the entrance. (The word *sarsen* probably comes from *saracen,* or, simply, strange or alien; the term "Heel Stone" is derived from a mark on the surface that resembles a man's heel.) The Heel Stone is the only one to have survived from the first circle of stones that appeared here around 1800 B.C., and was erected exactly in line, along with other stones, with the point at which the sun rises above the horizon during the summer solstice.

Between 1700 and 1600 B.C. the construction of the second stage of Stonehenge began. Blue stones were transported from Wales and erected in two concentric circles. This was the work of the so-called Beaker Folk, farmers from the Continent. The construction of Stonehenge III began after 1600 B.C., when the blue stones were moved and 80 huge sarsen stones were transported here from the Marlborough Downs. These were formed either into a ring of upright stones, connected by carved lintels, or an inner horseshoe shape.

Later (also part of Stonehenge III) an oval arrangement of blue stones was erected within the sarsen horseshoe, and a block of sandstone, also from Wales, was erected in the center. It became known as the Altar Stone. Finally, sometime around 1300 B.C., the residents rearranged 19 blue stones into their current configuration.

A word of advice: As with Salisbury cathedral, try to visit Stonehenge when the rest of the world has decided to skip it. Dull, even rainy, days are good; misty or foggy ones are better still. It all helps to get the imagination working. Even when the site is closed, however, it is possible during daylight hours to see a certain amount of Stonehenge from the road. For further information contact the shop-cum-information center at the site. Tel: (8095) 62-31-08.

BATH

The only sad faces you'll see in Bath are those belonging to people who have allowed themselves only one day to see the city. It's worth a whole week, but it *is* possible to get the flavor of the city in a day. Train travellers will find that the station is close to the heart of things. Just walk north along Manvers Street until you see the **abbey**, which is famous for its light, bright interior and its delicate fanvaulting. The mainly 16th-century structure was restored in the 17th century. The Pump Room and the Roman Baths are virtually adjacent to the abbey, and you get to Pulteney Bridge, for example, from the abbey by walking east toward the river and then left along Grand Parade. On a day trip you will have to resist the temptation to linger over lunch in one of Bath's elegant restaurants, and even this genteel and self-conscious city has sufficient fast-food restaurants and pubs with food where you'll find enough sustenance to keep you from flagging.

Even in history-rich Britain few places offer such an immediate hands-across-the-centuries link with the past. The Romans are omnipresent. It was they who first exploited the health-giving qualities of the water that fell on the nearby Mendip Hills about 10,000 years ago and now bubbles up from the earth at the rate of 250,000 gallons a day.

The **museum** created around the excavated remains of the **Roman baths** (which came complete with the equivalent of today's Jacuzzis, saunas, and Turkish baths) is exceptional. Not surprisingly, the grateful Romans also created a temple to Sulis Minerva: Sul was an ancient Celtic deity and Minerva the Roman goddess of healing.

But it was the 18th century that created the Bath that today has such a powerful hold on visitors. The influx of outsiders looking for the elixir of life made massive redevelopment possible, and the soft, crumbly local stone was ideal for a comparatively quick transformation of the place, which was completed with skill and a keen aesthetic sense. Jane Austen, when she first came, disliked the squeaky clean look of the new buildings, but these have now mellowed to form one of the handsomest cities in Europe.

Of course, the city is best seen on foot—unless you take a horse-drawn carriage (which are found at the bottom of Milsom Street) or an open-top bus tour. Because it takes you right out of the city into the surrounding hills, one advantage of the latter is that it offers distant views down into and across Bath. These buses are highly visible, and can be picked up at several points.

The city is indeed friendly to walkers, and if time is limited consider a conducted walking tour, best joined at the Pump Room (tickets from the tourist information center, recently moved to Unit G1, the Colonnades, 11– 13 Bath Street; Tel: 0225-46-28-31), which includes entrance to the Pump Room and the Roman Baths (where you'll probably have a separate, and extremely well-informed, guide), saving time and hassle. A further advantage is that you can ask your guide all sorts of questions to help you get the most out of the limited time at your disposal: about pubs, fast-food restaurants, and shops (especially antiques shops, many of which are high class but nonetheless sell good-quality pieces that will not have you calling your bank for an urgent cash transfer).

Should you want an interesting angle on the city without actually walking, consider an hour-long riverboat trip from the Pulteney Bridge. These fit well into a day-trip schedule. The boats leave every hour on the hour between 11:00 A.M. and 6:00 P.M., with evening trips in July and August.

A walking route covering places not to be missed might start at **The Royal Crescent**, created by John Wood the Younger between 1767 and 1775 and probably inspired by Bernini's Colonnade around the Piazza San Pietro in Rome. The **Royal Crescent Hotel** is right in the center of the elegant crescent: lunch here is elegant as well, but, of course, will eat into your time.

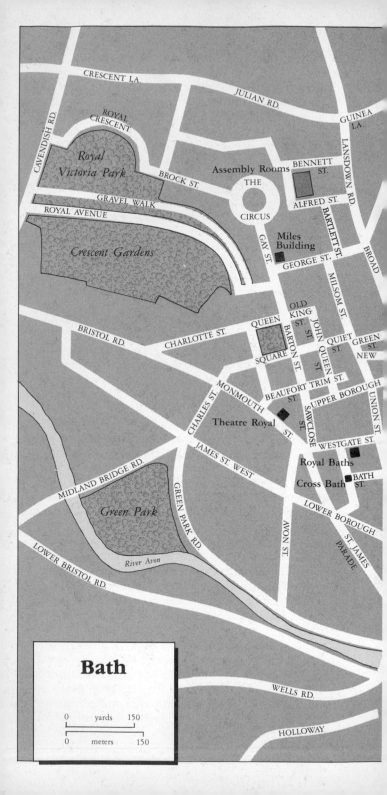

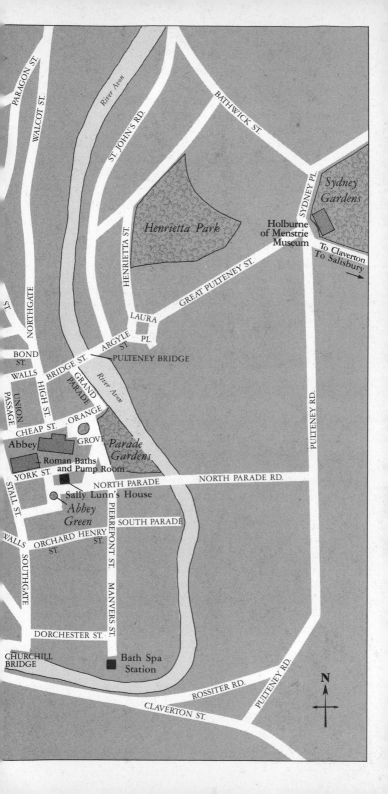

With or without lunch here, you'll experience the elegance of a Royal Crescent interior at **No. 1 Royal Crescent**, a museum maintained in great style by the Bath Preservation Trust. The handsome stone houses of the Circus (not the Big Top type) are in the classical 18th-century tradition. A few yards away are the **Assembly Rooms**, once the haunt of Bath's high society, and now housing an exceptional costume museum that is scheduled to reopen after major renovations in April 1991. One contemporary costume is added to the collection every year.

There is good antiques hunting in and around **Bartlett Street**, and as you walk down Milsom Street you will hear echoes of Jane Austen, who referred to this street in *Northanger Abbey*. Actually, she referred to "the prettiest little hat you can imagine" in a shop window here, but you are also likely to notice the excellent bookshops—useful for souvenirs and guidebooks. In *Persuasion,* Sir Walter Elliott "counted eighty-seven women without there being a tolerable face among them." Also in Milsom Street, it's worth seeing the **Octagon Chapel**, famous for being so comfortable that some pews even had their own fireplaces. It is now the headquarters of the Royal Photographic Society.

From the bottom of the street you can hail a horse-drawn carriage; the usual route goes via Pulteney Bridge (perhaps the single most photographed structure in Bath, and the second oldest river bridge in Britain, after Lincoln's, to have houses built on it) to the **Holburne of Menstrie Museum**. Inspired by the works of Italian Renaissance architect Andrea Palladio, Robert Adam designed the bridge in 1770. The Holburne of Menstrie Museum is named after Sir Thomas William Holburne, who amassed a collection of fine paintings—among other things—including works by Gainsborough, Stubbs, and Turner.

A short walk from here, at the end of North Parade Passage and then into York Street, you'll find the house of Ralph Allen, who bought several stone quarries and organized much of the development of the city. Do not miss quiet, tree-shaded, and often overlooked Abbey Green, nearby, which is close to the Roman Baths. The **Crystal Palace** pub on Abbey Green is convivial and has good food.

Unfortunately, the restoration of the city's 17th- and 18th-century baths (Cross Bath, Hot Bath, and the Beau Street Bath) has been suspended, and they can only be seen from outside. (Go via Bath Street, past the tourist information center.)

Retrace your steps up Bath Street and you'll find the best souvenir hunting around Northumberland Place and Union Passage—a fascinating traffic-free rabbit warren of small shops and cafés. Turn left at the top of Union Street into Upper Borough Walls and you'll come to the Theatre Royal. Almost next door is the house once occupied by Beau Nash's mistress, Juliana Papjoy, now a restaurant known as Popjoy's (nobody seems to be able to explain the corruption of the name).

Apart from establishments already mentioned, day visitors are recommended (partly for reasons of time) to the **Moon and Sixpence Wine Bar** at 6A Broad Street, **Le Parisien** on Old Bond Street, and—for Japanese dishes— **Chikako** on St. John's Place.

Worth a detour (even on a day trip) is the **American Museum**, Claverton Manor, on the outskirts of the city. There are 18 rooms set out with American furniture dating from the mid-17th century to the mid-19th century, as well as galleries devoted to glass, pewter, and silver. Occasionally special weekends are devoted to such themes as the Civil War, the War of Independence, and the Native American heritage. For details, Tel: (0225) 46-05-03. To get there by public transport take the number 18 bus from the abbey or the bus station as far as the university; from there it's a five-minute walk (ask the driver for directions).

During late May and early June you may want to extend your day well into the evening, as that is when the annual **Bath Festival of Music and the Arts** is held. Every year there is a special theme, and 1991 musically celebrates both the bicentenary of Mozart's death and the dramatic changes in Eastern Europe. There's also a jazz program and a fringe festival, and not all events are evening ones. For details, Tel: (0225) 46-22-31 or 46-00-31.

Should you be tempted to spend the night in Bath, you may be able to find accommodations on short notice, although there is no guarantee. You are more likely to find a room at one of the larger hotels, such as the **Francis Hotel** on Queen Square, a Georgian building that was partly rebuilt after it was hit by one of the few Luftwaffe bombs to fall on Bath. It has a particularly spacious restaurant. Another possibility is the **Hilton National** on Walcot Street, a fairly functional hotel in which some of the more than 100 rooms have a river view.

GETTING AROUND

Windsor

By car, leave London via Hammersmith and follow the M 4 to Junction 6. It's a 40-minute train ride from London's Paddington Station to Windsor and Eton Central; the trip takes 55 minutes from London's Waterloo to Windsor and Eton Riverside. You can also reach Windsor by Green Line bus from Victoria Coach Station.

Winchester

Winchester is about 65 miles from London by rail, a trip of just over an hour; the round-trip fare is about £11. Trains leave from Waterloo Station, which lies on London's Bakerloo and Northern Underground lines. From Winchester's train station it is only a ten-minute walk southward via Station Road and Upper High Street to the heart of what remains of the ancient city. The approach is as uninspiring as old Winchester is impressive. You can also travel by long-distance bus from London's Victoria Coach Station, travel time about an hour and a quarter; round-trip fare is about £8.50.

It is possible to combine a day trip to Winchester and Salisbury, but if you are coming from London it will require an early-morning start and a late return. You'll need to change trains at Basingstoke, and you should be prepared to wait up to an hour for connections.

Salisbury

Salisbury is accessible by train from London's Waterloo Station, which lies on the Northern and Bakerloo Underground lines. The trip takes approximately an hour and a half. The round-trip fare is about £14.

You can also go by long-distance bus (National Express) from London's Victoria Coach Station. The journey takes about two and three quarters hours, and the round-trip fare is approximately £10.50.

A busy full-day alternative is a conducted coach tour from Evan Evans. Costing about £32 per adult, this includes all entrance fees (to the visitor center at Stonehenge, for example) and takes in Bath and its main attractions as well as Salisbury and Stonehenge. Details from Evan Evans, 26–28 Paradise Road, Richmond, Surrey TW9 1SE; Tel: (081) 322-2912.

For regular bus service from Salisbury to Stonehenge, see the end of the Salisbury section, above.

Bath

Bath is well known for its speedy rail connection to London's Paddington Station, which lies on the Circle District and Metropolitan lines of the London Underground system. Although it is 107 miles from London by train, Bath can be reached in about an hour and a half. The train station is convenient to the city center, and a further bonus is that it is an elegant building in its own right. The round-trip fare is about £20.

Bath is also accessible by long-distance bus (National Express) from London's Victoria Coach Station. The journey takes about three hours, and the round-trip fare is approximately £11.25.

ACCOMMODATIONS REFERENCE

Salisbury

▶ **Rose & Crown Hotel.** Harnham Road, **Salisbury** SP2 8JQ. Tel: (0722) 279-08; Telex: 47224; Fax: (0722) 33-98-16.

▶ **White Hart Hotel.** 1 St. John Street, **Salisbury** SP1 2SD. Tel: (0722) 274-76; Fax: (0722) 41-27-61; in U.S., (800) 223-5672 or (212) 541-4400.

Bath

▶ **Francis Hotel.** Queen Square, **Bath** BA1 2HH. Tel: (0225) 42-42-57; Telex: 449162; Fax: (0225) 31-97-15; in U.S., (800) 223-5672 or (212) 541-4400.

▶ **Hilton National.** Walcot Street, **Bath** BA1 5BJ. Tel: (0225) 46-34-11; Telex: 449519; Fax: (0225) 46-43-93.

NORTHWEST

OXFORD

Visitors to Oxford, 59 miles northwest of central London, tend to arrive with a ready-made image in mind: Matthew Arnold's description of "that sweet City with her dreaming spires." That is not always what they find, particularly if they arrive by public transportation. Emerging from the railway station, passengers are confronted by a brewery and an old jam factory. The latter, once the source of Oxford's famous marmalade, now does at least house an antiques market where the atmosphere is friendly and there are bargains to collect. Bus travellers are likewise dropped in one of the city's more nondescript quarters.

The best way to get a feel for Oxford is to find a vantage point with an overall view. One such spot is where the main streets, St. Aldate's, Queen Street, Cornmarket, and the High, converge, at Carfax. The 14th-century **Carfax Tower** (all that remains of St. Martin's Church, which was demolished in 1896) is open to visitors, who, when they have wound their way up the spiral stairs, will find all Oxford laid out before them. This is where you should begin your tour of Oxford.

MAJOR INTEREST

Carfax Tower
University colleges
Radcliffe Square
Bodleian Library
Bookstores on Broad Street
Sheldonian Theatre
Science Museum
Ashmolean Museum

To the east of the tower, High Street—always known as "the High"—curves away to the distant hills. To the north is Cornmarket Street. Between these two streets is an enticing array of domes, pinnacles, and towers. St. Aldate's, to the south, is dominated by the ornate Tom Tower, marking the entrance to Christ Church College. Beyond it is the Thames, or (as it is more popularly known in its passage through Oxford) the Isis. To the west are sadder sights: Queen Street leads to a mishmash of modern shopping areas and parking lots. The old castle also lies this way, but the romantic battlements are now the site of the local jail, and all that remains of the Norman fortress is a grassy mound.

From the Carfax Tower, the areas that reward exploration are apparent. The rich golden stones of the old, which on a sunny day seem to glow with their own inner light, offer a far greater lure than the neon and plastic of the new. Thus, visitors to Oxford are drawn to the city's main claim to fame, its ancient university.

Travellers here frequently ask to be directed to the

university, only to be told that it is all around them—as you can clearly see from the top of Carfax Tower. The university is made up of 35 separate colleges, each with its individual history and traditions, yet all growing from a single root. To understand the system you must step back some 800 years. Medieval learning drew its strength from the church, which was the major center of study and which controlled virtually all forms of education. By the 13th century Oxford was home to a guild of teachers, the Universitas, whose students were housed in communal halls. From these grew the colleges, each with its chapel for prayers and its quadrangles, around which were grouped rooms for students and teachers. Common facilities, such as libraries, soon developed to serve all the colleges. But the heart of the teaching system remained the tutorial, the meeting of teacher and student in the comfortable, informal surroundings of a college room.

Great variety exists among the colleges, certainly in appearance. There are grand colleges, with architecture so classically formal it approaches pomposity, and others where you might feel you had strayed into the garden of some old country mansion. To understand the colleges, it may help to take a little time at the beginning of the tour to look at one in detail.

Christ Church College

As you descend Carfax Tower and walk south on St. Aldate's, the first college you come to is Christ Church. The site originally held an Anglo-Saxon nunnery, but the church was rebuilt several times before the Norman church of St. Frideswide was begun here in the 12th century. In 1525 Cardinal Wolsey arrived with typical bravado and plans to demolish all that was old and raise a new college with a new chapel. The cardinal's fall brought a change of plans and patrons. Henry VIII took over, and Cardinal College became Christ Church. In the process, St. Frideswide's was saved, first as the college chapel, later as **Oxford Cathedral**.

Given its powerful patronage, the college was inevitably built on a grand scale and improved and developed over the centuries, with much of its present formal beauty due to the influence of Sir Christopher Wren. The formal entrance, topped by the tall **Tom Tower**, is intended to impress the visitor, and it does. Each evening during term

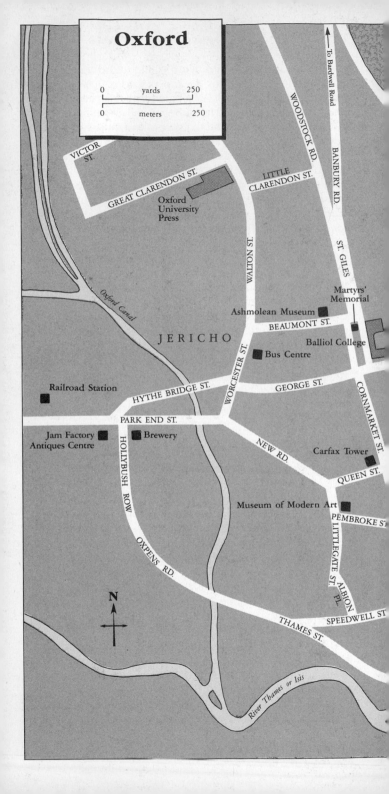

Oxford

| 0 | yards | 250 |
| 0 | meters | 250 |

VICTOR ST.

WOODSTOCK RD.

To Bardwell Road

BANBURY RD.

GREAT CLARENDON ST.

LITTLE CLARENDON ST.

Oxford University Press

WALTON ST.

ST. GILES

Oxford Canal

JERICHO

Martyrs' Memorial

Ashmolean Museum

BEAUMONT ST.

Balliol College

WORCESTER ST.

Bus Centre

Railroad Station

HYTHE BRIDGE ST.

GEORGE ST.

CORNMARKET ST.

PARK END ST.

Jam Factory Antiques Centre

Brewery

HOLLYBUSH ROW

NEW RD.

Carfax Tower

QUEEN ST.

Museum of Modern Art

PEMBROKE ST.

OXPENS RD.

LITTLEGATE ST. ALBION PL.

N

THAMES ST.

SPEEDWELL ST.

River Thames or Isis

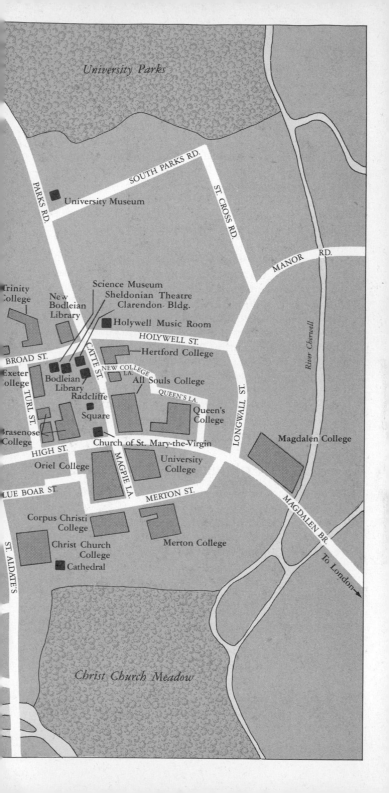

time the great bell in the tower tolls 101 times, once for each member of the original founders of the college.

Once inside the quad you find yourself in an enclosed space, the self-contained world of the college. All around are the buildings that house students and dons, but the sheer size of the open grounds prevents any sense of claustrophobia. Meanwhile, the eye is drawn to the tower and spire of the cathedral. Thus, the architecture expresses both the college's religious and scholarly heritage. Christ Church has an air of spaciousness, fronting a wide street with the open green of Christ Church Meadow alongside. Beyond the main quad are subsidiary quads and such important buildings as the college kitchens.

Famous alumni of Christ Church include the mathematics tutor C. L. Dodgson, better known as Lewis Carroll, who might have been amused by some of the antics of 20th-century undergraduates: A swan was once discovered languishing in Tom Quad, formally attired in black bow tie; on another occasion, when Dean Lowe of Christ Church landed in Christ Church Meadow in a helicopter, he was greeted by a choir of undergraduates singing "Lo, he comes in clouds descending."

Christ Church creates its own unmistakable atmosphere, just as every other college at Oxford does, and if it can boast of former members as diverse as Lewis Carroll, William Penn, and W. H. Auden, so can they.

Other Colleges and Landmarks

If you go back up St. Aldate's and then take a stroll east down Blue Boar Street, a quite different sense of space and time develops. The noise of traffic recedes, and the narrow lane briefly opens out into Oriel Square, bounded by the **Peckwater Quad** of Christ Church and Oriel and Corpus Christi colleges. What is at once so striking is that Oxford really is a mixture of quite disparate styles: **Oriel** is grandly Jacobean, while **Corpus Christi**, altered and enriched though it has been over the years, has a feel of almost domestic intimacy. It is typical of Oxford that there should be curiosities to look out for, such as Corpus Christi's pelican sundial with its strange perpetual calendar.

Beyond the square, the way continues its ever more secretive path up cobbled Merton Street past **Merton College**, which received its first statute in 1263 and is generally regarded as the oldest of the colleges—though the claim is strongly contested by two others, Balliol and

University. Merton can at least claim to have some of Oxford's oldest buildings, and nowhere do you feel closer to the Medieval heart of the university than in **Merton Chapel**, with its beautiful stained glass.

Merton Street bends through a right angle, and the mood changes again, quite dramatically, for there at the end is the High, dominated by colleges and two churches set among many old houses of character (virtually all now converted to shops). To the west are crowded city streets, to the east openness and light—no accident, but, rather, a reflection of the fact that the former lay within the old city walls, the latter outside them. To the east the view is dominated by **Magdalen College** (pronounced *maudlin*), its elaborate stonework gleaming from a recent cleaning. Magdalen is the focal point for one of Oxford's most popular traditions. Each May Day morning at 6:00 a hymn is sung from the tower, signaling the start of a pre-breakfast round of roistering that fills the surrounding streets, not to mention the surrounding pubs, which are opened early for this one day of the year. From here you can hire punts to explore the River Cherwell. A favorite excursion is to punt down to the **Victoria Arms**—universally known as the Vicky Arms—for a well-earned pint of beer on the lawn. It takes approximately two hours from Magdalen Bridge. A shorter, one-hour trip is possible by hiring a punt upstream at Bardwell Road.

Heading west down the High toward the city center the scene is one of rather formal grandeur, with the Classicism of **Queen's College** striking the dominant note. But to reach the core of the university complex you must turn off the High onto Catte Street and follow the latter to **Radcliffe Square**. An urban space that captures the imagination, the square owes its impact to the genius of Nicholas Hawksmoor, who suggested that the library, the **Radcliffe Camera**, be built as a rotunda. His own design was not used, however, and the work was given to James Gibbs, though both men received fees. So there it sits like the hub of a wheel, positively inviting you to look outward to the splendors on every side.

To the south is the **Church of St. Mary-the-Virgin** with its tall tower. The main body of All Souls College comes into view to the east, and Brasenose College is to the west, while to the north is the Bodleian Library. But it is not just the magnificence of the buildings that gives the square its special character: The Camera is the principal undergraduate library, so it is constantly surrounded by a clutter of bicycles and a whirl of students who are there to work, not merely to gaze.

The **Bodleian Library**, a research library used by scholars from all over the world, is rather more solemn. Statistics, for once, do give some notion of scale: five million volumes, spread along 81 miles of shelving, with seating for 2,078 readers. What statistics cannot do is convey the air of antiquity of a library whose heart is now four centuries old. Modernization has been slow. Heating was introduced only in 1821, which is why the oath all new readers must take includes a vow "not to bring into the Library or kindle therein any fire or flame." Visitors who want to see the oldest part of the library must make arrangements in advance, but it is well worth the effort. Visitors should call the Bodleian (Tel: 0865-27-71-65) and book a tour; there are four a day, starting at 10:30 A.M., from mid-March to the end of October, with limited visits in winter. No children under 14 permitted.

Broad Street

Opposite the Bodleian is New College Lane, spanned by Oxford's version of the Bridge of Sighs, which unites the two parts of Hertford College.

Those tempted to explore will find ever more secluded alleyways, one of which, St. Helen's Passage, ends surprisingly at a country-pub-come-to-town in the shape of the thatched **Turf Tavern**. Just around the corner at the end of Broad Street is one of the undergraduates' favorite pubs, the **Kings Arms**, where you can choose between the big open bar at the front and the cozy paneled back bar, which until very recently was exclusively a male preserve. (Still reserved for men is the famous bathing spot on the Cherwell, Parson's Pleasure, where gentlemen can bathe in the nude.) Those who prefer wider vistas will certainly find them in **Broad Street**. Close at hand is the **covered market**. Stalls originally cluttered and blocked the surrounding streets before they were moved into this specially built market hall. Here the colleges buy their provisions; many of the stalls sell very traditional English food—from the specialists in game, whose stalls, in season, are festooned with pheasant and partridge, to the sellers of English cheeses.

But Broad Street also caters to a quite different need: For book lovers, it is as close to heaven as they are ever likely to get. Here virtually anything can be found, from the most esoteric textbook to the latest paperback. There are shops specializing in art books, children's books, and even antiquarian books. **B. H. Blackwell**, the world-famous bookshop on Broad Street, is nearly as much an Oxford institution as the university itself. Trinity, Balliol, and Exeter colleges manage to squeeze in among the booksellers and still leave space for a small group of historic buildings, such as the Sheldonian.

The **Sheldonian Theatre** was not designed as a theater in the modern sense but as a site for ceremonials. The first work of Sir Christopher Wren ("the first" in the sense that it was the first to be begun; Pembroke Chapel at Cambridge, though completed earlier, was started later) soon found other uses. Home for a time to the university press, it later became a concert hall and remains one today. The Sheldonian and the delightful little **Holywell Music Room** up Holywell Street are part of Britain's musical history—Haydn performed here and so did Handel. In July there is the **Handel in Oxford Festival**; hearing the composer's works in the ornate setting of the Sheldonian is not unlike hearing Mozart's music performed in Salzburg.

Broad Street is a cheerful place, but it has had its moments of horror. An iron cross outside Balliol marks the spot where the Protestant martyr Thomas Cranmer, archbishop of Canterbury, was burned at the stake in 1556, and an old gate in Balliol quad is still said to show the scorching of the flames. Bishops Hugh Latimer and Nicholas Ridley were also burned nearby, and all three are commemorated in the Martyrs' Memorial in St. Giles.

Opposite the memorial on Beaumont Street is Oxford's best-known hotel, the stately and very traditional **Randolph**. Those looking for something less overwhelmingly grand need only walk up St. Giles to the ivy-covered **Old Parsonage** (closed until March 1991) at the end of Banbury Road. Along here, too, are two of Oxford's favorite, if contrasting, restaurants. **Brown's** has good food at reasonable prices and is invariably bustling, noisy, and crowded—but full of atmosphere. **Gee's Restaurant**, 61a Banbury Road, is very different: Housed in an elegant Victorian conservatory, it boasts one of the best and most sophisticated French menus in the country (to reserve, Tel: 0865-535-40 or 583-46). Another popular restaurant in this area is **Munchy Munchy** at 6 Park End Street. Its plain appearance gives no hint of the exotic flavors of Ethel Ow's authentic Indonesian cooking.

Broad Street has one more building of note, not perhaps the grandest but one that has a fascinating history. The tiny **Science Museum** building, which now holds an array of beautiful old scientific instruments, began life in the 17th century as home to Elias Ashmole's Cabinet of Curiosities, the world's first public museum. The Ashmolean collection outgrew its old quarters and found a new, Classically styled home on Beaumont Street—it is not unlike a British Museum in miniature. The **Ashmolean Museum** today covers a wide range of exhibits, from Egyptian mummies to 19th-century paintings. The ceramics are particularly fine, and among the gems of the art collection are a number of beautiful, haunting paintings by Samuel Palmer.

During the mid-19th century Oxford decided it needed a natural-history museum, and again a new style was pioneered, an almost riotously elaborate Gothic Revival design by Benjamin Woodward and John Ruskin that used the new building materials of iron and glass. This, the **University Museum**, is on Parks Road. As well as housing the natural-history collection, it is home to the Pitt-Rivers Collection of ethnography, an extraordinary assemblage of objects from around the world, including such bizarre items as shrunken human heads.

The 20th-century all but abandoned architectural elaboration, and the **Museum of Modern Art** on Pembroke Street is housed in a converted warehouse—very bare, very austere, but a perfect setting for its constantly changing exhibitions. The restaurant in the basement is a popular place for a lunchtime snack, and the diners are often as colorful as the pictures on the walls.

A new addition to the Oxford scene, opened in the spring of 1988, combines something of the museum world with a good deal of show business and high-tech wizardry. At **The Oxford Story** on Broad Street, visitors follow the evolution of the university and meet some of the great thinkers and personalities who have been "up at Oxford."

University Oxford is what most visitors rightly wish to see. There is another city, however—the city where William Morris began making motorcars, the city of little terraces that run down to the canal in the area known as **Jericho**. This maze of narrow streets was once home to the working-class families of Oxford but now has become fashionable. The past is nevertheless preserved in simple pubs such as the **The Bookbinders Arms** on Victor Street—a reminder that the Oxford University Press is not very far away. Oxford is still a city where town and gown both have important roles to play.

WARWICK

The historic town of Warwick and its magnificent castle hold a magnetic attraction for visitors the year round. Both have been the setting for major events in England's history, and Warwick has been the administrative capital of the county for centuries. Although the castle is rightly the focus of any trip to the town, the town of Warwick itself, 96 miles northwest of London and beyond Oxford, has a particular charm and intimacy rarely found elsewhere. It is relatively small and contains many places of interest that can easily be visited in an afternoon.

MAJOR INTEREST

Warwick Castle—especially the tour of the private
    apartments
Lord Leycester's Hospital
The Beauchamp Chapel in St. Mary's Church
Hiring a boat at St. Nicholas's Park on the River
    Avon
Regency town of Leamington Spa

Warwick began as an Anglo-Saxon village standing on a sandstone outcrop above a natural ford across the River Avon, just west of its confluence with the River Leam. In A.D. 914 the town was fortified against the invading Danes by the Mercian queen Ethelfleda, daughter of Alfred the Great.

Later, in 1068, two years after the Norman Conquest, William I ordered castles to be built throughout his newly conquered kingdom, and a typical "motte and bailey" castle was erected here. A tall wooden tower within a stockade was built on the man-made sandstone mound that still stands to the west of the present-day castle, and the town's inhabitants would take shelter within the castle's bailey whenever danger threatened.

Throughout the centuries the town remained an important trading center because of its good strategic position, but it also gained status as a result of the increasing importance of the castle and its inhabitants. An especially notable period in the castle's history was its occupation by the mighty Beauchamp family, who began a massive rebuilding program in the mid-13th century and continued to improve the castle until the end of their tenure in 1445.

For several hundred years after this the castle remained a vital link in the defense of the kingdom, a position ensured by its location at a strategic crossing place on the river. Successive kings awarded the castle to their allies and confiscated it from their enemies, which resulted in its buildings constantly being enlarged and improved upon. Today it presents to the visitor one of the finest arrays of fortified buildings in the country. Castellated battlements and awesome towers spread over the hillside between the town and the river, surrounded by superb gardens and enclosing an enormous mansion at their heart.

Warwick castle became the subject of controversy in the 1970s when the present earl of Warwick sold a number of the family heirlooms and, finally, the castle itself, together with the remainder of its magnificent contents. The buyers were Madame Tussaud's—the owners of the famous waxworks museum—and, despite initial fears, they have proved extremely successful at making the castle a commercial success without compromising its historic integrity. They also have an ongoing policy of conservation and restoration as well as of buying items associated with the castle.

As one of Britain's major tourist attractions, the castle is filled to the brim with visitors in high summer (queues to see the state rooms and private apartments have been known to stretch beyond the castle walls), so avoid visiting then if at all possible. However, if a visit in summer is unavoidable, take pleasure in knowing that you'll be seeing the grounds at their best; you will also often be able to see special events, such as Civil War enactments or falconry displays, on the grounds. If you want to avoid the worst of the summer crush, visit in the early morning; Thursdays and Saturdays are said to be the least crowded.

The Castle

Unlike for many other historic sights, a winter's afternoon can be one of the most rewarding times to visit Warwick castle. Visitors are few and the tour of the **private apartments** can be thrilling. The apartments have been arranged to replicate a royal weekend house party that actually occurred here in June 1898—complete with life-

like models of the guests and appropriate sound effects.
(Guests included the Prince of Wales—later King Edward
VII—Lord Curzon, the young Winston Churchill, and a
clutch of dukes and duchesses.) It is one of the most well-
presented exhibits of its kind, and visitors may feel like
invisible party crashers who have travelled back in time
as they walk around the house looking in on small groups
of guests as they chat, listen to music, or dress for dinner
in the guest bedrooms. All the rooms are furnished as
they would have been in 1898 and dressed with the
paraphernalia of late-19th-century living.

The rest of the mansion consists of the 14th-century
Great Hall and the various grand State Rooms (including
the State Dining Room), which were used for formal
entertaining. Nearby is the supposedly haunted Watergate
Tower, and there is a splendid armory near the gatehouse. If you are not claustrophobic you can visit the
gloomy dungeon with its instruments of torture.

Visitors coming by car can park on the grounds to the
west of the castle, just off the Stratford Road (A 46). If
there is space in it, you might try a more convenient car
park off Castle Lane, just above the castle and closer to the
town center. Castle Lane is also the most convenient route
for those arriving in town by train: All visitors enter the
castle via the main entrance and gift shop in the stables
on Castle Lane. Contact the castle directly for information
about the special events that occur throughout the summer season (Tel: 0926-49-54-21). The tour of the castle
and grounds will take at least three hours. On July and
August afternoons an open-top bus tour of Warwick
leaves the stables coach park every 45 minutes; for details, Tel: (0789) 29-44-66.

Warwick Town

You can get a fine view of the castle if you walk to the
"new" Banbury road bridge, which was built in the 1780s
to replace the old bridge at the foot of the castle walls.
This made possible the survival of the delightful collection of old buildings in Bridge End across the river.
Fortunate visitors may be able to view the beautiful private gardens at 55 Mill Street, just east of the castle
(occasionally open for charity), which also afford a magnificent view of the castle and the remains of the old
bridge.

However, by far the finest view can be obtained from

the river itself. Small rowboats and some charming, anti-quated motorboats can be rented from the ever-helpful Mike Harrison and his family, who run the boathouse in St. Nicholas Park, across Banbury Road from the castle, from Easter to September (Tel: 0926-49-47-43). The set-ting is magical. The park is full of delightful attractions for the whole family and makes a great spot for a picnic. The Jacobean mansion housing the **St. John's House Museum**, on its northern edge, is worth a visit for its interesting examples of social history, including a full-size Victorian schoolroom.

The most historic part of the town itself is contained within a triangle of roads north of the castle centered on St. Mary's Church: To the north is Priory Road, which runs along the southern edge of Priory Park (the priory build-ings are no longer here; they were shipped to the U.S. in 1926); to the east is St. Nicholas Park and Coten End, which leads toward the town of Leamington Spa (see below); to the west, Bowling Green Street runs from Theatre Street down to West Gate, one of the town's original gates; and to the south is the castle and its fine grounds, which stretch along the banks of the River Avon.

The base of this triangle is the High Street (leading into Jury Street), which separates the town from the castle and joins the East and West gates—the original entrances to the Medieval walled town. Although the town's outline has survived, fire destroyed many of the original build-ings in 1694. As a result, most of the houses date from the late 17th and early 18th centuries.

The fire also destroyed the main body of **St. Mary's Church**. Its nave and tower were rebuilt in the early 18th century. However, the jewel of the church—the 15th-century **Beauchamp Chapel**—survived, and should not be missed. This striking and richly decorated chapel was built between 1443 and 1464 in accordance with the will of Richard Beauchamp, the fifth and greatest of the earls of Warwick. In the center of the chapel lies a gilded bronze life-size effigy of the earl lying on an elaborately carved tomb of Purbeck marble. Among the "weepers" around the tomb is Richard Neville, who married Richard's daugh-ter Anne and was later known as "Warwick the Kingmaker." (Anne is seen grieving over his corpse at the beginning of Shakespeare's *Richard III.*) Later earls of Warwick and their families are also commemorated here, most notably Queen Elizabeth I's favorite, Robert Dudley, earl of Leices-ter, and his wife, Lettice. In the far corner of the chapel is the tomb of their only son—the "noble impe"—who died aged six. His tiny suit of armor is in the castle's Great Hall.

Among the most interesting of Warwick's ancient buildings are **Oken's House**, near the castle—now a world-famous doll museum—and **Lord Leycester's Hospital**, by the West Gate. Home to retired military veterans since 1571, the hospital was founded by Robert Dudley, earl of Leicester, in a group of buildings that also houses the former Guildhall (built by Richard Neville in 1450) and the candlelit Chapel of St. James, which is built over the town's West Gate. The half-timbered, overhanging façade has an impressive and much-photographed lean, and if you walk through the tiny passage between the houses you will discover a charming inner courtyard. The buildings date from between the 12th and 16th centuries.

The **Brethren's Kitchen** here serves excellent light lunches and homemade teas from Easter to September (closed Sundays). A number of other tearooms can be found along Jury Street, or try the charming little **John Paul's** tearooms at 5 New Street. For a more substantial meal, eat at the excellent **Fanshawe's** at 22 Market Place; Tel: (0926) 41-05-90.

The Warwickshire Museum (local and natural history of Warwickshire) is housed in the Market Hall on Market Square. A weekly market and the annual Mop Fair in October are still held here. Like many other such halls, this once stood on arcades (now filled in) that sheltered the market stalls.

Around Warwick

A mile north of town, at Guy's Cliffe on the Coventry Road, the **Old Saxon Mill** steak house is in an unusual building and has tables outside by the old mill wheel. From here there is a spectacular view up to the gaunt ruins of an 18th-century mansion where the great actress Sarah Siddons worked as a young girl. Inside the Old Saxon Mill you can eat overlooking the river or have a drink while you watch the water rushing underfoot. Go for the setting rather than the food. Guy's Cliffe itself is named after the legendary hero of the Dark Ages, Guy of Warwick, who ended his days as a hermit in the caves above the river.

Dramatic ruins are now all that is left of the great castle at **Kenilworth**, about 4 miles north of Warwick. This once-formidable royal stronghold was dismantled by Cromwell's troops at the end of the Civil War. The 12th-century keep of the castle and its outer curtain wall were originally surrounded by a vast man-made lake, which acted as a defensive system in the early Middle Ages. Later, the lake became an important asset for entertainment and leisure, culminating in the three visits of Queen Elizabeth and her 400-strong retinue to the castle when it was the property of Robert Dudley, earl of Leicester. The most well-documented of these was the July 1575 visit, which formed the background for Sir Walter Scott's novel *Kenilworth*.

Today the lake has been drained and the buildings are decayed and roofless, but their sheer scale is very impressive indeed, and you can still see the walls of John of Gaunt's Great Hall, the massive gatehouse, and the stables erected by the earl of Leicester. You may find your visit enhanced if you have already been to the World of Shakespeare exhibition in Stratford, which illustrates Elizabeth I's triumphal procession to Kenilworth in 1575. Make sure, too, that you have a close look at the postcard sold here that shows a drawing of Kenilworth as it was during Elizabeth's visit. There is, in addition, a small exhibition in the stables.

A couple of miles east of Warwick is the elegant Regency town of **Leamington Spa**, as charming as Warwick but with a completely different atmosphere: Here the visitor is transported to the early 19th century, with its gracious, well-lit houses and spacious streets. Leamington, like Bath and Cheltenham, came to prominence on the late-18th-century wave of enthusiasm for "taking the waters." By 1814 several baths had been built, together with the large, handsome buildings housing the Pump Room, the Assembly Rooms, and the Public Baths. The town continued to prosper in the 19th century, a fact well illustrated by the broad avenues and crescents lined by handsome houses, which are embellished with porticos and ornate iron balconies.

Although two distinct towns, Warwick and Leamington Spa are divided only by their suburbs and the River Avon. Buses between the towns are frequent and are marked with the letter "C." Leamington's spacious elegance and excellent shopping make it a more attractive place than Warwick for an overnight stay—try the moderately priced **Lansdowne Hotel** on Clarendon Street for excellent accommodation and dinner. Those looking for an inexpensive meal should try **Alastair's Bistro and Wine Bar** on Warwick Street or **Rooster's** on Oxford Street. (See Getting Around at the end of this section for more on travelling between Warwick and Leamington Spa.)

STRATFORD-UPON-AVON

If you only have time for one excursion out of London, Stratford-upon-Avon should be high on your list. This charming little town only 8 miles or so southwest of Warwick was the birthplace of Shakespeare, and many buildings here associated with his life have been superbly restored. These houses and their contents today provide a fascinating picture of life in Elizabethan and Jacobean times. A day spent in Stratford can give visitors a very special insight into England's heritage—both rural and urban—as well as a more complete picture of the world's greatest poet-dramatist.

Ninety-six miles northwest of central London, Stratford has been a place of pilgrimage since the early 18th century, when interest in Shakespeare's oeuvre started to grow. Although a steady stream of visitors came to the town, it was not until the famous actor and impresario David Garrick organized the first Shakespearean Festival in 1769 that the town received the widespread attention that it still enjoys. There are many places of interest to visit here, ranging from the superbly preserved houses associated with Shakespeare to such oddities as the Teddy Bear Museum.

MAJOR INTEREST

Shakespeare's Birthplace
New Place and Hall's Croft
Anne Hathaway's Cottage
Mary Arden's House
Shakespearean plays at the Royal Shakespeare
    Theatre

If you only have a day in Stratford and you are travelling from London, you will probably want to visit all the Shakespearean properties, and maybe even fit in a play in the evening. It is possible to organize all this yourself, but the most efficient and least time-consuming method is to take advantage of the many services offered by the Guide

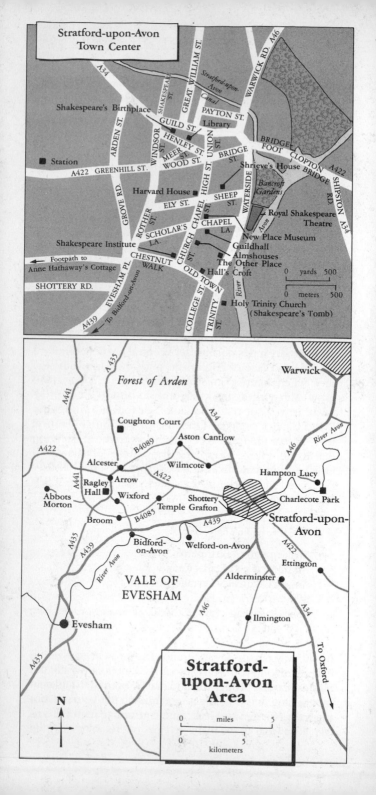

Friday company in Stratford. You can contact them at Civil Hall, Market Place, 14 Rother Street, Stratford CV37 6EF; Tel: (0789) 29-44-66; Fax: (0789) 41-46-81; or at Bridgefoot by the Pen and Parchment pub.

In any case, the best way to start your visit is by following the route taken by Guide Friday in their open-top buses. Each bus is accompanied by a knowledgeable guide who recites a prepared commentary between each of the stops on the tour. Your initial ticket (bought at the Guide Friday office or on the bus) is valid all day. You can get off one of their buses at any of the stops, spend as long as you like at any of them, and then rejoin the tour on another bus. The buses travel the route every 15 minutes in summer and every 30 minutes or hourly in the winter months. The tour starts at Bridgefoot, outside the Pen and Parchment public house (although you can join it at any point). It then meanders through town, stopping at or near the major attractions, before heading west to Anne Hathaway's Cottage in the nearby village of Shottery, and Mary Arden's House in Wilmcote, also nearby, to the north of Stratford. Of course, you can also walk the tour, as laid out below, except perhaps for the sites in the nearby villages.

A recent attraction that should be taken in at the beginning of a visit is the lavish sound-and-light presentation called **The World of Shakespeare**, on Waterside. This is designed to illustrate the everyday life of the Elizabethans and is a great help to the visitor touring other Shakespearean sites. However, this spectacle, with its life-size tableaux, is due to be sold, so its future is uncertain. For further information, Tel: (0789) 26-91-90.

The first stop on the bus tour is at the end of the pedestrianized section of Henley Street, where you will find the town's principal place of pilgrimage, **Shakespeare's Birthplace**. The house has been a popular attraction for 300 years, although nowadays visitors are no longer offered pieces of the bard's chair as expensive souvenirs. (Early commentators noted that the chair must have been unusually large, judging by the number of people who received pieces over the years.) The house is entered through a modern visitors' center and a garden that has been planted with the trees, herbs, and flowers mentioned in Shakespeare's plays. Inside, there are a number of exhibits that illustrate Shakespeare's life and work, and the house is furnished with Elizabethan and Jacobean furniture throughout.

Shakespeare's Birthplace, together with four other Shakespearean properties in the area, is owned and run by the Shakespeare Birthplace Trust, which also operates an extensive library, a records office, and a specialized bookshop at the visitors' center. Entry tickets can be bought to the individual sites, but it is cheaper to buy an inclusive ticket for all of the properties (available at any property). These other four sites are Nash's House, with the gardens of New Place; Hall's Croft; Anne Hathaway's Cottage in Shottery; and Mary Arden's House and Countryside Museum in Wilmcote.

Shakespeare's own house, **New Place**, where he lived during his retirement until his death in 1616, was demolished by its cantankerous owner in the 1760s. Its foundations are at the corner of Chapel Street and Chapel Lane, opposite the historic Guild Chapel, and now form part of a very pleasant garden, part of which has been planted as a colorful Elizabethan knott garden. **Nash's House**, next door, was the property of Shakespeare's granddaughter, Elizabeth Hall, and her first husband, Thomas Nash. It is now the local history and archaeology museum. The **Guild Chapel** dates back to the 15th century, when the town was developed by the influential Guild of the Holy Cross. A religious foundation, the guild was dissolved in 1547, but by then it had already built the chapel, a series of almshouses, and the King Edward VI Grammar School, which Shakespeare attended less than twenty years later. The school, on Chapel Street, is still in use today.

Shakespeare's daughter, Susanna, married a physician with an extensive medical practice; their house, **Hall's Croft** on Old Town Street, is the last of the Shakespearean properties in town. This fine Tudor house has some exceptional Elizabethan and Jacobean furniture, but its main interest is its dispensary and other exhibits that illustrate the state of medicine in those times. In addition, the garden at Hall's Croft is a particularly pleasant place to have morning coffee or afternoon tea.

If your time is limited you should go straight to Hall's Croft from New Place, leaving the Royal Shakespeare Theatre for later in the day. However, only a few minutes' stroll south from Hall's Croft is **Holy Trinity Church**, the beautiful Medieval parish church where Shakespeare was both baptized and buried. This is worth visiting to see Shakespeare's grave and bust. The bust was made within seven years of his death, while his widow and many of his friends were still alive. Every year on the Saturday closest to Shakespeare's birthday (April 23rd) invited guests, including actors, local officials, and foreign ambassadors, celebrate the day by walking in procession to the church to lay flowers on the Bard's tomb. If you can plan your visit to Stratford to coincide with the occasion, you will miss the summer crush of tourists and, at the same time, see some of the true life of the town.

Another time to avoid the crowds is autumn, when the Mop Fair is held (on or near October 12). Now largely a modern amusement fair, originally this was an annual hiring fair during which crowds of indoor and outdoor farm servants would come into town to be engaged for the year.

From Hall's Croft the bus tour heads west out to the village of Shottery, where Shakespeare did much of his courting. If you have time you can take a pleasant stroll from the croft through fields out to Shottery and Anne Hathaway's Cottage. The walk is signposted from Evesham Place (opposite Chestnut Walk north of the church). **Anne Hathaway's Cottage** in Shottery is a perfectly preserved thatched cottage that was the family home of Shakespeare's wife, Anne. The house stayed in the Hathaway family for several generations and still contains much of its original furniture. It is staffed by some extremely knowledgeable guides and surrounded by a superbly kept, old-fashioned English garden. Just across the road from the cottage is the charming **Cottage Tea Garden**, where visitors are served tea and light snacks in a lovely little garden by a stream.

Whereas Anne's parents were yeoman farmers, Shakespeare's parents were a comparatively wealthy couple. His father was a glover and tanner and his mother, Mary Arden, was the daughter of a prosperous farmer. The Ardens' attractive farmhouse in the village of Wilmcote (4 miles northwest of Stratford) is now a museum of farming and rural life, and is the next stop on the bus tour. This is the largest of all the properties associated with Shakespeare, and, like the others, it has been immaculately preserved and, in places, reconstructed.

The farm outbuildings behind **Mary Arden's House** now contain the **Shakespeare Countryside Museum**. This is an extensive museum of farm and country life and is linked with the restored Glebe Farmhouse next door, which illustrates Victorian and Edwardian domestic and farming life. The large complex is full of interesting objects and warrants an hour or so of your time. In the summer you can also see frequent local craft demonstrations. The museum operates a café in summer, or you can get good bar food at the **Mason's Arms** nearby. A short stroll to the east is the Stratford-upon-Avon Canal, and just south of here a series of eleven locks takes the canal down into town.

Back in Stratford, visitors may well find that they have had enough of Shakespearean connections for a while, however fascinating. If so, other places worth a visit are the **Brass Rubbing Centre** in Avonbank Gardens, near the theater, the Teddy Bear Museum, and Harvard House. The late-16th-century **Harvard House**, on the High Street, is now owned by Harvard College. Erected by the grandfather of the college's founder, John Harvard, it contains a fascinating collection of books, pictures, curios, and period furniture.

If you have children in tow, the **Teddy Bear Museum** on Greenhill Street is a must. This rickety little four-story building is crammed to the rafters with teddy bears of every shape and size. Among the many bears on display are those donated by famous people—from royalty to rock stars. Stratford also abounds with antiques shops well worth browsing in. As in all tourist-oriented haunts, you ought to shop around, however.

The tourist information center at the corner of High and Bridge streets is worth visiting for any further information. Down by the River Avon is Bancroft Gardens. From here, or just across the footbridge on Swan's Nest Lane, you can hire boats or take a short cruise on the River Avon or the Stratford-upon-Avon Canal, which branches off the river at this point.

Nearby, and dominating the riverbank, is the large brick **Royal Shakespeare Theatre**, built in the late 1920s to replace the Victorian Memorial Theatre, which burned down in 1926. The shell of the older theater still stands, and the **Swan Theatre**, a replica of a Jacobean playhouse, has been built within it. The Swan generally puts on plays by Shakespeare's contemporaries or followers, such as Marlowe. It also houses the RSC (Royal Shakespeare Company) collection of paintings, costumes, and other mementoes, and is open daily. Tours of the collection and the backstage areas are offered in the afternoons. There is also a modern theater here, **The Other Place**, which stages contemporary productions. As of this writing, it is being rebuilt and is scheduled to reopen sometime in 1991.

Plays are performed from the end of March to the end of January, but advance booking is highly advisable at any time. The RSC also offers a variety of stopover packages that include theater tickets, meals, and accommodations. Information about these can be obtained from RST Restaurants, Royal Shakespeare Theatre, Stratford-upon-Avon, Warwickshire CV37 6BB. The box office is open from 9:30 A.M. to 8:00 P.M. on performance days; Tel: (0789) 29-56-23, or 26-91-91 for 24-hour booking information.

Theatergoers and others can dine at the theater, either at the **Box Tree** restaurant overlooking the river or at the more informal **Terrace** restaurant. Just over the road is the popular actors' pub, the **Black Swan** (known locally as the "Dirty Duck"). For those who would rather eat in the center of town, the **Slug and Lettuce** pub-cum-bistro on Guild Street is a lively alternative, with an excellent range of dishes, in spite of its unappealing name.

Legend has it that the young William Shakespeare poached deer on the grounds of nearby **Charlecote Park**, east of Stratford, and deer can still be seen grazing in the landscaped park. Whatever the truth of the legend, the magnificent Tudor mansion in its great park is well worth visiting for itself. Still the home of the Lucy family, the house is the property of the National Trust, which opens the ground-floor rooms to the public. A short video that gives a very attractive picture of some of the house's history can be viewed in the bakehouse. Watch it before going on an extended tour of the impressive Victorian living rooms, the vast kitchen and brewhouse, and the museum of local and family relics; open from April to October. Visitors without a car can either take a taxi from Stratford or catch the X18 bus, which leaves hourly from Stratford's Wood Street.

GETTING AROUND

Oxford
Oxford, 57 miles northwest of London, can be reached by rail from Paddington Station, by bus from Victoria Coach Station, and by road via the A 40 and M 40. Rail service is frequent during the day, and the trip takes a little more than an hour.

Warwick and Stratford

If you want to travel to Stratford or Warwick by car from London, then starting sometime in 1991 you should be able to drive almost all the way along the newly completed M 40 motorway from west London. At junction 15 you can turn north to Warwick and Leamington Spa or south to Stratford-upon-Avon. However, before you start check that all stretches of the new motorway are completed. The journey should take less than an hour and a half. If you want to travel on the M 1 motorway, turn west at junction 16 and go via A 45 and A 425 to Leamington Spa and Warwick, and then on to Stratford via A 46 and A 439.

If you are not travelling by car, the fastest way to Warwick or Stratford is via the "Shakespeare Connection" intercity rail service from London (Euston Station). The fast train to Coventry takes about an hour, and Guide Friday has a special connecting bus that goes from Coventry to Stratford via Kenilworth Castle, Leamington Spa, and Warwick. The total travel time is usually under two hours and there is a special late-night coach to pick up theatergoers from Stratford. You can, for example, leave London (Euston) at 8:40 A.M., arrive in Stratford at 10:35 A.M., do a day's sightseeing, attend a performance at the Royal Shakespeare Theatre in the evening, and arrive back in London in the early hours of the morning. For details contact British Rail (Tel: 071-387-7070) or Guide Friday (Tel: 0789-29-44-66).

Three bus companies run trips to Warwick and Stratford from London: National Express (Tel: 071-730-0202); Evan Evans Tours Ltd. (Tel: 071-930-2377); and Frames Rickards (Tel: 071-837-3111).

Although Leamington Spa, Warwick, and Stratford all have railway stations, they are on different branch lines, and Leamington Spa is the only one that can be reached directly by rail from London (out of Paddington Station). Although relatively scenic, these lines can provide both slow and infrequent service. Both Snowhill and Moor Street stations in Birmingham have direct trains to Warwick and Leamington Spa, or to Stratford, every hour. For details, telephone British Rail in Birmingham (Tel: 021-643-27-11).

Once you have reached Stratford or Warwick, sightseeing on foot is both easy and rewarding. However, if you want to rent a car to go further afield, this can be arranged locally. Guide Friday in Stratford can arrange car rentals through the major international companies, such as Hertz or Avis. Alternatively, they may be able to arrange personal tours in a car driven by a qualified guide.

Regular Midland Red buses (X16) also run hourly (every two hours on Sundays) between Wood Street, Stratford-upon-Avon, and Coventry via Warwick, Leamington Spa, and Kenilworth Castle. The X18 bus goes from Wood Street, Stratford, to Leamington Spa via Charlecote Park. For details telephone the Midland Red bus information service (Tel: 0788-53-55-55).

ACCOMMODATIONS REFERENCE

Oxford
▶ **Old Parsonage Hotel**. 3 Banbury Road, **Oxford** OX2 6NN. Tel: (0865) 31-02-10. (Closed until March 1991.)
▶ **Randolph Hotel**. Beaumont Street, **Oxford** OX1 2LN. Tel: (0865) 24-74-81; Fax: (0865) 79-16-78.

Warwick
▶ **Lansdowne Hotel**. 87 Clarendon Street, **Leamington Spa** CV32 4PF. Tel: (0926) 45-05-05; Telex: 337556; Fax: (0926) 45-00-83.

Stratford-upon-Avon
▶ **Stratford House Hotel and Shepherd's Restaurant**. Sheep Street, **Stratford-upon-Avon** CV37 6EF. Tel: (0789) 682-88; Fax: (0789) 29-55-80.

NORTH

CAMBRIDGE

In the perpetual pairing of Cambridge with Oxford, Cambridge always comes second. It is Oxford and Cambridge, or even Oxbridge, but never the other way around, except perhaps in the specialized world of the scientist. This is perhaps a reflection of history, for the university at Cambridge began with an exodus of scholars from Ox-

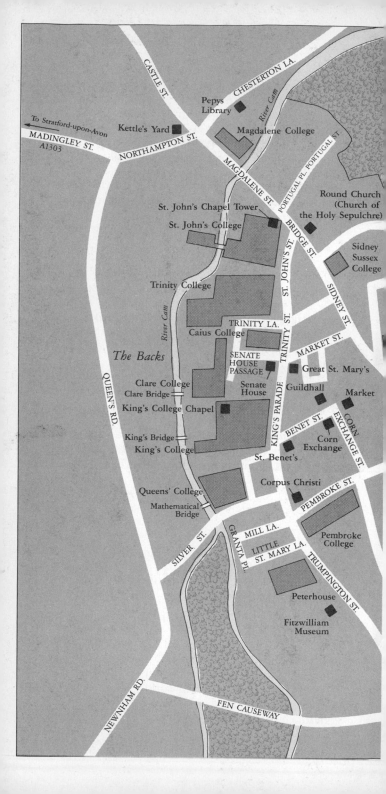

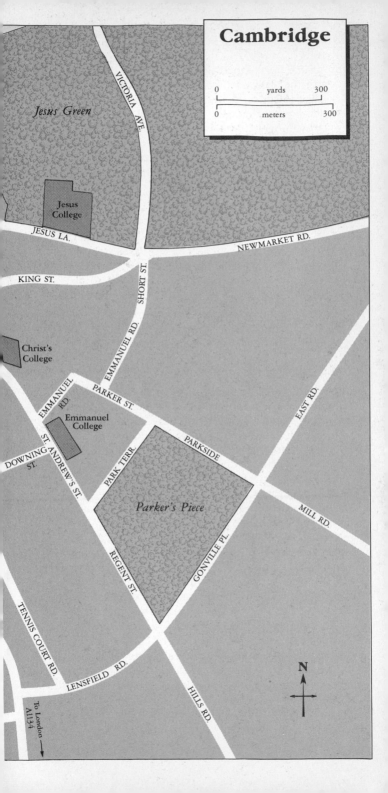

ford after a quarrel between town and gown at the beginning of the 13th century. Yet, paradoxically, Cambridge
contrives to appear the older city, more closely tied to its
Medieval past. Here, the influence of the university is
overwhelming; it is an inescapable presence in a way that
is never quite the case at Oxford. But if it is the university
that has made Cambridge the fascinating and beautiful
place it is today, it is the River Cam that first brought the
city into being. It was at the crossing of the river that the
settlement of Cam-bridge grew, and it is the river that
today threads together the different parts of the city's past
to make a coherent whole.

MAJOR INTEREST

The Backs
University colleges
King's College Chapel
Kettle's Yard
Round Church
Fitzwilliam Museum

From the river, the visitor passes **the Backs**, which are
exactly what the name suggests—the green space in back
of the colleges, along the river's edge. But the unimagina-
tive name gives no notion of the enchantment here,
where the stone towers and turrets of colleges and chapels are reflected in the quiet waters of the Cam. By far
the best way to take in this view is from a punt, the
traditional narrow, flat-bottomed boat propelled by pole.
These can be hired either by the bridge at Magdalene
Street or by Mill Lane.

It is also possible to take "chauffeured punts" and let
someone else do the poling. Those who choose to be
punted rather than punt may fancy themselves in some
English Venice, a feeling reinforced as you pass under
Cambridge's bridges, particularly the local version of the
Bridge of Sighs at St. John's College. The oldest bridge, at
Clare College, was built in the 1630s, and the oddest is
the Mathematical Bridge at Queen's College. A shapely
wooden arch, it was constructed entirely without nails
from straight timbers that notch together like a Chinese
puzzle. It was certainly a puzzle that proved too complex
for generations of drunken undergraduates. They were
capable of dismantling it, but putting it together again was

quite beyond them. Eventually, the authorities had to step in, and the bridge sections are now bolted together.

The views of the colleges from the Cam include what is perhaps the city's most famous—**King's College** and its Chapel. The latter is on every tourist itinerary and deservedly so, for it is one of the great buildings not just of Cambridge but of the world. Its majesty is apparent from the outside, but its true glory is its interior.

Cambridge University is, like Oxford, the sum of its colleges, and while there are many similarities in organization, there are subtle differences as well. Colleges in both universities are usually built around squares, but what is a quad at Oxford is a court at Cambridge, and undergraduates here never have tutorials—they go for "supervisions" instead. For visitors, however, the most obvious difference lies in building materials: Whereas in Oxford stone rules, here warm red brick dominates. Most of the colleges are open to visitors except during the examination period, which runs from early May to mid-June. But even when they are closed, much of the colleges' magnificence is on display. Indeed, it is the cumulative effect of the college architecture that gives Cambridge its unique atmosphere, and that visitors tend to remember far more clearly than any nice points or fine details.

The geography of Cambridge is comparatively simple. Starting in the north, below the river crossing of Bridge Street, the main road divides. One branch becomes Sidney Street, changing to St. Andrew's Street and continuing as Regent Street. The second branch, starting as St. John's Street, continues on as Trinity Street, King's Parade, and Trumpington Street. Both these routes are lined with colleges, and the space between is given over to town affairs, to the Guildhall, the Corn Exchange, and the still-flourishing market—a proper market with stalls selling everything from fresh meat to fine books.

Exploring the Colleges

Beginning a tour of Cambridge on the far side of the Cam, at Magdalene Bridge (originally Great Bridge), the spot where the Roman road crossed the river, you come first to **Magdalene College** (pronounced *maudlin*), founded in 1542. Although it is not one of the grander colleges, the splendor of its Renaissance gateway can be admired, while the extremely Gothicized church can be left to those with enthusiasm for heavy-handed Victorian restoration. The college has much of interest besides its architecture. The **Pepys Library** contains Samuel Pepys's bequest, which includes the famous diaries written in the author's unique shorthand and the more easily deciphered pocket book of Sir Francis Drake. In the 17th century there was a strong Puritan element in the college, and one member who left for the New World, Henry Dunster, went on to become the first president of Harvard College.

Magdalene and its immediate surroundings show how rich and diverse the charms of Cambridge can be. You could spend a contented day without straying more than a few hundred yards from here. Magdalene Street itself has a wealth of ancient buildings. Look, for example, at number 25, now a shoe shop but basically a timber-framed Medieval building with an upper story jutting outward and embellished with lovely, ornate carving. Just north of the crossroads, on the corner between Northampton Street and Castle Street, is one of the city's most surprising finds, known somewhat prosaically as **Kettle's Yard**. Here is the house of the art collector Jim Ede, who died in 1990. Nothing on the outside prepares you for the interior. This really is a home, not a museum, so arranged that the visitor feels the owner might turn up at any moment to resume residence. Ede bought the then-unfashionable and unwanted work of his contemporaries—from Gaudier-Brzeska to Ben Nicholson—and he had special affection for the paintings of the Cornish primitive Alfred Wallis.

Across the bridge, visitors who enjoy exploring back streets will find an area that once housed college servants but now comprises what the local real-estate agents would call "desirable residences." It also has its oddities and surprises. On the corner of Portugal Street, an aged police notice announces that hand carts and trolleys are not allowed in, while nearby Portugal Place has a genteel terrace that ends with the High Victorian Gothic of St. John's chapel tower. Back on Bridge Street is the popular student pub the **Baron of Beef**, and just a little closer to the city center is another of Cambridge's more pleasing oddities. The church of the Holy Sepulchre is usually known simply as the **Round Church**, for the very good reason that it is indeed round. Dating from about 1130, it contains a ring of stone heads—from fiercely mustachioed warriors to even fiercer demons—that stare down at the visitor.

The Round Church stands by the point where Bridge Street and St. John's Street diverge, at **St. John's College**, which boasts one of the most attractive and ornate gatehouses of all the colleges. Typical of many, it was built of both red brick and stone. In addition to a statue of the saint, the gatehouse bears a variety of heraldic emblems, from Lancastrian roses to mythical creatures with horns and tusks known as yales. They are the emblems of Lady Margaret Beaufort, under whose will the college was founded in the 16th century. These you might expect, but the builders had a sense of humor. A field of marguerites makes a visual pun on the founder's name, and among the daisies is a rabbit hole with a fox disappearing down one end and a rather smug rabbit popping out the other.

St. John's Street leads to Trinity Street and **Trinity College**, where you might notice that the heraldic ornaments on the great gate are the same as those at St. John's—not surprising, because Henry VIII was Lady Margaret's grandson. The statue of Henry clutches an orb in one hand and—thanks to generations of undergraduates—a chair leg in the other. Trinity's **Great Court** is the largest in Cambridge, and college athletes test their prowess by attempting to run a circuit while the clock is striking 12:00—as depicted in the film *Chariots of Fire*. The apple tree on the lawn is descended from one that stood in the garden of a former member of Trinity, Sir Isaac Newton. Opposite Trinity Great Gate is **Heffer's**, long established as the university's main bookshop.

Trinity Lane is one of those curved, narrow ways that promise fresh delights just around the corner. Here it leads on to **Gonville and Caius College**, begun by Mr. Gonville and enlarged by Dr. Caius and usually known simply as Caius (pronounced *keys*). It has three gates: The undergraduate enters in Humility to Tree Court, passes through Virtue to Caius Court, and leaves the college via Honour. The lane leads on past Senate House Passage and the 18th-century Classical formality of Senate House itself, where university degrees are conferred in a ceremony that, because of the numbers involved, takes two days. After that comes Clare College, closely followed by King's.

King's is a delight, but the **King's College Chapel** is the inevitable focus of attention. Seen from across the Backs it is majestic; up close the detail is revealed; and inside the full splendor appears. It might never have been so splendid but for the turbulence of Medieval life. The chapel was begun in the 15th-century reign of its founder, Henry VI, but the long and bloody Wars of the Roses caused numerous interruptions, and it was completed by Henry VIII. His devices—the Royal Arms, portcullis, Tudor rose, dragon, and greyhound—can be seen everywhere in the building. More important, English architecture had reached a period of great elaboration; hence we have what is literally the chapel's crowning glory, the intricate tracery of the beautiful fan-vaulted roof. The chapel's proportions are noble and the vast areas of stained glass send a warm light washing over the intricate details of carving and tracery. If you left Cambridge having seen nothing else, you would go away content.

King's has an appropriate companion in nearby **Queens' College**, named after its two founders, Margaret of Anjou and Elizabeth Woodville. Where the former college is all grandeur, the latter has a feeling of pleasant domesticity, with buildings of mellow brick that could be part of a country house.

Back on Trinity Street, now become King's Parade, the clock on **Great St. Mary's Church** rings the hours with a familiar chime, for it is the same as Big Ben's at Westminster—although first struck at St. Mary's. Church bells are also cause to visit St. Benet's Church, where modern bell-ringing, or change-ringing, was begun. There are two ways of ringing bells. The simplest is one in which the bells play a melody. In change-ringing, however, the bells ring peals, each one differentiated from the next by the order in which the bells are rung. It is a system of great, almost mathematical, complexity whose nearest musical equivalent might be a Bach fugue. Change-ringing, still widely practiced in English churches, was invented by a parish clerk at St. Benet's named Fabian Stedman. Another reason to visit the church: It boasts a Saxon tower, the city's oldest building.

Where King's Parade becomes Trumpington Street, water courses run down deep gulleys on either side. These once brought drinking water to the city's center, and the man largely responsible was Thomas Hobson, who owned extensive livery stables. His customers were forced to take whichever horse was nearest the door, a practice that gave rise to the expression "Hobson's choice."

Off Trumpington Street is Pembroke College, with a chapel by Sir Christopher Wren that was the first of his architectural works to be completed—giving Cambridge a Wren "first" to set beside Oxford's Sheldonian Theatre.

Nearby **Peterhouse**, the oldest of the colleges, dating to 1281, has a famous curiosity. Looking up at the top of the building near the church, you can see an iron bar across a window. The poet Thomas Gray had it placed there to anchor a fire-escape rope. This proved too tempting for his fellow undergraduates, who put a tub of water at the bottom and yelled "Fire!" He was so upset by the experience that he packed his bags and moved to Pembroke College.

Trumpington Street leads on to the **Fitzwilliam Museum**, which has the solemn appearance associated with much Victorian architecture, having been built in 1848. Once past the somewhat dourly tiled entrance, rather reminiscent of a grandiose public lavatory, you will find a fine collection of art and antiquities, with the work of French and English Impressionists doing a great deal to lighten the overall sense of darkness that seems to pervade the museum. There are temporary exhibitions mounted throughout the year and special exhibitions and concerts during the Cambridge Festival.

If, by now, you are tempted by the thought of afternoon tea, then the thing to do is to leave the Fitzwilliam for **Fitzbillies**, Cambridge's most famous tea shop, at 52 Trumpington Street, or, if the riverside still exerts its appeal, then the **Garden House Hotel** on Granta Place for cream tea on the lawn stretching down to the water. The Garden House is also recommended for an overnight stay. The **University Arms** on Regent Street is another excellent accommodation.

Those on the lookout for something equally traditional but a little stronger than tea might care to sample the beer at the 17th-century coaching inn known as **The Eagle**, on Benet Street. And if a full-scale meal is in order, there is no shortage of restaurants, from the excellent Chinese fare of **Tai Cheun** on St. John's Street to the Swiss fondues at **Flames** on Castle Street. Fine though international restaurants are, visitors to Cambridge are more likely to want something as English as a punt on the Cam, and what could be more English than a cricket pavilion? **Hobbs Pavilion** restaurant on Parker's Piece is just that, though the proprietors cannot guarantee you will have a match to watch.

GETTING AROUND

Cambridge, 55 miles north of London, can be reached by rail from Liverpool Street Station, by bus from Victoria Coach Station, and by car via the M 11. There is frequent train service; the trip takes approximately one hour.

ACCOMMODATIONS REFERENCE

▶ **Garden House Hotel**. Granta Place, Mill Lane, **Cambridge** CB2 1RT. Tel: (0223) 634-21; Telex: 81463; Fax: (0223) 31-66-05.

▶ **University Arms**. Regent Street, **Cambridge** CB2 1AD. Tel: (0223) 35-12-41; Telex: 817311; Fax (0223) 31-52-56.

THE COAST OF FRANCE AND BELGIUM

Less than 10,000 years ago, before the melting waters of the Ice Age raised the level of the sea and drowned the plains between France and Great Britain, you could have walked from the coast of one country to the other. When, a few years from now, the Channel Tunnel is transformed from bore to reality, you may even be able to do the same again. In the meantime you'll have to settle for a boat. But the ride is such a short one that hopping over to the Continent, just for the day, is a favorite excursion for the British, at least for those living in London and the southeast. With frequent sailings from several British ports, combined with regular train service from London to those ports, it is just as easy for visitors from abroad to add a taste of France or Belgium to a holiday in the London area.

MAJOR INTEREST

Boulogne
The Haute Ville
A walk around the ramparts
Basse Ville specialty shopping
Cathedral·
Place Dalton market

Calais
Town Hall
Parc Richelieu
Restaurants

Dunkirk
Museum of Fine Arts
Malo-les-Bains seaside resort

Dieppe
Seafood restaurants
St-Jacques historic area with cathedral
Saturday morning market
Castle

Bruges
Horse-drawn carriage tour
Belfry
Breidelstraat lace shops
Michelin-rated restaurants

Cherbourg
Basilica
Old town
Normandy cuisine

The proximity of northern France to Britain does not imply the slightest compromise in its Gallic ambience. In fact you could drive for hours on end into the French hinterlands and not discover anywhere more French than the Channel ports and their immediate environs.

You get a whiff of France from the moment the ferry nudges past the end of the harbor walls with their complement of red-nosed fishermen wearing berets and smoking yellow-paper hand-rolled cigarettes. You'll swear you hear them muttering Gallic curses as your ferry's propellors churn up *their* patch of La Manche ("The Sleeve"), as they call the Channel, disturbing all the *poisson* that were just about to take a bite of hook.

The simplest way to book is to choose your port, then the means of travel (where there are alternatives), and then walk into any British travel agent's office. A day round-trip excursion ticket from the British port costs around £10. Only a few agents, however, are able to sell the train ticket between London and the British port; for that you need to go to the railway station. At Victoria Station you can buy both rail *and* ferry, hovercraft, or Jetfoil tickets from the offices on platform 8 on the morning of departure—though leave yourself a few minutes to spare, as the lines can be long, especially during the peak summer months.

The choice of routes and sailings is enormous. For speed you can't beat the hovercraft services, the "flying cushions," which cut the crossing time by more than half, between Dover and either Calais or Boulogne. But the disadvantage is discomfort. There is no room to roam on a hovercraft, the interiors being modeled on the lines of an aircraft. There are also no money-changing facilities, and no shops or restaurants (soft and hard drinks are brought to your seat, but not tea or coffee). When the sea is choppy the journey can be unpleasant, although when it's *too* rough they switch you onto a ferry.

An alternative to lingering in the ports is to rent a car and explore some of the surrounding area. As with Britain, the variety of scenery packed within small pockets of French territory is enormous, and each port will plug you into a distinctive brand of countryside as well as towns of enormous historic interest. Northern France has been, over the centuries, one of the most fought-over patches of land in the world, and it has plenty to offer its visitors.

BOULOGNE

Less than a two-hour sail from England, the port of Boulogne offers living proof that France really does begin just across the Channel. All things considered—ease of access, range of shops and restaurants, and overall ambience—it is arguably the best choice for the day-tripper.

Boulogne is really a two-in-one town, an old and a new. Crowning a hilltop, and easily spotted from the approaching ferry long before it pulls into the docks, stands the largely intact old Medieval city, the **Haute Ville**. From within its 13th-century ramparts, Boulogne feels more like a small provincial town buried in the rural heartland of France than a city that is just a swift ferry ride from British shores. The old town comes complete with narrow, winding, cobbled streets, with lots of interesting specialty stores lining the rue de Lille; a 13th-century belfry attached to the 17th-century town hall; a castle built in 1231 to defend the town walls against the threat of invaders; and a grand 19th-century cathedral built on a Norman crypt.

A leisurely stroll around the ramparts, with a pause to look down from any of the four bow-fronted gateways or 17 towers to admire the horizon of the town's high-pitched rooftops or the views of the docks and the distant surrounding forests, will take anywhere between 30 and 40 minutes. On the clearest of days you can just make out the coast of Britain.

Boulogne's Basse Ville, or new town, lies at the foot of the old town, and was largely rebuilt after hefty damage was done by Allied bombs during World War II (487 bombs landed here, destroying some 5,000 buildings). The waterfront is home base not only for the ferries but for the hundreds of trawlers that make Boulogne the largest fishing port in Europe; they unload some of the catch on the quai Gambetta, a scene that Edith Piaf used to enjoy from her apartment.

Travel on a Wednesday or a Saturday and you'll catch the tail end of the market on place Dalton, a sightseeing trip in its own right. Pity the poor rabbits, calmly nibbling grass in their hutches, unaware they are up for sale at 25 francs per kilo.

High on the agenda of any day-tripper to France is a good lunch, and Boulogne's restaurants will not disappoint. Two worthy of special mention are owner-chef Tony Lestienne's thoroughly modern **La Matelote** on boulevard Ste-Beuve (Tel: 21-30-17-97) and **La Liégoise**, much favored by the upper echelons of the local business community, on rue Monsigny (Tel: 21-31-61-15).

CALAIS

Calais is the nearest gateway to England, the quickest to reach, and is served by an armada of ferries that seem to shuttle in and out as frequently as commuter trains.

Although Allied bombers laid waste to much of Calais' Medieval charms, many of the town's older buildings cleverly, some say miraculously, managed to survive the assault. They include the most spectacularly flamboyant building, the town hall, fronted by Rodin's statue of the Burghers. The town hall, a red-brick, Flemish Renaissance Revival building in gâteau style, appears far more ancient than its 20th-century construction. How on earth, you may wonder, did the architects manage to persuade the straight-laced city burghers to accept their plans for such a wild fantasy of a building?

The oldest building in town is the Tour du Guet, built in the 13th century on the place d'Armes to keep an eye on shipping movements in the Channel. It is, unfortunately, closed to the public (the authorities don't want British visitors to look nostalgically back at the white cliffs). But you can walk around the delightful Parc Richelieu and watch the locals play *pétanque,* or boules, as we know it, or visit the **War Museum**, housed in one of Hitler's bunkers that was used as the German navy's main telephone exchange in northern France.

British day-trippers in France fall into two distinct categories. There are those who grab a full breakfast on the morning ferry, make do with coffee and perhaps a bag of *frites* during the day, and hold out till early evening for real English fare on the ferry home. For others, the day starts as one long fast until the moment that the first crumbs of genuine baguette fly like shrapnel across the restaurant table.

At the **Côte d'Argent** (Tel: 21-34-68-07) you can dine on fish soup, coquilles Saint-Jacques, sole meunière, French cheese, chocolate mousse, coffee, an aperitif, and wine for around 150 francs, a fraction of its British equivalent (assuming you could ever find such a thing), and the meal will be served in great style. Sole, for example, comes on a huge, beautifully painted platter beneath a silver tureen that looks like a czar's helmet. The restaurant is located on the **Plage de Calais**, an apron of sandy shoreline sufficiently broad to be the venue for sand-yachting races. With hundreds of tiny old-fashioned wooden changing huts, it is one of the best beaches along the entire coast.

Although nowhere near as attractive a town as Boulogne, Calais' strength lies in its two shopping centers: between the place d'Armes (where those without a car are deposited by the ferry bus) and the main street of rue Royale; and at the northern end of boulevard Jacquard just beyond the town hall, then along boulevard Lafayette. Among the best of the specialty shops are **La Maison du Fromage**, which sells more than 200 brands of cheese; **Au Royal Chocolat** for delicious cream-filled Leonidas chocolates from Belgium; **La Madrague** for a host of pretty household items; **Descamps** for luxurious bed and bathroom accessories; and **Cupillard** for its excellent range of kitchenware, including cast-iron Le Creuset pans and casserole dishes.

DUNKIRK

Dunkirk (Dunkerque in French) is France with a Flemish accent. Flemish influences are everywhere evident, from the style of the buildings to the unpronounceable names of some of the shops, not to mention items on the restaurant menus. The Belgian border, never a real, cultural dividing line, is just up the road—nearer, in fact, to the town center than Dunkirk's own ferry port.

Dunkirk was badly damaged during World War I and virtually devastated during Operation Dynamo in May 1940, when the mass evacuation of Allied troops from the Continent took place. Its reconstruction afterward was with an eye more on commercial slickness than on aesthetics, though a few old buildings, including the town hall, the belfry, the Medieval Leughner Tower, and St. Eloi church, survived. The **Museum of Fine Arts**, bang in the center of town on place du Général de Gaulle, contains several important collections of Flemish and Italian paintings from the 17th century, while in the basement there is a display of souvenirs, documents, and a diorama detailing Dunkirk's role in both worlds wars (closed on Tuesdays).

Dunkirk's trump card is **Malo-les-Bains**, part seaside resort, part residential neighborhood, a 20-minute walk north of the center but a world away from its heavy maritime commerce (Dunkirk is France's largest port after Marseille and Le Havre). The broad Digue de Mer promenade, backed by cafés and crêperies, brasseries and restaurants, runs alongside three miles of beach that stretches all the way to the Belgian border. A good place to eat here is **La Mer du Nord** at 3 rue du Leughenaer, near the water.

DIEPPE

The prettiest and most Gallic of the Channel ports, Dieppe is characterized by narrow streets and historic houses clustered around the harbor and behind its pebble beach. It is also France's oldest resort, popularized by the duchesse de Berry in the early 19th century when she made seabathing socially acceptable for ladies.

The town lies at the end of a route aptly known to many Parisians as the Road of the Sea. Dieppe has, in fact, long billed itself as the *plage de Paris*. Spreading out to the west as far as the castle and an intimidating line of cliffs is a deeply shelving pebble beach backed by a gusty promenade, the latter separated from the main hotels by La Pelouse, a broad ten-acre swathe of grass.

There are more good-value-for-money restaurants squeezed into Dieppe than in any other Channel port. Specialties include *sole dieppois* and *marmite dieppoise,* a fish soup (dieppoise style means cooked in cream and wine, or sometimes cider), as well as scallops. In fact, half the scallops eaten in France come from the waters off Dieppe. The **Marine,** a nondescript modern restaurant on the Arcades de la Poissonerie, serves very good fish. The owner has what the French call a British mustache; see if you can spot him.

The most interesting shops lie in the historic St-Jacques area around the cathedral. On Saturdays the area is the scene of one of the best markets in Normandy. Dieppe's **castle** houses a gallery of paintings by Pisarro, Monet, and other Impressionists who came to capture Dieppe's light, as well as prints by Braque—who spent his last years nearby—and a collection of locally made ivory carvings.

For those in search of character, a nice place to spend the night is the **Hotel Windsor** on the boulevard de Verdun. Its grand, old-fashioned staircase is hung with pictures of transatlantic liners; the rooms are large and many have sea views, although the furnishings tend to be frayed at the seams.

BRUGES

The best reason for going to Belgium for the day is not Ostend, the Channel port, but Bruges, which is a swift train ride from the port. Bruges is the best-preserved Medieval city in Europe, and the best way to plug into the ancient mood is from a horse-drawn carriage. A bowler-hatted driver will guide you along lime- and willow-shaded canals, over hump-back bridges, and down cobblestoned alleyways lined with fine gabled houses, merchants' mansions, ornate guildhalls, and other manifestations of the success of the city's ancient trade.

The more energetic can tackle the 366 steps to the top of the belfry in the Grote Markt, the town's main square. If you reach the summit just as the 47-bell carillon peels, your ears will tingle all the way to your boots. The place for lace, a local specialty, is Breidelstraat, while Steenstraat is lined with shops full of delicious Leonidas and other locally made chocolates (one shop is called **Suker-buye**, "sugar-belly").

For lunch there's a choice of some 30 Michelin-rated restaurants to choose from, more per square mile than in any other provincial city in Europe. Try the **Huyze Die Maene** (House of the Morn) at Markt 17 for elaborate dishes and a magnificent view of the floodlit Markt. A longer visit, in fact, may seriously damage your health, but if you want to spend a night try the **Navarra** hotel on St. Jacobsstraat, a 17th-century former palace that was restored in 1983. Napoleon nearly slept here—a special swan staircase was built for the occasion, but he didn't show up.

CHERBOURG

Cherbourg is some two and a half hours from Portsmouth, but the ride on board the current holder of the Blue Ribband for the fastest transatlantic crossing (a claim disputed by some parties in the U.S.) makes the time seem to fly.

Cherbourg sits on the northerly tip of Normandy's Cotentin Peninsula, that stubby thumb of land that pokes up into the Channel to the east of Guernsey and Jersey islands. The historic town center lies just a few minutes from the ferry terminal across the harbor bridge. Directions to town could not be simpler: Turn right as you come to the first set of traffic lights.

Although you're soon on dry land, Cherbourg is still a city built on water; over the years the center has expanded around its dockland heart. The sea is everywhere, even lapping the main railway station at the aptly named Criée au Poisson, where the local catch is unloaded every morning to be auctioned.

Away from the dock area are remnants of the older town that, unlike the harbor, which was heavily blitzed by the retreating Germans, survived the ravages of war. Many of the buildings date back to the 16th and 17th centuries, and several of the narrow, often cobblestoned streets have been pedestrianized for the benefit of shoppers (those that aren't are usually highly congested with traffic). Pretty well everything of interest to the visitor is contained within this compact heart, an island of interest surrounded by the tall structures of post-war Cherbourg.

Cherbourg is in Normandy, home of delicious food, especially if you like your fish served straight from the sea and don't mind risking an assault on the arteries by the heavy cream and butter sauces that are the basis of the cuisine here. Besides being famous for its crayfish, prawns, and saltmarsh-grazed lamb, Normandy is also apple country, which means *tartes aux pommes* and Calvados brandy. Restaurants in Cherbourg itself are not plentiful, but they are good. They are mostly found on the streets around the old basilica, one of the seedier parts of town (especially seedy on a Saturday night, when fishermen and visiting sailors do most of their drinking).

The huge fishing net and tray of live crabs in the window of the **Café de Paris** on the Quai Caligny is an unambiguous clue to the principal items on the menu in this long-standing restaurant with 1930s decor and a reputation that extends far beyond the city limits. Overlooking the port, the café serves such specialties as sea snails, *raie beurre noisette,* and lobster. Tel: 33-43-12-36.

If you decide to spend the night, a decent choice right beside the port is the **Hotel Mercure**, a modern, businessperson's hotel on the Gare Maritime.

GETTING AROUND

Entry Documents
For France: Citizens of the United States and Canada require valid passports but not visas for tourist visits of 90 days or less. Citizens of Australia and New Zealand require passports *and* visas; to obtain a visa, check *well in advance* of a trip with the nearest French consulate. Residents of EC countries require only a passport or an identity card.

For Belgium: Citizens of the United States, Canada, Australia, and New Zealand may enter Belgium for tourist visits of less than 90 days with valid passports; citizens of EC countries may enter with a passport or an identity card.

Local Time
France and Belgium are one hour ahead of the U.K.

Telephoning
The international country code for France is 33. The country code for Belgium is 32.

Electric Current
Current in both France and Belgium is 220V, 50 cycles AC; North American appliances will need a converter and a plug adapter; British appliances will need a plug adapter.

Trains to Dover
Trains from London to Dover leave from both Victoria and Charing Cross stations. For the most part, trains from both go only as far as Dover's downtown station, Dover Priory, which is some distance from the embarkation areas; courtesy buses and taxis operate between the station and the harbor. There are, however, some trains from both Victoria and Charing Cross that go directly to Dover Harbour; check the timetable at the British Rail Travel Centre at either of those two London stations, at the International Rail Centre at Victoria Station, or call (071) 834-2345.

Boulogne
You can travel to Boulogne by ferry via either Folkestone (with Sealink; Tel: 0233-64-70-47, 1 hour and 50 minutes) or Boulogne (with P&O; Tel: 0304-20-33-88, 1 hour and 40 minutes), but the best service for day-trippers is the hovercraft from Dover (Hoverspeed; Tel: 0304-24-02-41), which takes 40 minutes and costs about £10 round-trip. Aim to catch the 7:45 A.M. train from Victoria Station to Dover Harbour, which connects with the 11:35 "flight" to Boulogne, arriving in Boulogne just in time for lunch. There is a free bus from the hoverport at Le Portel into the town center. The return "flight" leaves Boulogne at 7:05 P.M., connecting with a train that will get you back to Victoria Station around 9:00 P.M.

(These times and carriers are selected from among many options to give you an idea of the possibilities.)

Calais
Again, the Hoverspeed (Tel: 0304-24-02-41) crossing from Dover is the quickest, taking only 35 minutes. The Sealink (Tel: 0233-64-70-47) and P&O (Tel: 0304-20-33-88) ferries from Dover take around 1 hour and 40 minutes. None of the services dovetails into the train timetable, but London (Victoria or Charing Cross)-to-Dover (Priory Station) services are very frequent, as are buses, which shuttle arriving passengers to the port (some trains go all the way to Dover Harbour). You could, for example, catch the 7:30

A.M. train from Charing Cross to Dover Priory, arriving in good time for the 10:30 A.M. P&O ferry.

Dunkirk

The Sally Line (Tel: 0843-59-55-22) ferry sails from Ramsgate at 9:00 A.M. and takes 2 hours and 30 minutes to cross the Channel. The main drawback is that you have to get up in time to catch the 5:50 A.M. train from Victoria Station to make the most of the day. At Ramsgate you have to catch a taxi to the port, a ten-minute ride from the station. The ferry docks at the western end of the vast Dunkirk port, 13 kilometers (8 miles) from the town center— farther, in fact, than the distance between town and the Belgian border—but Sally operates a free shuttle bus into town. Although the sailing time is long, Sally Line ships are among the most comfortable on the Channel. Return on the 5:00 P.M. sailing, which will get you back to London at 10:32 P.M.

Dieppe

There is only one good reason for not going to Dieppe for the day: The trip from Newhaven on Sealink-Dieppe ferries (Tel: 0273-51-22-66) takes four hours. The most sensible approach is to stay overnight on the British coast in nearby Brighton (see elsewhere in Day Trips) and catch a morning train along the coast to Newhaven in time for the 7:00 A.M. sailing, returning on the 6:00 P.M. ferry.

Ostend/Bruges

Travel by ferry to Ostend takes nearly four hours, but there is an appealing alternative, the Jetfoil, a variation on the hydrofoil, operated by P&O (Tel: 0304-20-33-88) from Dover. This takes 1 hour and 40 minutes for the crossing, then another few minutes for the train to Bruges. To make the most of the day, catch the 7:45 A.M. train from Victoria Station to Dover Western Docks, which connects with the 9:35 A.M. Jetfoil, arriving in Ostend at 12:15 P.M. local time. The Bruges train leaves Ostend at 12:34 P.M. and arrives in Bruges at 12:48. For the return journey catch the 6:54 P.M. train from Bruges and you'll wind up back at Victoria at 10:04 P.M.

Cherbourg

The new wave-piercing 74-meter catamaran service from Portsmouth is operated by Hoverspeed (Tel: 0304-24-02-

41); the trip takes three hours. The vessels sail from Portsmouth at 9:00 A.M., the last one returning at 9:15 P.M. (though you need to catch the 1:45 P.M. to be sure of connecting with a same-day London train to Waterloo Station, a half-hour trip). (For Portsmouth itself, and getting to Portsmouth from London, see elsewhere in Day Trips.)

ACCOMMODATIONS REFERENCE

► **Hotel Mercure.** Gare Maritime, 50100 **Cherbourg,** France. Tel: 33-44-01-11; Telex: 170613; Fax: 33-44-51-00.

► **Navarra.** St. Jacobsstraat, **Bruges,** Belgium. Tel: 34-05-61; Telex: 81037; Fax: 33-67-90.

► **Hotel Windsor.** 18 boulevard de Verdun, 76000 **Dieppe,** France. Tel: 35-84-15-23; Telex: 770741F.

CHRONOLOGY
OF THE HISTORY OF
LONDON

The Ancient Past

London stands on a site where two spurs of gravel jutted out to face each other across the Thames, making the river fordable. This was the lowest crossing point on this section of river, and was used by people as long ago as the Stone Age, which began around 12,000 B.C. and lasted for 10,000 years. Hunters once pursued mammoth where commuters now chase after taxis, and these early wandering inhabitants left behind flint hand axes and arrowheads as evidence of their presence. There are few reminders of the Bronze Age, which lasted from roughly 2000 to 500 B.C., but by the time the Iron Age had arrived around 500 B.C. there was a permanent settlement in the area. This was a time of a strong Celtic presence in England, the Celts are the people we consider to be the first "British" race. Eventually, a fort was established, guarded by a rampart and ditch on what is now Wimbledon Common. Its inhabitants might well have been the first settled Londoners.

The Romans

The Romans (55 B.C. to A.D. 409) brought new standards of civilization to Britain, establishing cities joined together by a network of well-made roads. Their houses had surprisingly "modern" amenities, including baths and under-floor heating.

- **55–54 B.C.**: Caesar's expedition.
- **A.D. 43–47**: Claudian invasion and conquest of southern England.

- **50**: Foundation of London (Londinium).
- **61**: Revolt of Queen Boadicea of the Celtic Iceni people. Londinium burned to the ground. The revolt is soon crushed, rebuilding begins, and Londinium is established as the capital of the province.
- **c.200**: The city walls are constructed.
- **c.340–369**: Barbarians from continental Europe raid the British Isles.
- **409**: Revolt against Constantine III and the end of Roman rule in Britain.

The Dark Ages and the Anglo-Saxons

The withdrawal of the Romans from London brought the Dark Ages. The name should not be thought of as indicating a period of barbarism, but rather as reflecting our lack of detailed knowledge of the period. The city was, it is true, only a poor shadow of its former self as the great public buildings fell into disuse and ruin. Invading armies—the Angles, the Saxons, and the Jutes, now generally lumped together as the Anglo-Saxons—from three parts of Germany played their part in adding to the destruction. Understandably, the more peaceful settlers generally preferred the country to the town. Gradually, however, London began to regain its former importance, though it was to suffer further raids by the Vikings from across the North Sea. The arts were represented by rich ornamental work, such as that found in the Sutton Hoo ship burial, now in the British Museum, and by the superb illuminated manuscripts of the Christian church.

- **c. 450**: First Saxon settlements in the British Isles.
- **457**: Celtic refugees from the southeast settle in London.
- **604**: First description of London as a Saxon town, subject to the king of Essex. Æthelbert of Kent establishes a bishopric, and Mellitus becomes first bishop of London.
- **616**: Mellitus driven out, and London reverts to paganism.
- **656**: King Sigebert of Essex converts to Christianity, and Finan becomes new bishop of London.
- **675**: Work begins on the first St. Paul's cathedral, under the direction of Bishop Erconwald.
- **839**: First Viking raid on London.

- **851**: Viking fleet attacks London and burns the city.
- **872**: Danes occupy London.
- **878**: Alfred the Great defeats the Danes and restores London to the kingdom of Mercia.
- **896**: New Danish invasion repelled.
- **994**: Olaf Tryggvason of Norway and King Swein of Denmark join forces to attack London, but the city stands firm.
- **1014**: Danes again in control of London.
- **1016**: London regained under Canute.
- **1042**: Saxon Edward the Confessor crowned, and begins work on Westminster Abbey.
- **1066**: King Harold marches through London after defeating the Danes at Stamford Bridge; English under Harold then defeated by William of Normandy at the Battle of Hastings.

Normans and Plantagenets

The first priority of the Norman conquerors was to consolidate their rule, and inevitably a particular emphasis was placed on the defense of the capital. Early fortresses here consisted of a motte and bailey; the motte, or mound, was topped by a wooden tower and surrounded by the bailey, or courtyard, with its protective moat. In time, the wooden tower was replaced by a stone keep, exemplified by the famous White Tower of London. The Roman walls of London were used as the basis for the fortification of the Norman city.

The Normans also brought with them elaborate religious rituals that required large churches, cathedrals, abbeys, and monasteries. Norman supremacy in church architecture had already been recognized under the Saxons by the use of Norman builders to work on Westminster Abbey. Now, however, churches were to reach even greater magnificence as the massive simplicity of the early churches gave way to the complexities of the full-blown Gothic. The nave of the rebuilt Westminster Abbey is an outstanding example.

London became the great trading and commercial center of the country. Outside the city, in what are now suburbs, the feudal society was based on the lord of the manor, who gathered his wealth from the labor of the villagers. The great lords fought against each other; secular power struggled with ecclesiastical power; and even the monarchy was subject to a series of dynastic struggles within the ruling Plantagenet line. To this could be added international wars and the long struggles of the Crusaders in the Holy Land, all combining to make it a period of seemingly endless turmoil.

- **1066**: William I crowned in Westminster Abbey.
- **1080**: Work begins on the White Tower of London.
- **1086**: The Domesday survey records many of the present London districts as settlements, for example "Stratford-atte-Bowe" and "Stevenhethe," or Stepney.
- **1087**: Coronation of William II.
- **c. 1090**: Construction of the Great Hall of Westminster Palace.
- **1100**: Coronation of Henry I.
- **1135**: Coronation of Stephen.
- **1141**: During the civil war between Stephen and Matilda, Matilda (Henry I's daughter) takes possession of London, but the townspeople revolt and she flees to Oxford. Fulham Palace becomes the home of the bishop of London.
- **1154**: Coronation of Henry II, the first Plantagenet king.
- **1163**: Edward the Confessor canonized. Pilgrimages to his tomb in Westminster Abbey begin.
- **1189**: Coronation of Richard I (the Lionheart).
- **1191**: Henry FitzElywin appointed first mayor of London, an office he holds until 1212.
- **1199**: Coronation of John.
- **c. 1200**: Lambeth Palace built for archbishop of Canterbury.
- **1215**: King John lays down Charter, specifying mayors to be elected annually. Signing of Magna Carta.
- **1216**: Accession of Henry III. During his reign London is established as the capital and permanent seat of government.
- **1245**: Work begins on rebuilding Westminster Abbey.
- **1272**: Accession of Edward I during his crusade.
- **1274**: Edward I returns to London.
- **1290**: First Parliament meets at Westminster. Expulsion of the Jews from England.

- **1292**: Lincoln's Inn founded to train lawyers.
- **1307**: Accession of Edward II.
- **1327**: Deposition of Edward II in favor of his son, Edward III.

The Late Middle Ages

This was a period marked by wars at home and abroad: the dynastic struggles between the houses of York and Lancaster—the Wars of the Roses—following the Hundred Years War against France. As wars need to be paid for, there were numerous increases in taxation, which called forth violent responses, notably the Peasants' Revolt, during which London was stormed, the prisons thrown open, and the houses of the rich sacked. To add to the misery, the country was ravaged by the Black Death, which reduced the population as a whole by a third. In spite of this catalog of horrors, the arts thrived. Architecture had one of its most exuberant periods of development as exemplified by the styles known as Decorated and Perpendicular, both characterized by elaborate tracery. It was also during this period that English literature was born. In part it looked back to a world of mythical chivalry, the celebration of which reached its highest achievement in Sir Thomas Malory's *Morte d'Arthur;* but there was also a new interest in everyday life. Among Chaucer's pilgrims in *The Canterbury Tales,* who amused themselves on a pilgrimage to Canterbury by telling stories along the way, were many characters who could have been drawn from the everyday life of London. Literature was given a further boost when William Caxton set up the country's first printing press in an alley near Westminster Abbey.

- **1337**: Start of the Hundred Years War.
- **1348**: Beginning of the Black Death.
- **1357**: The Black Prince brings the captured king of France back to London after the Battle of Poitiers.
- **1377**: Coronation of Richard II.
- **1381**: Wat Tyler leads the Peasants' Revolt and marches on London.
- **c.1386**: *The Canterbury Tales* completed.
- **1397**: Richard "Dick" Whittington becomes mayor of London for the first time.
- **1399**: Accession of Henry IV.
- **1411**: London guilds combine to build Guildhall.

- **1413**: Accession of Henry V.
- **1415**: Henry V escorted back into London by mayor and aldermen after his triumph at Agincourt.
- **1422**: Accession of Henry VI.
- **1435**: Jack Cade leads rebels against London.
- **1461**: Edward of York marches on London and is declared king. He becomes Edward IV. Lancastrian Henry VI exiled.
- **1470**: *Morte d'Arthur* completed.
- **1477**: Caxton prints his first book in London.
- **1483**: Death of Edward IV and alleged murder of the young princes in the Tower of London. Accession of Richard III.
- **1485**: The Wars of the Roses end with Richard III's defeat at the Battle of Bosworth. Henry Tudor crowned as Henry VII.

The Tudors

The accession of Henry Tudor brought an end to the strife and turmoil that characterized the Wars of the Roses. In the peace that followed, prosperity, based on a growing overseas trade, came to London. The arts flourished in this new atmosphere. Ecclesiastical architecture saw the last great flourishes of the Gothic style, epitomized by the brilliance of Henry VII's chapel at Westminster Abbey. Other religious houses were reduced to ruin by Henry VIII's break with Roman Catholicism. Secular architecture, too, saw dramatic changes, as the rich and powerful came out of their fortresses and built new palaces of a previously undreamed-of luxury. (Cardinal Wolsey's Hampton Court boasted a thousand rooms.) The arts likewise thrived. The miniaturist Nicholas Hilliard provided jewel-like portraits of the age, while the composer William Byrd gave British music a distinctive voice. But it was in the new London theaters that the arts achieved what now seems a Golden Age. Of the great dramatists of the age only one, Ben Jonson, was a native Londoner, but the capital drew in other men of genius, such as Christopher Marlowe and William Shakespeare.

- **1486**: First royal naval dockyard begun at Deptford.
- **1503**: Work begins on Henry VII's chapel, Westminster Abbey.
- **1509**: Accession of Henry VIII.

- **1515**: Cardinal Wolsey appointed lord chancellor.
- **1519**: Hampton Court completed.
- **1531**: Construction of St. James's Palace.
- **1533**: Henry VIII marries Anne Boleyn, who was later to be executed on Tower Green.
- **1536**: Dissolution of the monasteries. Many London monasteries pulled down. Others are put to new uses: The monks' refectory hall at Westminster Abbey becomes the dining hall of Westminster School.
- **1547**: Accession of Edward VI.
- **1553**: Accession of Roman Catholic Mary Tudor. Sir Thomas Wyatt leads rebellion in favor of Lady Jane Grey. After fighting in the streets of London, Wyatt is defeated.
- **1558**: Accession of Protestant Elizabeth I.
- **1573**: Birth of Ben Jonson.
- **1576**: Burbage builds London's first theater.
- **1577**: A second theater is built on Curtain Road, Shoreditch: first performance here of *Romeo and Juliet* and *Everyman in His Humour*.
- **1587**: Execution of claimant to the throne Mary Stuart, Queen of Scots.
- **1588**: Elizabeth I addresses fleet at Tilbury before it engages the Spanish Armada.
- **1599**: Overseas traders found East India Company in London.
- **1603**: Death of Elizabeth I.

The Seventeenth Century

This was a period of dramatic change in England, and particularly in the capital. The Stuarts lost the throne in the Civil War and regained it at the Restoration, and the century ended with the throne secured for the Protestant House of Orange. It was a time of contrasts and conflicts—austerity and flamboyance, Protestantism and Catholicism. Many left the country to seek freedom in the New World. For London it was a time of devastation and renewal. The plague years were followed by the Great Fire, from which a new London rose. The Gothic past was left behind and new architectural idioms, both Classical and Baroque, came to the fore. The new London was developed by such masters as Inigo Jones, who designed the Queen's House at Greenwich, and Sir Christopher Wren, whose St. Paul's

Cathedral was to dominate the city skyline until the age of the skyscraper. In music, Henry Purcell reigned supreme.

- **1603**: James VI of Scotland, a Stuart and son of Mary Stuart, crowned James I of England.
- **1605**: The Gunpowder Plot conspirators attempt to blow up Parliament.
- **1608**: Thames freezes over; great "frost fair" held on river.
- **1613**: Work begins on New River to provide first water supply for London.
- **1619**: Inigo Jones's Banqueting House begun.
- **1625**: Accession of Charles I. Ceremonial return to London in state barge ruined by torrential storm.
- **1642**: Charles I attempts to arrest five Members of Parliament in the House of Commons. Civil War. Charles loses control of London.
- **1649**: Execution of Charles I outside the Banqueting House.
- **1653**: Oliver Cromwell becomes Lord Protector.
- **1660**: Restoration of Charles II.
- **1662**: St. James's Park redesigned in the French style and opened to the public.
- **1665**: The Great Plague.
- **1666**: The Great Fire of London.
- **1675**: Work begun on St. Paul's Cathedral.
- **1685**: Accession of James II. Edict of Nantes revoked: French Protestant refugees (Huguenots) settle in London.
- **1688**: Accession of William and Mary.
- **1689**: Purcell's *Dido and Aeneas* performed in Chelsea.
- **1691**: Lloyd's insurance company formed in Edward Lloyd's coffeehouse on Lombard Street.
- **1694**: Formation of Bank of England

The Eighteenth Century

The period tends to be associated with the name "Georgian," for George I came to the throne in 1714 and George III was still there when the century ended. Inevitably the name suggests an urbane Classicism in architecture and decoration, as seen informally, for example, in Church Row, Hampstead, and formally in the Paragon, Blackheath. It was the age of Adam, Sheraton, Chippendale, and Wedgwood. Musical life was dominated by Handel. In literature, the novel was born in the works of Richardson, Fielding, and Sterne, and toward the end of the century Romanticism flourished in the hands of Blake and Wordsworth. A different view of London appeared in the works of William Hogarth, whose Gin Lane showed a London steeped in debauchery. It was also an age of great change: Britain lost a colony in the American Revolution but began building a new empire in India. More dramatic still were the profound changes brought about by the Industrial Revolution, which began to gather momentum in the second half of the century.

- **1702**: Accession of Queen Anne.
- **1714**: Accession of James I's great-grandson George I from Hanover in Germany.
- **1715**: Handel's *Water Music* composed for Thames pageant.
- **1719**: First general hospital built at Westminster.
- **1727**: Accession of George II.
- **1733**: Westbourne River dammed to create the Serpentine in Hyde Park.
- **1739**: London gets a second Thames bridge at Westminster.
- **1749**: Henry Fielding takes his seat as a Bow Street magistrate.
- **1751**: Act raising the price of gin limits the ruinous effect of cheap drink.
- **1753**: Thomas Chippendale establishes his furniture works on St. Martin's Lane.
- **1759**: Opening of the British Museum.
- **1760**: Accession of George III.
- **1761**: Robert Adam appointed as architect to the royal works.
- **1785**: First issue of *The Times* appears.
- **1794**: Work starts on Grand Junction Canal, linking London to the Midlands.

The Nineteenth Century

In many ways, the new century saw a continuation of trends begun in the previous period. Industrial development continued, particularly in the field of transport. London's Docklands began a long period of expansion, and by the end of the century the city was at the hub of a complex rail network. The great railway stations, such as Paddington and St. Pancras, are among the capital's finest

Victorian buildings. As the Georgian age passed and the Victorian age began, a new style in architecture found favor—the Gothic Revival, epitomized by the House of Commons. Literature, from the gently ironic novels of Jane Austen to the teeming world created by Charles Dickens, continued to be the leading artistic medium. It is perhaps a commentary on the times that 1851 saw both a celebration of Britain's leading role in world affairs in the Great Exhibition and the start of Mayhew's chronicles of the desperate poverty of many of the capital's citizens.

- **1802:** West India Docks opened, first of a series of new docks.
- **1808:** Trevithick demonstrates his steam locomotive in London.
- **1811:** Work begins on Waterloo Bridge.
- **1812:** John Nash begins new design for Regent's Park and Regent Street.
- **1820:** Accession of George IV.
- **1835:** Opening of new Houses of Parliament.
- **1836:** First steam railway in London. Dickens publishes *The Pickwick Papers*.
- **1837:** Accession of Queen Victoria.
- **1843:** Opening of the first tunnel under the Thames.
- **1851:** The Great Exhibition in Hyde Park. Henry Mayhew begins work on *London Life and the London Poor*.
- **1863:** The first underground railway opens.
- **1864:** Work begins on the Embankment, covering London's new main sewer.
- **1888:** London given a new governing body: the London County Council.
- **1890:** First electric trains run underground.
- **1895:** Trial of Oscar Wilde at Bow Street.

The Twentieth Century

The role of London in the life of the country has changed in the present century. Trade and manufacturing have declined as the emphasis has shifted toward the financial institutions. Two World Wars have taken their toll, and the bombs of the Blitz brought greater changes to the face of the city than any event since the Great Fire. Equally important has been the role of transport, with the airplane and especially the automobile changing the whole pace and pattern of life. The confidence shown by the builders of the past has only rarely been matched in more recent times, most notably in buildings such as the 1930s Underground stations and the Lloyd's Building of Richard Rogers. In the arts, literature has continued to play a dominant role, but music, which had declined, has experienced a revival. The visual arts, too, have fared well, and now have an appropriate setting in the recently refurbished Tate Gallery. The new arts of cinema, radio, and television have become increasingly dominant.

- **1901:** Death of Queen Victoria and accession of Edward VII.
- **1906:** Suffragettes establish headquarters at Clement's Inn.
- **1910:** Accession of George V.
- **1914:** Outbreak of World War I.
- **1918:** Armistice ends World War I.
- **1922:** First radio broadcast from London.
- **1924:** The first Empire Exhibition at Wembley.
- **1929:** First public television broadcast from London.
- **1936:** Death of George V, abdication of Edward VIII, and accession of George VI.
- **1939:** Outbreak of World War II.
- **1940:** Battle of Britain, and start of the Blitz.
- **1945:** End of World War II.
- **1951:** Festival of Britain. Beginnings of South Bank arts complex.
- **1952:** Accession of Elizabeth II.
- **1963:** Establishment of National Theatre in London.
- **1986:** New Lloyd's building opened.

—Anthony Burton

INDEX

FOR THE BEST IN PAPERBACKS, LOOK FOR THE

In every corner of the world, on every subject under the sun, Penguin represents quality and variety—the very best in publishing today.

For complete information about books available from Penguin—including Pelicans, Puffins, Peregrines, and Penguin Classics—and how to order them, write to us at the appropriate address below. Please note that for copyright reasons the selection of books varies from country to country.

In the United Kingdom: For a complete list of books available from Penguin in the U.K., please write to *Dept E.P., Penguin Books Ltd, Harmondsworth, Middlesex, UB7 0DA*.

In the United States: For a complete list of books available from Penguin in the U.S., please write to *Dept BA, Penguin*, Box 120, Bergenfield, New Jersey 07621-0120.

In Canada: For a complete list of books available from Penguin in Canada, please write to *Penguin Books Ltd, 2801 John Street, Markham, Ontario L3R 1B4*.

In Australia: For a complete list of books available from Penguin in Australia, please write to the *Marketing Department, Penguin Books Ltd, P.O. Box 257, Ringwood, Victoria 3134*.

In New Zealand: For a complete list of books available from Penguin in New Zealand, please write to the *Marketing Department, Penguin Books (NZ) Ltd, Private Bag, Takapuna, Auckland 9*.

In India: For a complete list of books available from Penguin, please write to *Penguin Overseas Ltd, 706 Eros Apartments, 56 Nehru Place, New Delhi, 110019*.

In Holland: For a complete list of books available from Penguin in Holland, please write to *Penguin Books Nederland B.V., Postbus 195, NL-1380AD Weesp, Netherlands*.

In Germany: For a complete list of books available from Penguin, please write to *Penguin Books Ltd, Friedrichstrasse 10-12, D-6000 Frankfurt Main I, Federal Republic of Germany*.

In Spain: For a complete list of books available from Penguin in Spain, please write to *Longman, Penguin España, Calle San Nicolas 15, E-28013 Madrid, Spain*.

In Japan: For a complete list of books available from Penguin in Japan, please write to *Longman Penguin Japan Co Ltd, Yamaguchi Building, 2-12-9 Kanda Jimbocho, Chiyoda-Ku, Tokyo 101, Japan*.

WHEN TRAVELLING, PACK

WHEN TRAVELLING, PACK

All the Penguin Travel Guides offer you the selective and up-to-date information you need to plan and enjoy your vacations. Written by travel writers who really know the areas they cover, The Penguin Travel Guides are lively, reliable, and easy to use. So remember, when travelling, pack a Penguin.

☐ *The Penguin Guide to Hawaii 1991*
0-14-019923-3 $10.95

☐ *The Penguin Guide to Ireland 1991*
0-14-019928-4 $11.95
(available December 1990)

☐ *The Penguin Guide to Italy 1991*
0-14-019932-2 $14.95
(available January 1991)

☐ *The Penguin Guide to London 1991*
0-14-019936-5 $12.95
(available February 1991)

☐ *The Penguin Guide to Mexico 1991*
0-14-019926-8 $14.95

☐ *The Penguin Guide to New York City 1991*
0-14-019931-4 $12.95
(available January 1991)

☐ *The Penguin Guide to Portugal 1991*
0-14-019935-7 $12.95
(available April 1991)

☐ *The Penguin Guide to San Francisco &
Northern California 1991*
0-14-019930-6 $12.95
(available December 1990)

☐ *The Penguin Guide to Spain 1991*
0-14-019937-3 $14.95
(available March 1991)

☐ *The Penguin Guide to Turkey 1991*
0-14-019938-1 $14.95
(available April 1991)